A COUPLE OF COPS

A COUPLE

On the Street,

in the Crime Lab

OF COPS

GEORGE CUOMO

Random House
New York

The accounts in this book are true, but the names of some criminals, victims, and their families have been changed.

Grateful acknowledgment is made to the Putnam Publishing Group for permission to reprint excerpts from *High Hopes: The Amityville Murders* by Gerard Sullivan and Harvey Aronson. Copyright © 1981 by Gerard Sullivan and Harvey Aronson. Reprinted by permission.

Library of Congress Cataloging-in-Publication Data

Cuomo, George.
    A couple of cops : on the street, in the crime lab / George Cuomo.
      p.   cm.
    ISBN 0-679-41851-2 (acid-free paper)
    1. Police—New York (State).   2. Criminal investigation—New York (State).   3. Police—New York (State)—Interviews.   I. Title.
HV8143.C86 1995
363.2´09747—dc20   94-33571

Manufactured in the United States of America on acid-free paper

98765432

First Edition

BOOK DESIGN BY DEBORAH KERNER

For Sam Vaughan
who's made a difference.

CONTENTS

CONTENTS

SECTION I

THREE COUSINS

WE GREW UP TOGETHER in the north Bronx of New York City, not dirt poor but hardly middle class, when little was expected of children beyond acceptable behavior within the family and an early willingness to earn one's way outside it. John Cuomo is a year older than me; Al Della Penna three years younger. Since I had only sisters, John and Al were essentially my brothers. Along with the other cousins, we've remained good friends over the years. John's mother, Al's mother, and my father were siblings, all three born in the Bronx of immigrant Italian parents.

John's and Al's families shared a house in the Pelham Bay section of the Bronx. Mine lived a short bus ride away near Castle Hill. We all got together on weekends, shared picnics, beach days, vacations, holidays, family occasions. My mother, of German descent, was the only non-Italian in this extended family, but she was very close to her sisters-in-law, John's and Al's mothers.

John and Al both dropped out of high school, while I received a bachelor's degree from Tufts and a master's from Indiana, and ended up a writer and professor.

John and Al became cops, although of very different sorts, after passing their police exams on the first attempt, an unusual feat for persons with so little education.

John rose to detective second grade in the NYPD, spending twenty years in the toughest areas of the city with the Narcotics and Robbery divisions. He was then arrested and suspended from the force on charges of bribery and official misconduct until . . . well, that story is ahead.

Al has completed over thirty years with Long Island's Suffolk County Police Department, where he's a detective sergeant and chief firearms examiner. He also heads a crime-scene unit responsible for on-the-spot investigations of major crimes, particularly homicides.

On their jobs, both have learned to be shrewd, practical, wary, and very tough, tougher certainly than I've ever had to be. They've spent their adult lives dealing with crime and criminals, with the maimed, the dead, the drugged, and both the manipulators and the victims of the drugged. As Al, a really sweet and thoughtful guy, says of his early days patrolling a beat, "If someone's coming at me, I'm gonna make damn sure I deck him before he decks me."

In talking about his current work in the Crime Lab, Al is analytical. He defines terms and responsibilities, notes parallels, classifies types of evidence. He's less interested in the sequence of events than in concepts and categories. As chief firearms examiner, Al is responsible for the handling, labeling, testing, and storing of all firearms items involved in any crime in Suffolk County, which comprises the eastern half of Long Island and has a million and a half residents.

A past president of the International Association of Firearms and Toolmark Examiners, Al teaches college and Police Academy courses in criminalistics. He began our first interview by listing, without my asking, his three different jobs—firearms examiner, crime scene investigator, criminalistics professor—and his work in each. He then outlined the structure of the County Crime Lab.

Johnny is less articulate in some ways, less sure of his vocabulary, less interested in books and theories. He's the most jovial and physically exuberant of all the cousins, a guy who finds it hard to sit still. He loves golf, poker, gambling casinos, teasing, practical jokes. At the same time, he's a pure story-teller. At our annual weekends he'll entertain all the cousins with more accounts of his adventures than Al has probably told in a lifetime. Invariably, Johnny's stories begin, "There was a guy in this casino down in Atlantic City that used to . . ." Or, "I was in my office one afternoon on this really dead shift when a woman with her kid comes in and . . ."

When we were preparing for this book, I asked Johnny for a brief summary of a gambling incident he'd mentioned. He went on at great length even though I kept reminding him that I only needed a synopsis, a few highlights. Much later, when I said *now* he could give me the complete, unabridged version, he took the same amount of time to cover the same details, as if to say: *That's it. That's the story. It's the only way I can tell it.*

Al likes to know what I'm looking for so he can collect his thoughts, check his notes and files, and is reluctant to say anything without the documentation to back it up.

But any kind of glib distinction between them seems too easy. Sure, Johnny was a tough, gruff street cop. Al has become a meticulous scientific investigator. But I've spent too many years writing novels to feel comfortable putting labels on characters, or cousins, and even though this isn't fiction, I'm still counting on Johnny and Al to show who they are by what they say and do.

The book deals mostly, but not solely, with their police experiences. I've always been fascinated by narratives, by the way stories grab us and hold us and eventually, in the best of circumstances, justify the attention we've given them. I hope these narratives will not only prove compelling but will tell us something about ourselves, and about the police that we both love and hate, rely on and distrust. I'm interested in Al's and Johnny's stories about the violent and hateful, and sometimes weirdly comic, ways we behave toward each other, and about the ugliness we're so ready to leave for the police to clean up. Most of all, I'm interested in what life is like for two different kinds of cops, and what their experiences and attitudes and complaints and jokes reveal about our cities and suburbs and criminals and victims, and ultimately about themselves and us.

The three of us have talked about this book for years, but other books and other matters intruded, and I didn't decide to go ahead with it until a hot summer day in Springfield, Massachusetts, where I was giving a talk about writing at a literary festival. Al and his wife Carrie attended, up from Long Island for the weekend. I mentioned to the audience that I'd never understood why people came out to hear writers talk about themselves. Writers, I pointed out with the confidence of one who really *knows*, lead incredibly dull lives, spending their best hours sitting at a machine with a keyboard, surrounded by other people's books and blank sheets of paper. I then pointed out Al, told them what he did for a living, mentioned Johnny too, and said in one of those flashes of pure, spur-of-the-moment insight, "They should be up here; their lives are ten times more interesting than mine."

Although I'll make some comments from the sideline, this book belongs to them. Their sections are in their own words, taken from the thousands of pages of transcripts produced in interviews in New York and Arizona. In shaping this material, I took full responsibility for the selection, emphasis, and organization required to preserve the integrity of their accounts while giving both their individual stories and the book as a whole a narrative cohesion. I haven't, though, tried to hype things up with either literary pretense or TV fakery, and would like to think the book deals honestly with the realities of their worlds. Working on it these past few years, I've felt a real responsibility, not only to them and their lives, but to those lone and shared memories that have come alive again for me, and I hope for them too.

I'd like to think that the book gives a genuine picture, on duty and off, of a couple of guys who didn't start out with much, who earned honors and awards while going where they wanted to go, and had some interesting experiences along the way.

—GEORGE CUOMO

WINE AND CHEESE

WHEN A SUSPECTED HOMICIDE occurs anywhere in Suffolk County, a forensic investigation unit is dispatched to conduct an on-the-spot search for physical evidence. If Al's on call, he'll lead the unit whether firearms are involved or not, since on these occasions he acts not merely as a weapons expert but also as the senior crime-scene investigator. It's a prestigious, much sought-after assignment, with only a few lab specialists qualified for the responsibility.

And Suffolk County is no longer the quiet, remote area of our youth, when it embodied the New Yorker's idea of "the country." Comprising the farther reaches of Long Island, gradually narrowing as it stretches out into the Atlantic to form New York's easternmost finger of land, Montauk Point, Suffolk's nearly one thousand square miles were once devoted largely to truck farming. After World War II, the county went through a period of suburban growth, with acre after acre of planned "communities," distinguished from one another largely by the bucolic names dreamt up by the developers. Large-scale commercial and industrial expansion followed. With a million and a half residents, Suffolk now ranks among the top ten United States counties in population, personal income, and retail sales.

In almost every way, it's a city, a large city, but not the traditional high-density eastern model. It's more like Phoenix or Los Angeles, a sprawling metropolis crisscrossed by freeways, where large individual towns, not neighborhoods, provide both the diversity and the divisions typical of a contemporary American city. Suffolk has its white areas, black areas, Hispanic areas, its tenements, apartment houses, working-class homes. Some suburban developments are still being built, some are clearly showing their age. It has garden co-ops and waterfront condos, Victorian mansions and country-club estates, industrial parks and office complexes, colleges and high-tech labs, and one huge glittering shopping mall after another. It has a thousand miles of shoreline and God knows how many beaches and marinas and yacht clubs, along with a couple of America's better-known ocean resorts in Fire Island and the Hamptons. It still has farms out on the eastern tip, still produces Long Island potatoes and Long Island ducks, still hauls in tons of fish.

Finally, and predictably, with all its other big-city attributes, Suffolk County experiences a major city's incidence of violence and crime.

Since violent crimes typically occur after midnight, Al admits with a quick smile that his life would be easier if people did their dirty work during normal hours. It's not just jumping out of bed to a screaming phone at three A.M. It's tough on his wife Carrie, alone at home wondering where he is, when he'll get back, what kind of mess he's walked into.

Being roused in the middle of the night also means he'll arrive tired and bleary, generally after a full daytime shift, maybe even overtime and a late dinner, with no more than a couple of hours' sleep. Once called out, he'll usually work through the night and well into the next day.

The timing was perhaps the most unusual aspect of Barbara Lambert's murder. Word of it reached headquarters early in the afternoon on a torrid midsummer day when a policeman reported a woman "found dead by her husband in her home with a knife stuck in her." Otherwise, Al said, the case was fairly typical.

AL DELLA PENNA ➡

THE CREW AND I logged in at 3:42 P.M., about three hours after the report came in. That's about as quickly as we get to a homicide, because a number of steps have to precede the call to us. The initial police officer on the scene immediately reports to his supervisor, probably a sergeant, that he's found a body. If the sergeant makes an on-site determination of a suspicious death, he then alerts the precinct detectives. It's only after the detectives show up and make their assessment of possible foul play that Homicide is summoned, along with the specialized crime lab units such as ourselves.

Geography also plays a part. In this instance, we were only about ten miles away, but Homicide and ID had to travel some three times that distance over the almost always busy Long Island freeways.

We joined the Homicide supervisors and detectives already at the scene, the dozen or so patrolmen, the police ID team, the Public Information officers.

Everybody's naturally trying to do their own thing, and since it's my job to recover evidence, my preeminent concern is to preserve the sanctity of the crime scene in the midst of the chaos. Hell, if the ID photos show a book on a table in one shot and on a shelf in another, even a half-asleep defense lawyer could get that evidence, maybe the whole case, thrown out.

Of course, I'm well aware that the first officer on the scene must exert every effort to protect human life. If he finds someone wounded, he calls for medical aid and offers every immediate assistance, even if it messes up the evidence I'll be looking for. The area can also be disturbed by doctors or EMT personnel trying to help the victim. I always tell my seminars that a patrolman should be able, within minutes after arriving at a crime scene, to suggest to medical personnel the best route to the victim. Often the most obvious path is also the most damaging. A less apparent but equally efficient route can usually be found that would protect the evidence.

You've also got to expect neighbors and passersby to rush up to check out all those patrol cars and emergency vehicles with their sirens and flashing lights, so you're always concerned with crowd control, keeping the rubberneckers at a distance. Then there's the reporters and cameramen monitoring police-radio frequencies, who often get there before we do. Nowadays, they've got miniaturized microphones and recorders that possess incredible range. They've got zoom lenses and hypersensitive film that works without a flash in any kind of light. More than once I've seen a dramatic picture of me in the morning paper when I'd swear no camera got within a hundred feet of me the day before. And newspaper people, of course, aren't concerned about violating the scene. They want news. I want evidence.

Even the police ID photographers can cause problems. They always get first crack at things because you want everything recorded on film before anyone, including us, is allowed to touch, tag, or collect anything. The ID people are as careful and agile as you could want, but even the most experienced forensic photographer, intent on doing his own job right, can accidentally crush a minute piece of evidence under his heel.

WHEN WE WERE GROWING UP together, the fact that Al was a few years younger than Johnny and me seemed pretty important, and we were into our twenties, I think, before we stopped viewing Al as the kid. He still looks the youngest. His hair is deep black and combed straight back, and although the three of us are all around six feet tall, Al's the trim one, with a thinner, more angular face, a quicker, more agile step. He still wakes up every morning at five and runs a few miles before his standard breakfast of coffee and cold cereal. He then heads off to teach his eight A.M. class at Suffolk Community College before beginning a full shift as Firearms chief at the Crime Lab.

At work, Al's considered something of a fashion plate, and although he scoffs at the idea, he never shows up in anything that might undermine that reputation. He favors dark business suits, dress shirts, ties that are stylishly narrow or wide, muted or colorful. His black shoes glisten.

Beneath his suit jacket Al wears a leather holster with his 9-mm semiautomatic pistol, a magazine of extra cartridges, a pair of handcuffs. Even though he's not worn a uniform for years and spends most of his time in his office or laboratory, Al looks and acts very much like the cop he's been most of his life. He can be laughing or joking, but his face changes instantly if something catches his attention. His stare is hard and steady, his eyes narrowing as he focuses on a gun he's turning over in his hand, a report, a person's expression. You can't miss his intensity, his concentration, his alertness.

As his wife Carrie points out, Al always parks his car nose out in the slot at their condo to save a few seconds in an emergency. The habit is so ingrained, she says, he even does it with rental cars on vacations. The Lambert murder, of course, didn't require Al to roar away from home in the middle of the night. Since the report came in while he was at work, he simply turned away from his dual microscope and hurried to the site in his fine suit and tie, as head of the county's crime-scene investigative team, riding in the Crime Lab van with his two assistants.

BARBARA LAMBERT WAS FIFTY, her husband Dan a few years older. Since their grown children were off on their own, the two of them lived by themselves in a very nice neighborhood of fairly expensive homes. Dan was an engineer who designed Air Force training systems for a defense contractor. Barbara worked as a librarian in a large corporation. From all indications, they enjoyed a quiet life, two stable, decent people who got along well with each other and everyone else.

As soon as the Homicide detectives arrived, which was before I got there, they wanted to question Dan Lambert, but the guy seemed really distraught and had been taken to a neighbor's. They'd also taken the family dog there, just to get it out of the way. Everybody naturally sympathized with the grief-stricken husband and realized how much he needed to be left alone to pull himself together. But he was the one who'd discovered the body, who might know something that we needed right now, not tomorrow morning. The more time you let go by, the more you have to depend on luck, or some dumb move by the guy you're after.

So a couple of Homicide detectives dropped in at the neighbor's, and Dan agreed to talk to them. The day, he said, began normally. As always, he and his wife ate breakfast together before he drove off to work. Barbara's job started later, so she'd stay behind to straighten up the kitchen and then shower before leaving for work herself.

Now, like most of us well-trained husbands, Dan Lambert would usually phone his wife during the day. You know, Hi, how's it going, who's picking up the chicken for dinner? This morning when he calls to say he'll be late for dinner because of a racquet-ball date, her office says she hasn't arrived yet. At eleven o'clock? He quick dials home to see what's up, only the phone just rings and rings. He doesn't like this at all, so he tears out of the office, slams the pedal, and drives home in record time.

He gets there around noon to find the garage door open and her car gone. Now he's really shaken. His wife is a very fastidious woman who'd never drive off without closing the garage. The front door's locked, so Dan uses his key to let himself in and runs frantically through the house looking for her. He sees her purse on the couch in the den, with her little lunch bag right next to it. He can't believe she'd possibly drive off without her purse. At the bedroom door, he freezes. His wife's on the floor, the carpet, with towels wrapped around her face and head and her hands tied behind her. She's lying face up, naked, with a knife sticking out of her throat. The room is an absolute shambles, with drawers pulled open and clothing flung around, with blood and fecal material everywhere. As soon as he recovers from the shock, he calls the police.

It's a compelling story, but Homicide hasn't yet had a chance to verify it. As a practice, the immediate suspect is whoever might stand to benefit, and in marital situations you think of girl-friend/boyfriend combinations, of inheritances, of people desperate enough to murder their way out of some hopeless predicament. So the detectives naturally look first at Mr. Lambert. They're respectful of his apparent grief but watch and listen to him very closely, looking for giveaways, for slips. You might have a guy here who's carefully planned the whole thing. He does in his wife, tosses stuff around to make it look like a robbery, and moseys off to work. A few hours later, he makes his customary phone call, puts on his panic face, and races home. Oh my God, she's dead, the poor thing, I always loved her so!

It wouldn't be the first time, right?

AL'S RELATED ALL this steadily, without melodrama or sarcasm, in his dry, deep voice. He hesitates occasionally, searching for the phrase he wants, pulling one side of his mouth back to make a little clicking sound—tension? distaste? a kind of verbal shrug? We're at his condo, downstairs in his wife Carrie's office. A tenured professor at Suffolk Community College with a doctorate in psychology, Carrie also maintains a private therapy practice in this room. But she has no clients scheduled this Saturday morning and has offered us the space. Al sits back on a deep couch, legs crossed, papers on his lap and next to him, while I face him from an overstuffed chair, each of us working on coffee.

It's a pleasant, comfortable room, and seems at the moment a wholly inappropriate setting for Al's story. I'm not even sure how eager I am to hear any more details about Barbara Lambert's death. As someone who turns away from the screen during gory movies, I've begun to feel—knowing how stupid it sounds—that I'd have preferred a nicer, more sanitary murder.

"You said you wanted something typical, that we deal with all the time," Al points out, and resumes his story with a cool, dogged attention to all the details.

WHEN MY CREW AND I arrive that afternoon, most of the officers are congregated on the sidewalk or in the driveway, with patrolmen keeping street traffic moving and holding off the reporters and neighbors and everybody else crowding around. Of the fifteen or twenty cops on the scene, maybe ten are from Homicide. To maintain that kind of presence, sometimes a shift is kept overtime, or the next shift called in early. The trash collectors have come that day, and the Lamberts' big lot and double-driveway house has been roped off with yellow police streamers looped around the garbage cans at the curb, around trees, around the four-foot chain-link fence enclosing the property.

Only authorized personnel are allowed within the yellow streamers, and up to this time none of the investigators have entered the house. Even before the ID crew is sent in for their pictures, a team of senior officials conducts a walk-through, and at 3:50 in the afternoon the ID chief, Detective Sergeant Wayne Muller, and myself, as chief forensic investigator, are led inside by Detective Sergeant Kevin Cronin, Homicide shift supervisor. Our aim is to familiarize ourselves with the site, to view the body and the surrounding conditions, to note the more obvious indications of what's happened.

We go carefully. You hate like hell to see someone on the loose that you know damn well took an icepick to auntie, so even though you don't want to waste time, you don't want to miss anything either, or screw something up.

First of all, we try to develop a general sense of the layout. You know: wood-frame ranch on a single lot, kitchen, living and dining rooms, two bedrooms, utility area. Nicely furnished, very clean, meticulously kept up, almost pristine, which immediately focuses my attention on some fibrous material on the floor near the front door. It's a reddish material, just a few fibers that seem out of place on the light-colored rug. That's exactly the sort of thing I'm looking for, anything that stands out by seeming unusual or out of place. I also notice some blades, particles, of grass in the hallway and then, almost like a trail, all these burnt paper matchsticks and little cylindrical units of cigarette ash. It's as if some flicked-off ashes stayed intact when they hit the floor. The trail goes through the central hallway to the living room and toward the kitchen, even into the bathroom itself. In the kitchen, my eye is caught by the bent louvers of the open window over the kitchen sink.

In the living room, I see a piece of cheese on the floor, its plastic supermarket wrapper partly pulled back, and I wonder what it's doing in the living room instead of the kitchen.

While making these preliminary observations throughout the house, we're also establishing an approach to the body on the bedroom floor. Let's not walk where we see those items on the floor, let's go this way instead.

The bedroom, of course, gets most of our attention, since that's where the body is and where the homicide seems to have occurred, since there's no blood anywhere else in the house. The bedroom itself is a god-awful mess, with blood and feces all over the carpet, where this woman's lying on her back with a knife sticking out of her throat, her head and face completely wrapped in towels, her legs spread, her hands trussed behind her. She's short and very heavyset. We note several stab wounds in her stomach and chest and blood soaked through the towels around her head. We spot a standard claw hammer on the floor near her.

The open dresser drawers and all the clothing and articles thrown every which way contribute to the general sense of mayhem and chaos. Despite the several other powerful odors, I smell something like wine, and sure enough, there's a liter-size bottle of Riunite on the dresser. We're also intrigued by a large mirror that's been taken off the wall and left leaning, face in, against a dresser.

We don't touch anything. We just look, point things out to each other, make notes, think of an approach to take later.

As soon as we complete our walk-through, we move out and photographers take over. I won't get back in for the hour or so they'll take to produce their videotapes and at least four stills of each room and a lot more of the bedroom, plus numerous close-ups of the weapons and other items and areas that caught our attention on the walk-through, and of the body from every conceivable angle. All this has to be done before anything is marked or tagged or even touched. We want the photos to record the scene exactly as found. To do this, they'll produce three or four hundred stills to be printed on proof sheets, with the more interesting and revealing shots then blown up in color.

By now it's late afternoon, and while the photographers are inside I take my first tour of the exterior, which has already been photo'd by ID. Out there, with everybody around, the camera people are careful not to get extraneous persons into their shots, especially policemen. The feeling is that the presence of anything extra compromises the purity of the scene and taints the picture as evidence.

The Lamberts' backyard, enclosed by the chain-link fence, abuts a wooded area that serves as a very wide right-of-way leading up to a highway, which you can't see or hear from the yard. Since there's a good chance the bad guy came or went by that route, we'll have to comb through it tomorrow. It's too late today to round up enough search personnel before dark.

On my outside tour, a Homicide detective points out a metal chair on the wooden deck, backed up to the open kitchen window with the bent louvers, so that increasingly appears to be the point of entry.

I take a look at Dan Lambert's Toyota in the driveway but don't see anything of interest. A close inspection would take too long right now. Later on we can easy enough put a hook to it if we're interested. It's always better working out of the dust and wind and weather, with controlled lighting and lab conditions.

Kevin Cronin, I find out, will remain in overall charge, but Detective Robert Henn, also of Homicide, will actively run the investigation. I've not seen Henn yet, which is typical at crime scenes. By the time I get there, the head guy is already off somewhere questioning people, organizing his troops, getting on whatever trail he's got as quickly as he can and leaving the on-site details to others.

At half-past six, with the photographers still inside, my crew and I grab a sandwich and some coffee. Sometimes, you know, you'll be at a scene an awful long time, and we generally get something from the corner deli or stop for a bite after we finish up. If we eat on the spot, we find some inconspicuous spot out on the perimeter, certainly outside the house. And we'll say to the press guys, Look, no pictures of us munching away against any kind of background, okay? You guys eat your sandwiches, let us eat ours, because the world just isn't going to understand.

Some of us use a nearby public phone to let our spouses know what's going on and when we might be home, which at the moment looks like pretty late. Cronin's got a cellular phone in his vehicle but we don't use that. Cellulars can be picked up on other units close by, maybe even reporters', and we don't want anything to end up in the papers, or being spread around by the neighborhood gossip. Even just saying we found this dead woman with a knife in her throat can cause trouble. If you end up getting a confession, you want to be able to say that the guy's admission of stabbing her in the throat reveals a knowledge of the crime that couldn't be picked up in some news report.

I generally try to stay away from the press and let the Public Information officers handle them, but the TV people will grab anybody they can. The stations send out these big vans with giant antennas for live, on-the-spot telecasts, and will do almost anything to beat their competitors onto the air. In this case, I manage to avoid both the newspaper and TV photographers, who are mostly using the wooded area to take shots of the house.

While I'm still waiting my turn inside, the chief medical examiner arrives. Dr. Charles Hersh is a Department of Health civilian who supervises the County Crime Lab, and is therefore my boss back at the office, where I'm one of the many department heads who report to him. Hersh himself doesn't generally show up at a crime, and has no doubt dropped by because of the whodunit nature of the case, plus the affluent neighborhood and the reasonable time of day.

Dr. Hersh has brought with him Dr. E. Stephen Bolesta, a young forensic pathologist, to conduct the preliminary examination under Hersh's supervision. Given that we're already into the evening hours, they both want to start right away. Only I don't want them in there yet, because a prelim necessarily involves moving the body. The doctor can't just report, Look, I found this lady dead on the floor with a knife in her throat, so I guess that's what killed her. Maybe there's a shotgun wound under those towels wrapped around her head, or poison traces, gunpowder burns, another knife in her back. Maybe she's been garroted or strangled. He's got to unwrap those towels, got to roll her over for a good look, and then, unless he wants someone sweating out the postmortem well past midnight, he has to rush the body back to the lab to get it under way. What makes Hersh even more impatient is that he's shown up in a suit and tie, figuring he's gonna be interviewed, gonna be on camera, and here he is being kept standing around on this really muggy ninety-two-degree day. At least I could take off my jacket and loosen my tie a little. But he's sweating and fidgeting and saying, What about the prelim? What about the post? And I'm saying, Please, just a little more time, we can't let you in there yet.

Thankfully, Kevin Cronin, the man in charge of the investigation, joins me in the stall, although neither of us has the rank or the authority to take on Dr. Hersh, a very classy, prestigious-type guy who as chief medical examiner is way up in the hierarchy, and who since then has moved on to the top M.E. position in New York City. Anyhow, there we are, telling him, Doc, you really can't go in yet because we haven't cleared the area or recovered any of the objects you'll have to mess up examining the body. I'm worried

about the fibers. I'm worried about the cigarette ashes, the matchsticks, the towels wrapped around her head, the knife in her
throat. I need to gather these items in a very pragmatic, unhurried
fashion and know that as soon as Hersh walks in, I stand to lose
everything.

Although Hersh is still fuming, he does agree to delay the prelim long enough to give us the chance, some eight hours after the
discovery of the body, to begin taking evidence, so I move back
into the house with my two young assistants, Joe Galdi and Sue
Ryan, both of whom have forensic-science degrees. Galdi special-
izes in biology and serology, including blood and seminal fluids.
Sue Ryan deals primarily in hairs and fibers.

We start in the bedroom, because once that room is cleared,
Hersh and Bolesta can get at the body. On our way, though, we
document the fibers near the front door, the matches and ashes,
the grass particles in the hall, by having photographers shoot
each of them alongside tags preprinted with identification numbers and two-inch ruler segments. We not only have to document
each and every item with pictures, but also by sketching and measuring off their exact locations. We also crosslist every item on a
standard recovery form, and there's no way all this can be rushed.
There are no shortcuts. We're talking about little piece-by-piece
bits of evidence, collected with the kind of precise, impeccable
documentation that can hold up under the most stringent challenges in court.

Depending on the size and type of item in various situations, we
can put them in plastic or paper bags, in boxes, crates, jars, canis-
ters, whatever's appropriate, since we always have a whole variety
of containers available in the lab van. We usually prefer plastic,
because it gives a more complete seal, but moist items with blood
or semen do better in paper, because it lets them breathe.

In the bedroom, we notice a number of objects showing a pat-
ternized imprint—small, fine lines, almost delicate, the sort of
thing you'd get from latex-type gloves with ridged palms. We even
find the print on the half-full Riunite jug on the dresser. The bot-

tle's been left open, and some of the stains on both the bed and rug give off a distinct wine odor. I'm beginning to wonder, What the hell are we dealing with here, a really sloppy boozer? That's what's happening at this point: even as we're dispassionately collecting everything of possible interest, we're also trying to piece things together. What does this mean? How did it get here? Does anything tie into anything else?

We also find on the bedroom floor a velvet-lined jewelry box that's obviously been rifled through and tossed aside. It too shows an imprint, but this one looks like a sneaker bottom. Maybe the bad guy stepped on it after grabbing what he wanted, which means that we now have to take all the sneakers and running shoes or whatever in the house in order to be able to prove, if the issue arises, that none of them made this mark. The sneakers would not be considered gross physical evidence, which encompasses anything apparently connected with the death, in this instance including such items as the knife in her throat and the claw hammer on the floor. The sneakers would be exclusionary evidence, objects that might enable us to rule out certain possibilities or explanations, such as the remote chance that someone as fastidious as Barbara Lambert may have, while wearing sneakers, stepped on her jewelry box under God knows what kind of circumstances. In much the same way, we may or may not have exclusionary evidence with the fiber on the rug, the ashes, the matchsticks. Did the Lamberts produce any of those bits and pieces, or were they brought into the house by the killer?

It occurred to us that maybe those matches weren't just used to light cigarettes. Maybe the murder occurred in the dark, and the guy didn't want to turn on any lights. Only she, Barbara Lambert, the body . . . looked too *fresh* for that time frame.

I keep saying he, or the guy, out of sheer force of habit. At this point, with everything still up for grabs, we certainly couldn't rule out the murderer being a woman. But I'd have to say, given my own experience and the hundreds of years of collective experience of everyone else intensely involved in this case, that you would have one hell of a lot of grizzled detectives absolutely flabbergasted if we ended up with a *she*. Politically correct or not, we're thinking of, looking for, *him*.

We're also becoming more and more convinced that Dan Lambert is not the guy we're interested in. What would he gain from all this rigmarole? Could he have possibly produced and then coolly walked away from this whole gory mess with such complete control and dispassion? And what possible use to him would be the towels wrapped around her head, let alone the wine splashed all around and the cheese on the living room floor? If he wanted to dispatch his wife, all he had to do was pull open a few dresser drawers, toss some jewelry into a nearby river, and make sure he kept looking as innocent as possible. We're very aware that Dan Lambert is an intelligent, educated man, a successful engineer logical enough to realize that every complication he introduced would increase the chance of screwing up. Stomping on jewelry boxes? Wine bottles? Supermarket cheese?

All told, we spend maybe four hours collecting in the bedroom, where we take the claw hammer, the jewelry box, the mirror leaning against a dresser, a hair dryer found on the bed with its electrical cord cut off and missing, more matches and cigarette ashes, the jug of Riunite, the stained and smeared rug and bedding items, the sneakers in the closet. With no conviction of their pertinence but just to cover ourselves, we also gather fiber samples and a clean piece of rug, a pair of sandals, a piece of earring found on the floor, various toiletries and articles of clothing, underwear, stockings, gloves, and scarves, some still in the drawers, some strewn about.

We do not touch the body, the towels around the head, the knife in her throat.

Finally we collect samples of the fecal material. It's not that unusual for burglars to defecate in a room, not necessarily out of spite or some further violation of the place. Their nerves get so tight, so jangled, that they're overcome by this urge to defecate and just drop their pants and let it go. We also know that a strangulation victim's sphincter muscles will involuntarily release, so we'll check the postmortem report for bruises around Barbara Lambert's throat.

For our purposes, we doubt the fecal material will prove of value. The lab probably won't even be able to determine if it's his or hers. Feces are generally nonidentifiable, unless the sample contains an amount of blood because of a wound or internal or rectal bleeding. Although fingerprints, hair, footprints, teeth, even signs of past injuries or operations, provide identifying characteristics, the bacterial contamination of fecal matter is so great it rarely reveals anything.

As soon as we finish in the bedroom, my two assistants fan out into the other rooms, since Dan Lambert has given us carte blanche to look everywhere, and I lead Drs. Hersh and Bolesta along a safe path to the body. I stay with them as Bolesta, closely watched by Hersh, performs the prelim. Usually only one pathologist is present, so I always try to assist during the exam, helping to move the body and handle clothing and other items, but primarily to document evidence as it's removed. I also don't want the doctor doing anything I don't know about. If in turning the body he smears blood on a shirt, I want to record that so there won't be any eventual confusion about when and how that stain occurred.

The pathologist will always remove the victim's clothing to look for hidden wounds, but the only covering on Barbara Lambert's body was the towels around her head. When Bolesta removes the serrated kitchen or steak knife from her throat, I tag and seal it in a plastic bag. ID will dust it for prints, but all they'll probably find is more of that ridged pattern from a latex glove. Dr. Bolesta and I turn the body over and examine the two black belts and electric cord binding her wrists behind her. He removes and hands them to me to document and bag.

We then come to a ticklish point as the two doctors discuss whether they should now remove the towels from Barbara Lambert's head. I say, Let's leave the unwrapping wait until the post, when we'll have better light and can unfold her, so to speak, as carefully as possible. Happily, Bolesta agrees, preferring to work under optimum conditions. In that case, Hersh says, she'll have to stay wrapped until tomorrow, because it's gotten to be ten o'clock, too late to start a post. He has a point, but we all know that Homicide will be working around the clock and needs all the help we can give them. And, hell, we haven't even seen her face yet, can't even positively identify her as Barbara Lambert. And how do we know she hasn't got a shotgun blast in her face that Homicide really should know about?

We agree to transport the body to the morgue to remove the towels, but leave the postmortem till morning.

While we're waiting for the morgue wagon, I check with Joe Galdi and Sue Ryan to see what they've found elsewhere. In the kitchen, they show me a set of knives on the wall near the sink that seem to match the knife from Barbara Lambert's throat. They've taken one which we'll later compare with the weapon via precise measurements, number of serrations, things like that. More than likely the intruder also picked up the claw hammer within the house, since it's not something normally carried as a weapon. Galdi and Ryan have also come up with a package of yellow latex gloves from the cabinet under the sink, a look-alike left-hand glove found in the workroom, a ceramic duck and several flowerpots from the sill of the entry window, some matches from the stove. As a routine measure, they've collected the water from the kitchen drain and the two downstairs bathroom drains. If the intruder washed himself, we might find traces of the victim's blood in the traps. We always have to think of later on. Maybe the guy confesses that after stabbing her he washed up in a certain sink, and later tries to disavow it. It's nice to be able to show that of the four sinks in the house, only the one he mentioned contained residue of the victim's blood.

While we're collecting, other people are naturally doing their jobs, and I hear that Homicide has pretty much ruled out Dan Lambert as a suspect, based on his cooperation and his totally convincing behavior. In addition, investigators have talked to Dan's boss and some coworkers and neighbors. Everyone says the same thing: the Lamberts were a nice couple, nice grown kids, no marital, financial, psychological problems. No indication that either one was running around or mixed up in anything. Even their cars were a tipoff. Although both made good salaries, she drove a four-year-old Oldsmobile, now missing, while he had a mid-range Toyota.

The hubby insists he can't imagine who'd want to kill his wife. Neither can anyone else, so even though we haven't verified any missing items, the thesis of a burglary that got out of hand looks increasingly good. The murder, in other words, was an unforeseen consequence, because Barbara Lambert had been unlucky enough to be home at the wrong time. Burglars will generally ring the bell before breaking in during daylight. Did Barbara answer or call out? If she had, he'd probably have bolted on the spot.

Homicide hopes that our guy's local, in their files somewhere, maybe even known to their informants. Their job then would simply be to discover which burglar, among the scores of thousands throughout metropolitan New York, had decided that morning to slip into this nice house belonging to Barbara and Dan Lambert. If the guy happened to be from somewhere else, just passing through, they'd mainly have to pray that along the way he did something real dumb.

Around ten-thirty P.M. the morgue wagon arrives, and the attendants prepare the body for the trip. I ask them not to use just the standard combined stretcher and body bag because I don't want the body placed directly on anything. Most hospitals use washed sheets to keep the stretcher and body bag clean, but I'm concerned with trace evidence and want to avoid even the slightest pollution, so ask them to cover the stretcher with a new, clean shroud. We have blue ones, made of a coarse paper. I have them put the body on top and wrap and enclose it with the shroud. This way I can respond if someone challenges the hairs and fibers we might find. So, with the bloody towel still wrapped around her head, Barbara

Lambert's remains are zipped into the bag and rolled out to the morgue wagon.

Before I follow it back to the medical examiner's building in Hauppauge—which also houses the Crime Lab, including my Firearms unit—I ask Homicide to put the whole Lambert residence and area on hold until we get back in the morning. After all, we still have to tend to the removal of the towels at the morgue, which will likely take us past midnight. We've been working since early morning and are so hot and bone tired that everything else is gonna have to wait overnight.

At the morgue we unwrap the first, outside towel, which is bound with torn strips from a different towel and swaddles her head and face. Beneath that we find yet another towel, knotted directly around her head, giving us a total of five separate pieces of material. Bolesta hands me each one to tag and bag. We can see that she's taken a series of crushing blows to the head, probably from the claw hammer we found. The doctor also checks the bruises around Barbara Lambert's throat and doesn't believe they're pronounced enough to indicate strangulation. Maybe someone started to strangle her, then switched to the knife and the hammer to finish her off.

After relaying this to Homicide around one A.M., we call it a night and head home.

A few hours later during the early morning postmortem, Dr. Bolesta takes oral, anal, and vaginal swabs to be examined by a serologist for traces of seminal fluid. He does a close exterior examination of the body to note and photograph all wounds, bruises, scars, anything unusual, and to recover any hairs or fibers that might have come from her killer. He also takes samples from under her fingernails. He performs a full autopsy, making surgical cuts to determine the depth and severity of her wounds and the organs affected by them.

Cause of death: Multiple stab wounds to trunk, blunt impacts to head and ligature compression of neck.

Manner of Death: Homicide (Stabbed, struck on head and strangled.)

Findings that clear-cut are always reassuring, but neither the autopsy nor anything else we turned up during the first day of investigation gives us much to go on.

To initiate a search of the wooded area behind the house, I ask the Police Academy to send out the whole class of recruits to pick up anything of note. Of course, you have to be selective in gathering evidence. One time we turned the recruits loose in a tavern parking lot and ended up with huge bulging trash bags of cigarette butts. What was I supposed to do, have Serology test a few thousand of them for saliva traces?

It wasn't that bad this time, but the group did come back with an awful lot of cans and bottles and other junk, none of which proved of any use whatsoever. But we had to give it our best shot. We couldn't just ignore it.

Once we learn that neither Lambert smoked, we can assume we're working on a heavy smoker who, given all the matches he used, must have spent a lot of time in the house. But we had practically nothing else to go on. He left no butts behind to be tested for saliva, no items brought in with him. The knife in Barbara Lambert's throat definitely came from the kitchen set. Dan Lambert identified the claw hammer as his own, and said that his wife usually draped her latex dishwashing gloves over the faucet, where the intruder probably saw them when he climbed in.

The burglary explanation is solidified by the list of missing jewelry Dan Lambert compiled, but no one expects his descriptions to do much good. Burglars fence off jewelry as quickly as possible, and by now the gold and silver has probably been melted down, the stones popped from their settings. Nothing else seems to be taken.

The lab results corroborate some of our assumptions but don't cause any excitement. The fibers on the rug came from one of the towels wrapped around Barbara Lambert's head. The two black belts binding her hands were cut halves of a single belt, the electric cord came from her hair dryer, the grass in the hall no doubt from the backyard. No useful prints anywhere inside, no seminal traces on the body, no inconsistent fibers or hairs.

But ID did come up with a clean, sharp print from the outside of a locked living-room window. Maybe the guy tried that window before finding the kitchen one open. The Trace Lab also provided a glimmer of hope when they determined that the jewelry box print hadn't been made by any of the sneakers in the house. That might give us a link to the intruder, although by now he'd probably have gotten rid of everything he'd worn. Even if he hadn't, the print wouldn't help us find him. At best, it'd only solidify the case against somebody we'd tracked down through other means.

Those means being employed Thursday morning, twenty-four hours after the murder, include sifting through innumerable files to check the records and tendencies and whereabouts of known area burglars, resuming the door-to-door canvass of the neighborhood, and setting up roadblocks on two adjacent thoroughfares, where commuters are flagged over and asked if they saw anything suspicious yesterday. Someone mentions a guy in a leather jacket walking away from a broken-down motorcycle, and the police check out local service stations and cycle shops. A woman says she saw Barbara Lambert out very early walking her dog. Someone else says she saw a young white man from that general area, who she knows as Terry Harrington, walking *his* dog at about the same time. A few other ho-hum leads turn up, but nobody's impressed by any of them until one of the local cops, a Third Precinct detective named Bob Hammond, pipes up. Hey, wait a minute, I know that Harrington guy, he's a real dirtbag that you oughta check out.

Terry Harrington turns out to have priors for burglary and gun possession, so everyone immediately perks up, because that immediately marks him as the *type* of guy who probably committed the crime. Unfortunately, from our point of view, the same could be said for a lot of other guys whose names have been dredged up from the files. Harrington's in his twenties, medium height but muscular and strong, a real tough kid from an Irish family, living at home with his parents and a younger brother and sister. The one thing that sets him apart from the others we're checking out is that Harrington's neighborhood, although a lot less affluent, is only blocks away from the Lamberts', which places him closer to the victim than any other potential suspect.

Certain legal considerations come into play when you have a target of possible suspicion, so you have to move carefully. If you officially start talking to that person, you have to give him the standard advisatories, which if he's got any brains will immediately signal him to shut the hell up. What sometimes transpires then, although it's not usually owned up to, is a technique known as *scooping.* The police will snatch a suspect or potential suspect off the street, preferably at night when his family and friends figure he's out somewhere and won't start worrying. They don't arrest him, don't accuse him, don't rough him up or anything like that. They just want to talk to him, preferably while driving around in a squad car, without creating a lot of paperwork or procedural complications, in order to develop information, either about that person or his acquaintances, or about various events.

With this in mind, the police start looking for Harrington at local hangouts, even though it's still early in the day. They even stake out his house in the hope of scooping him coming or going. All this is still very low key, and when they don't run into him anywhere, they just shrug and move on to other things.

That afternoon we receive word that Barbara Lambert's missing Olds has been recovered some fifty miles away in the heart of New York's theater district, apparently abandoned there only hours after the murder. We have the vehicle towed out to the Suffolk County impound yard, and I head there with some ID people to check it out. The car's an investigator's dream, as neat as the house, with none of the piles of debris and crap, none of the squashed beer cans and old comic books and last week's underwear that you usually have to wade through. In this car, any little

thing would stand out, and as soon as we open the door I spot a
good-sized, cohesive cigarette ash on this nice neat passenger-side
rug, which right away gives us a tentative connection with the
guy inside the house. This pleases the hell out of me, although
from the beginning we've always assumed that whoever took Barbara Lambert's car had to be the guy who killed her. But we have
to deal with proof, an airtight case, and up to now we haven't
come up with anything to connect her death in the house with the
disappearance of the car. Maybe we're getting close to doing that,
although we have to consider the possibility of more than one person being involved. So far nothing has ruled that out, but our gut
feeling has always assumed a lone culprit.

I take a lot of lifts from the car seat with adhesive tape, looking
for fibers that might connect with what we found inside the house.
In a messy car, I probably wouldn't even bother. I also pick up the
brake and accelerator pads, looking for similar material and
maybe even footwear prints to match what we found on the jewelry box. Meanwhile, the ID people come up with a lot of prints, including some beauties on the rearview mirror. They could be hers,
of course, but since Barbara Lambert was quite short, the car thief
probably adjusted the mirror. Could someone who'd been so careful not to touch anything in the house except in latex gloves become so careless in a stolen car? We're certainly hoping so, and
anxiously wait for word from the ID lab.

Boom-o, we hit the jackpot! The mirror prints not only match
the ones from outside the locked living-room window, but the
computer turns up as the odds-on match for both sets a certain
Terry Harrington, the dirtbag we've been trying to talk to, although with no particular urgency. So at eleven P.M. on Friday
night, two and a half days after the murder, Homicide initiates a
serious round-the-clock stakeout of the guy's home. They're not
even sure he's inside, but at this point they're absolutely committed to unearthing Harrington, and are not about to overlook anything. They're reluctant, however, to just go up and knock on the
door, or even try a disguised phone call. If he's not there, they
don't want the family tipping him off. Besides, the cops are very

much aware of his priors for gun possession, and understand how jumpy a guy facing a murder rap can get when he sees the police closing in.

Even with evidence as convincing as Harrington's prints in Barbara Lambert's car, we still can't put him *inside* the house, where the murder took place. He could always claim he left the prints on the living-room window when he looked in to make sure the coast was clear before stealing the car. So all right, he could say, you got me, send me up for grand larceny because I certainly never went inside and killed anybody. So that becomes our prime task: putting Harrington inside that bloody bedroom.

As I've said, most burglars will ring the bell of a house even if it looks empty, and we figure Harrington must have done it when Barbara Lambert was taking her post-breakfast shower. She doesn't hear it, doesn't respond, and Harrington confidently heads around the back, tries the locked living-room window, discovers the open one leading into the kitchen. Maybe he grabs the kitchen knife when he climbs in, maybe he comes back for it after realizing someone's home. The latex gloves he probably dons right away, not wanting to leave prints regardless.

You'd think he'd bring gloves, rather than hope to luck out finding some inside. But burglars have their own mentality. People see a break-in type as some shrewd, well-organized guy with a nylon stocking over his face, slipping inside in the middle of the night with a little pinpoint flashlight and a leather belt with loops of ingenious tools. Well, sometimes they bring things, sometimes they don't. But even with no more than a screwdriver and a pair of pliers from their car trunk, a regular tire iron for a jimmy, you'd figure they'd be smart enough to force a lock rather than throw a rock through a window. But a lot of them throw rocks.

What you're generally dealing with are just plain stupid or bored or high kids walking down the street when suddenly, *Bang!* the lightbulb goes off in someone's head and he blurts out, Hey, let's rip off that house there. That's one reason burglars are so frustrating from our point of view, their penchant for the spur of the moment. They spot an open window or a ladder against a house and figure, Why not give it a shot? So they sidle into the backyard and smash a window and leave messes everywhere, help themselves from the fridge and liquor cabinet, touch everything in sight, grab whatever they can, and beat it.

Why aren't they caught more often then, if they're so sloppy? When you factor in the frequency of burglaries in a given area, and the hours of police work it takes to do a really thorough job of digging and looking and reconstructing, simple arithmetic says we can't exert maximum effort on every two-bit break-in that comes along. Remember, the intensity of our concern with Barbara Lambert didn't result from her being burglarized. We were all out there because she was murdered.

Still trying to develop a credible sequence for the killing, I go back to the two towels wrapped around Barbara Lambert's head, which match those terrycloth fibers near the front door. The underneath towel was knotted by being folded into itself, the way a woman might do up her hair after her shower, before using the blow dryer. She was probably still in the bathroom or else would have heard Harrington clambering through the kitchen window and probably scared him off before he even got in.

Once inside, Harrington must have heard the shower running—another moment when most burglars would have fled. Burglars don't like being seen, don't want any contact with anyone. They're totally consumed with getting in and out as quickly and smoothly as possible, with no detours, no surprises of any kind. But Harrington made a decision. He could have turned tail and run. He probably should have. But he didn't. He stayed.

Who knows why?

At some time after encountering the naked Barbara Lambert, Harrington placed another towel, like a full mask, over her head and face and tied it with strips torn from a third towel. This would have been when those tiny fibers near the front door attached themselves to his clothing or shoes. Either before or after this, he bound her hands behind her with the belt pieces and the hair-dryer cord. At some subsequent time, he stabbed her with the knife from the kitchen, hit her with the claw hammer from the workroom, and tried to strangle her with his hands, in some order that we still could only guess at.

The purse found on the couch in the den raised more questions than it answered. I mean, it was so undisturbed, with her sandwich and yogurt container right alongside. Yet Harrington must have seen it, must have dumped it out looking for money, for car keys. How could a guy who'd made such a mess of the bedroom leave the purse so orderly? Why the hell he took the mirror off the wall is also beyond us. Did he consider stealing it and then change his mind or just forget about it?

The sneaker print on the jewelry box wasn't leading us anywhere either. Everything Harrington had been wearing must have been stained with blood and fecal material, and since we found no evidence of either in the Olds, he must have dumped his clothes before he even got into the car. Did he toss everything into a bag and drive off barefoot in his skivvies, and then abandon the car in Manhattan?

The cheese on the living room floor and the bottle of Riunite on the bedroom dresser presented still more puzzles. Sure, wine and cheese, maybe we're dealing with a real gourmet here who had an attack of the munchies and grabbed the cheese from the fridge, bit off a hunk, and tossed it aside, washing it down with the Riunite. Only none of that guesswork pans out. Serology tests the cheese for a protein present in salivary juices and for blood or other substances. Our odontologist examines it for tooth marks. ID dusts the plastic wrap for fingerprints. Nothing, nothing, nothing. So we just hang on to the cheese, along with everything else we've taken, hoping it'll eventually justify our efforts.

While I'm trying to piece together a scenario based on what we've collected, the stakeout at Harrington's house continues for over twenty hours with no sign of the suspect. Then on Saturday evening the surveillance team radios headquarters that Terry has left with another man in the family car, and that they're tailing it.

They're quickly joined by Detective Henn and two other Homicide detectives, and when the car pulls into the Grand Union Shopping Center, Henn and the others close in and make the arrest. Terry Harrington is not armed and offers no resistance.

The passenger, Harrington's father, isn't held, but he also surprises the detectives with his passive behavior. Usually, when a kid's had criminal experience, his family knows all the right moves, and the minute someone gets nabbed the relatives are on the phone rousing up their lawyer. Not only doesn't Harrington's father call anyone, but apparently no one else does either, because throughout that long night, when a lot of heavy stuff is going on, no lawyer contacts the police on Harrington's behalf. You get the impression the family's already written the guy off.

At first, when Harrington's informed he's being arrested for the murder of Barbara Lambert and read his rights, he insists he doesn't need a lawyer because he hasn't done anything wrong. At headquarters an hour or so later he changes his story and gives an oral confession, transcribed by a detective who also notes that Harrington keeps lighting and smoking cigarettes, flicking the ashes off to one side.

I didn't think anyone was home. She saw my fuckin' face. I had it all worked out she was going to give everyone a different description of me, but when I was leaving she flipped. I got real mad and choked her with a towel. I wanted to make sure she was dead so I stabbed her in the chest with a steak knife and hit her on the head a few times with a hammer. To make sure she was dead I stabbed her once more in the throat.

The police want it in his own handwriting, and Harrington obliges, all witnessed and sworn to and notarized by an arresting detective. Any confession or other document carries a lot more weight when it's notarized, so all cops are notaries. I am.

Terry Harrington's handwritten confession runs six pages, and includes his signed acknowledgment of his right to remain silent, his awareness that anything he says can be used against him, his right to a lawyer even if he can't afford one, etc., etc. He also answers and initials three specific statements saying that he understands his rights, wishes to talk to the police anyhow, and does not wish to contact a lawyer. For good measure, the bottom of each page is signed by Harrington and notarized by Detective Pat Paladino, the attending officer. Everybody is very conscious of procedure, and careful not to undermine the testimony in any way.

I Terry X. Harrington do give the following statement. I am 22 years old and was born in Nassau County New York. I now live at ———. I live there with my mother Anne, my father Walter, my brother Sean, and my sister Sheila. I work as a carpenter for ———, in ———. I am not working right now.

On Wed Aug —, I was at my home, I was feeling very low I had no money and wanted to get high. I decided to break into the house up the street. As I was walking my dog I saw that the house had no cars around and took the dog home.

I went to this house, it was white, I went around to the back through the side gate, I went to the cornor window in back and looked in. I saw that no one was home and then put a chair near the window to climb in. I took off the screen the window was open and moved some of the stuff on the ledge around. As I was about to go in I saw yellow rubber gloves on the sink. I grabbed a steak knife and started to look around the house. I was looking for the bedrooms to get jewelry and cash. As I walked in the bedroom, I woman was standing there naked, she was drying her hair, she scream and I grabbed her. I made her sit on the end of the bed. She was covering her face, and I pull the towel over her eyes. She lifted the towel as I was going through the jewelry boxes, I took the mirror off the wall then, she told me she had money in her pocketbook. I made her go with me to get it, we went to the living room and told her to sit down.

She got her wallet out and a $5 bill and a few ones. I then looked and found more. I made her go back to the bedroom, the dog was with us all the time, I didn't want the dog to follow me so I got cheese and gave it to the dog. We then went to the bedroom again, *the woman was telling me wear to find the jewelry now. I tied her up with a belt from the closet and a cord that I cut with the knife. I didn't want her to call anyone and I cut up the towel and gagged her with it. I was leaving then and she said take the car and she told me how to open the garage door she could still talk a little.*

We agreed that she would tell everyone a opposite description of me. As I was leaving she flipped and I got real mad and put a towel around her neck and pulled on it.

She passed out I let go, and she pissed and shit, she was still breathing, so I pull on it some more. I wanted to wash her off so I poured wine on her, I don't know why. I wanted to make sure she was dead, so I stabbed her in the chest with the steak knife. I also stabbed her in the stomach a few times. I was scared and didn't know what to do, I then got a hammer and hit her in the head about 5 or 6 times. Just to make sure she was dead I stabbed her in the throat, she was on the floor then and took the car keys I had taken when I took the money from her pocketbook.

I then drove to New York City to Canal St and allen off of Houston. I had a guy that I knew from before, his name is John, I sold stuff to him before when I did burgs. I sold him a women's gold ring with a green stone and gold earrings and gold chains and braclets. I think there was some other rings too, I got about $700.00 for all the stuff, I bought crack off a guy at 43rd street and 8th Ave in Manhatten. I bought $600.00 of crack. I wanted to go home then and took the train because I had dumped the car on 45th street. I threw away the shirt I had on because it had blood on it in garbag bags on 44th St. I had bought a shirt on 43 St and 8th Ave, it is a blue tee type shirt, my blue shorts that I had on are a my house now.

When I got home on thursday I had no money or crack left. I am now giving this statement to Detectives Pat Paladino & Joseph Acquara. I have read it and swear it is all true.

The details were convincing, and Harrington also provided knowledgeable comments on several crime-scene photos. But we were all sure that even while admitting his guilt to the murder, Harrington was covering up certain other aspects of his behavior, because every time he was questioned about sexual abuse of Barbara Lambert he simply refused to answer. He also made, according to Detective Paladino's report, a last-ditch attempt to spread the blame:

> *After speaking with his parents at telephone number ——————, he again confessed to the murder of LAMBERT, but prior to ending his conversation with his parents, he, in question form, stated on the phone the name of BILL GARGAN, "BILL GARGAN?" After completing his telephone conversation he stated that his friend BILL GARGAN assisted him in the murder. When asked why he didn't mention GARGAN earlier he stated, "I just remembered." HARRINGTON then proceeded to go over his entire earlier rendition substituting BILL GARGAN'S name as co-defendant, doing parts of the murder he had earlier attributed to himself.*

Nobody gave any credence to the idea of an accomplice. Harrington was our man, and now we had his confession. We'd even solved the cheese on the floor, although the wine business was still questionable.

To some extent, all this shows the value of the neighborhood police, in this case Bob Hammond, that people often look down on. I mean, you have a major crime, a big uproar of publicity, so you bring in all your big shots and the fancy up-to-date technology of your specialized squads. But the local cops are the ones out on the beat, day after day, dealing with the burglaries and brawls and 7-Eleven stickups, with all the pain-in-the-ass hotheads and troublemakers, so when some neighbor mentions this dirtbag down the street, it's the local detective who hoists the red flag and points everybody in the right direction.

Of course, Harrington himself did us a big favor by taking off the latex gloves in the Olds. What'd he think—we'd scour the house for prints but not the car? Some yeggs, like I say, aren't too impressive in terms of brainpower. And then instead of getting as far away as possible, he hangs around the old homestead until the cops collar him, and then spills the whole story over and over again, orally and then in writing and then before the videocam, every word signed, sealed, and delivered. I came, I saw, I killed. Christ, it's like Julius Caesar.

Only you have to be very wary with confessions. Even if the guy pours it all out in the kind of detail that you couldn't make up if you tried, the courts have to be happy with every single moment of how you spent your time getting that statement or they'll throw the whole thing out and put you back on square one. All cops know this and try real hard to avoid any kind of sloppiness, but these issues are very delicate, very borderline, and sometimes very frustrating.

With Harrington, the cops clearly bent over backwards to keep everything legit, but the key issue became the absence of an attorney. The guys from Homicide swear that neither Terry nor his father ever mentioned calling any lawyer, that they gave Terry all the proper advisatories, and that when they got to the station house Harrington *wanted* to talk and wasn't the least interested in an attorney, as attested by his signing the proper document acknowledging and waiving his rights. I believe them, partly because Harrington's behavior is perfectly plausible in terms of my own experience. Some two-bit punk suddenly finds himself in deep, serious shit, and the pressure gets to him. When he's picked up it's almost a relief, and he's more than ready, even eager, to get it all off his chest.

Still, the introduction of the lawyer issue means we're now dealing with a potentially questionable element in our otherwise very solid case. Even with both written and videotaped confessions, a lawyer might still insist that the only thing his client told the police *of his own free will* was that he desperately wanted to consult with counsel, and that the cops said, Well, if that's how you feel, we'll just hang you by your feet outside this sixteen-story window until you change your mind and sign these papers we happen to have handy.

This uncertainty, of course, means we can't just say, Okay, we got a confession, case closed, let's all go have a beer. It's still imperative that we gather every possible piece of evidence, so that we're damn well ready to make our case solely on that evidence, with no reference at all to the confession.

And remember, we're cops. It's like I tell my wife when she gives me a hard time about the hours and the scares and the jangling phones in the middle of the night. I say, Hey, Carrie, don't razz me. I'm out there doing battle against the forces of evil. So she laughs and I laugh and that's the end of it. But we really hate to see some ultimate scum like Harrington turned loose, for whatever reason, after all the awful things he did to a nice lady like Barbara Lambert, who did not, by any stretch of anyone's imagination, deserve to have her life end in all that blood and shit and horror. And for what? So Terry Harrington can afford a goddamn fix that'll let him forget for a couple of hours what an absolutely worthless human being he is?

So back at the lab, at all the labs, we're still struggling to understand exactly what happened, looking for that one little insignificant detail that might open everything up like a rose. You've also got to remember that we're professionals, and want very much to master our craft, our art, whatever you want to call it. We want to learn everything there is to know about slobs that break into homes to slash people with knives and knock their brains in with hammers. We want to know more than they do themselves about what makes them tick. Maybe years later it'll give us that one flash of insight we'll need to find and send away another atrocious slob from exactly the same mold.

Often things catch our attention for odd reasons. Like, Barbara Lambert was such a meticulous person. Even in her terrified state, naked in front of some wild guy flashing a knife at her, she digs out the money and car keys for him and yet we still find her purse in a perfectly orderly state, sitting next to her yogurt and sandwich on the couch.

The dog business is weird, too, Harrington tossing it a chunk of cheese to mollify it. All during this violation of its territory, this gruesome attack on its mistress, the mutt's apparently loose in the house and of no goddamn use whatsoever. It doesn't even seem to have touched the cheese. It must have been some real nothing Fido-type dog that just ran off and quivered under the couch the whole time. I've seen dogs become more violent being dragged out of their hiding spots than they'd ever been defending their presumably beloved owners.

The sequence we finally put together had Harrington first holding Barbara Lambert face down on the bed while tying her hands behind her and wrapping the towel around her head to keep her from studying his face and maybe recognizing him from the neighborhood. He then sets about ransacking the room but notices in the mirror that she's peeking through the towel to watch him in the mirror, so he yanks it off the wall and turns it around. And then at some point we're convinced he gets horny and starts trying to have sex with this naked woman, and when he's got her on the bed, attempting to rape her, maybe holding her down by choking her, she becomes so terrified she loses control of her bowels. He then becomes infuriated and pulls her off the bed onto the cleaner carpet. We're sure he didn't stab her on the bed, because there's no blood there. And then the wine comes in, because nothing else seems to explain it. He says in his confession, I wanted to wash her off so I poured wine on her. Well, why on earth would he do that if he was just going to leave her there, grab the jewels, and run? He wanted to wash her off because he wanted to have sex with her, no matter how much he insisted on denying it afterward.

Of course, we got no semen at all on the rape kit. Our guess is that Harrington either gave up or lost the desire.

Only why would a guy who freely acknowledged maiming and killing this woman refuse to admit sex was involved, when we're almost positive it was? Well, he was a real macho-type guy, lifting weights and wearing T-shirts to show off his bulging biceps. We think there's no way this hardass muscle man's gonna admit to getting horny over some older, kind of matronly woman. Can you imagine him going off to prison with that on his record? He wants to say, Hey, look, I was burgling this place and this fat old lady, she got in my way, so I stabbed her, I beat her to death. Because that, you know, that's macho, that's big-time tough nut. The other cons would look up to him for that.

As to why he finally decided to kill Barbara Lambert, we're almost sure it was because she'd gotten too good a look at him. He says in the confession that she kept swearing she wouldn't turn him in, ever, ever, but he must have said to himself, I've gone too far, and there's only one way I can absolutely guarantee she won't sic the cops on me. . . .

I'm naturally not the only one looking for more evidence, and on the Monday after the arrest Homicide detectives pay a visit to Terry Harrington's brother Sean. They spot him walking toward the local gas station for a pack of smokes, and he's surprisingly willing to help out. He gives them a signed statement that around seven-thirty on the morning of the murder his brother Terry returned to the house after being gone for a few hours and quickly changed his clothes and left again. After that, he says, Terry was gone for a day or two. He mentions problems between Terry and the rest of the family, and notes that his brother kept a knife in his room and a gun in the house.

A couple of days later, a store clerk in midtown Manhattan identifies Terry Harrington from a photo as the guy who came into her store on the afternoon of the murder, remembering him as a muscular type in a tank-top shirt.

The continuing investigations also give us some confirmation, if we really needed any, of the kind of dirtbag we're dealing with. Two nights after the murder a patron was dragged out of a local bar and severely beaten and robbed by two young men. Again from photos, the victim identifies one of his assailants as Terry Harrington. So does the doorman at the bar:

A little while after Terry Harrington arrived at the bar he got into a pushing/shoving incident with an old spanish guy who was drunk. They were yelling at one another and the old man left, but he was followed out of the bar by Harrington.

A confrontation started across the street by the Funeral Home. There was a lot of yelling, pushing and shoving. It looked like the old man didn't want to be bothered because he sat down on the ground. Harrington was persistent in bothering the old man. The old guy got up and started running across the street and Harrington followed and caught the old guy and grabbed him and threw him to the ground. The old man hit his face on the ground and was bleeding. I called for help and pushed Harrington off the old man but he was acting cocky and yelling and still trying to get at the old man. I punched him in the chest, and he was pushed by others and went down to the ground, then ran away. The old man was taken to the hospital in an ambulance.

Homicide also checks out Bill Gargan, the friend mentioned as an afterthought by Harrington. They get a warrant to search his home and vehicle, take prints of his sneaker bottoms, question him at length. Gargan admits knowing Harrington but vehemently denies any connection with the crime, saying he was home asleep at the time of the murder. Everything supports Gargan's alibi, and Homicide clears him, giving us one more sign of what a sweet guy we had in Harrington, who'd drag a friend in on a murder charge on the basis of absolutely nothing.

In yet another canvass of the area, the police encounter a neighbor woman who says Terry's mother spent several hours at her house on the morning of the murder, complaining about problems with her children and appearing very nervous. Eventually she provides a handwritten statement about Mrs. Harrington's visit:

At about 10:30 A.M. I was home when my neighbor, Anne Harrington called me on the phone . . . We started talking and she started to tell me her family problems. I asked her if she wanted to come over to my house and talk and she said yes.

Anne told me that her son, Terry, had frightened her that

morning. She said Terry was reading a telephone book at the kitchen table and she was looking over his shoulder and he said something like What are you looking over my shoulder for? He said it in such a manner that it frightened her so much that she stayed in the laundry room and was afraid to come out.

She started to talk to me about Terry. She said when she came out of the laundry room Terry had left the house and she didn't know where he went.

She stayed at my house for about three hours. While she was there Sean, her other son, came to the door and said another neighbor called and said there were TV cameras & police down the block. He then said Sheila said it was probably Terry.

When he said that Anne went white. She got real excited and said, The neighbor said it was Terry? and Sean said No, Sheila said that, and left.

Anne asked me What could it be and asked me to go and find out. I told her she should go and she said that if she went Terry would get involved.

Anne stayed in my house and I went and spoke to a neighbor and she told me there was a murder. A woman had been knifed to death.

I left immediately and went back to my house and told Anne. She went white again and she looked feignt. I suggested she go find Terry. She started to tremble. She said she was going home to find the knife and he would have had blood on his clothes, wouldn't he? She asked me if I saw blood on him when he came home and I said, no, I didn't think so although I wasn't sure.

IN TALKING WITH AL about the Lambert case, I avoid the obvious comment: Christ, all this for seven hundred dollars' worth of crack, and the next night the guy's so bored he's beating up an old man in a bar. I do, however, give in to the obvious question, and receive the obvious answer.

No, Al readily admits, the police would not have gone after the murderer with such single-minded intensity if the victim had been some poor, all but nameless black street person robbed of a pack of cigarettes and the few dollars in his pocket and left beaten to death in some gutter. Fewer Homicide detectives would have been sent to the scene, less time spent collecting evidence—how much could you find in a gutter anyhow? The chief medical examiner would hardly be expected to show up. Al wouldn't have been so fussy about the morgue wagon stretchers and shrouds.

Al remembers a course he took once, taught by a high-level police type who pointed out that certain murders, involving the wrong people in the wrong parts of town, have always been routinely treated by everybody as *misdemeanor* homicides.

The reporters sometimes like to ride cops about this. But where, Al asks, were *they* last week in the rain at four A.M. when the derelict's body was discovered in the gutter? At least the cops showed up. The crime-scene team was there. Homicide detectives checked the area and questioned anyone who'd talk to them. A pathologist from the medical examiner's office dragged himself out of bed to declare the guy dead and perform a prelim. All this while the reporters, if they were on duty at all at that dreary hour, were comfortably ensconced back at headquarters working on their hot coffee and crossword puzzles, perfectly content to wait until somebody got back with all the information they needed for the story that they knew damn well wouldn't get more than an inch or two back among the used-car sales and radar-detector ads on page 17.

Of course, the reason the reporters aren't out there is simple enough: none of us regular folks—the TV-watching, newspaper-reading public—gives a damn whether they are or not. The blame, if that's the word, goes right up the line until it reaches us. The police chiefs, the editors, the politicians, don't really care because they know we don't.

Al remembers a letter in some paper about the beating and rape a few years back of that woman jogger in Central

Park. The writer complained about all the editorials saying what a horrible crime it was. Wouldn't it have been just as horrible no matter who the victim had been? Sure, but the reason the jogger case shook most people was their identification with the jogger. The same with Barbara Lambert. She could have been their sister, wife, mother, gruesomely violated and battered and murdered by some lowlife drug addict. Get the son of a bitch. String him up.

If they even bother to read that two-inch story on the dead body in the gutter, most people will shrug. After all, there's no connection with themselves, with their friends and families, and so because they're not interested, neither are the press or the politicians or the police. But of all those groups, the police are the only ones who *have* to pay attention, who *have* to be out on that cold and rainy and dirty street at four A.M.

Maybe the best way to understand the realities of police work is to acknowledge its dual nature. The cop on the beat is hired in the hope that he may help to prevent crime and thereby maintain some semblance of civility and safety. In trying to do this, he spends most of his time among the impoverished and the disenfranchised, where the drug and crime cultures intersect and flourish.

The job of the investigator—the detective, the evidence gatherer, the laboratory specialists who've been trained in pathology and serology and firearms examination—is to solve specific crimes after they have been committed. Typically this involves tracking down a young man who's emerged from his own neighborhood, eluding the cop patrolling that beat, to infiltrate other neighborhoods and commit crimes against people like Barbara Lambert.

Looking back on the Lambert case, Al provides a couple of final thoughts. "Remember how we had to fight to keep Dr. Hersh away from the body until we could get in to gather our evidence? Well, Cronin and I were both called on the carpet for that, and reprimanded for keeping the medical examiner from doing his job. We said we were just trying to do our own jobs, but were chastised anyway." Al feels he was eventually vindicated by a recent change in department procedure. Now, the MEs aren't even summoned to a homicide until the crime-scene team has the chance to gather its evidence.

Al's even more satisfying postscript: Terry Harrington was convicted of second-degree murder and is now serving twenty-five years to life, his various appeals all denied. Al testified at length during the trial, withstanding challenges from the defense on a number of points, including the eventual disintegration of a piece of evidence—the cheese.

SATURATING HARLEM WITH OP TWO-FIVE

"I ALWAYS WANTED TO be a policeman," Johnny says, reaching for his diet soda. The two of us are standing in the kitchen while he cooks lunch, three hamburgers popped straight from the freezer into an electric fry pan, one for me, two for him. His wife Jeannette is working at the Wilkes Gallery, a successful custom-framing and arts-and-crafts shop that they own and operate together in Northport a few miles from the house. Johnny's a big man, in his sixties now, someone old-time reporters wouldn't be able to resist describing as a "burly ex-cop." His short gray hair curls as tightly as a Brillo pad. He's still a powerful man, still physically active, playing golf almost daily through the summer, although for years he's been troubled by bad knees, which eventually will need surgery.

"Jeannette keeps after me to cut down," he says, putting his two patties on a single bun and loading on the ketchup and relish. I follow him into the living room, his limp reminding me of the way his father walked at the same age. We settle into upholstered armchairs, balancing our paper plates.

It's a large, tastefully furnished room (Jeannette's touch) with fine rugs, unusual lamps and end tables, a suburban home with a wooden deck over a spacious pool, with trees and bushes and lawns that Johnny faithfully tends.

We chat casually until we finish eating, and then Johnny settles back to tell me of his first days as a cop out on the streets of East Harlem.

JOHN CUOMO ➡

I FIRST TOOK the written test for the NYPD when I was around twenty-one, but then got drafted into the Army and sent to Texas for basic training before I could take the police physical. I tried to get into the MPs, but the Army put me in radio school.

For me, a big attraction of the police was that they judged you on performance, not schooling. I'd pretty much finished my education by age fifteen, after less than two years at two high schools, so didn't have much choice of long-range jobs. After growing up in the Depression, we were all looking for something steady, where you weren't afraid of being tossed out when things got slow, the way our fathers always were, and you could eventually count on a decent pension. Since the chances of a poor Italian kid without a diploma weren't all that good in business, a lot of my friends were attracted to civil service, with the brighter ones, I noticed, often going into the police. That became my ambition, not to rise up to detective, which was way beyond my expectations, but just to get on the force, to prove myself good enough to become a street cop.

Jeannette and I were married by the time I got out of the Army, and right after my discharge I went to work as a bus driver for the Transit Authority while waiting for the next police test. The pay was good, especially with overtime, so I looked upon bus driving as my backup, because I knew how tough it was getting on the police. About thirty thousand applicants took the test with me, from which they published a list of fifteen hundred eligibles based on a passing score on all three tests, written, physical, and medical. For the physical, you had to carry a 120-pound weight through a full obstacle course. You had to broad-jump, do pectoral lifts with 45 pounds in each hand, situps with 90 pounds behind your back. Of course you trained for this, and studied for the written.

Today it's a lot different. On the physical, for instance, they don't even make you carry a weight, you just have to run the course. As for the written, one of my friend's sons brought home a recent police test. What three colors are used in New York City traffic lights? That was an actual question. We had to do math and know about the city and state and even national government. If the president and vice president both died, who would take over? They asked us things like that.

Anyhow, I came out five hundredth, which put me in the top one-and-a-half percent of the thirty thousand applicants, and the top one-third of the fifteen hundred eligibles. That was high enough for an appointment, but not until the following year, so I took my onetime use of veteran's preference points to move up to three hundredth and receive my appointment that year. I was overjoyed because I wanted it so badly, and because a lot of people had gone out of their way to tell me I'd never make it.

My class spent about four months at the Police Academy. You learn a lot there, but they don't really prepare you to go out on the street by yourself. What they give you is the basics, plus the theory, most of which turns out to be bullshit. The most practical training you get is from the tours of duty in grays, as sort of apprentices. You'd be assigned to traffic, or ball games, parades, various occasions or celebrations, but always supervised by an experienced officer. In class they used script presentations that were supposed to prepare you to react to different situations. In a domestic dispute, say, how you should respond, what you should say to the husband or wife to resolve the situation. But we were already beginning to sense that when you walked into a bloody kitchen at three o'clock in the morning somewhere down in Harlem—well, you usually had to just throw all that out and fend for yourself.

That's where they sent every one of us, not only into East Harlem but into a single precinct there. For the first time in history, in what the department and the newspapers called a bold new experiment, the whole graduating class in 1954—some two hundred and fifty newly sworn patrolmen—were assigned to the Two-Five Precinct, which was supposed to be one of the most violent and crime-ridden areas in the city.

Nothing like that had ever been tried before, because each graduating class would be spread out over all forty-one precincts. They were using us to see if absolute saturation could cut down on crime and protect the victims of crime within a heretofore very bad neighborhood. Prior to this, the Two-Five was undermanned, if anything, without even the manpower to cover the precinct with radio cars. And they'd never send out foot patrolmen at night, it was just too dangerous. In other words, the city had more or less given up on that area.

Then all two hundred and fifty of us showed up, maybe a little shiny-faced and green but wearing police uniforms and carrying weapons, and overnight the precinct had five or six times as many police as they did the day before. And the Two-Five was small, maybe a square mile all told in northern Manhattan, from 110th to 125th Street, and from the East River to Fifth Avenue. Even so, it contained three distinct sections of black, Italian, and Puerto Rican residents, with practically no overlap. Blacks just didn't go into the Italian neighborhoods, and vice versa.

Even the crimes were different. You had a lot of petty street crimes in the black and Puerto Rican neighborhoods, but very little in the Italian stronghold, from about 112th to 116th Street on the East Side, where you had a lot of old tenements, clubs, groceries. But the big-time crime bosses lived there and ran narcotics and gambling operations. All the major gambling banks were located in that area. Later on when I got into Narcotics, I learned that the tenement building next to this very famous Italian church, Mt. Carmel, was used by drug couriers who hid and picked up their shipments from behind a radiator. That really got me—only a few feet from this world-renowned church.

Of course, I was as raw as could be at the time, and had no inkling of anything like that. Like most of the others, I had never been to a black or Puerto Rican neighborhood before. To be honest, I'd have to say that as a kid growing up in the Pelham Bay neighborhood of the Bronx, I never knew a black person and was pretty much taught to fear them. I remember people saying they'd stopped picnicking or whatever in Pelham Bay Park, only a few blocks from my home, because the blacks were going there now.

In fact, it was at the Academy that I had my first real contacts with blacks. There weren't as many of them on the force as you have now, maybe around 10 percent, but there were never any clashes. Over the years I worked with a lot of black officers, and I can really say that it was the police force, that a lot of people think of as antiminority, that gave me the opportunity to know and respect blacks. But that came later for me, as opposed to something I brought with me from the beginning.

It wasn't just in the racial area that I was naïve. I was twenty-three years old and ignorant about all kinds of things. Narcotics, for instance. I never even knew anybody who used marijuana. I didn't know what marijuana looked like, or what it was supposed to do for you, where you could buy it, how much it cost. I remember reading about some actor—I think Robert Mitchum—being charged with marijuana use and thinking, What the hell is that all about? Is the guy some crazy drug fiend or what?

Most rookies were in the same boat, more ignorant than seems possible nowadays, and there we were, plopped down into a Harlem we hardly knew existed, that could have been some mysterious country on the other side of the world. Where's 119th Street? Where's Lenox Avenue? Where the hell are we?

Within the operation, you were assigned to a very small foot patrol, which you walked alone, although you regularly had visual sightings of another patrolman as you moved from block to block. You might have, say, both sides of Third Avenue from 110th to 113th, and would go halfway down the block on each cross street. The guy patrolling Second Avenue would be doing the same, so you'd see each other. Each patrolman was also assigned one of the fifteen or twenty call boxes spread through the area, and you called in regularly. That way the station would hear from at least one patrolman in a given area every five or ten minutes. A lot more patrol cars were also assigned to the precinct, manned by veterans who would be constantly driving around looking for signs of trouble and ready to answer calls for help.

We were fully apprised of all these procedures ahead of time and could appreciate that it was a well-thought-out system. Still, starting out there gave us a very strange and funny feeling. Just putting on the uniform for the first time is something you never forget. And naturally it rained like hell that night, and since there weren't enough lockers we had to commute to work already dressed, which meant that my brand-new blues were absolutely drenched by the time I *arrived* at the station house.

You could really feel the excitement, along with all the tension and nervousness, as everybody sat around the damp-smelling muster room waiting for our tour to begin. Various guys played cards or dominoes or just bullshitted with each other to pass the time, including this fellow Dick Manning, who later became, and still is, a very good friend of mine. He was playing dominoes with his cap tilted back when this veteran cop strolled in. We didn't even know who the old-timer was, but later on discovered he was this really dumb guy who people could never believe had actually passed the test because he was such a jerk. Anyhow, he just strolled into the muster room as cool as can be, not only with his gun out but actually twirling it, cowboy style. We were positive he had to know what he was doing, because none of us would have dared try that with a loaded pistol. He seemed to be having a lot of fun swinging it around his finger until suddenly this incredible explosion rocked the room and Dick Manning's hat actually flew off his head. It was like a movie, like a joke, the hat flying off like that, and then someone picked it up and, Christ, there's this perfect round bullet hole in the front. Maybe three inches lower and it would have got him right in the forehead. We still talk about that. There we were, all these jumpy probationers trying not to turn into a bunch of nervous ninnies on our first patrol, and one of us almost gets his head blown off by another cop. During my next twenty years on the force, nothing even close to that ever happened again.

Nor did I run across anything that exciting out on the street. Mostly I remember the rain coming down in torrents and keeping me soaked for eight solid hours. I didn't even know enough to get under something, to step into a hallway. I figured I couldn't let anything interfere with responsibility to duty, which was walking my beat, so I walked it the whole goddamn time even though, on a night like that, you'd have to be an awful dumb crook to be out there causing trouble.

The experiment lasted a few months and really seemed to be successful. The criminal element wasn't used to operating with cops all over the place, especially this bunch of gung-ho kids trying to make their way, butting into things and pulling people in for everything from really minor stuff up to serious assaults, none of which ever got much noticed before. We hounded the street thieves and hookers and drug pushers, the people fighting or shooting or stabbing each other in bars and gambling clubs. Although the number of arrests went up, the number of reported crimes actually went down. Before we got there, the cops wouldn't even bother with something like car theft, which was very commonplace at the time. But now you had a couple of hundred cops writing down for every tour the alarms, that day's fresh list of stolen cars, and then keeping an eye out for them on the street.

To keep an eye on all these rookies, the department naturally sent in a lot of brass, captains and lieutenants and sergeants, so at all times we had to look and act really sharp. Before every tour we'd muster for a military-type inspection, where a lieutenant would walk between the lines for a very close look at everyone, and you'd get all kinds of hell if you weren't impeccably groomed with your uniform and all required equipment in perfect order.

Like all precincts, the Two-Five had its own internal structure and mode of operation that had developed over the years, and even with all these new superior officers coming in, the old-timers

still maintained a lot of their previous authority over their own little regimes. In the Two-Five, for instance, Lieutenant Mangello
was a real legendary character. Everybody called him Mangy—
with the real Italian pronunciation, *Mon*-gee—and for years he'd
run the precinct with a very strong personal hand. If there was
trouble anywhere in the Two-Five, especially within the Italian element, whoever was on the desk would say, Hey, let's get Lieutenant Mangello in on this. You'd bring in a bookmaker, a thief, a
numbers runner, a corner drug dealer, any kind of action at all,
and Mangy might say, Hey, take him in back and come see me.
You'd get the guy out of earshot and explain to Mangy why you'd
brought him in. He'd listen and maybe say, Okay, fine, go book
him. Or he might say, Go upstairs and get yourself a cup of coffee
and I'll talk to him. When you came back, Mangy might say, Go
back on patrol, everything's taken care of, and you'd look up and
see the guy you brought in strolling out the front door.

No one disputed Mangy. He'd been born and raised in the district and knew everybody who lived there and exactly what kind of
business, legitimate or otherwise, they were involved in. He never
explained his reasons for what he did, although sometimes he
might shrug and say, It's okay, kid, I know the family, nice family,
nothing to worry about. And it wasn't just the Italians. He kept
tabs on the blacks and Puerto Ricans too, knew all the varieties of
activities, the good families and the bad, the decent kids and the
punks.

Nowadays people might say Mangy's palm was just being
greased by the guys he let walk, but I think that misses the point.
Sure, Mangy had lots of friends around, including the business-
men, the store owners, and around the holidays he'd get little gifts
from those people. That was true of almost everyone except us
young kids, who didn't stay there long enough for Christmas. But
the regular patrolmen would always be taken care of. The grocer
or the guy who ran the garage or the bowling alley, he'd say, Let's
give the fella a hat for Christmas. That was the term: a hat, meaning around twenty-five dollars. You could buy yourself a nice hat
for that amount. Or they'd give you a bottle of liquor, a couple of

tickets to a ball game, whatever. The store owner might bump into the patrolman on the street and say, Hey, did Louie see you? Did Louie take care of you for the holidays?

A person in Mangy's position no doubt did better with gifts than the cop on the beat. But that didn't mean he was on the take. Mangy ran the precinct the way he did, deciding who got booked and who didn't, who got listened to and who didn't, because he had more experience and knowledge than anyone else and saw it as his legitimate responsibility to take charge. It was the old way of doing things, like with Tammany Hall in New York or Mayor Daley running Chicago with a very personal day-to-day control over everything. I don't remember how many times Daley got re-elected, but I suspect if the people in the Two-Five had the chance, they'd have kept electing Mangy for as long as he wanted to run.

Out on the street, of course, you didn't have Mangy around to tell you how to handle everything that came up. We didn't even carry radios in those days, but had to use the nearest call box or public phone to contact the station in an emergency. We were very much on our own, without the immediate help a patrolman can sum-mon today, even though we hardly knew one end of a nightstick from the other. We learned from our mistakes, and from the veter-ans. Not that the old-timers ever said much. They didn't see them-selves as teachers, or even talkers. They'd say, Don't worry, kid, just watch me, and whatever I do, you do. We watched them real close, because we knew we had to pick up things very quickly if we wanted to survive out there.

Sure, we had a uniform and everything, but the sidewalks were crowded with people who'd grown up in this environment, who knew their own neighborhoods, whether black or Italian or Puerto Rican, in a way we'd never know them. We were absolutely in the dark about drugs and numbers and gambling scams, about stickups and knifings and what people with gunshot wounds re-ally looked like, about street kids who very casually accepted all kinds of violent behavior as a part of everyday life. When you sud-denly found yourself dropped down in the middle of all this, your whole life and attitudes changed. People sometimes ask how long it took to get used to what you saw. I don't think you ever got used to it. You had to learn to deal with it, though, as a regular part of your job.

Another early incident that always stood out in my mind also involved someone who later became a dear friend, Howie Hundgeon. Howie was a hardnosed radio-car operator in the Two-Five with about two years already on the force. Well, I was on patrol very late one night when someone rushed out of this tenement building yelling, Help! Help! and as soon as I entered I saw this guy above me on the second-floor landing. You have to remember that I was still very inexperienced, and to me he presented a really alarming sight, this great big guy, clearly out of his skull, screaming down at me, Come on up here, you mother! Come on up and I'll kick your fucking ass in!

I couldn't see if he had a gun or a knife up there, couldn't tell if he was drunk or drugged up or whatever, so was more than a little leery about approaching him. Only that was my job, to deal with people like that, and if I was going to be a cop, I would have to be ready to do it. But I had barely started, somewhat cautiously, up the stairs when the door behind me slammed open with a loud bang and these two policemen busted right in on us, Howie Hundgeon and his radio-car partner, neither of whom I'd ever seen before. Without a second's hesitation they rushed past me and pounded up the stairs, Howie leading the way. Before the guy up there had any chance to attack them, Howie whacked him with his nightstick and yanked him away from the banister he was clutching, and the next thing I knew the guy was tumbling down the stairs.

Howie accomplished all this without saying a word. He immediately recognized, you see, that I didn't have the situation under control, so his first order of business was to protect me by taking command. Then he asked, You all right, kid? I told him I was and he said he'd call an ambulance for the guy, who was groaning and muttering on the floor, and that I should make out an Aided Card, which was the form you used when you aided someone who required an ambulance. And that was it, they just took off and left me there to sort out the situation and think over whatever lessons I'd learned.

Guys like Howie Hundgeon who operated radio cars in the Two-Five hardly got a chance to catch their breath, let alone grab a coffee and talk things over, what with these hotshot probationary cops calling in all the time over things nobody had ever been around to report before, an ambulance here, somebody hurt in a fight, a wife having a baby, a crowd outside a bar. You also had plenty of more serious matters, like a Ten-Thirteen, Assist Patrolman, which always brought a very heavy response, especially if linked with Shots Fired, or Cop Shot, anything of that nature. Everybody dropped whatever they were doing and rushed to the scene. I've been on an Assist Patrolman in Harlem where as many as thirty radio cars showed up.

Gradually some of us began to move into the radio cars, not as operator but as recorder, the number-two man who handled the radio and assisted the operator any way he could. Maybe you'd get a couple of car tours a week, and when the operator wanted a break you'd get your turn behind the wheel. Being mobile like that and responding to calls from patrolmen, you saw twice as much in one night than you would a whole week on foot, which really quickened your pace of learning about things.

The most common instance you ran into was the domestic dispute, which could be punching and beating up, but was often the husband or wife stabbing one another during an argument, usually after a drinking bout. It was often a serious wound, somebody slashed in the stomach, the face, the arms. When you got there they might still be yelling and screaming, each accusing the other of starting the fight or running around or drinking or gambling away their money. But as soon as you arrived they'd start yelling at you, and all the friends and neighbors crowded into the hallway or living room or kitchen would start yelling at you too, defending one person and demanding you arrest the other, or telling you not to arrest anybody but to mind your own business and leave them both alone.

Given the explosiveness of the situation, especially in a black neighborhood with you and your partner the only whites in sight, your other real concern was to protect yourself and not be dragged into the melee, which is exactly what would happen if you started blaming or arresting anybody, especially since you almost always got two absolutely contradictory versions of what had taken place. If the male cut the female, his friends would be all over you shouting it was her fault, she was a bitch, she was running around, she came at him with the knife and got cut when he tried to grab it away. If the female cut the male, which you ran into just about as often, her friends would be screaming exactly the same things at you. According to what the Academy taught, you were supposed to gather evidence, interview witnesses, and take statements, but you could spend hours writing everything down without getting any closer to solving anything, so you just tried to settle the situation down as quickly and cleanly as possible. If you actually spent all night trying to sort everything out and ran in either the husband or wife with a whole notebook full of explanations and accusations, the desk officer would laugh you out of the room. Jesus, he'd think, we really have a dumb greenhorn here! The veterans would tell you that when one or both of the couple sobered up in the morning, the injured party would almost always tell the police to forget it. Everything's okay now, they'd say, skip the whole thing.

Today, with all the new attitudes and awareness about battered wives and violence in the home, that seems hard to believe, but at the time, especially in the poorer, rougher neighborhoods, it was extremely rare for a husband or wife to press charges against each other, over anything. Of course, the whole situation of people beating each other up in their own homes was something completely alien to me, and part of what I mentioned before about getting accustomed to a different way of life than I grew up with.

Detectives seemed to me a breed apart in those days, almost like some kind of sacred person, and when you dealt with them it was like walking on eggshells. If one said, Hey, kid! You! Get over here!

you came running, Yes sir, yes sir, what is it, sir? You always called them *sir.* They were mostly in their thirties and forties, whereas we were in our early twenties, and they had so much experience and smarts and confidence that it was hard to believe that at one time they'd also just been ordinary greenhorns.

They all had well-known reputations which they'd developed over the years. You felt they could handle anything that came up, and it was an important part of their reputation for you to believe this. You would never see a good detective lose control or look unsure of himself. Of course, certain detectives had bad reputations too, including the heavy drinkers, known as slosh guys, and the ones you couldn't depend on or that would let their personal problems interfere with their work. Dependability and trust were particularly important, because you had to rely on each other, and if the other guy had his mind somewhere else, it could be a very dangerous thing for all concerned.

And a detective, or anybody in law enforcement, had to have the reputation of being a man of his word. You dealt with all kinds of people, and every one of them had to know that when you said something, you meant it. If you told even the lowest punk, Look, I'll meet you at Alfonso's tonight at eight, you made damn sure you showed up, no matter what. You knew that if you reneged even just once, your word would lose its value and nobody would want to deal with you about anything.

Being a policeman was really different back then, maybe worse in some ways but better in others. For one, the communication with the public was better. The police and the people were closer, more knowledgeable and respectful of each other. I think that was even true on the black/white issue. True, the black neighborhoods had mostly white cops, but not exclusively, and both black and white officers considered themselves policemen first and worked together without problems, and also worked with all the decent neighborhood people who were being hurt most by the crime. You also stayed in one area longer, which gave you and the residents a chance to get to know each other. A father might come up and say,

Billy's getting kind of wild these days, he's out all night and we don't even know what kind of crowd he's with. You wouldn't just let it ride, but would keep an eye out for the kid and try to help him straighten out. As time went on, though, you'd be given more area to patrol, and get shifted around more often, and would just become another outsider not to be trusted.

I have to laugh, but when you say today that parents might actually come up to a cop to ask for help with their kid, people don't believe it. They think you've just got this rosy glow about the good old days. But when I started out, being a street cop was an honorable position, not only in our minds but in everybody's. Many times people asked me for all kinds of help, even when I was just this fuzzy-cheeked kid in the Two-Five. At first, because I was right out there on the street, it happened with both blacks and whites. Later on in other mixed precincts it would be mostly whites who came in, because blacks would not want to be seen talking to a white Narcotics detective. If the next day I made a drug bust, even if it was totally unconnected, it would not look good and they would be fearful of retribution. What you'd get would be anonymous calls from people concerned about their neighborhood, tipping you off that the super of such-and-such a house on East 119th was selling drugs to young kids. Then they'd quick hang up without another word.

As time went on, there was less and less informal contact. Everything became more cold and suspicious between the blacks and whites and various Hispanics. By the time I retired, the Puerto Ricans and Cubans and South Americans were all on different sides of the fence from each other and from everybody else.

During my first years, for instance, women would come in and even talk about sexual things their husbands would make them do, or about him going to some whorehouse, all kinds of stuff. We had to be what you'd now call a counselor, although God knows we weren't trained for that. But people back then had nowhere else to go, except maybe the church, and people would tell us stuff they wouldn't be caught dead saying to a priest. All the social and psychological agencies you have now, the help groups for battered women and runaway children and drug addicts, we had practically none of that. So we did the best we could to listen to people and calm them down, point out the various things they could do and whatever services were available at the time.

I'm not saying we were altogether good Samaritans. You could never let yourself lose your hard edge, your wariness, your sense of having to protect yourself at all times. Still, I think a good part of a policeman's job is like being a nurse. I'm sure I've got as many prejudices and misconceptions, pro and con, as the next person, but I always believed that a policeman's job was to help people, not check first to see if they're black or white.

Oftentimes this got you into situations that couldn't by any stretch of the imagination be considered pleasant. Years after the Two-Five, my partner and I were patrolling in a squad car out of the Detective Division in Brooklyn when a frantic cabbie pulled up and showed us this guy in the back seat, a black guy, that had been stabbed so bad most of his intestines were hanging out. He flopped into my cab before I realized he was hurt, the driver said. Take him to the hospital, do what you want, just get him out of my cab. It must've been three in the morning, a bitter, icy night, and I remember having to watch our footing while transferring him from the cab into our back seat, which believe me wasn't the least bit easy or neat, because the guy was bleeding and his intestines were oozing and bubbling up. The nearest hospital happened to be a private one, and the woman at the desk behind these locked glass doors said they wouldn't accept emergency cases. Even though we were police officers, she refused to open the door and told us to take him to a public hospital. So with this guy bleeding and gasping horribly in the back seat we drove into downtown Brooklyn to this other place, where we helped the orderlies get him out of the car and onto a stretcher for the emergency room. We wrote it up: Felonious assault, unknown assailant or assailants, victim unable to be interrogated. It took us hours just to clean up and dry out the back seat, and we figured all that messy running around was just a lost cause anyway, because the guy had to be a goner. But when we called the hospital the next day they said, Oh, no, he's fine. The doctor fixed him all up and we'll release him in a couple of days.

In a similar instance we were summoned to a fourth-floor walk-up apartment to assist a female assault victim. She was an extremely large black woman who'd also been badly stabbed in the abdomen. She was fully conscious, though, sitting very unruffled on a kitchen chair holding her intestines in her hands. We got a wet towel to make it easier for her to hold everything in until the ambulance arrived. Then we helped the orderlies get her downstairs. She weighed well over two hundred pounds, and we carried her down on the kitchen chair, with the two ambulance men and us each holding one chair leg. She'd gotten weaker, so one of us had to use his free hand to keep the wet towel in place. She just sat up there above us on the chair, sort of moaning softly, almost like humming, as we struggled and lurched down all those narrow twisting flights of stairs to get her out of there without the whole bunch of us crashing down in a heap.

Maybe the first thing I learned in the Two-Five was that whatever you dealt with on a given day—beatings, stabbings, rapes, suicides, auto wrecks where you found people all bleeding and mangled up inside, screaming in agony with bones sticking through their skin, homicides where you have to deal with someone who's been shot in the head, with brains and body fluids all over the place—you just can't bring any of that home to your wife and children. I always told Jeannette a cop had to be two different people, with two different personalities. At home, I tried to be your average husband and father. With Danny, Marianne, and Bobby, I got involved in Little League and CYO baseball, in school football. I coached teams, umpired and helped raise money, worked on maintaining the fields. For a time, I was Big Brother to a boy a couple of years younger than Danny whose father was in a mental institution. I'd see him once or twice a week and sometimes take Danny along, so the three of us could go to a ball game or get a soda together or whatever. I bought him a bat and glove and we'd just go out and hit a ball around sometimes. I also used to help run the Big Brothers' annual picnic. Now, there were occasions at work when I could be open and friendly like that, but a lot of the time I had to act out that other part of me, with that other, harder, distrustful personality, or I would never have lasted or maintained my sanity.

Over the many years since, Operation Two-Five has become kind of legendary in the annals of the police department, partly because it was the first ever saturation attempt like that, and because it was considered a tremendous success. The department, in fact, repeated the identical procedure in some other precincts, where it produced the same increase in arrests and decrease in crimes. Because every time the saturation was employed, the drug dealers and pimps and petty thieves immediately felt the effect of our presence, and so did the regular law-abiding residents of those areas, who appreciated the safety and security of knowing that twenty-four hours a day they could count on a patrolman walking a beat nearby.

Eventually, other sides of Operation Two-Five also came to light, that nobody could have predicted ahead of time. For one, a number of that group eventually got arrested for one reason or another—including me. Some of us got our names cleared, some got in serious trouble. On the other hand, only a few of all those Academy graduates remained patrolmen throughout their careers. And over the years, they probably made more important arrests and received more awards and commendations than any comparable group. A great many moved up to detective or even lieutenant or captain, often very quickly, and usually in the much-prized Narcotics and Homicide squads. One guy even became assistant chief of detectives.

Maybe it'd be an interesting research study for a university or something, whether the record compiled by those rookies afterward was the result of that unusual early experience. One thing

certain is that we were a special group in many ways, but personally I haven't the slightest explanation for either the good or bad
things that happened to us afterward.

Some of the guys, as I said, remain dear friends to this day, like
Dick Manning and Howie Hundgeon and his wife Angie, and others too. Some Op Two-Five graduates became quite famous, like
Sonny Grosso, who I was very close to back then and who helped
get me assigned to Narcotics. He played a major part in the French
Connection drug case that they based the movie on, and then took
early retirement to become a very successful movie and TV pro-
ducer himself. But for most of the guys back then, I have no idea
what they're doing now, or if they belonged to the group that
moved up or the group that got in trouble, or even if they're still
alive. What we ought to do, I often think, is trace everybody down
and invite them to a big gala reunion, so we can see who shows up
and find out what happened to everybody since.

IN HIS OFFICIAL REPORT, an obviously proud New York City
police commissioner, Francis W. H. Adams, said, "Operation
25—to the best of our knowledge—represents the first time
that an urban police department has ever tried in this way to
determine precisely what constitutes adequate policing."

He presents impressive statistics, such as a 50 percent re-
duction in robbery, burglaries, grand larceny, auto theft, felonious assaults, incest, frauds, arson, forgery, etc. With some
crimes, he said, "It is desirable to show an increase in . . . vio-
lations which testify to the alertness and effectiveness of
policing . . . disorderly conduct, gambling, prostitution, narcotic cases and the possession of dangerous weapons." Here
he reported the desired growth in both crimes reported and
arrests.

And the more sweeping investigations made possible by
the additional police, he said, led to great increases in the solution rates of reported crimes.

My own research into law-enforcement data some years

ago produced a thoroughgoing skepticism about all crime statistics. Besides the ambiguity and elusiveness of what is supposedly being catalogued, all too often the evidence is assembled and the conclusions presented by people with the greatest interest in those conclusions, and the strongest desire to buttress their own preconceptions. Commissioner Adams, for instance, openly admits that "we in the department have always believed that good order and peace are possible given enough men. For that reason we decided to put this belief to the test of practical demonstration."

In his own words, we have a demonstration rather than an experiment. It can hardly be a surprise that Adams then used his own analysis of his own statistics to support his plea for more money for more police to cut down on crime.

"We have shown, beyond question, that crime can be drastically reduced in this city. We have shown that it is possible to have peace, security, dignity and order in the City of New York. We have shown that we can establish what Mayor Wagner has so clearly described as a climate of law and order, the kind of climate without which we can never hope to solve such complex problems as juvenile delinquency and similar social ills."

The reference to juvenile delinquency seems almost quaint now, but the findings from Op Two-Five are so decisive that even if skewed by self-interest, they remain impressive enough to make their point.

As for Adams's conviction that complicated social dilemmas can be solved in a simple, straightforward manner, such radiant optimism still lives. Op Two-Five took place in 1954, when Dwight Eisenhower was President. A few months ago, in 1994, President Clinton proposed bringing crime under control by putting a hundred thousand more police on the street—citing the same reasons, pretty much, that Commissioner Adams mentioned forty years ago:

"This community was on the verge of becoming a city of violence and crime. . . . For the first six months of 1954 there was an increase of about 11 per cent in major crimes over the first half of 1953. Now I have the equally unpleasant duty of reporting to you that crime continues on the rise in New York. As I have made clear many times, the lack of law and order in this city is chiefly due to a shortage of at least 7,000 men in the police department. . . ."

Yet none of this history, let alone the juggling of all those numbers and percentages, gives any sense of what it must have been like for a twenty-three-year-old rookie cop to step onto the rainy, windswept Harlem streets for the first time, not only willing but eager to take on challenges and obligations and risks that neither I nor my friends want any part of.

SECTION II

W O R K I N G   Y O U N G

LIKE MOST KIDS we grew up with, all the cousins started working early and went through the gamut of typical kid jobs featuring long hours, grumpy bosses, lousy pay. Yet I think we all felt good being able to do something outside the home that some stranger was willing to pay us for. At that time, in those families, I don't think the idea of complaining about a *job* ever occurred to us. When you reached a certain age, school simply became less important, work more. If you contributed to the family's welfare, no matter how modestly, it showed that you were levelheaded and responsible, not some scatterbrain full of foolishness. And if while making your way you had to cut a few corners in school, or even quit altogether, what was so terrible about that?

J O H N   C U O M O ➡

I MUST HAVE BEEN about ten when I started delivering groceries at the A & P for tips, then took over my older brother Alfred's job in a tailor shop for maybe three bucks a week and an occasional ten-cent tip for delivering the clothes. I went to work in a drugstore for a couple of dollars more, and on Saturdays would bring half of it home to my mother and stop off at the bakery to pick up a cake or something as a special surprise.

Around my fifteenth birthday, during World War II, I was hired by Woolworth's as a stock boy, and turned out to be the only male except the boss, who was too old to be drafted, in a store full of women. The boss took a shine to me and got me into their management training program at fifty dollars a week, an awful lot of money back then, especially for a fifteen-year-old who lied about his age to get hired in the first place.

But it was full-time, more than full-time, because they had me doing everything under the sun, including staying late after the women left to mop all the floors and shelve fresh stock for the next morning. The only way I could work those hours and make that money was by dropping out of school, but you had to be sixteen to do that, so I just stopped going. I let my parents think I was still just working after school and tried to intercept the letters the school was sending home. Eventually my mother figured out what was going on, only here I was, bringing home this incredible amount of money, so I don't remember her making too much of a stink.

My real mistake was bringing into the store a good friend of mine, who was sort of a cutup and caused me to lose some favor with the manager. Between that and the war ending, making it easy again to hire men of normal age, the job faded off. For a while I went to Staten Island every morning to shape up as a longshoreman, and got a construction job dipping lumber into creosote vats for those great stretches of Quonset huts being built as temporary veterans' housing out in Brooklyn. There was good money in that too, but the unions naturally preferred taking on returning vets as opposed to bunch of kids.

My big break came when the War Assets Board opened up a huge complex of Quonset huts at Westchester Square to sell off wholesale lots of surplus government supplies, uniforms, mess kits, tools, tents, vehicles, anything except firearms, and my friend Ally Wadman's sister, who worked at the food concession, got us jobs in the café. When a similar War Assets place opened in Jersey, the café owner asked if we would run that for him, which we did very successfully and eventually bought him out. We weren't even eighteen yet, but had this very profitable café with a grill and counter and a full kitchen in back, where we served breakfast and lunch, including platters of doughnuts and sandwiches piled up for people flocking in on their coffee breaks saying, Give me sixteen coffees and sixteen Danish to go. When War Assets ran special sales, hundreds of cars would start lining up on U.S. 1 at midnight to get in early, and we'd work all night getting ready for the crush. Even on regular days, we got up at four A.M., so it wasn't easy, but we were making so much money we didn't know what to do with it. Sometimes after a big day we'd tally up eight hundred, twelve hundred dollars, and finally went so far as to open a bank account back in the Bronx, so we could deposit money there on weekends. Before that we never had bills or accounts or debts. We didn't understand bookkeeping so just paid cash for everything.

We had eight, ten thousand dollars in the bank when in 1947 the first new cars since before the war started rolling off the lines, and we bought a brand-new Chevrolet convertible, a very racy maroon car with a white top. It was really funny, these two kids strolling into the showroom and saying, Okay, we'll take this one, and putting down this paper bag with five or six thousand in cash. The dealer must've figured us for couple of gangsters, but he took the money.

What with the car and the bank account, Ally and I were living pretty high off the hog, going up to Yonkers to play the trotters, treating ourselves to fancy restaurants, but we never became spendthrifts. We weren't big gamblers or drinkers or party guys, we just had a lot more money than most kids our age.

With War Assets winding down, we looked for other opportunities. Owning a restaurant or bar looked like a good deal, but we were too young to get a liquor license. Vending machines were just coming into prominence, and we also gave that some thought. Meanwhile, I'd been giving my mother more money every week than she'd ever seen before, and she was squirreling it all away until she and my father combined it with everything else she'd squirreled away over the years to buy the house on Parkview Avenue, which I think cost five thousand dollars, about what we'd paid for the convertible.

A few odd jobs followed, and then I met Jeannette when we were both working at Orchard Beach. She'd gotten her high-school diploma from the Villa Maria Academy, this very high-rated Catholic girls' school in the Bronx, where they were taught by French nuns and everything. Even though I didn't have any kind of background like that, we began keeping company and before long I bought out Ally's share of the convertible and sold the car to buy an engagement ring.

Then in 1951, at age twenty-two, I got drafted into the Army—the same day as a whole bunch of my friends, since they used to call up a whole neighborhood at one time. Jeannette and I got married after I finished basic training, and we lived in Texas together until my two years were up and I could come back home and take the police exam.

AL DELLA PENNA ➡

GROWING UP, I never got along that well with my family. My father, of course, was drunk a lot and got worse as time went on, eventually losing his longtime job with the Transit Authority, which he'd pretty much held all through the Depression. It was practically impossible to get fired in that kind of bureaucracy, especially with a strong union, so that was an indication of how bad he'd gotten. He left after that, just disappeared, when I was in my teens, and I don't think anyone heard anything until years later when my mother was notified that he had died in a California veterans' hospital.

Actually, I didn't have that much trouble with him, as long as he left me alone. I was something of a wild, impatient kid, always wanting to go my own way without interference from my mother or anybody else, and always felt caged up at home. I'm sure my mother wanted the best for me, and I'm sure my older sister Jo did too, but I just felt under someone's thumb all the time, being told what I ought to be doing for my own good.

To give some idea of what passed for thinking on my part back then, just prior to turning seventeen I was talking with my hanging-around-the-Bronx-type friends who told me that one of the ways to score with girls was to join the Marine Corps Reserves. You get this uniform, they said, and you show up at Fort Schuyler Thursday nights for a few hours and then head for Westchester Square in your uniform and take your pick of the girls. Maybe I was ripe to buy into this because at the time I had the most unglamorous of my many teenage jobs, in a fresh-poultry store on Buhre Avenue, which provided little of the aura designed to attract female attention. So I joined the Marine Reserves on my birthday, while still in high school, and two months later, in June 1950, the North Koreans moved across the 38th Parallel, and Truman activated all the Reserve units, including mine.

It wasn't until I was many years older, and hopefully wiser, that I could look back and think, Hey, that's how kids end up being killed in wars—they want to strut around in fancy uniforms to impress the girls.

I was lucky enough to survive, though, even managed to learn a bit about myself in the process. Since I was assigned to a weapons battalion, I also learned something about the workings of a variety of handguns, rifles, and machine guns.

When I got out after a couple of years, I had no desire to go back with all the seventeen-year-olds at Christopher Columbus High. My father had disappeared by then, and I wanted to strike out on my own. I moved to Long Island and for four years remained pretty isolated from my family until after I met and married Mary, who helped get us all back together. So did Johnny, who'd call and say, Look, Al, why don't you get in touch with your mother? I didn't necessarily do it right away, but he helped edge me in that direction.

During that period away from the family in my early twenties, I bounced back and forth between factory jobs, hauling heavy material around, and working on a poultry farm, where I'd been hired on the basis of my experience in the poultry store. In addition to raising and slaughtering turkeys, I also got involved with artificial insemination, definitely a new experience for me. After Mary and I got married and started a family, though, I settled in at Air/Marine Motors, which produced small auxiliary motors for boats and airplanes, working my way up to head of production control for the whole factory.

By then, Johnny was already flourishing on the police, and took it upon himself to educate young Cousin Al in the ways of the world—in his own typically understated fashion. Al, he would say, no matter how good you think it is, any factory job makes you a factory worker, and no factory worker's worth a pimple on a policeman's ass. Then he would add, Only you have to pass a really tough exam and you probably couldn't manage that.

He wanted me to join him on the NYPD but I had no interest in working in the city, so took the Suffolk exam, where the county-wide merger of township police departments made for new openings. The written test was similar to the one in the city, and maybe I just wanted to show Johnny that I damn well *could* pass it, although I'm not sure I was actually all that confident.

What mainly worried me was the physical. They had a rigid 20/20 vision requirement, which I knew I could never meet. So the whole thing was just a lark, on the part of this big shot pulling down the handsome sum of nine thousand a year at Air/Marine. Then they notified me I'd passed the written and the medical with flying colors and only needed the physical to make the list. Suddenly I really did care. I'd do anything for that job, and when it came time for the physical I was a nervous wreck from wanting to pass it so bad. I was also very discouraged, because I knew I hadn't the slightest chance of doing so.

Was the uniform part of the attraction, meaning I wasn't really any smarter than I'd been in high school? Who can say deep down, but I like to think it was more than shiny buttons that drew me so strongly in that direction.

On the appointed day I joined your typical group exam, a bunch of naked guys moving from one station to another with the doctors patting and poking and sticking things into you. I'm doing fine, moving along with everyone else, but all the time dreading the guy with the eye chart.

Now, even with lots of openings, Suffolk had far more applicants than they could possibly take, so it wasn't like WW II, when the Army desperately needed cannon fodder and would take anybody who made it through the door. And all the other examiners had been very thorough and businesslike, but when I finally got to the eye doctor he must have had more important things on his mind. *Cover one eye and read the chart!* he barked, but in this very bored and mechanical voice of someone who'd been sitting there saying the same thing all day long. Maybe he was paring his fingernails or studying the *Daily Racing Form* or dreamily gazing off into space waiting for the time to pass. Whatever he was doing, I could see he wasn't paying the slightest attention to me. So I conveniently neglected to cover either eye and leaned and stretched and inched forward as far as I could and started barking the letters from the chart right back at him. I got maybe halfway through when he stopped me short with *Okay, next!* and scribbled his initials on my form. I was out of there like a shot, and then the realization hit me: Take that, Johnny, you old son of a bitch! I'm a cop!

Starting pay was five grand a year, and Air/Marine offered me ten to stay on. We had three kids by then, but Mary said, It's your decision, Al, you gotta live with it, and I was sworn in a month later and started walking my beat.

SINCE MY OLDER SISTER Marie died of polio when I was five, and my younger sister Rita wasn't born until I was thirteen, I was an only child for a long time, and for many of those Depression years my mother used the kitchen table to make artificial flowers at the going rate of a penny or so a dozen. Afterward she worked as a late-night cleaning woman at the Century Association, a private men's club in downtown Manhattan whose membership included presidents, governors, generals, artists, writers, Broadway stars. I guess my most vivid recollection of my mother, who as I write is approaching her ninety-second birthday, is that she never had it easy, and never complained.

My father, an honor student at Townsend Harris, a special high school open only on the basis of a very competitive citywide exam, had to leave the school in his first year, at fourteen, when his father died. He then struggled through his twenties and thirties, and through the Depression, via one precarious job after another until he finally settled in at Taller & Cooper as a precision grinder, where he worked until he died of pneumonia at fifty-three, after shrugging it off as a cold and going back to work, where he suffered a final collapse.

Growing up, I was much closer to the Italian relatives than to the Vogts on my mother's side, because none of my three German uncles had children my age. My early jobs were like my cousins': a meat-and-vegetable market, the Rogers Peet clothing store across from the New York Public Library, the Taller & Cooper factory practically under the Brooklyn Bridge, where my father served as union steward and helped me get hired. I continued working there either full- or part-time, both in the shop and in the front office as an advertising and PR writer, even after my father's death.

Besides the hard times our parents went through and our own early jobs, other parallels for Johnny and Al and me include our brief interludes of military service, relatively early marriages, and large families. Finally there's the fact that we all either gave up or turned down better-paying jobs in order to do what we wanted. In my case, while working for my master's degree at Indiana University, I was offered a position as head of toll collection for the newly opened Indiana turn-pike, based on my experience in the manufacture and sale of that equipment at Taller & Cooper. I turned down the better-paying job to stay in graduate school. Johnny and Al did it to become cops.

SIX BIG ONES

THE DEFEO MURDERS became the most notorious homicide case in which Al's work as a firearms expert played a significant role. The crime occurred in 1974 and received massive media coverage. Even *The New York Times* carried the story on page one for several days running, and included lengthy sidebars under such time-honored tabloid headlines as NEIGHBORS RECALL DEFEOS AS "NICE, NORMAL FAMILY." Before long the story received sensational treatment in such novels and movies as *The Amityville Horror. Good Housekeeping* also readily exploited the material. The one factual book, *High Hopes* by Gerard Sullivan, the prosecutor, and Harvey Aronson, has long been out of print.

Al remembers the case, he said, not only because of its notoriety, but because it left him with questions that he still can't answer.

The public fascination with the case, including the haunted-house spookiness of its weirder manifestations, probably springs from several causes. But maybe the simplest explanation was summed up by the Homicide detective who welcomed Al to the spacious DeFeo home with *Hi, Al, we got six big ones for you this time.*

A L D E L L A P E N N A ➡

I WAS LIVING in Brentwood then, and late on the night of the thir-teenth of November, I received a call at home reporting a homicide in Amityville and was asked to head right out with my crime-scene investigative unit. I took my own car, arranging to meet my two crew members there with the crime-scene van. I hadn't paid much attention to the address, and more or less assumed I was being sent, as I usually am on homicides, into the poorer section of town, where the shootings and knifings are just one more sign of all sorts of obvious social and economic difficulties and disloca-tions. But when I arrived on the scene, the street already a chaos of flashing lights and emergency vehicles, I found myself in one of the older, more affluent areas of Amityville. The house in question was particularly impressive: some type of colonial, three stories high with an actual name sign hanging from a little post out front—"High Hopes"—and featuring expanses of landscaped lawns with a swimming pool out back, Virgin Mary statues, huge old trees, a fancy upstairs sun deck enclosed with a filigreed rail-ing. Like many opulent South Shore homes, this one backed onto one of the canals that finger their way in from the Great South Bay. That way the owners can have a boat, a boathouse, right on their property, as this one did. Everything spelled money, maybe with some showing off to boot.

Even with the detective's mention of *six big ones*, it didn't really dawn on me what I was getting into. The realization took hold when he and Dr. Howard Adelman, the deputy chief medical ex-aminer, walked me through the house to view the bodies. It was the most awesome homicide scene I'd ever encountered. We had six family members murdered in one house at one time, including the mother and father, two daughters, and two sons. Just in its basic essence, it was a difficult concept to grasp.

By the time I arrived, the police had been on the scene for some hours and had already identified the victims and developed some background material. The DeFeos were a relatively prominent family. The murdered father, Ronald DeFeo, Sr., worked as service manager at his father-in-law's automobile dealership in Brooklyn, Brigante-Karl Buick. The name rang a bell, since Michael Brigante, besides heading up a very prosperous business enterprise, was active in various civic and charitable causes and apparently well connected politically.

Since I'd been dispatched there not specifically for firearms work but as head of the crime-scene unit, I immediately went about the business of collecting evidence. Back then, however, our commitment to the protection of the site was nowhere as meticulous as it's become since, say by the time of the Lambert case some fifteen years later. So I surveyed the situation along with the Homicide detective in charge mainly to get a general sense of what had happened, and to search for obvious signs of gross physical evidence, such as the presence of weapons or live or spent ammunition. There was no attempt, really, to seek out the trace residues or stains or stray fibers that we'd be looking for today. Besides, in a big home like that, occupied by two parents and five children, you obviously had a much messier and less helpful condition than we found at the Lamberts'.

We had to move quickly on the walk-through because Homicide was anxious to get the bodies to the morgue for postmortem conclusions on the exact cause of death, and in the hope of recovering bullets or fragments from the bodies, all of whom had obviously been shot.

We started upstairs, where all the bodies had been found in upper-story bedrooms. As we climbed to the first landing, we passed this whole series of gold-framed paintings on the wall, obviously family members in different poses and groupings, the parents, two girls, three boys. From the first landing I could see two bodies, one male and one female, lying face down on the large bed in the spacious and expensively furnished master bedroom. Both had their hands stretched overhead, not straight up but clasped, palms on the sheet, to form an arch over their heads. They'd already been identified as the father, Ronald, Sr., and the mother, Louise, both in their forties. She was dressed in a nightgown. He wore only boxer shorts. He looked no more than average height but probably weighed close to three hundred pounds. Each had been shot twice in the back. Since Ronald, Sr., had no shirt on, I was able to view his wounds without disturbing the body. The bullet holes were big and traumatic enough to indicate a powerful weapon. In both bodies, some lividity had set in—a kind of grayish-blue cast to the skin indicating that the victim had probably been dead at least a few hours.

Down the hall we viewed the bodies of the two boys in the bedroom they shared. One was twelve, one seven, dressed in T-shirts, pajama bottoms. One, I remember, had a Knicks logo on his shirt. Like the parents, both boys had been shot in the back—but only once—and were also lying face down on their beds with their hands identically stretched and clasped overhead. It appeared to be a typical room of young boys: an inflated Pepsi bottle, grungy sneakers tossed about, wallpaper featuring guns and globes, even a pattern of soldiers on their pillowcases.

On the top floor we viewed the two girls, aged thirteen and eighteen, in their separate bedrooms, these in pastel colors with flower designs, jigsaw puzzles, a stuffed panda. Again, the bodies were face down on the beds, in nightgowns, each shot with a single bullet in the cheek or face, as if maybe, lying on their beds, they'd turned to look at—maybe even plead with—whoever was about to kill them. Both wounds were large and bloody, again indicating a powerful weapon at close range. Incredibly, their hands were clasped overhead in that same eerie manner.

The overall effect of the questions raised was almost numbing: six members of the same family murdered, executed, in exactly the same way, in four different rooms on two separate floors of the house. No signs of forced entry, of scuffles, of robbery, of any kind of molestation of the victims. How *cold and efficient* it all must have been. Eight shots fired, six people dead, all probably killed immediately, from the look of the wounds they received. Conceivably, four different people, one in each room, had committed the murders at almost exactly the same moment. As soon as we got a chance to collect and examine the bullets, we'd be able to deal with that possibility—which would necessitate four different guns being used. If there'd been only one gun and one murderer, how the hell had anybody been able to systematically move through all those rooms killing these people one by one? A gun as big as the one we were surely dealing with would have made a godawful noise. After the first shot killed the first person, wouldn't the other five scream, beg for mercy, hide in a closet, jump out a window—anything to escape from whoever was firing off this humongous weapon?

And then there was the real lulu of a question: what kind of person, with what kind of motivation, could be capable of killing these parents and kids alike by taking them out one by one with what seemed to be no more emotion than someone aiming at a row of ducks in a shooting gallery?

Well, before I'd even begun recovering evidence, Homicide already had one guy in their sights—although he hadn't yet been officially designated as their prime, A-number-one, first-class bad-guy suspect: a twenty-three-year-old named Ronald DeFeo, Jr. He was the son of the two murdered parents, brother of the four murdered boys and girls, and the only member of the immediate family still alive.

Ronald DeFeo, Jr., known to most as Ronnie, was the person who, around six-thirty that evening, had called the Suffolk County police to report that everyone else in his family had been murdered. After the police discovered that his incredible report was indeed correct, they were naturally quite interested in talking with him further. Pretty average in height and weight, Ronnie presented a somewhat disheveled appearance to the cops, with a full head of wild black hair, heavy sideburns and mustache, a large, sharply pointed black beard. His eyes also seemed to have a strangely disturbing expression, and the interrogating officers agreed that Ronnie had no doubt recently consumed a certain amount of alcohol. Nonetheless, he seemed quite willing to relate his story to the officers.

The night before, he said, he'd slept at home without hearing or noting anything unusual, and woke early that morning, Wednesday, to go to work at Brigante-Karl Buick, the dealership on Coney Island Avenue owned by his maternal grandfather, Michael Brigante. He was employed there as a helper in the service department, washing cars, changing oil, and generally making himself useful to the mechanics and to the service manager, who happened to be his father, Ronald, Sr. His father generally drove separately to work, he informed the police, and when the older man did not show up that morning, neither Ronnie nor anyone else gave it much thought. The father often went off on business without checking with his colleagues.

Ronnie left at the end the day, still without seeing his father, and dropped in for a couple of drinks at Henry's Bar, a few blocks from his house. He went home around six-thirty and said he was horrified to find his mother and father murdered in their beds. Overcome with panic, fearing that the killer might still be in the house, he raced back to the bar and told his friends what he had seen. Several accompanied him back to the house, where they discovered the additional bodies of his brothers and sisters and immediately called the police.

Even before I arrived, the police had begun wide-ranging investigations along every possible line of pursuit, which would continue and intensify over the next few days. Investigators sought out and talked to relatives. They attempted to question every one of the more than fifty employees at Brigante-Karl Buick. Policemen—and no doubt reporters and cameramen too, judging by the TV and press coverage—knocked on doors throughout the neighborhood and visited every bar and tavern within a couple of miles. Since there'd been no sign of a murder weapon inside the house, teams searched the immediate grounds and other possible dumping spots nearby. Divers explored the muddy bottoms of creeks and inlets. One unit combed all the nearby wooded areas with a metal detector.

What they were looking for was *everything*—about the victims, about the sole surviving son who'd discovered the bodies, about anybody in the world connected to this family, about the time of the deaths and the sequence and methods and activities of the killer, and finally, and most important for me, about any firearms and ammunition used in the murders.

All the standard procedures, in other words, had been set in motion, and in a case of this magnitude they were clearly being pursued with extra zeal.

Meanwhile, on that Wednesday night, still only hours after the report of the murders, I set about making whatever contribution I could to the overall effort by revisiting the various bedrooms. My crew, following others earlier in the evening, set about collecting the usual items we picked up in those days, which would include any sheets or bedclothes or rugs that had been bloodstained, along with cigarette butts, ashtrays, anything lying around or in the trash containers that looked in the least bit unusual. And since I was already struggling with the idea of all six victims being eliminated without any resistance whatsoever, we were also looking for any signs that they had been sedated with some kind of drug. As a matter of course, the stomach contents of the victims would be taken during the autopsies to be analyzed in terms of what and when they'd eaten before they died, and the presence of any suspicious substances, but you're always trying to approach possibilities from as many directions as possible, and to latch onto information as soon as you can. I therefore made sure my crew understood that I particularly wanted everything out of the sinks and drains, plus any dishes and silverware and glasses and cups that hadn't been washed, any food left on dishes, any scraps or leftovers in the garbage pails.

Personally, I focused on ballistic evidence. After all, we had six people down with eight bullets expended, and no murder weapon in sight. So I'm looking for cartridge cases, for ammunition, for anything that can help us pinpoint the weapon or weapons we were looking for, because the sooner I can do that the happier everyone else is going to be. Luckily, it wasn't long before I came up with a couple of interesting finds.

Often in a shooting, I'm dependent on the postmortem for the recovery of ammunition from the victim's body. But in this case, just judging by the traumatic wounds, I thought the bullets might have gone right through the victims. I didn't know for sure, because I couldn't turn any bodies over to check for exit wounds. But as soon as they began removing corpses, I started probing mattresses and checking under beds, and I found a single bullet embedded in one boy's mattress.

That it had passed cleanly through the body was another sign of a powerful weapon, but only the presence of powder burns and residues on the skin would tell whether or not it'd been fired at close range. With a high-powered rifle, the loss of projectile velocity is so minor it isn't even calculated until after maybe a hundred yards, so the wounds themselves weren't enough to indicate the killer's distance from the victims.

Since the whole situation had been immediately recognized as a big event, with all sorts of top brass on the scene, when word got out that I'd found one of the bullets, the chief of detectives of the Suffolk County PD immediately sought me out. He was an old Scotchman, and he kept saying in this really thick burr, *What can you tell me? What can you tell me? We have nothing to go on.* Of course, I had nothing to go on either, except this one bullet I'd just recovered from the bed area, so all I could offer was a strict eyeball identification. But you can often come up with something just on that basis. So I covered myself by warning that it was strictly a first reaction, but said that I'd almost swear the bullet came from a .35-caliber Marlin hunting rifle—a gun designed for hunting full-fledged wilderness game beasts like bear and moose and deer, where you needed all sorts of range and power and penetration.

My relative confidence in identifying the bullet wasn't the result of any kind of legerdemain on my part. At that time, and still today, Marlin was unique among manufacturers in reference to the spiral grooves, or rifling, cut into the inside of their rifle barrels to impart a spinning motion to the bullet. They used many more grooves in their weapons than other manufacturers, really fine incisions designated as microgrooves, and it was the presence of

these, along with the size of the bullet, that indicated the Marlin
.35. Still, it was only an educated guess. There's no way, except microscopically, that you can even approach 100 percent certainty.

Within the next few hours we recovered more bullets, both in
the house and from the bodies, all of which appeared the same, although it was solely on the basis of my identification of that first
bullet that Homicide concentrated on searching for a Marlin .35,
instead of having to check out every conceivable firearm they
might run across.

The fact that we hadn't yet found the right weapon in the house
didn't mean it wasn't still hidden in there somewhere, so we continued combing through the various rooms, and in the course of
that search created a couple of situations that later became major
issues at the trial.

During the Lambert investigation, you remember, I said we were
able to turn the whole house inside out looking for evidence because we'd received a carte blanche to do so from Dan Lambert.
But we always have to be aware that any kind of search, like just
about every other police activity, is governed by very precise legal
definitions and restrictions relating to the privacy rights of the occupants. At a homicide, for instance, we can go through the house
and grounds but *only* to look for suspects and for dead or injured
victims. We can't use the occasion to gather evidence, since that
would violate the privacy rights of the residents. We can open
every door and scan closets and attics and storage areas, but again
only to check for suspects or victims. If we come across a diary on
a desk, for instance, we can't flip through it. Nor can we look inside drawers, cabinets, briefcases, anything like that. Thus the
whole house, with the exception of the crime scene itself—the
Lambert bedroom, the several DeFeo bedrooms—would be pro-
tected against unauthorized search or seizure in order to protect
the privacy of the surviving occupants, Dan Lambert then, Ronnie DeFeo this time.

As police, we often find this frustrating, but can understand it.

The mere *possible* implication in a crime doesn't open every aspect of a person's life to unbridled scrutiny. What about the local padre, the straight-arrow businessman, the shy schoolmarm—don't they deserve protection from cops ransacking their booze or dirty pictures or secret love letters?

But any gross physical evidence in open view—a gun in the garage, a bloodied baseball bat in the cellar—is fair game, although we can't actually confiscate even those items without a search warrant from a judge based on our having seen, during a legally limited open-door exploration, something we have reason to believe was involved in the commission of a crime.

Given all these strictures, police have naturally developed ways of getting at evidence beyond the strict limits of allowable search. In other words, they sometimes cut corners, not necessarily to trample anyone's rights but because someone's been murdered and it's their job to find out who the hell did it, usually under heavy time pressure and in the face of considerable difficulties. Suppose an investigator notices a laundry basket in a hallway; he lifts the cover for a peek and sees a pair of bloody dungarees. Wow, he says, and quick slams it shut. What's he supposed to do, pretend he never saw anything? What he does is tell a judge he has cause to believe valuable physical evidence might well be found in certain locations. Usually, that'll do it, and then whoever found those dungarees at, say, 12:16, will return with warrant in hand and officially record sighting them at 3:49.

You have to understand, though, that judges aren't the least bit anxious to give the police a free hand. What they'll say is, Okay, you cite probable cause, and I'll take your word this time, but you sure as hell better find something germane, because I'm not interested in authorizing wild-goose chases.

As far as admissibility is concerned, judges will often just let the jury weigh the disputed evidence or confession or whatever against the other evidence presented to them. It's much like Detective Della Penna testifying that a certain bullet was fired by a certain gun. That statement can never be an absolute. In the final analysis, it's merely something a jury takes into consideration along with everything else they've heard. Maybe they don't like the snide look on my face and choose not to believe a word I say. It's the same with our claim to a voluntary and legal confession, or to a pair of bloody dungarees discovered at precisely 3:49. The judge will often just let the jury make the crucial decision.

In the course of our search of the DeFeo house, we went into Ronnie's room. As far as we knew, nothing criminal had taken place there, but for obvious reasons we were interested in taking a look, and this was the issue that later arose: did we have the right to even enter that room? But we did enter it at the time, and took a good look around. As the oldest of the three boys, Ronnie had his own room, the walls decorated with posters and road signs, a big girlie picture, a painting of a sailboat. We also noticed, though, a couple of items that became the basis of the challenge to our presence in that area.

An open bottom dresser drawer clearly exposed a charred teaspoon.

Now, that's how addicts cook heroin: they bend a teaspoon and light a match under it, put in a little water, a little powdered heroin, and cook it up until it liquefies. Then they draw the liquid up into a syringe and inject it into their arms. I'm not sure if we recovered the spoon at that point or merely recorded its presence in our notes, but either way we were eventually challenged as to whether we found the drawer open, which we did, or pulled it opened ourselves to look inside.

We also spotted in a little alcove of Ronnie's room a gun rack on the wall containing a .22-caliber rifle and a shotgun, with a .22-caliber pellet rifle leaning against the wall nearby. Because they were too small to have caused the wounds we'd witnessed, none of these interested us as much as the two empty cardboard rifle boxes we observed in a corner. One was labeled for a .35-caliber Marlin which, if my earlier appraisal was correct, matched the *class* of weapon that had fired the murder bullets. This produced the biggest challenge, not to the discovery itself but to the exact *time* of that discovery.

It has to be borne in mind that whole slews of other investigators on this very big case were pursuing their own paths as I was pursuing mine. Most notably Homicide detectives were talking to Ronnie, first as a material witness, since he'd discovered the bodies, and later on as a designated suspect. At some point in this continuing process, he was asked about possessing weapons. I was not involved in this end of things and don't know exactly how the question was phrased. Since these were high-level detectives of considerable experience, I assume they were careful not to sully the procedure by phrasing questions in ways that might invalidate the answers. So they probably did not ask, *Did you own a Marlin .35?* which would subject them to the charge of trying to incriminate him. They probably didn't even ask whether he'd ever owned *any* weapons. Most likely they'd pursue the inquiry along the more neutral lines of, *Were you ever aware of the presence of weapons of any kind within this house?*

At some point in the process, though, they asked him about a .35-caliber Marlin, and that's where the crucial issue of timing comes in. Exactly when—during the course of all those frantic, simultaneous, overlapping investigations and searches and interrogations—did they introduce this specific question?

Now, my inference as to the type of weapon, based on the spent bullet found in the boy's mattress, was absolutely clean, since that piece of evidence obviously came from one of the rooms where a crime had been committed. But suppose that when I found that bullet I really had only the foggiest notion about the kind of weapon that had fired it, but then subsequently found the Marlin .35 box and used *that* to make my identification. Even that would be okay if I came across the box in a legitimate manner. But the defense would later very vigorously challenge my mere presence in Ronnie's room, demanding that we establish that my identification of the bullet, and the questions to Ronnie about the possession of a .35-caliber Marlin, both took place *prior* to, and thus could not have been prompted by, my possibly tainted sighting of the gun box.

Of course, I had no inkling of these future challenges at the time, and if you asked me now to swear on a stack of Bibles as to the exact sequence of events during those chaotic hours after the discovery of the six bodies, I'd have to say that I'm simply not sure. We had an awful lot of people running in and out of that house, a lot of rumors and information flying back and forth. For instance, when I make a discovery in the heat of an investigation, I don't stop and write up a formal report to be transmitted to all interested parties. Hell, I got things to do, I have to keep working, keep looking for more and possibly better pieces of evidence. Most likely I just say something to one guy, the officer in charge if I can find him, or one of my assistants or his assistants, in the hopes they'll pass the word along to the interested parties.

We're therefore forced to work under a very unstructured system of disseminating information—including guesses and assumptions—that usually isn't sorted out and made sense of until hours or days later when the actual reports *are* finally written and filed. So who knows what happened in exactly what order that night? We certainly tried to follow the rules of investigation, because we're always concerned about the trouble we can cause if we don't. But could someone have ever so slightly adjusted the sequence of events? Of course they could, but I simply wasn't the least bit aware of what kind of questions they were asking Ronnie while I was working as hard as I could recovering bullets from the bedrooms and trying to find the actual murder weapon.

Maybe the final word on the gun box, legal considerations aside, is that a person would have to be stupid beyond belief to leave in his own room the goddamn box in which he received the goddamn rifle that he used to kill the six people closest to him in the whole goddamn world.

His mother, his father, his eighteen-year-old sister, his thirteen-year-old sister, his twelve-year-old brother, his seven-year-old brother—why in heaven's name did Ronald DeFeo, Jr., do it? That was always the question, and believe me, all of us struggled mightily with it, in the hope that it might lead us to some final understanding or explanation. As to *whether* Ronnie did the deed, none of us doubted that after the first few hours.

Rarely are you that confident on the basis of a single spectacular find. You usually depend on a gradual buildup, an accretion of details, with something here and something there eventually fitting together with lots of other things from other places. So all right, from my direction, the biggest strike against Ronnie was that gun box in his room for a weapon of the exact size and type not only for the first bullet we found, but ultimately for all the bullets recovered from the house and the bodies. So that arrow pointed straight at Ronnie. But what if someone else—stranger, friend, mobster, whoever—had gained entrance and used Ronnie's Marlin to shoot up the place? So the ballistic evidence needed a lot of help from other directions.

I remember being in each of those bedrooms for a long time that night, looking for anything I could find and also methodically reconstructing the path of each bullet that we recovered, working particularly with the ID photographers, peeling back mattresses to make sure they got pictures of where the bullets went through, where they struck the wall or the floor or whatever, making sketches showing the angle of each shot, the position of the bodies, where the person who fired that shot had probably been standing. I also worked closely with Dr. Adelman in the removal of the bodies, making sure we had complete notes on the bedding and blankets and clothing.

Not only were all victims lying face down with their hands over their heads; except for the father, they were all found under a blanket or sheet that the bullets went through. So they'd all been killed in bed, not somewhere else and then deposited there. With the seven-year-old boy, his sheets had been ripped up around the top, near his hands, and we wondered if that might reflect a convulsive reaction to being shot, or whether he'd clawed at the sheets in terror as he lay there waiting to be executed.

Like almost everything else we saw, that again brought us back to that basic puzzle of how anyone could possibly have killed all these people in all these beds without a single sign of a struggle or attempted escape by any of them, even though the murderer had to go from room to room and floor to floor knocking them off in turn with an incredibly noisy weapon. Could he possibly have drugged all of them at their final meal? The postmortem analysis of stomach contents would give us a definite yes or no on this, but even before the lab reports came in we shied away from the Agatha Christie elements of this theory. You'd have to be a phar-macological wizard to drug six people without their knowledge, from a man who eventually weighed in at 270 to a preteen boy and girl barely a third that size, and with such precise dosages that they all stayed conscious just long enough to put on their night-clothes and climb into bed, at which point they all conveniently dropped into stupors. And why, if they were drugged, did they all fall into bed on their stomachs, with their hands stretched over-head? Why on earth did they all do that even if they *weren't* drugged?

Another initial possibility that we briefly contemplated had him rounding them all up and shooting them together at one spot, a hallway maybe, and then dragging each to his or her own bed. From the beginning, this seemed even more implausible than the drugs, considering the copious amounts of blood he'd have to have cleaned up, since we'd found none in any hallway. And once I started digging bullets out of mattresses, and tracing their paths through mattresses, the absurdity of this explanation became ap-parent. Even so, just to make sure, we did a luminal test of the nonbedroom areas by spraying the floor with a chemical that re-acts with even the most minute traces of blood to give you a pro-nounced fluorescence under darkened conditions, and got absolutely no reaction at all. The fact that we even considered something this farfetched gives a good indication of how desper-ate we were for some kind of explanation as to how this incredible scenario could have transpired.

Okay, maybe he used a silencer, so none of his future victims could hear any of his previous shots. I'd seen military silencers designed for snipers that substantially reduce the noise caused by the exiting bullet and the blast of expanding gas that follows it. But this muffling effect is achieved via a device that envelops the gun barrel by being screwed onto the tip with an extremely tight seal. Both the enveloping silencer and the threaded barrel are expensive and very hard to come by, and not even the best of them are totally effective. Even so, the idea couldn't be dismissed out of hand, although I for one never gave it much credence.

Gradually through that long first night, certain crucial pieces of the story came to light, mainly through ongoing interrogations that enabled us to move beyond these areas of pure speculation. This is what always happens, at least when you're lucky. You start with nothing but crazy hunches and Agatha Christie guesses while you're waiting for someone, somewhere, to dig up something resembling a solid piece of evidence.

One of the first breakthroughs again involved ballistics, so I right away got called in when a friend of Ronnie's told Homicide he'd recently sold Ronnie a .35-caliber Marlin. That in itself wasn't that much of a revelation, because the gun box in his room had already pretty much tied him to the ownership of that kind of weapon. What caught everyone's attention was the recollection of Ronnie fiddling around with the gun at the fellow's house and accidently discharging it, leaving a hole in the floor. If we could get our hands on that bullet and match it to ones dug out of the mattresses and bodies, we'd have made a huge step forward. Instead of just saying the fatal bullets came from the *type* of weapon Ronnie possessed, we'd be able to prove they came from the *specific* rifle he'd bought.

So off we headed for the friend's house in search of that all-important bullet—Ronnie's friend, a Homicide detective, and myself. It was now very much the wee hours of the morning, but we had no hesitance in rousing the friend's family out of bed in order to pull back their living room rug. When we did, I found myself staring with great excitement at this neat little hole in the hardwood floor. No, the friend said, they'd never bothered with the bullet itself, because the house, like a great many South Shore dwellings, was pretty much built on sand and only had a little crawl space underneath. I still vividly remember scuttling under there with a flashlight to find the little circle of light coming down through the hole, and then digging into the wet sand with my bare hands and sifting it impatiently through my fingers. It was November, though, and cold as hell under there, and wet, and pitch dark except for the flashlight, and densely populated, at least in my imagination, with every manner and form of creepy-crawly lowlife and vermin—clearly a ridiculous situation, especially since I was having no success at all finding anything. Eventually I gave up and crawled out and told the Homicide detective I'd done my best but we needed to get someone under there with the right tools.

That didn't happen until the next day, when the Emergency Service Group arrived. They're the police unit that gets, as a kind of last resort, into all kinds of bizarre situations, like dealing with guys threatening to jump off telephone poles or ledges or bridges, or extricating people from wrecked cars with the Jaws of Life. They're also heavily armed with a lot of special firepower and serve as our SWAT-type team. Basically, they're equipped with just about every tool and implement you can think of, including floodlights and a lot of digging equipment, so under the house they went and later the next day they delivered to me in the lab a beautiful specimen that microscopically matched all the other bullets. That allowed us to establish beyond doubt that the Marlin .35 rifle Ronald DeFeo, Jr., had purchased from his friend—wherever it might be now—had fired the bullets that killed those six people.

That's jumping ahead, though, since there was still a lot going on at the house that first night, as the chief investigators began to agree that Ronnie was their man and ultimately classified him as the prime suspect. But they'd been talking to him from the beginning, and for a while at least, claimed they were keeping him sequestered partly for his own protection. The reasoning here isn't as artificial as it might sound. Until they knew who the killer was, they couldn't rule out the possibility that Ronnie, the sole surviving family member, might still be on the killer's list.

How long that assumption went on, I don't know, because I was busy with my own work and not involved in the interrogation. But I do remember that before the winter sun rose the next morning, Ronnie, with the generally eager help of some friends, had talked himself into very deep trouble. This transpired despite the fact that Ronnie had in no way been cut off from advice and consultation. Michael Brigante, Ronnie's maternal grandfather, who owned the Buick dealership and was considered the family patriarch, came by, as did one of his sons, the slain mother's brother and thus Ronnie's uncle, who happened to be a lawyer. But the lawyer uncle never claimed to represent Ronnie, and both men may have been too overwhelmed by the family tragedy to give Ronnie much in the way of coherent counsel.

The investigators also learned, from the first officers on the scene, that the family's huge dog had been locked up outside the house in a rough shed used for the metal garbage cans. The police put the animal in a car to await the arrival of the dog handler, and I was asked to check out the shed. All I found was an incredible amount of dog hair, which seemed to indicate that the dog had been locked in there for some time, all the while trying to get out in the worst way. Various neighbors reported hearing a lot of loud barking on the previous night, Tuesday, which by now seemed the likely time period for the murders. Finding the dog locked away would certainly be consistent with some stranger or outsider being the culprit, but the cops also heard from several sources that the dog and Ronnie absolutely hated each other, so he too might have been interested in getting it out of his way.

Oddly enough, none of the neighbors bothered by the dog barking seemed to have heard any of the eight shots from the Marlin .35, which normally would make enough noise to wake an elephant. Did this get us back to the silencer theory? Maybe not. It

was November, after all, with the houses all shut tight behind double storm windows in a well-treed neighborhood with plenty of
space between them. The neighbors may well have heard the dog
in the flimsy outside shed but not the shots inside the cocooned
house.

But the people in the next bedroom?

At some point along the way, maybe reacting to the fact that the
police knew he owned a .35 Marlin, and to whatever internal
pushing and pulling was going on inside his head, Ronnie confessed. Not just once or twice, but several times over a period of
many hours. Sometimes he would retract what he'd already said.
Sometimes he would add new details, or even create wildly diverse
versions of what he did and why he did it. Would any of this be of
any value, with practically every statement being contradicted by
some other statement? What we needed, obviously, were revela-
tions that only the murderer could make, and every possible corroboration of his basic admission of guilt. But the scariest part of
a confession being thrown out is that, under what's known as the
fruits-of-the-forbidden-tree theory, any and all evidence you
gather *because* of an invalid confession goes right out the window
with the confession itself.

Now, some of these developments occurred throughout that
first night, some the next day or the day after. I don't recall the sequence in every instance, because what really mattered was that
they all followed, and were essentially outgrowths of, Ronnie's
various confessions.

In the basic story that he related to Homicide, Ronnie said he
murdered the family the night before, Tuesday, and then left the
bodies exactly where they were on Wednesday morning to go to
work at Brigante-Karl Buick, and that he came back that evening
and pretended to be shocked at the "discovery" of the bodies. In at
least one confession he added an after-work visit to some girlfriend's place to do drugs. The girlfriend confirmed this, adding
that he called home a couple of times and made a point of telling
her, *I don't know why nobody's answering there.*

To the cops, Ronnie both looked and sounded distinctly weird, but neither the girlfriend nor any of his coworkers or tavern friends reported sensing anything unusual about him on Wednesday. Maybe he was just no weirder than usual. Certainly all his planning and preparation, the incredible patience he showed throughout the day, the careful establishment of his presence at various places, were hardly signs of someone raving out of control or under enormous psychological pressure. It's hard to believe, isn't it? A guy could wipe out his whole family in one incredible bloodbath and go through a whole goddamn day as if nothing had happened. You'd think he'd have shown *something*.

In some of his confessions, Ronnie said he acted alone and shot everybody himself. Other times he claimed someone else helped him kill everybody, or even forced him to do so against his will. Most of this was extremely vague, up and down and all over the place, without the kind of convincing details we were desperately hoping for. A clear picture of his motivation would have helped our cause immensely, but he was just as contradictory and disorganized on his reasons for the killings as he was on everything else.

Financial gain, of course, always has to be considered. Ronald, Sr., was heavily insured, and various cousins and such said he kept large sums of money in the house, on the order of twenty or thirty thousand dollars. In one of his confessions, Ronnie actually declared that was why he killed him, to get the money for drugs, and then killed everybody else because they would have been witnesses. He never liked or got along with his father, he said, who all his life had yelled and screamed at him and beat him up over nothing.

Much of what the police had learned independently seemed to support a view of the father as, at the least, a very strict and controlling parent who maintained a tight rein over his oldest son. At the Buick dealership, for instance, Ronnie wasn't paid any more than any of the other essentially unskilled workers. Yet he seemed to have money for booze and drugs and girlfriends, because the father would slip him a hundred bucks or so as long as he behaved himself. If the father didn't like something the son did or said, he'd not only slap him around but cut off the goodies too.

The investigators also learned that Ronnie was on probation for stealing a boat motor to replace one that he'd wrecked on his father's boat. The probation officer checked his pay slips from Brigante-Karl Buick to make sure he was working regularly.

After hearing about the father's habit of keeping a lot of cash around, we looked around for likely spots and discovered at the entrance to the master bedroom a little saddle under the rounded wood sill that meets the bottom of the door. We pulled it up to reveal a long, narrow strongbox underneath. It was empty, and the investigators never got a straight story from Ronnie about what he'd done with any money he might have taken. Maybe it's all buried out on the Island somewhere, twenty or thirty grand waiting for someone to find it while digging for bait or watching his dog bury a bone.

When asked about his motives, Ronnie gave some really flippant answers. He killed the older sister because she always spent too much time hogging up the bathroom. And the younger sister annoyed him because she was so sloppy about everything. A couple of even these hardened Homicide detectives were taken back by the vehemence of his anger toward his father, mother, and sisters and brothers alike. Fat fucks, he called them. Fucking pigs. His mother's cooking, he said, tasted like shit.

When Ronnie told the investigators where he'd dumped the murder weapon in a nearby canal, I was again sent looking, this time accompanying the marine scuba guys. Recovering the gun would be a real coup, especially if we found it through his directions. That would provide almost unassailable corroboration.

But you face real difficulties trying to recover an object from a body of water. In general, a canal would be easier than a river, but the canals from the Great South Bay generally have enough depth to carry some of the bigger private boats, so we're probably talking ten feet or so, and maybe forty or fifty feet across, so it's not exactly like looking for a bar of soap in the bathtub. The scuba guys try to mark a path that they can follow back and forth across the canal in parallel lines, so they're not just aimlessly circling around. A lot depends on how murky the water is. If it's too muddy and roiled up, or with strong tides that will almost immediately bury an object in silt, they really can't do a visual search and have to resort to feeling and groping. You can't really use a magnetic device, because it'd bring up everything but the kitchen sink. Any body of water you could mention, certainly anything within a few hundred miles of New York City, probably has enough junk down there to fill Yankee Stadium a few times over.

We had another suspect one time who threw a gun off a dock, and we spent hours trying to re-create the situation, the arc and distance and that sort of thing, by throwing rocks about the same weight as the weapon to see how far would they would go, trying to calculate such factors as how aerodynamic a gun would be as opposed to a rock of the same weight. Surprisingly enough, we actually recovered that weapon, but probably as much through luck as anything else.

Bridges are the worst. If you feel the need to dispose of a murder weapon someday, find a nice big bridge spanning a lot of deep, fast-running water and just give it a fling. No one'll ever see it again in this lifetime.

In the DeFeo case, the good Lord was with us, and one of the scuba people came up with the weapon, which was immediately placed in my hands. The first thing I checked was the end of the barrel. No outside threads, so no silencer. (I've heard people talk about muffling shots by firing through a bunched-up pillow, but my response is that you'd better make sure you're wearing good heavy fireman's boots, because no pillow's going to absorb the tremendous heat generated at the end of a gun barrel without bursting into some pretty spectacular flames for you to stomp out.)

As soon as I'd checked the barrel for threads, I gave the weapon a quick bath in regular water to rinse off as much salt as possible, then submerged it in kerosene to stop any further oxidation. Leave it out in the air any length of time and you give yourself a major rust problem.

Once I got it back to the lab, I painstakingly disassembled the rifle piece by piece, being careful not to damage or disable anything, in order to eliminate the tiniest traces of hidden rust. I then did a function test of all mechanisms to make sure the weapon could be safely fired. You don't want anything blowing up in your face when you're just trying to determine the markings it imparts to a bullet. All of this takes hours. In a lever-action Marlin like Ronnie's, you've got thirty or forty individual pieces to deal with one by one, most quite small and delicate and all interlocking with a very small tolerance.

I got each piece as dry as possible, gave everything another very thin coat of oil, and reassembled the weapon for a test-firing, hoping to duplicate on the test bullets the exact marking found on the murder bullets. My major worry was that the salt water had eaten away at the lands and grooves that form the rifling pattern in a gun barrel. Any significant corrosion could also alter the microscopic scratch marks inadvertently produced during manufacture. Because they're so small and numerous, these tiny *striae* can be vital in authenticating a perfect match between bullets.

So with some trepidation I used the weapon to test-fire several bullets identical to the murder specimens into our water tank recovery system, and put the test and murder bullets under the dual microscope.

Since I had a lot of items to work with, and there'd been some loss of clarity due to the saltwater erosion, it took me days to run all the tests. Eventually, though, I was able to substantiate the exact matches we needed. The gun from the canal, which could only have been recovered with Ronnie's precise directions, had without question fired all eight bullets used in the six murders.

The investigators also produced some additional, although less conclusive, evidence based on Ronnie's confessions. After the murders, he said, he drove into Brooklyn and dumped a bunch of stuff down a sewer across from a Shell station on Ninety-sixth Street near Seaview Avenue. Again his map skills were faultless, and we recovered in excellent condition a rifle carrying case, a pillowcase containing various items of bloodstained clothing, a box or so of live ammunition, and all eight spent casings from the murder scene. Some casings were also stained with blood, probably having fallen into pools of it when they were ejected. Ronnie had collected all of them from the several bedrooms, another sign of how methodical he'd been.

It ought to be emphasized, in talking about the value and admissibility of confessions, that the recovery of both the rifle and the casings would have been almost impossible without Ronnie's help. And if he'd waited another week or so before owning up, our chances of finding anything in a testable condition, or even finding it at all in the context of continual tidal movements and sewer flow, would have long since vanished.

During the course of their very intensive background checks, Homicide learned that about two weeks before the murders Ronnie had reported to the police that he'd been robbed while transporting several thousand dollars' worth of receipts from Brigante-Karl Buick to the bank. The police working on the case had suspected from the beginning that Ronnie had faked the robbery in order to get money for drugs. There'd also been talk of money being missing from the business on other occasions in which Ronnie might have been involved.

As to why Ronnie wasn't accused in these instances, or why the investigations were not carried to final conclusions, it might have been due to the fact that his father and uncle, both of whom had a lot of civic and community connections, were not anxious to pursue any possible charges. I remember finding in the dresser in the master bedroom an incredible collection of PBA and detective-association membership cards, miniature police badges, receipts for all kinds of contributions to police organizations. My guess is that some friend in the police hierarchy tipped off the father to their suspicions about Ronnie, and Ronald, Sr., said, *Look, I'll take care of it, all right? I'll beat the shit out of him and teach him a lesson and that'll be the end of it.* The cops probably figured, What the hell, it was just the family's money being stolen in the first place.

So maybe, a couple of weeks before the murders, Ronnie's father administered to his son, who he outweighed by a hundred pounds, one final beating which maybe got crazy mixed-up Ronnie thinking about getting back at the old man in real world-class fashion.

Although we never took it seriously, the concept of Ronnie drugging the family made for a lot of breathless speculation in the newspapers. Then the autopsy reports on stomach contents showed absolutely nothing, ending that line of theorizing, except for some of the more sensational tabloids that contended Ronnie had come up with an exotic drug that knocked people out for specified periods of time without leaving a trace.

Ronnie's several mentions of someone else being involved didn't exactly surprise us. We saw it with Terry Harrington, and generally see it a lot. Suspects seem eager to spread the blame to make themselves look less guilty, either morally or legally. Like Ronnie, they'll even insist the other guy made them do it, as if to say, I would never kill my whole family *alone.* They don't understand that if you have fifty guys involved in a murder, you have fifty guys facing homicide charges.

But you've got to double-check anything a suspect says. In this case, for instance, another intruder might explain some things. The cohort could have held various family members at gunpoint while Ronnie wiped out the others, making them all lie down just so in their own beds when their time came. It was as good an explanation as anything else we'd come up with, although you still had to wonder about a whole family being slaughtered without *any* signs of panic or attempted escape, of vomiting or defecation or tearing their hair out. Except for the blood strewn about, the rooms and the bodies were all perfectly clean and composed.

And what would be the incentive for someone else getting involved in six murders alongside the guy who'd clearly be the most likely suspect? Money, probably, another druggie desperate for immediate cash. And of course Ronnie wouldn't necessarily have advertised the deal as including any murders. The other guy might have just figured on a quick, neat robbery.

Even though a second suspect had a certain plausibility, everyone on the case was convinced that Ronnie acted alone. It wasn't just a matter of a gut feeling. We checked for prints and footwear impressions, for serological evidence on cigarettes and glasses and receptacles, for any sign of an outsider's presence, and never came up with a single credible piece of evidence putting anyone else in the house. Ronnie never named who this person might be, which would have led Homicide to check out his alibis and possibilities, but they interrogated everybody they could find without developing a single lead along these lines.

Throughout, Ronnie remained vague and contradictory on any number of points, but some of the things he said could make your hair stand on end. When they asked him to reconstruct the shooting of his youngest brother, the seven-year-old, Ronnie sort of shrugged and said he remembered that after shooting the kid he could see his feet twitching on the bed.

IN HIS BOOK *High Hopes,* prosecutor Gerard Sullivan talks of the difficulties of getting a conviction in a "motiveless" crime. He didn't want DeFeo declared innocent by virtue of insanity; he wanted him convicted on six counts of second-degree murder.

In the course of his trial preparation Sullivan received some tapes from the Brooklyn district attorney's office that had been obtained during a secret investigation the rackets bureau was conducting. He was told they might have some bearing on the Amityville murders, and Michael Brigante's voice was indeed heard often on the tapes, although he was not himself being investigated. Brigante's comments indicated that nephew Ronnie had killed the whole family for the money and jewelry in his father's strongbox, which Sullivan welcomed as a step toward establishing a motive. But even more pithily Brigante labeled his nephew "a nut job," which Sullivan was not quite so happy to hear.

ABOUT A YEAR LATER the pretrial hearing began, which promised to be more important than the trial itself. Its purpose was to let the judge rule—with no jury yet seated—on the defense lawyer's motion to exclude DeFeo's confession and all other statements he'd made to the police. Obviously this went to the heart of the prosecution's case. If the confession was thrown out, then all the evidence we'd collected on the basis of it would be thrown out too, under that fruit-from-the-forbidden-tree concept I mentioned earlier. So out would go the rifle rescued from the canal and the casings and ammunition recovered from the Brooklyn sewer. Without all that, the prosecution might just as well pack up and go home.

The defense also claimed DeFeo had been unconstitutionally prevented from obtaining proper counsel from the lawyer/uncle who showed up that first night. This charge, too, would have crippled the prosecution. If a suspect is denied counsel, no information gained after that denial can be used against him. Finally, for good measure, the lawyer charged police brutality.

After a week of arguments pro and con, the judge denied all defense motions. That pretty much sealed DeFeo's fate, even though the trial itself eventually went on for seven weeks, the longest in Suffolk County history at the time, with over a hundred exhibits and more than fifty witnesses, including numerous policemen, friends, neighbors, relatives, and psychiatrists. A great deal of time was spent on sometimes conflicting testimony dealing with Ronnie's sanity or lack thereof, with the general consensus seeming to be that although he was not legally insane, he sure was, as the cops felt from the beginning, one very weird kid.

My own testimony went on for a couple of days and dealt mainly with the firearms items and the methods I'd used to reach my conclusions about them. My most important conclusion, obviously, concerned the Marlin .35, established by other testimony as having been purchased by Ronald DeFeo, Jr., and fished out of a canal by following his directions. I was able to testify that this weapon, to the exclusion of all other weapons in the world, had been employed in the killing of these six people.

It was a satisfying experience, partly because the wide publicity the trial got brought the whole idea of firearms evidence a good deal of favorable recognition, particularly since we'd been able to produce conclusive evidence from a weapon recovered from the bottom of a saltwater canal.

In New York State, first-degree murder can be charged only if the victim is a police officer or the killer is already serving a life sentence. So Ronald DeFeo, Jr., was convicted of six instances of second-degree murder and sentenced to Dannemora on six concurrent sentences of twenty-five years to life. He'll be eligible for parole in 1999, at age forty-eight, although in remarks at the sentencing the judge made it pretty clear that he didn't think a parole, ever, would be an awfully good idea.

IN *HIGH HOPES*, prosecutor Gerard Sullivan writes:
Before the day ended, I had introduced another expert to the jury—Detective Sergeant Alfred Della Penna, chief of the Suffolk Police Department's firearms identification section. Jurors liked to play amateur detective, and Della Penna was their meat; a sleuth who made scientific deductions on the basis of physical evidence. He was an ex-Marine completing a Master of Science degree, and he was understated but authoritative in the witness chair. All that, and Della Penna was so dapper that it was a running gag to ask him [outside the courtroom] whether he loosened his tie when he cut the lawn. As usual, he was wearing a three-piece suit set off by a pocket handkerchief, but I suggested that he change his tiepin, which was a gold replica of a Thompson submachine gun.

During Della Penna's testimony, fifty-seven exhibits were introduced, including the death bullets. (I would call him later in the trial with the murder weapon when a proper foundation had been laid as to its recovery.) The ballistics sergeant described his retrieval of the spent bullets—telling, for instance, how he opened Mark's and John's box springs with a scalpel. His expertise was evident when I asked what produced his preliminary determination that they were fired from a .35-caliber rifle, probably a Marlin.

"The type of rifling that was left on the bullets," Della Penna explained. "The rifling being the channels or grooves which are transposed from the inside of the barrel to the bullet. These channels and grooves are placed inside the barrel to give it trajectory and flight and stability. And as the bullet passes through the barrel, they are transposed onto the bullet."

In describing other material he brought to the police lab, Della Penna told of finding hairs inside the garbage shed at the back of the DeFeo house—where, I had told the jury, Ronnie had tied the sheepdog during the murders. "On the inside of the shed," added the sergeant, "there were two swinging-type doors that led into the shed, and these doors appeared to have been damaged or scratched similar to the type of scratches that are produced by an animal."

I asked if he could tell how fresh the marks were. "They appeared to have been fresh, as did the hair in that particular shed," Della Penna answered.

It sounded much like Al, although I have the distinct feeling that he's never cut the little patch of grass behind his condo, with or without loosening his tie.

The stricture that a novelist tie up all the loose ends in the final chapter is no longer as prevalent as it used to be, but I'm not sure how comfortable I'd be with as *many* lingering questions as we've got here: the sequence of the murders, Ronnie's ability to proceed unimpeded from one victim to the next, the identical positions of the bodies, the lack of any indications of terror or escape. Beyond these factual uncertainties lie the even murkier challenges concerning Ronnie's state of mind. Did he intend from the outset to kill off everyone, or just his father, as he claimed in at least one confession, with the others simply falling victim to his fears that they'd bear witness against him? Maybe he'd only intended to steal money from his father and somehow stumbled into all that horror through some incredible mishmash of derangement and misadventure, of fear and desperation and ineptitude. But if he hadn't planned his actions, how in God's name had this guy, whose all-around klutziness was well established, managed to carry out all those execution-style murders with such pitiless efficiency?

It was this efficiency that became a major point of contention at the trial. After lengthy testimony from Ronnie's friends relating numerous incidents revealing his "irrational" behavior with friends, family, and bar patrons, the defense and prosecution brought on their hand-picked psychiatrists. (The two doctors, Sullivan notes in his book, had opposed one another at any number of trials; testifying against each other was apparently one of their specialties, and a form of competition both enjoyed.) The question, of course, was whether or not Ronnie had been legally insane at the time of the killings. The defense psychiatrist naturally said he was, citing Ronnie's almost lifelong pattern of irrational behavior and concluding that "as a result of a mental disease the defendant at the time lacked substantial capacity to appreciate the wrongfulness of his acts."

The prosecution psychiatrist predictably came to the opposite conclusion, based in large part on Ronnie's efficient behavior during the commission of the crime. He must have known right from wrong, the doctor said, must have been aware of the criminality of his acts, or else he wouldn't have so carefully disposed of the evidence that he knew would incriminate him. But didn't Ronnie have to have *something* wrong with him to do what he did? He had an antisocial personality, the doctor told the court, which was a personality disorder, not a mental illness, and therefore not an indication of legal insanity. The jury, apparently, agreed.

Whatever legal purposes were served by his efficiency as a murderer, it remains to haunt us. A police officer at another mass-murder scene, this one with seven victims, commented, "There's a lot of evidence when you shoot that many people." Yet despite the untiring efforts of the police, if Ronnie hadn't confessed, if he hadn't left that rifle box in his room, if he hadn't accidentally fired a bullet through his friend's living-room floor, if he hadn't told the cops exactly where to find the gun and the ammunition he'd dumped, he'd probably have walked away a free—and rich—man.

If his lawyer had managed to throw out all those confessions, Ronnie would today be somebody's crazy neighbor.

Al doesn't apologize for the loose ends. It's not his job to answer every doubt. The world's a messy, inexplicable place. Crimes can be particularly messy and inexplicable, and neatness doesn't count, either for the criminals or the cops.

Unaware at the time of Al's connection with the DeFeo case, and never a horror-movie fan, I missed Hollywood's 1979 treatment of the case, *The Amityville Horror*, based on Jay Anson's "study in para-psychology and demonology." I couldn't dig up the book, but my local video-outlet clerk, who must have been a baby at the time of the murders, knew the film well: a real cult classic, she said, although her computer indicated that the print of "the first one" got worn out and wasn't replaced. But they did have numbers II and VI.

According to her, *seven* films, the last as recent as 1992, grew out of the DeFeo murders—distinguished by roman numerals and subtitles like *The Possession*, *The Demon*, *The Evil Escapes*, *The Curse*, and so on. Since she assured me that the first version was by far the best, I asked for it in several other stores. All the clerks knew the film, although none could find a copy, and all stocked at least a couple of the sequels. I finally tracked down the original in a massive out-of-town outlet. "You'll like it," that clerk promised.

It wasn't all that bad, with Rod Steiger, Margot Kidder, and James Brolin heading the cast, music by Lalo Schifrin, and an effectively eerie opening sequence showing the dark DeFeo house on a stormy night with lights flashing on in different windows as loud gunshots rang out. The next morning the six shrouded bodies are removed and the hard-bitten cops shake their heads over the kind of world in which something like this could happen.

That's pretty much the end of the film's concern with police work. After that we get a lot of nostril-flaring otherworldly stuff transpiring within the house, haunted as it is by both the six victims and the spirit of the murderer. All of this naturally scares the bejesus out of the young family that now lives there. Even the secular and rational priest/psychiatrist/exorcist played by Rod Steiger ends up hearing, and being demolished by, the voices that the murderer says drove him to kill. That's pretty much the movie's explanation of the "motiveless" crime: those haunting, bloodthirsty voices.

WHITE SHIELD DAYS

JOHN CUOMO ➡

BACK THEN, AFTER YOU SERVED your apprentice time on the streets, the way I did with Operation Two-Five in Harlem, you almost always got assigned to the Youth Squad with all the other rookie patrolmen and were known as a white shield. You got a regular beat, though, and learned how to handle whatever came along. Generally, rookies spent a year, two years, on the Youth Squad before getting their gold shields.

I got mine after three or four weeks, and it happened like this.

The first surprise was that as a white shield, I wasn't sent to the Youth Squad but instead to the Narcotics unit of the Detective Division in the Bronx. Exactly why, I don't know, but there I was, twenty-four years old and walking the street as part of the Narcotics Squad, just beginning to know my way around, when late one afternoon my partner and I went to the nearby precinct headquarters to phone the Detective Division that we were going off duty. You were allowed to do that, call in from a convenient precinct instead of having to travel to headquarters every time you signed in or out.

While we in the station house up there in the Bronx, a couple of off-duty cops came in wearing civvies, and one of them had all this blood streaming from his face, dripping all over his jacket and shirt. Naturally everybody, including us, crowded around to find out what had happened.

The bleeding guy said he'd gone to his sister's apartment in Harlem because she'd tipped him off that her boyfriend had showed up with a large quantity of heroin. He went there with this other cop, who I knew from working in Operation Two-Five in Harlem. Both these guys were black, which of course wasn't unusual, but these two had a bad reputation on the street, and even with their fellow officers. They weren't just tough and hard-nosed, which cops were expected to be, but real mean, vicious guys.

When they got to the sister's apartment house, the bleeding cop said, his buddy stayed downstairs while he went up to his sister's apartment. The boyfriend was still there, and managed to surprise him by clubbing him with something—he didn't know what—opening up one whole side of his face, which immediately started gushing blood. To make matters even worse, the boyfriend grabbed the cop's service revolver and ran off with that and a quantity of heroin from the apartment.

Much worse than the injury was the missing gun. In those days, and still, for an officer to give up his weapon was a terrible, terrible thing, shameful for the cop himself and reflecting badly on the whole force. You never knew what the guy might do with the gun, and the officer that lost it couldn't help but feel responsible for anything bad that happened.

So the whole station was immediately alarmed. The detectives called the commanding officer and even got word down to the borough commander, who's very high up in the hierarchy, in charge of the whole borough. Whenever the borough commander got called in on anything, you knew it had to be big. Being just a raw patrolman, I was really impressed, because I'd never seen so much hubbub before.

Meanwhile, the bleeding officer was sitting there holding a bloody towel to his head as the detectives pumped him for information. Do you know who the guy was, do you know his name, do you know where he is? And the cop kept saying, No, all I know is he surprised me and laid me out cold and ran off with my gun. Then he said, Wait, the guy's got a nickname—what the hell was it now? Kicky. That's it, his nickname's Kicky.

After listening to all this with the rest of the guys, my partner and I looked at each other and figured maybe instead of going off duty we'd just head down to that neighborhood in Harlem where the cop's sister lived and see if we couldn't find some drug dealer that people called Kicky.

Neither one of us, by the way, was in uniform. Even though I was just a white-shield patrolman, as a member of the Narcotics Squad in the detective division, I worked in civilian clothes. Not only that, but I was driving my own personal car.

I know—it's almost ludicrous to think about now, but that's how it was those days. Everyone in Narcotics except supervisory personnel used their personal vehicles. It was like an unwritten law, and when you first started out, you naturally fell in line with the more experienced people. No one knew how it started or the reasons behind it. As far as I knew, the department simply never authorized us to use official vehicles. And if you weren't given a squad car, but still had to patrol this huge section of the Bronx covering three to five precincts, and to be prepared to engage in hot pursuit into other areas, including other boroughs, what were you supposed to do? Hail a cab? Take the subway?

So everyone in Narcotics used their own cars, rotating with the one or two other guys on their team. I don't think anyone ever sat down and analyzed the financial or other ramifications. Here we were patrolling all over the place, chasing narcotics dealers, cutting off their cars, forcing them to the curb, without ever really giving any thought to who'd be responsible if we ran somebody down, or smashed up our car or got hurt in an accident. Somebody probably could've sued the city for millions, to say nothing of what our personal insurance companies would've thought if they'd seen us screeching between el pillars on Southern Boulevard and fishtailing around corners chasing drug dealers.

Maybe the oddest part was how we got reimbursed for all the gas and wear and tear during an eight-hour patrol. We never once got automobile expenses of any kind. But at the end of every month you were allowed to put in an account in the form of your arrest record. Not mileage—you never entered mileage. You'd just list the arrests you made during that period, and would get paid fifteen dollars for a felony arrest, seven-fifty for a misdemeanor. You had to make the arrests yourself. If you just assisted your partner in making one, he got the money, not you. To keep anyone from being tempted to go around arresting people just for the money, you could only get a maximum of ninety-nine dollars a month. In essence, that was to cover your car expenses, although you had to justify it with your arrest record.

Actually, the ninety-nine dollars was listed on your report as "Money used for information received from informants leading to arrest." A really important arrest would sometimes bring you another twenty-five. Every borough commander had a special fund for paying informants, although nobody knew where it came from or how much it actually amounted to.

Narcotics was the only squad in the city that did this, because we were the only ones using our own vehicles. The old-timers told me how to fix my car up with stuff from a certain army-navy store, where you could buy sirens that had been used on trains during the war and blinking lights for your grill, along with buttons that turned them on from the dashboard. Whenever we were in pursuit or answering an emergency call, we'd blast out the siren and get the lights flashing. Sometimes we'd even get them going when we were just on our way to some meeting downtown, flying down the East Side Drive cutting off cars right and left.

All these years, I kept that siren in the garage, but when we packed for Arizona, I got rid of it. Maybe I shouldn't have.

Another thing people don't realize is that we never got overtime. You might get involved in something and work twenty, thirty hours straight, but that didn't matter. Overtime pay didn't begin until 1974, right after I retired. I spent twenty years on the force without receiving a single minute of overtime.

This is just background. Anyhow, my partner and I forgot about going home, left the bleeding officer at the station house, and drove up to Harlem in my car. All we did was just start asking people we saw hanging around on the street if they ever heard of a guy called Kicky. Sure enough, we eventually found this guy who said, Gee, I know Kicky, and described him to us. We asked if he knew where Kicky hung out, and he said this bar over on 110th and Fifth.

You never really know why someone's willing to talk to a couple of cops like that. I mean, we weren't putting any pressure on anybody, but just asking around. Maybe he figured that if he did us a favor, we might return it someday. Maybe he hoped there'd be something more immediate in it for him, or just had a grudge against Kicky.

Whatever his reason, he sounded pretty convincing, so we got him in the back seat of my car and drove back to the Bronx precinct station house. My partner stayed outside with the guy and I went in and told the detectives, Look, we have an informant and think we know where Kicky is. Two detectives said, We'll come along, so the five of us, four cops and the informant, crammed into a regular squad car and roared back to the bar in Harlem.

We sent the informant in alone to see if Kicky was there, and after a few minutes he came out and sidled up to the squad car and said, Sure enough, he's in there, standing at this certain part of the bar. So the three other officers and myself moved into this really crowded, noisy bar, everyone jam-packed together in an incredible mass of humanity. Almost all were black or Puerto Rican because the bar sat right on the border between the Two-Five precinct and the Two-Eight, one black and the other Puerto Rican. We threaded our way through and grabbed and cuffed Kicky and hustled him out to the car before anybody could figure out what was going on, and once again zoomed back to the precinct in the Bronx.

This time when we got there all hell had broken loose. The chief of detectives was on his way up. The borough commander was ac-

tually already there. Every cop in the precinct was angry and really feeling the heat, first of all because an officer had been assaulted and wounded, and secondly because the guy who beat up
on him was still running around with a bunch of heroin and the
officer's service revolver.

So they were all very happy to see us drag Kicky in there, and
the detectives really jumped on the opportunity to question him.
Of course, in those days, especially in an explosive or high-pres-
sured situation such as this one had become, the detectives would
sometimes resort to what was termed physical interrogation.
Whether they did so or not in this case, before long Kicky decided
to reveal where the gun was, and also the eight ounces of heroin
he said he took from the cop's sister's apartment in a hatbox. He
also gave his version of what had actually happened. Even though
I was still pretty green, from the beginning I hadn't felt really comfortable with the original story from the bleeding cop, and Kicky's
version struck me, at least in some aspects, as maybe closer to the
truth.

First of all, Kicky said he wasn't just the boyfriend of the cop's
sister but was actually living with her while dealing in drugs. And
when the sister tipped off her brother, it wasn't for the cops to
arrest him for dealing, but because she wanted them to come
and steal the heroin from Kicky to sell it themselves. But Kicky
somehow got wind of what was about to happen, or just smelled
something funny, so he surprised the brother and absolutely cold-
cocked him and ran off with his gun and the hatbox containing
the heroin.

He stashed away the gun and the heroin, he said, at the apartment of a woman friend, and would take us there if we wanted.
That was exactly what we wanted, so the three of us hopped into
my car and drove down to Harlem once more, recovered the gun
and the heroin, and for the last time that night drove back up to
the Bronx precinct house.

By this time it must have been close to midnight. We'd been set
to go off duty at five, so in less than seven hours we'd managed to
get the guy, get the heroin, and get the gun, which just about

everybody at the station, including the higher-ups, seemed very pleased about.

The exceptions were the two cops who'd gone to the sister's apartment in the first place, because now everybody's interest suddenly shifted back to them and certain questionable aspects of their story.

For one, why would two off-duty cops have gone to the apartment on their own like that? They stuck to their story, that they'd been tipped off by the sister and had gone to arrest the drug dealer, but by now most people seriously doubted that. More likely they were planning to say, Give us the heroin or we'll arrest you, using that as a threat and then hoping to make a quick killing with the eight ounces, which even wholesale was worth a few thousand dollars.

I don't think they ever got charged, though, because all that was just a speculation that couldn't be proved, so whatever they had in mind, they got away with it, except of course for the cop who got the bloody whack on the face.

For me, it was a big break. The next day the borough commander called me down to his office and said, Listen, how much do you want me to give this guy, referring of course to my informant and the fund he had for paying people like that. I don't remember exactly what we agreed on, maybe a hundred dollars or so, very good money in those days. And that was legitimately for the guy, not for me, and I gave it to him the next day. My own reward came a week or so later when I was invited down to the chief of detectives' office to receive my gold shield after only a few weeks on the street, making me a detective third grade. It wasn't only prestigious and something I was real proud of, but meant a nice raise and got me on the path to making detective second grade, which I did before too long, which brought even more money both in salary and eventually in retirement.

I still remember the big ceremonial. Maybe a half-dozen guys were getting early promotions, and the chief of detectives would call up each one by name and say, Detective Jones, you encountered two armed gunmen on the street and by your heroic response . . . You know, really brave and impressive stuff. I'd just been lucky, I figured, and remember feeling very awkward in the middle of all that hoopla, being rewarded for something that really wasn't all that outstanding. I feel even more so now, because I can think of dozens of other cases where I worked ten times as hard, took all sorts of chances, put all my experience and knowledge to work for days on end, and came up with nothing.

SHOOTING AT TREES

WHEN AL GOES OUT as leader of the laboratory's crime-scene unit, he joins a dozen or more specialists from other police units in a flurry of high-pressure activity. Time counts. Mistakes cost. Hunches, split-second decisions, favorable breaks, risky assumptions—all affect those critical first hours. When he acts solely as firearms expert, Al often remains on the fringes of the action. In one homicide investigation, with someone else's unit handling the evidence search, there seemed to be no need for Al's expertise for the simple reason that no one could find the murder weapon, or even the fatal bullet. No-gun cases, Al says, are usually lost cases.

This murder took place in a comfortable North Shore house where, according to the initial report:

On June —, 19—, at 2130 hours, unknown perpetrator fired a shot through the front den window striking the victim FRANCES PATTERSON below the left ear, killing her. The shooting had been called in by the victim's eleven-year-old son, who'd been sitting on the carpet with his younger sister, watching TV at his mother's feet. The boy said they heard what sounded like a firecracker and saw that their mother was bleeding from the face. The daughter, only eight, fled to a neighbor's while the son phoned the police.

A L D E L L A P E N N A ➡

I WASN'T EVEN DISPATCHED to the scene until the following morning. Even though the investigators hadn't yet produced any firearms evidence, it was a weapons case nonetheless and they hoped I could maybe come up with something. By the time I arrived, some twelve hours after the murder, the body had been removed but everything else was undisturbed. I got a rundown of the status of the investigation from Bob Amato, a Homicide detective I knew who'd been put in charge of the case, and from Detective Sergeant Robert Misegades, his immediate superior. They also showed me around the house and grounds. The family room was one of those down-a-few-steps split-level affairs, a big room with a sofa, on which Mrs. Patterson had been sitting, facing the TV across the room, when she was shot. The windows were halfway above-ground, and the bullet had been fired through one of them, leaving a hole in the glass and screen. Outside, that window was mostly hidden behind some bushes in front of the house. I poked around out there, of course, not so much looking for evidence, as every inch of the area had already been scrutinized, but just interested in the exact angle of the shot, the view of the room and occupants that someone would get crouching out there. Given the short distance and the unobstructed line of fire, you wouldn't have to be much of a marksman to pick off somebody from that vantage point. Still, it was a matter of taking a shot at the woman with two kids practically in her lap. How could you be that confident of not hitting them, not bringing them down on a ricochet? This thought really struck home when I learned that the immediate and only suspect was William Patterson, estranged husband of the dead woman, father of those two kids who'd been sitting at her feet when the bullet whizzed by.

As always when children are involved, investigators face a real dilemma. The Patterson children had already been through enough shock and horror to last a lifetime. Yet the cops had a murder on their hands, and the kids were the only witnesses. On the night before, shortly after the murder, Amato had sought them out at a neighbor's, where they were already asleep. They were awakened but not told that their mother was dead. They still believed she'd just been hurt by a firecracker, since the relatives who would have to tell them the truth hadn't yet arrived. The younger girl seemed tired and confused and fell back asleep, and Amato pretty much let her be. From the eleven-year-old boy he learned that Mrs. Patterson had been expecting the father, who now lived in Atlanta, to arrive in the morning to take care of some legal business having to do with their separation.

Questioning of relatives and neighbors that night and the following morning turned up the information that the feelings between William Patterson and his estranged wife were quite bitter. So the first matter of business was to find out whether the guy's planned arrival the following morning meant that he was already in town when the shooting occurred. The detectives checked the local motels and the flights from Atlanta, but couldn't find his name.

The question of the guy's whereabouts was answered by William Patterson himself when he showed up at the house the next morning about the same time as me. After one look at the still-heavy crowds, at all the policemen and emergency vehicles, he ran up to the nearest patrolman and cried out, *What going on? I'm William Patterson and my wife and kids live here!* The patrolman said, *You'd better talk to the detectives in charge,* and at this Patterson moaned, *Oh my God, she's been sh———*

That's it, just *sh,* but obviously he was about to say *shot.* At that moment, nothing about the cause of death had been released, so in the first words he uttered the guy put the spotlight right on himself. (This, of course, is why police often withhold information as long as possible. The media doesn't like it, but it can be a real help when only you and the guy you're looking for know exactly what happened.)

Under questioning by Misegades and Amato, Patterson explained that he'd come north to declare bankruptcy, because he's had job troubles and can no longer afford alimony and upkeep for the wife and kids. He left the day before, right after going rafting with his woman friend down in Atlanta. In fact, he jumped into his car to drive straight up without even changing clothes. Only, the cops noted that for shoes he was wearing this polished pair of wing tips. Rafting? In wing tips? Sure, he told them, he doesn't own any sneakers. Nothing terrible about that, of course, but maybe a tad strange, a trim and active guy in his thirties without a pair of sneakers somewhere in his closet.

Now, he'd just arrived on the scene and obviously hadn't been labeled a suspect yet. The police were just interrogating him as the husband of the deceased. But the guy, who otherwise didn't seem all that dumb, just kept digging himself into a deeper and deeper hole.

When they asked him the exact time of his arrival and where he'd stayed overnight, the guy said he got in early the night before, and since he had some apprehensions about his wife's behavior, the first thing he did was drive to the house to make sure everything was all right with her and the children. All he did, though, was go to a rear window and peek in on the wife and kids watching television, with their dog nearby. He hadn't knocked at the door or anything to let them know he was around. All he'd done was make sure everybody was all right by just looking in on them like that.

This, of course, put him right at the house on the evening of the murder.

After peering through the window, he said, he drove to a rest area on the Long Island Expressway, where he slept in his car until morning. Again, the interrogators perked up, knowing that the highway police, as part of their routine patrol, periodically keep tabs on cars parked late at night in rest areas. So they called in on that and word came back that no car resembling Patterson's, or with Georgia plates, had been observed in any rest area overnight.

All through that first morning, Patterson kept saying how broken up he was over his wife's murder, but these were veteran detectives, with real expertise in evaluating demeanors. Unanimously, they found his grief less than convincing.

Patterson may have begun to sense this, because at one point he actually said that if they were wondering whether he killed his wife, he could assure them he didn't. He'd never owned a rifle in his life and didn't even know how to operate one. This really raised their eyebrows. Not only hadn't it been announced that she'd been shot by a rifle, but the police, including A. Della Penna, ace firearms expert, had yet to uncover a single piece of evidence indicating what type of firearm had been used.

Somewhere along here, Misegades asked Patterson if he'd submit to a polygraph test, particularly in regard to the time he arrived in New York and what he saw through the rear window. Patterson refused. Misegades asked me about having him submit to a Firearms Residue Test, which would have entailed wiping his hands for signs that he'd recently fired a weapon. Since a whole day had elapsed since the shooting, I said it was too late to bother swabbing for residues. We'll ask him anyway, Misegades said, to see his reaction. His reaction was very firm. No way was he going to let anybody wipe down his hands.

Before he turned me loose on my own search, Misegades took my arm and said, Al, come with me a minute. He led me around to the back window that Patterson said he'd used to peek in on his wife and kids in the den. Take a look, Misegades said, and I crouched down and did. This window didn't have a screen, just these folding wood shutters on the inside. I saw a pool table in another section of the downstairs area, but no matter how much I scrunched from one side to another I couldn't see the couch or the area around it.

We had a now-widowed husband who admitted driving a thousand miles to see his now-dead wife about the financial burdens of supporting her, who displayed an unconvincing show of grief while revealing far too much knowledge of the murder, and who seemed to lie about a lot of details. But not all liars are murderers, and Patterson hadn't admitted anything criminal or revealed anything to prove he'd killed his wife. Of course, he'd hardly produced an airtight alibi either. What we had, in other words, was one very likely suspect, but no evidence whatsoever.

While Amato and the others pursued their interviews and background checks, I set about trying to give some help on the firearms aspects. The neighborhood sumps and sewers and woods and Dumpsters and drainage basins had already been searched, giving us a lot of nondescript sneakers and other junk but no weapon. Although I'd eventually confirm this myself when I got the chance, I was also told that the size of the wound indicated a big bullet, heavy-duty stuff, powerful enough to pretty much take out the bottom of her skull before exiting on the other side of her neck. Still traveling with enough force to go right through the couch, the bullet ended up fragmenting so completely against the cement wall of the den that no useful or identifiable pieces of it had been found.

We took the window screen that the bullet had been fired through and got good pictures of the hole in the glass window. No footwear impressions had been found out there on the grass, nor any objects we could connect to the assailant. And since there were no cartridge casings around and only a single shot seemed to have been fired, I didn't think we were dealing with a semiautomatic-type weapon, which would discharge each expended casing after firing. I was leaning toward a single-action type, similar to a hunting rifle, where the casing remained inside until you levered it out.

When I looked at the tiny bits of copper and lead that had been collected in the way of bullet pieces, my immediate reaction was that we should have had more. Even if some shreds were too small to be recovered, I still felt we'd missed something. Even what we had told us something, however, because the presence of copper pieces supported the premise of a high-powered rifle. In that type of weapon the high speed of the bullet going down the barrel produces a great deal of heat, so the manufacturers will envelop the lead bullet with heat-resistant metals like copper or steel to keep the lead from losing its shape. And these bullets will often fragment into separate lead and copper bits when they hit something hard, as they did here. We always want the copper, which is what makes contact with the inside of the barrel and therefore acquires the unique markings we depend on for identification.

So far, none of the copper shreds I'd seen were anywhere near large enough to be useful, so we gave the rec room yet more close search. Still nothing. In frustrating situations like that, you thank God for little favors. Sometimes even the puniest, dinkiest find is worth cheering about because it beats anything else you've come up with. Having given up all hope of identifying the murder weapon from any of those fragments, I started going through the other items that had been picked up and came across a plastic baggie containing a small, flat, circular piece of metal with tiny, irregular, sharply pointed edges sticking up along its circumference. It'd been labeled *Earring*, which seemed plausible enough. The size was right and its jagged condition could easily have been caused by the bullet, which had struck the victim right below the ear. Only the thing intrigued me, and I kept looking at it from every angle. Finally I said right out loud to no one in particular, *That's not an earring, that's the base of a bullet.*

By *base* I mean the circular back part of the bullet, which in this case still had a few really tiny, splintery portions of the sides attached to it. It was too small to show anything to the naked eye, and I wasn't optimistic about learning much more under the microscope, but it was all we had, so I headed off to the lab with it.

That evening, almost exactly twenty-four hours after the murder, Misegades received a call from a lawyer who said he'd been engaged to represent Mr. William Patterson. Misegades said the police had offered Patterson a polygraph test, and that it might be in his best interest to submit to one if he had nothing to hide. The lawyer said he'd consider it, and reminded Misegades that from this point on the police could only question his client in the presence of his attorney.

Patterson never did take the test, but even if he'd failed it miserably, we wouldn't have changed our investigation. Polygraphs can be challenged even more easily than confessions, and can be thrown out for all sorts of reasons at any time, up to and including the final appeal.

Neither the arrival of the lawyer nor the debate over the polygraph particularly grabbed my attention. I concentrated solely on that little trace portion of bullet, spending a great many hours trying to identify whatever impressions existed on the fragment successfully enough to at least be able to associate it with a certain *type* of weapon. But these rifling patterns are not made on the base of the bullet, which comprised most of my sample, but on the sides, of which I had only the tiniest shreds.

My method of measuring these minute engravings entails the use of a special microscope with a micrometer attached, which allows me to view a bullet or bullet fragment while manually adjusting the micrometer jaw openings until they conform to the groove width displayed on the sample. These of course are very fine, very precise measurements, and you can't just document a single groove. You have to repeat the process again and again with every marking you can find. It's slow and painstaking under the best of circumstances, and when you're dealing with a portion that's not only tiny but also twisted and distorted, you can't be sure of coming up with anything at all.

In this instance, just by naked-eye examination of the size of the back portion, I felt I could probably ballpark a caliber somewhere in the .35-to-.38 range. After extensive microscope measurements, I began to detect a particular rifling pattern that appeared characteristic of a .35-caliber rifle manufactured by the Marlin Firearms Company—the same type that had been used in the DeFeo murders some years earlier.

We maintain an extensive collection of both new and expended

shell in the lab, so I referenced some .35-caliber bullets that had
been fired from Marlin rifles to see if the dimensions matched
closely enough for me to make a call. You're always cautious
about committing yourself because you want a very high degree
of consistency, and the meagerness of the sample was a real concern. I also would have welcomed more replication, say with three
or four items to work with, or even one whole and complete sample. And at the back of your mind, you're always conscious of the
possibility that someone, somewhere, might have developed a rifling pattern that you'd simply not run into yet and therefore are
not considering in your conclusion.

All in all, it was an extremely tough call, and I remember being
nervous about it, knowing full well that Homicide had nothing
else to go on in the way of physical evidence and therefore would
lean heavily on whatever I told them. Even though I knew how
anxious they were waiting for some kind of word, I kept viewing
the same markings and taking the same measurements over and
over. Even then I was very guarded in my report, letting them
know that although I'd done my level best to give them whatever I
could, the findings were not so decisive that I'd want them hanging their whole investigation on it. What I said in essence was that
the markings on the sample fragment were *consistent with* it being
fired from a Marlin .35-caliber-class rifle with lever action.

If we actually had a potential murder weapon in hand, that information could have been immediately helpful in ruling a certain
gun either in or out of consideration. Believe me, they searched
and searched for a weapon but just couldn't come up with anything. My involvement in the case therefore seemed over.

Homicide of course stayed on it. With the lawyer involved, they
couldn't question Patterson anymore, but Amato arranged a second interview with Patterson's eleven-year-old son down in Georgia, where he and his younger sister were now living with their
father—who we were pretty sure murdered their mother. The son
recalled the first program they'd viewed that evening, which of all

things turned out to be *CHiPS,* about the California Highway Patrol. Well, it came on a half hour later than the time Patterson
claimed he saw the family group watching television together, so
Patterson seemed to have been caught in another minor lie. The
son further remembered that the family dog didn't stir before the
shooting, although it always barked when a stranger came near
the house.

Although six weeks had passed since the mother's death, the
eight-year-old daughter was still so fearful and withdrawn that
Amato again declined to question her. It tends to remind you, especially when your basic contribution to a case consists of squinting into a microscope, that there are real people out there whose
lives have been horribly, and maybe permanently, mangled in
ways that maybe you tend to overlook, given your natural concerns about the progress of your investigation. (And it's not only
the victims whose psychological situation sometimes intrigues
you. More than once I would get an image of Patterson driving all
night and day from Georgia to Long Island with this big old hunting rifle stashed away in the trunk, thinking the whole time about
that instant when he'd get his wife in the gun sight and squeeze
the trigger. You wonder about funny things, like what kind of
music did he listen to along the way, was he aware of the scenery,
did he stop for meals and pay attention to the radio news? Did he
ever hesitate, ever think of making a U-turn and forgetting the
whole thing? Maybe all twenty hours was just one frozen blur during which he hardly blinked.)

On subsequent trips to Georgia, Amato talked to all the standard sources: the local police, Patterson's friends and neighbors,
coworkers and supervisors. He'd just recently gone to work for an
air-freight outfit at the Atlanta airport, at much lower pay than
he'd received for the job he'd recently lost.

Amato also interviewed the Atlanta woman Patterson had
been involved with. They'd apparently split, and she rather will-
ingly passed along a lot of background information. Her real contribution, though, was in handing over some unused bullets she

said she'd found in Patterson's apartment, although the guy had always denied ever owning a rifle. The fact that they were .35-caliber bullets certainly interested Amato, since they would have been appropriate for the kind of Marlin cited in my ballistic report.

Amato ran routine requests through ATF, the Alcohol, Tobacco, and Firearms division of the Treasury Department, which keeps track of gun permits and weapons sold in stores, but came up with nothing. Once you get past commercial transactions to just one guy selling to another, generally only handguns have to be recorded, not rifles.

Nobody Amato interviewed, including the ex-girlfriend, recalled Patterson showing any interest in firearms. He wasn't a hunter, wasn't a target shooter. This information could help, actually, indicating that he'd probably gotten his hands on the gun relatively recently. Amato spent days with local police officers going through the books of every gun shop and pawnbroker and business establishment that handled firearms in Atlanta and all of Clayton County. They checked every sale of .35-caliber Marlin rifles for the past six months without finding anything useful. Seeing how much time and energy Amato was spending on this lead, I remember saying a little prayer that I hadn't sent him and everybody else on a wild-goose chase.

Amato then got the idea of looking into those local throwaway tabloid *Pennysaver*s and such, where people list various items for sale. He asked Patterson's ex-girlfriend if she and Patterson had received a paper like that, and she said, Oh yes, the *Atlanta Advertiser.* Not only that, she further remembered seeing a copy on the back seat of Patterson's car with ads for rifles circled. She'd asked if he was planning to buy a gun, and he had said, No, he'd picked up the paper at work and someone else must have marked it up.

Right away Amato called the *Advertiser* for information on rifles sold through their columns. He'd have to look for himself, they told him, as they didn't keep track of the items listed or sold. Amato flew back to Atlanta and settled in at the newspaper office to go through every issue of the paper for the six months prior to the shooting, during which time an awful lot of rifles had been put up for sale. For every listing of a Marlin .35, Amato called whoever ran the ad to get the name of the buyer or at least a description of the person and the circumstances of the sale. Just for Marlin .35s, nothing else, and thank God the call I'd made based on that tiny shredded fragment paid off, instead of making me look like some kind of rank amateur.

He ultimately connected up with one Harry Allen Eastman, who lived in a small town just south of Atlanta and reported selling his Marlin .35-caliber lever-action with a 4× universal scope on June 21—barely a week before Frances Patterson was shot. He hadn't gotten the buyer's name, but the fellow talked like he came from up around New York somewhere.

Amato visited Eastman at his house, and the more he learned, the more promising things looked. For one, Eastman's description of the guy was right on. What happened, Eastman said, was the fellow showed up with a hundred forty dollars in cash, saying he wanted the gun to hunt varmints with—you know, pests of one kind or another, groundhogs or gophers or whatever might have taken a mind to tearing up your garden or digging holes in your pasture for your cows to break their ankles in. But Eastman knew that all you wanted for small animals like that was something like a .22, not a big old .35. He was also surprised when the guy proceeded to buy the gun after just looking through the scope, without even opening the breech. No one who knew anything about guns would ever do that.

The next day the buyer called back asking if Eastman would pick up a box of shells, saying he couldn't do it himself because he didn't have a Georgia driver's license. Eastman knew there wasn't any such requirement, but got the shells anyhow, for which the guy gave him twenty dollars, about twice what they cost.

Eastman's wife also saw the guy, and she too gave a description that fit Patterson. Amato had them study a photo spread, which is a collection of six or seven photos of people of the same age group that have similar general characteristics. You know, not with just one black guy, or one white guy, or one with a mustache or a big scar. You let people make their choice, then you cut and reshuffle the batch, like a deck of cards, and have them choose again, and then again. They both picked out Patterson, although Eastman was a little less positive than the wife. Both also provided written statements, and in hers Mrs. Eastman said she remembered commenting to her husband that it seemed strange, when the man came to pick up the shells, that he parked down the road, as if not wanting to give them a good look at his car.

All this went on over a period of months, with everything pointing straight at Patterson, who all this time remained free as a bird, with the two children still very much under his wing. Clearly we could establish his motive, and make him look bad on all his lies and contradictions. We probably could even, with the Eastmans now in the ball game, show that despite his denials Patterson had purchased a rifle of the make and caliber indicated by my lab tests. Only we still had absolutely nothing that would put that rifle in his hands outside his wife's front window or, more importantly, connect it to the fragment of the bullet that killed Frances Patterson, which I was keeping very carefully secured away in a plastic baggie.

The search for that link that we desperately needed veered off in a more peculiar direction than you'd ever expect in your typical homicide investigation.

In one of their numerous contacts, Amato, groping for straws, asked Eastman: That rifle you sold, did you ever use it for target practice anywhere? Well, sure, Eastman said. We used to hunt out of my father's place in Douglas County, and he's got these trees we'd shoot into for practice.

The next day a very excited Amato showed up at old man Eastman's place, accompanied by some county sheriff's people. It's important, when you're away from your home base, that you connect up with the local police. They know the landscape and the people and can keep you from a lot of fruitless driving around on dusty back roads that don't lead *anywhere.* They also help deflect the suspicion you're bound to run into as this New York cop nosing around where you don't belong, not even knowing a varmint from an orangutan.

The younger Eastman showed Amato a tree that he said ought to be just full of bullets, and Amato politely asked his father about cutting it down. Now, we're not talking about some magnificent, stately old specimen here. It was just your plain everyday dime-a-dozen scrub oak. But the old man played the real southern country boy not about to be hornswoggled by any city slicker. Sure thing, he told them, only if they're gonna just barge in and cut his tree down, they're damn well gonna have to pay him for it. And he wanted a lot, way more than the thing was worth, a hundred bucks, a hundred and fifty, something like that, saying how all these trees were real precious heirlooms that'd been on his property for generations. Finally they paid him what he asked, and we've actually got the receipt in the file. You know: one tree received, for such and such in U.S. currency, although the price listed was less than they actually shelled out because they didn't want it to look like they were throwing money around buying witnesses or anything like that.

Amato had the foresight to bring along some County Maintenance people, and he had them chop it right down. All he took was the trunk section from the ground up to maybe six feet, where Eastman said they'd find most of the target bullets. They left the rest behind at the old guy's insistence on keeping it for firewood.

Given that a sizable portion of tree trunk wasn't a type of evidence they'd much handled before, Amato called me to kick some ideas around, and between us we decided our first move should be to make sure we actually had bullets in there. They hauled the log to a local vet who had this X-ray machine for horses and cows— and who knows, maybe circus elephants too—only the pictures didn't show anything because the wood was too thick and dense. They nonetheless gave the vet twenty-five bucks for use of his machine and transported the log to County Maintenance, where they split it into smaller pieces, during which process they found and removed several bullets. Only they were working with axes and wood splitters, and Amato called them off before they messed up too many potentially useful specimens. Next they dropped in on the Georgia Crime Laboratory, where they had these smaller pieces fluoroscoped to locate the promising-looking objects buried inside. More carefully now, the lab technicians removed about a dozen objects, some bullets but mostly fragments, and sent them up to me for comparison against the bottom circle of the murder bullet.

Again, it was slow going, without much to work with. The samples represented a whole variety of different calibers, but the end result was we found no match at all. The Eastmans then said maybe some of the shots had been fired higher up in the tree, so they took another piece of trunk and split that up and took the pieces to a hospital X-ray department. Nothing showed, though, so they just tossed them.

At this point, the Eastmans, father and son, allowed as to how there was *another* tree, not far from the first, that they used to shoot at as well. By this time Amato and everyone else were pretty sure the old guy was nothing but a drawling country-boy hustler, but what could we do? We were still trying to associate Patterson with the bullet that killed his wife, and this looked like our one last best chance. So Amato headed out once more with the local gendarmes and tree choppers in tow, saying we would much appreciate cutting this one down too, because we got this crackerjack ballistics fellow up there in New York who just loves playing around with all kinds of little scraps and scrapings. The old man just chewed on his cud or corncob or whatever—I never saw him, I just have this picture of him in my head—and said, Oh no, this tree has my television antenna on it, along with several other vital electrical connections and transmission wires. I imagine Amato at this juncture taking a deep breath, something between a sigh of resignation and a snort of frustration, because what the hell, he's a police officer, and this is a piece of potentially very important information. Okay, he said, we'll pay you for it. This time the price is not only substantially elevated, but the old guy gives the knife one more twist by saying that in addition to paying for the tree they're going to have to replace it with a *telephone pole* so he can properly hook up his disrupted TV antenna and the other electrical connections. I don't know, Amato says, I can't just go around buying telephone poles without talking to my superiors.

What he did then was contact the county police, who said the Georgia Department of Transportation had a portable X-ray machine that they used to check out bridges for hidden cracks and faults. Amato wanted them to come out and make sure this second tree actually had something inside that looked interesting before he forked over any money for it. Only then he learned that the fees for transporting and using the machine would make the cost of buying the damn tree look like pocket change.

The idea was left in cold storage for almost a full year while other areas were explored by Amato. Up north, he organized more neighborhood searches and distributed thousands of fliers through local post offices, asking for help in locating the gun. He found counselors at two women's groups who reported that Mrs. Patterson had sought help because she was fearful of her husband and had received threats from him.

The following June, Amato even flew a hypnotist down to Georgia for a four-hour session that he hoped might help the younger Eastman recall more details about the man who bought his gun, maybe even produce 100 percent identification from the photo spread. It didn't do either. Amato took Eastman to the airport to secretly observe Patterson at work through binoculars. He still thought Patterson was the guy, Eastman said, but still wasn't absolutely positive. Again the wife seemed more positive about things, identifying a picture of Patterson's car as the one driven by the gun buyer. The hypnotist also tried his abracadabra on her, but it too proved unproductive and was abandoned when the session was interrupted by a neighbor dropping by for a friendly visit. (I always wondered, you know, what the neighbor thought was going on, with these cops and hypnotists and photo spreads all over the place.)

Since we were still mighty thin on physical evidence, Amato ultimately bought that second tree for a hefty price from the old geezer and threw in the installation of a new telephone pole as a bonus. I have to admit, I rode the ass off him. You suckers, I said, you fell for it, you bought a whole goddamn tree from that con artist. Cops are always quick to razz each other—although between you and me, I'd have bought it too. And boy, I'd have given my left arm to dig out just one pristine and beautiful specimen of a .35-caliber bullet that would solve all our problems, and maybe finally allow us to get on the ass of this guy who surely had spent all this time congratulating himself on this really perfect crime he'd pulled off.

This time they decided not to mess with hospitals and veterinarians and labs down there but just send the two bottom sections of trunk directly to me. Where the laboratory-analysis request form asks, *State what the material is, or is alleged to be,* they wrote, *2 wood logs,* which I'm sure had to be a first. We X-rayed them in the morgue, laying them down on the slab like bodies. The wood acted the same as flesh, letting the rays through to show these solid, bullet-shaped objects inside.

We still needed to split the logs into smaller pieces to work with, and boy, those logs were still so green and gummy that we ended up attacking them with anything we could get our hands on in the way of sledges and mauls and what have you—logging tools, not woodworking tools. The rest of the Crime Lab naturally got a big laugh out of me turning all these highly trained scientists and technicians into regular Paul Bunyans, whacking away with their axes while at the same time I'm hovering over them saying, *Careful now! Careful! We don't want to mess up any of those bullets!*

They did a great job and eventually we scooped out, as delicately as we could, maybe twenty separate bullets and identifiable metal fragments. Some .223s and .30s, obviously the wrong caliber, could be eliminated with one look. But there were .35s, too, including some that might have been fired in a Marlin, and I very painstakingly examined their rifling characteristics and any other microscopic attributes that I could find.

The unequivocal upshot of all this lab work, of all the time spent poring over newspaper ads to finally track down the Eastmans, of the whole business of chopping down and X-raying and lugging around and shipping north various scrub-oak logs, was unfortunately summed up in my report:

> *Microscopic examination and comparison of the previously sub-mitted bullet fragment (Frances Patterson death) with Items A1 through A3, B1 through B19, revealed that none of the bullets recovered from the two (2) logs had been fired in the same weapon as the "Patterson" bullet.*

It happens. You do everything you can, but you get no guaran-tees. You can perform the best police work in the world without producing anything even resembling evidence. Sometimes there just *isn't* any evidence. And sometimes, let's face it, you can stum-ble and bumble all over the place in your innate dumbness but still end up smelling like a rose because the bad guy, thank God, turns out to be even dumber.

In this instance, our major problem from the beginning, which we could never overcome, was that the shredded piece of bullet was all we had, and it wasn't much. If it had been whole, or larger, or in better shape, maybe I could have matched it to one of the tree samples. But that's pure speculation, as opposed to the hard truth, which was that those two logs probably represented the end of the line as far as evidence gathering was concerned. We had nowhere else to go.

The time had come, in other words, for somebody, not me, to make a decision. We were all convinced that William Patterson killed his wife in an act of premeditated murder, yet for well over a year we'd diligently explored every conceivable lead without com-ing up with anything beyond the circumstantial. And even there, the most damning evidence we had—Patterson's lying about the purchase of a .35-caliber Marlin from Eastman—depended en-tirely on the linkup established by nothing more or less persuasive than my identification of that tiny shred of murder bullet.

Do you simply let the whole thing drop, hoping that eventually something might fall in your lap, or do you haul the guy into court hoping you can nail him with what you have?

Late in October, sixteen months after that single shot fired through the basement window killed Frances Patterson, the Suffolk County prosecutor went before a grand jury and obtained a murder-two indictment against William Patterson. Did he do it with his fingers crossed, hoping for some kind of miracle along the way? I really have no way of knowing. But a few days later when Patterson was arrested at his Georgia home, he reportedly said to the sheriff's deputies, "I knew it would come to this."

You didn't have to be a legal genius to realize that Patterson's lawyer would immediately take dead aim on our lack of concrete evidence, with his number-one target for disparagement being my claim that a teensy piece of metal, originally identified by a trained crime-scene investigator as an earring, had actually been fired from a weapon that none of us had ever seen but that I, all by myself, after a whole bunch of scientific hocus-pocus, had declared *could* have been the murder rifle.

The first trial ended in a hung jury. In the second trial, the jury found both the circumstantial evidence and the ballistic findings sufficient to convict Patterson in his wife's death, with the judge then sentencing him to twenty-five to life.

AS AN AFTERTHOUGHT, Al mentioned an odd coincidence. Patterson graduated from Patchogue High School in 1961, where his close friend and classmate was Jeffrey MacDonald. Both were athletes and good students who went on to successful careers, MacDonald as a military doctor, Patterson as an air-freight executive. Patterson murdered his wife in 1982. The following year his old buddy MacDonald became the subject of *Fatal Vision*, the best-selling book by Joe McGinniss, later made into a movie of the same name. MacDonald's considerable notoriety at the time resulted from his conviction for shooting his wife and daughters to death in 1970.

THE ATTACHÉ CASE

IN ALMOST EVERY CASE he talks about, Al comes back to the critical concern of someone whose job is to collect evidence: it's got to hold up. Whether at a crime scene or working in his lab, he automatically assumes that everything he touches will end up being legally and technically contested. It gives him a curious double vision, always considering not only what he's doing at the moment, but how these actions will appear to a judge or jury a year down the road.

John, on the other hand, patrolling the most scarred city streets, has had to deal with all sorts of day-to-day surprises, drawing instinctively on his own resources, his own hard-won reservoir of shrewdness and experience. Much more than Al's, his life as a cop seems encapsulated in a series of distinct moments, each with its own beginning and end, its own completeness. He rarely has the time, and I doubt he's ever had the inclination, to view whatever's happening right before his eyes in terms of some future legal controversy over the precise meaning of the search-and-seizure provisions of the Constitution.

Yet it was John who got most notably caught up in this issue when a seemingly routine drug arrest was challenged all the way up to the United States Court of Appeals, leading to an important decision regarding the actions of the police in gathering evidence.

J O H N   C U O M O ➡

THIS WAS SOON AFTER I'd gotten my gold shield as a detective in the Narcotics Squad. Even though I was only twenty-five, I was the senior officer of a three-man team on patrol in the Bronx, since one partner was still a white shield and the other had just been assigned to Narcotics. We were working out of the Four-One precinct in the South Bronx, in the area nicknamed Fort Apache, which later became well-known from the movie by that name. It was mostly Puerto Rican at the time and included part of Westchester Avenue and Southern Boulevard, and probably featured more drug use than any part of the borough.

Our general procedure on routine patrol was to ride around keeping our eyes peeled until we saw something that looked suspicious. We'd then park and walk into the streets to check things out. This was a summer day, early in the evening but still light, and our attention was drawn to this female, whose name was something like Bridget, who was out on the street with her child of maybe three years old, holding his hand. She was one of the few people of Irish extraction in the area, with red hair, and although she was an addict, she wasn't that far gone and still had a nice appearance. She had been an informer of mine on prior occasions. We'd grabbed her one time with a bag of heroin and the works—you know, spoon and needle and eyedropper, the stuff you need to prepare and inject the dope—and instead of arresting her on possession, which was just a misdemeanor anyway, we agreed to leave her out on the streets. In token of that, she cooperated with us. When we saw her we'd ask how it was going and she'd sometimes have stuff to pass along. Like she'd say, Well, there's a guy in such and such a brick house dealing out of his apartment. This would allow us to institute a surveillance on the apartment and with any kind of luck make an arrest of a seller, as opposed to bringing in a simple user like Bridget.

We didn't go up to her this time because she was talking to a man we knew was a drug user and seller. She was probably trying to score, using the kid as a good guise, so we moved up to a house roof, which we'd sometimes do to gain a vantage point of the activities and individuals on the street. By the time we got up there, though, Bridget was alone on the sidewalk with the child, waiting, so we waited too. Before long the man, who wasn't Puerto Rican either, whose name was Harry something, sort of skipped out of a house and down the stoop to rejoin her. The three of them, with the little kid in the middle, started off at a good pace, so we hustled down from the roof and followed them. We stayed at a distance, not to let her spot me. Down the block they approached a big expensive car at the curb with Texas plates. For the first time they started acting suspicious, looking over their shoulders and up and down the street, but we kept hidden and she never made me— never recognized me.

The two of them and the kid hopped into the car, and we were pretty sure we were on to something, given the purposeful way they'd headed straight for this fancy out-of-state car, which zoomed away so immediately that there had to have been a driver in there waiting for them to arrive. We ran back to my car and followed them along Southern Boulevard up to Castle Hill Avenue, near where you grew up, George, only way out on the other side of Bruckner Boulevard, which now is covered with all those huge project buildings but back then was mostly empty land overgrown with weeds and bushes. In this particularly desolate section, they swung onto a little dirt road and stopped in a clearing.

Still far enough back so they hadn't made us, we parked around a bend and moved up as close as we could on foot while staying hidden behind the bushes. At this point we assumed Bridget was going to turn a trick for whoever was driving the fancy car, with the other guy, Harry, acting as her pimp. Therefore we expected to find Harry outside the car tending the little kid while Bridget and

the driver were doing whatever inside. I don't think she was a regular prostitute, but she was always out on the street and enough
of a junkie to have a real need to support her habit. Only when we
looked through the bushes we were astounded to see *her* standing
outside, again holding the kid by his hand, with the two *guys* inside. Then the driver got out, a young guy, blond, very well
dressed. He opened the trunk, bent in to take something out, and
rejoined Harry inside.

At this point we made our move to examine the situation face-
to-face. We didn't draw our guns because we hadn't seen anything hostile or threatening and were approaching just to make
inquiries. But the minute I stepped out of the weeds Bridget yelled
at the top of her lungs, "Holy shit, here comes Cuomo!" She ran to
the car window and shouted inside, "Here comes Cuomo!"

We were already at the car, though, and saw that the two guys
in the front seat were injecting themselves with heroin. We
weren't really surprised, because once we ruled out her turning a
trick, a drug deal was the next likeliest possibility.

From each side the other officers reached in and removed the
needles from the arms while I grabbed the works and made them
get out. Bridget rushed up to me and said, "You're not going to arrest me, are you?" I asked her what the hell was going on, and she
was so flustered she spilled out everything in one breath. Nothing,
we just scored for this guy, that's all, we just met him and he
wanted us to score for him, I don't even know the guy, I just met
him today for the first time in my life. Please don't arrest me,
they'll take away my baby, remember everything I did for you. And
on and on like that, with the child standing right alongside,
clutching her hand.

I wasn't about to make any promises, and turned to the blond
guy, who now had rolled down the sleeves of both his shirt and his
suit jacket to cover his forearm marks. He gave the impression of
being a young businessman, well-spoken and intelligent. Look, he
said, nothing's going on. I just needed a fix and I met these people
and they scored for me. I'm not in any trouble, am I? I told him he

certainly was, that I was placing him under arrest, along with the other guy shooting up in the car.

Then, without giving it much thought one way or the other, I asked him what he'd gone into the trunk for, and he said, It doesn't matter. What do you want to know for? I told him I was just interested in knowing if whatever was in the trunk had any connection with the illegal drug usage I had just witnessed, and asked him to open it up. When he refused, I took the keys and opened the trunk myself and saw an attaché case inside and asked the guy what was in it. He said, Money.

Money? I said. How much money? He said he didn't know, so I opened it up and my eyes must've popped out. The case was stuffed with tens and twenties and fifties, a lot still bundled in paper wrappers, and sitting on top of all this money was a loaded .38 revolver, along with a book on makeup and disguises.

I asked him where all this money came from, and he said, Look, I'll tell you the truth. Down in Houston I heard about this guy who made a lot of money as a pimp running some whores, so I went and burglarized his place at night. He had all this cash around and I took it out of his bedroom closet. He said he'd just driven up from Texas and hadn't even got around to counting it yet but figured it was maybe thirty, forty thousand dollars.

C'mon, I said, we're all going to the station house.

Wait, the blond guy said. Listen, I don't want to get in any trouble. Why don't you just take ten thousand for yourself and we can forget the whole thing. When I said we weren't interested, he offered us the whole valise of money to let him go, which convinced me we'd stumbled onto something a lot heavier than burglarizing someone's apartment.

I cuffed him and we escorted them all down to the station. I didn't say anything to the station personnel but went upstairs and called my superior officer, the lieutenant in the detective division, who was home at the time, and advised him that I had a suspicious situation, with a man in possession of a loaded gun and a huge sum of money. He said he'd come right over, and while we waited I charged the two men and the woman with possession of heroin and a set of works. Even though Bridget and Harry had obviously sold the blond man the heroin, a more serious charge, we hadn't witnessed the sale and couldn't have proved it. They underwent the regular processing and fingerprinting on the possession charge, with no mention of the money or the weapon.

Bridget and Harry had probably provided him with the works, too. People didn't usually travel with their own, because you could get arrested for that, so addicts would borrow what they needed from the dope dealer for a standard one-dollar fee. It was very dangerous for your health, of course, since nobody ever cleaned the needles, but that's the way they operated.

At most station houses, the *Daily News* delivery truck stopped by every night to drop off some copies of the morning paper, and while I was waiting for the lieutenant to arrive, one of the patrolmen looked up from his copy and said, Hey, there's been this big bank robbery up in Ridgefield, Connecticut, and a couple of guys got away with sixty thousand dollars.

Some of the money was still bundled in wrappers labeled *Ridgefield State Bank,* and when the lieutenant showed up he right away notified the FBI. On the basis of keys in the prisoner's possession from a motel in Fort Lee, New Jersey, the FBI discovered that he'd registered there under an alias, and even had business cards printed with that name, saying he and his partner ran a business that sold stainless-steel surgical implements. Motel records showed that he'd made a series of phone calls to a motel on Long Island, where the FBI not only picked up his partner but also the other half of the cash taken from the Connecticut bank. They also got another loaded gun.

All this happened within twenty-four hours of our spotting my informant and her friend getting into the Texas car, and within forty-eight hours of the bank robbery itself, during which period both perpetrators were arrested and most of the money recovered. The missing cash went for the fix the Texas guy purchased, along with two hundred additional dollars for a money order he sent to his mother. That always got me: he picks up thirty grand in a bank heist and plays the real big shot by treating his dear beloved mother to a couple of hundred bucks.

The other thing about the money was that when I got to the station house with the attaché case, I never myself counted it or put it under any special security. I don't even remember exactly where it was in the station house, or under whose control, but eventually they sat a bunch of clerical types around a big table to count every bill, and everything was still there, minus only the expenditures for the fix and the money order. I was very relieved, because by this time I realized how foolish it was to ever let that amount of money out of my sight. If someone had gotten sticky fingers, the suspicion would have immediately fallen on me. I should have slapped seals all over it and just taken a lot more precautions in general.

In those days, anyone arrested on a significant felony would be taken downtown to headquarters the next morning to appear in the daily lineup. The purpose was to allow detectives across the city to check out anyone arrested who might bear some resemblance to a suspect wanted on other open investigations.

When I escorted the prisoner down for the lineup, there were reporters everywhere, and the next day all the papers ran big stories and pictures about this big bank robbery that got cracked by this young detective who got suspicious up in the Bronx and came upon a whole attaché case full of money.

It turned out that the Texas guy was a Rhodes scholar, a brilliant student who'd gone to England and gotten a degree at Oxford. Him and his partner were professional bank robbers, both looking very neat and thoughtful and businesslike, the partner wearing glasses and everything. They traveled around the country using the surgical-instruments business cards as a cover, and had pulled off heists in California and Rhode Island and various other places. Earlier, though, the Texas guy, who'd actually grown up on Long Island, in the next town over from me, had served time in Sing Sing for some robberies of drugs from pharmacies on the Island.

When they were charged with Federal bank robbery, it wasn't

the Connecticut heist but an earlier one in Rhode Island that the Feds decided to try them on. But the evidence I had turned up would be crucial against them, so at the judge's preliminary hearing I was pretty much the key witness.

The sole purpose of the hearing was to decide whether I should have opened the trunk. That was it. The defense for the two guys said I had no right to do so, and therefore the spoils of my illegal search and seizure—the gun and the satchel full of money—could not be used against them in this trial or any other. But this trial was the crucial one. Suspects in a series of Federal bank robberies would just be tried on one of them. If convicted, they'd plea bargain all the other charges, which saved the government a lot of time and money while letting them declare a whole bunch of crimes solved. The one case was usually picked as the strongest the government could mount, so if they couldn't get a conviction on that, the government would usually drop the other charges and let the guys walk.

So either we got to use the evidence I found in the trunk or these guys would go free on the Rhode Island charges and probably everything else too. Even if independent evidence existed, it couldn't be used against them if they'd been apprehended by unconstitutional means. What we'd be left with would be two nationwide guilty-as-sin armed bank robbers facing nothing more than a misdemeanor drug-possession charge.

I spent a couple of days testifying at great length up in Rhode Island. Since I was the arresting officer who'd opened the trunk and then the satchel, I was naturally the prime target of the defense lawyers. I told them the same story I just told you, although they made me go over the same points again and again, with a lot of tough questions along the way. When did you do this? When did you do that? Did you do this before that or that before this? They really pressed me, but I stuck to recounting the events exactly as they happened.

The main point of contention became my assumption when I went into the trunk. The defense lawyers said I was just looking to grab anything I could find, and had no clear cause for investigat-

ing the contents of that part of the car. The prosecutors supported
me by saying that since I had seen the one guy go into the trunk
before I caught the two guys shooting up in the front seat, I'd
made a reasonable assumption that the dope had come from the
trunk. My search therefore was a logical and legal extension of my
arresting them for drug possession.

After I finished testifying, the defense lawyers surprised everyone by putting Bridget on the stand. I was really shocked to see her
walk in, and my immediate feeling was that they must have offered her money to come all the way up from New York and partic-
ipate in the trial. The other surprise was that they didn't even
question her about the trunk business. Instead they tried to dis-
credit me by having her testify that I insisted on searching her personal body, touching her undergarments and stuff, which really
infuriated me because it wasn't true at all. First off, I knew who
she was and knew she posed no threat of any kind, and therefore I
would have looked pretty silly to my partners if I'd tried to go
through the motions of searching her. Secondly, I'd dealt with her
a number of times before and this kind of issue had never once
come up.

I told the prosecutors to put me back on the stand, which they
did, and I testified to the fact that she had been my informant for a
period of time, which undercut her credibility as an objective witness, and she became very nervous at that point and disappeared
from the scene.

In the end, the judge paid no attention to Bridget's accusations
and upheld me entirely on the search issue, saying I had every
right under the circumstances to go into the trunk. The defense
wouldn't let it rest there, taking their arguments up to the U.S.
Court of Appeals. Eventually that court too supported me. The
ruling went on for pages and pages, sometimes in legalistic terms
but also in plain English:

*The rule that officers making a valid arrest of one or more
occupants of an automobile can, without a warrant, then and
there search the car including its trunk is reasonable not only be-*

cause of necessity in many cases but because a speedy search may
disclose information useful in tracking down accomplices still on
the move. . . . Detective Cuomo's spontaneous request for an ex-
planation was as investigative as anything could be; he was bound
to inquire as to the facts in order to ascertain what other persons
might be involved and where they and the stolen money might be
found.

Naturally I felt pretty good when the ruling came down. The two guys meanwhile were serving long terms, but they must have just been natural-born con artists because they were still full of great scams. They tried to escape from the maximum-security prison at Cranston, Rhode Island, but it turned into a comedy of errors that was like something from a Three Stooges movie. *Newsday* headlined the story JAILBREAKERS TRIP ON OWN MOP HANDLES. They actually carved a bar of soap into the shape of a gun, then blackened it with shoe polish and used it to overpower a couple of guards and take their uniforms. The guards were unarmed, so the two guys still didn't have a real weapon. They put on the guard uniforms and crossed the prison yard carrying some knotted sheets tied to a couple of mop handles, which they figured they'd use to hook onto the ledge on the prison wall. Of course there were towers on the wall, so they went up to one and pointed the blackened soap gun at the guard up on top and yelled that he'd better throw his gun down or they'd blow his fucking head off. By this time the whole place was onto these guys dressed like guards and running around with sheets and mop handles, so the sentry shouted back down that they'd better drop *their* gun or he'd blow *their* fucking heads off. Soon every guard in the place was charging them en masse, and they got tackled and overwhelmed and dragged back to their cells. They ended up with ten extra years for attempted escape.

God only knows where they are, or what kind of scam they're dreaming up now.

BIG BARRY
WEARS A BIG HAT

A L   D E L L A   P E N N A   ⇒

PEOPLE ARE SO USED to seeing TV cops crouching down with both hands wrapped around their guns as they blast away at everything in sight that they have trouble believing you when you tell them how rarely in all your years on the force you've ever drawn your weapon. Of course, I've been in the lab a long time, with less call to pull my gun than someone like Johnny. Still, for most policemen their gun, which unfortunately symbolizes them in the public mind, represents the *least* important part of their job.

In my own career, the occasion to draw my weapon has arisen, but only on widely separated occasions. The one that comes to mind happened barely a year ago, when I came within a flash of turning an already bloody scene into something even more tragic, not only for the guy in my sights but for me too.

It began with a triple murder at a restaurant known as Big Barry's, a typical huge Long Island steak house. I wasn't on call at the time, and therefore didn't go out with the crime-scene unit. The killings occurred around five A.M. and I wasn't called in until mid-morning. Nobody on the investigative unit was a ballistics specialist, and since there'd been a lot of shooting, they thought a firearms man might be of help.

By the time I arrived, the Homicide detectives were able to give me a pretty good summary of what had transpired, which of course made it much easier for me than barging onto a scene without the foggiest idea of up or down.

I'd eaten in the restaurant a few times, so had a general sense of the layout, at least in the public areas. You could spot the place a good distance away because outside it had this huge ten-gallon hat. Inside, the western motif was carried through with a lot of dark wood, wooden booths, that sort of thing. It was owned by a man named Barry, and I'd heard his ads on the radio, with his booming John Wayne voice. I later learned that he also appeared on his own TV ads, although I'd not seen them.

Like most restaurants, Big Barry's was cleaned every night in the wee hours after closing, in this case by a man and a woman, both Hispanic, who worked for a cleaning company. They would let themselves in around four A.M. to vacuum and mop and would be gone before the day staff showed up for lunch.

Big Barry was also having some inside painting done during the same nonbusiness hours, and for this he'd hired a couple of brothers, both Suffolk County police officers who moonlighted as painters to make ends meet. They'd arranged this morning to meet at the restaurant at five A.M., but the one driving the van with their equipment and materials apparently arrived a few minutes before his brother and started unloading, because when the second brother drove up he saw the van parked outside with its doors opened. He went inside looking and found his brother face down on the entryway floor, shot to death. He called headquarters, and the responding officers found the cleaning woman also shot to death, further inside in the dining area, and the cleaning man seriously injured with a stomach wound. He was taken to the hospital and died shortly thereafter, but survived long enough to say that the assailant was a Spanish-speaking man he'd never seen before, who was short and very slight.

Even though he seemed obviously dead, the police officer was also rushed to the hospital. I think everyone wanted to make sure they'd expended every effort to save his life.

Neither policeman did their painting armed. Officers used to be considered on duty around-the-clock and therefore wore their service revolvers everywhere. But the union said anyone on duty twenty-four hours a day ought to be paid twenty-four hours a day. Eventually the policy was relaxed, although many officers, because of their avocation, so to speak, still wear their guns off duty. But it's an option now, and the brothers probably figured the weapons would get in the way climbing up and down ladders. I'm sure they didn't foresee any need for them in a deserted restaurant. Hell, no one ever *expects* to be shot.

By the time I got there, only the woman's body remained on the premises. She hadn't been rushed off because she was indisputably dead, shot several times, including once in the leg and at least once in the chest and upper back. Another shot had gone through her hair, not actually wounding her but taking out a lot of hair. There was hair everywhere.

In general, I could see that a large amount of ammunition had been expended, with buckshot pellets and spent shells all over the place. Just from an immediate visual examination I could tell that the guy had used 00 Buck ammunition with its huge load of shot, between nine and twelve .32-caliber pellets packed into this very large casing. That means the target has to absorb the equivalent impact of being hit by a dozen .32-caliber bullets at once.

I set about to locate and collect all traces of firearms activity, including whatever pellets could be retrieved from the walls and ceilings and floors, even the furniture, along with all spent and ejected shell casings. I then used my sketches of locations to reconstruct the crime as accurately as possible, particularly in terms of the movements of both the assailant and his victims. I went down the stairs leading to the basement, where meat and other perishables were stocked in giant iceboxes and storage rooms, and even found pellets and shells at the bottom of these steps and a pattern of shots in the ceiling over the stairs. The woman must have been chased around by her killer, down into this huge basement and then up again, because her body had been found upstairs.

Tons of cops had been on the scene for hours, and being that one victim was a fellow police officer, there was no lack of zeal on the part of any of the investigating officers. So every inch of the place had been thoroughly scoured, but being the methodical guy that I like to be, I told one of the sergeants that I was going down to search out the basement.

It's been cleared down there, right? I asked.

Oh, yeah, the sergeant assured me. Nobody's down there, everything's fine. C'mon, I'll go with you.

So we moved down to this really dark and dank and kind of smelly cellar, practically like a huge catacomb, extending beneath the whole restaurant with various halls and doors and alcoves. The sergeant nosed around in one direction and I walked down this hallway in another when, not ten feet in front of me, a door swung open and out stepped this really short guy of very slight build—exactly the description we had of the suspect—with the hall light behind him totally obscuring his features.

It absolutely scared the shit out of me, so I grabbed my gun and practically screamed, Don't move, you little prick! Get up against that wall! Go on, go on, get up against that wall!

The guy immediately thrusts his hands up, but all he's saying is, Uh—uh—uh.

I'm still screaming at him, One step and you're gonna die! One move and you're gone!

Now the guy is saying, Okay—okay—okay—.

Just then I feel a little tap on my shoulder, and the sergeant sort of whispers in my ear, kind of apologetically, Gee, Al—that's Big Barry.

I just, the guy stammers, still barely able to talk, wanted a c-cup of c-c-coffee. Let me know when, all right . . . ? I c-c-can wait.

It really shook the hell out of me, realizing how close I'd come to actually shooting the guy. One wrong move and there'd have been four murders splashed over the papers the next day instead of three, and one sorry cop in a cell somewhere watching his whole career, his whole life, go right down the toilet. Still, the Homicide detectives kidded the pants off me. Like, didn't I ever see his TV commercials, where the same little runt went around in a big ten-gallon hat calling himself Big Barry? I tried to point out that since three people had been shot dead on the premises that morning, it would have been nice if someone had informed me that somebody was still working away in his office downstairs, whatever his name or size happened to be. They naturally would have none of it—you know, cop humor, black humor. He was just this little pipsqueak, they kept saying, that any real cop could have handled with his bare hands.

They found the assailant without much trouble—I think later that same day. He was the cleaning woman's husband. They'd fallen out and she'd been threatening to divorce him. In his apartment they found a number of guns, including a shotgun I was able to test out as the murder weapon.

He was a Cuban who'd come over on the Mariel boat lift in 1980, and at first he told the cops he was working for Castro, then that he was working against Castro. At one time he said he drove to the restaurant in a truck, another time he claimed he took a cab. He also kept insisting that he didn't go there to shoot her but to patch everything up. Given that he showed up with a loaded shotgun, a reasonable man might be inclined to doubt that part of his story. Eventually, at his trial, he went for an insanity plea, but no one bought it, and he was convicted in a pretty straightforward manner.

S U S P I C I O U S
O N   T H E   S T R E E T

J O H N   C U O M O ➡

WHEN YOU'RE WORKING narcotics on the street, almost everything
you get involved in stems from coming across something or somebody that just doesn't look right. That's what happened when we
zeroed in on the Texas guy and the woman addict and her kid and
ended up discovering a suitcase of money from a bank robbery.
Out on the street almost everything starts like that. You could say
it's pure luck, I guess, but a lot goes into creating that kind of luck.

For instance, what do we mean when we say somebody looks
suspicious? How can we tell? Well, sometimes it's nothing more
than a feeling you get, a sense that something fishy is going on.
There's also certain obvious giveaways that you're always alert to.
Gait, for one, the way a person walks. This is particularly true for
narcotics types, where you notice the turning of the head, a little
more tension than clean people usually show. You get a lot of anxious looking around, maybe a guy wanting to score, or a seller
searching for buyers and making sure no one's tailing him.

Even just hailing a cab can give away a person who's dirty. He'll be very impatient to jump in and get away, yet will take one last look over his shoulder to see if anyone's watching. Or you'll spot guys talking on the street, and very abruptly they'll rush off in different directions. If you just pull alongside a car at a red light and stare hard at the driver, immediately he'll look back at you, because he wants to know what you find so interesting. But a guy who's dirty will just keep staring straight ahead because he's hoping you're not really looking at him. We also felt we could spot a guy who'd been in prison. I don't know why, but an ex-con would usually have very rigid hands, hard hands. When you printed a man with a nice loose feel to his fingers, you could be pretty sure he wasn't a hardened criminal who'd served a lot of time. With ex-cons, you really had to work to roll their fingers for the prints, because they'd be so stiff and unbending.

Partly, you just make a point of remembering things. To this day, I'm still very good with faces. Cars too. I'll be driving along with Jeannette and I'll say, Did you see that guy in that car? She'll say, What guy? What car? With me, it's practically second nature after all these years.

Not that you're ever infallible. Maybe something looks funny but turns out perfectly okay. Narcotics patrols, of course, usually focus on your typically poorer and dirtier areas, where you're more likely to run into suspicious street action pertaining to drugs and other things. I can remember instances, though, in entirely different circumstances where this sixth sense or whatever went right into action.

One day in midtown Manhattan, in a very expensive neighborhood of high-class shops and restaurants, I spotted these two well-dressed white men in front of some very posh hotel, the Pierre maybe, putting suitcases into a car parked at the curb. Now, that's what you'd see in the hotel area hundreds of times a day. For whatever reason, this particular instance hit me the wrong way and I said to my partner, Hey, pull over and let's go see what those guys are up to. We hit the jackpot on that one. In one of those suitcases they had something like fifty thousand dollars' worth of money orders, along with the validating machine they'd grabbed in a post-office heist up in Massachusetts.

Another time, near Grand Central Station, we really stumbled onto something far weirder than we could ever have imagined. We noticed a man walking along with a plain cloth bag, that's all. He was just a little guy and you could tell that what he was lugging in the bag had to be very heavy. He also had that shifty nervousness about him, looking over his shoulder, so we followed him until he turned to go into this bank. We moved up and stopped him, and what we found in the bag was a real heavy load of coins, plus a long, straight piece of wire hanger with a little two-inch mesh net attached to one end.

He didn't seem too perturbed about being nabbed like that, and admitted that he had a scam going that he made a decent living out of. Nothing sensational, he said, but decent. What he did every day was wander through Grand Central Station, with hundreds of public telephones all over the place, and use the wire-and-net gadget to scoop out the coins. He was very good at it, he said, and must have been, because he'd been doing it for years and had never run into trouble until this day we spotted him lugging his bag.

At the precinct house, we learned why he was so casual about being caught. He was just small beans, he said, maybe clearing a hundred, two hundred bucks a day, but if we gave him a break he happened to know about a *real* operator, with a scam big enough to put his own little scheme to shame. So he fingers this other guy, who we follow up on and eventually bring in, and it was the truth—we'd gotten into something impressively big-time.

This second guy had been employed for years as the phone company's chief collector for those same phones in Grand Central Station. Now the first guy, with his little mesh bag, had been pulling out coins one at a time, which was laborious work that even demanded a kind of delicate touch, and so time-consuming I'm still amazed he was never caught at it. The phone company's collector had come up with something a lot simpler and easier, and far more lucrative. Actually, it was so simple we had to wonder if he could possibly be the only guy to think it up. Maybe the idea was too simple, and anyone trying to defraud the phone company felt they needed something more complicated.

This was a strictly average-looking business type, by the way, in his fifties, a veteran employee with an unblemished record making a modest salary and building up retirement credits. He lived in an unremarkable house with nothing, not cars or clothes or fancy vacations, indicating any extravagance.

His daily responsibility was to go through Grand Central collecting tolls from all the phone installations. As you'd expect, the top company brains had designed a foolproof collection procedure to protect against any funny business. Well, the guy's scheme worked like this. He would arrive with his official little cart full of the proper number of empty coin boxes. Pulling the cart from phone to phone, he would open them all with his special key to remove the boxes inside containing the coins. But he would not, as he was supposed to, replace each one with an empty box. Instead, he would move down a whole line of maybe twenty or thirty phones, taking each full box but not leaving an empty in its place. Then after a period of time he'd go back to the beginning of the line, reopen each phone with his key, and sweep out into his own container all the loose coins that had accumulated inside that space in the interim, and only *then* put in the empty box he should have put in right away.

Since the company only kept count of the sealed empty boxes he received each morning, and the sealed filled ones he brought back, no one ever suspected him of anything. We had no idea how many years he'd been bilking the company, but when they finally accosted him based on the tip we passed along from the other guy, they discovered Swiss bank accounts and all kinds of financial holdings. In the cellar of his little house out in Brooklyn they found *garbage* cans filled with coins that he hadn't even gotten around to sorting yet. They actually traced down over a million dollars, and God knows how much they just couldn't find.

To the best of my knowledge he was never prosecuted, or even indicted. The phone company didn't want the stockholders or board of directors knowing what was going on. They were probably also afraid of letting their other collectors know that such a scam was possible—after all, they couldn't redesign every public phone in the country overnight. So they confiscated all the money they could lay their hands on and just told him to disappear. I think maybe they had him deported. The whole thing was kept very hush-hush, although the precinct received a nice letter from the phone company thanking all the officers who contributed to the investigation.

I never found out if they actually redesigned their collection system, or just hoped the scheme was too simple and obvious ever to occur to anyone else.

When you worked a heavy drug area, you got to know the place very well, including all the corners and alleys and storefronts where drug transactions took place. You also became familiar with the habits of both the straight and dirty people. Around one P.M., for instance, you knew the junkies would wake up and head out looking for a fix, so naturally the dealers would be out too, and you'd get a good deal of action.

In those days, talking back twenty, thirty years, the main heavy drug was heroin, a deck of which you could purchase on the street for three dollars. A deck was a small quantity, enough for one fix, and it was sold in powder form in a little glassine envelope. The poorer addicts would scrape up the money to buy a single deck. The better-off users would pick up a half load or a load at a time, fifteen or thirty decks bound together with a rubber band, selling for forty-five or ninety dollars. Although you had thousands of people involved in the drug traffic, with all kinds of differences and variations, the general pattern of importing and distributing was fairly standard.

The basic unit of heroin was a kilo, approximately two pounds two ounces, selling back then for around fifteen thousand dollars, usually brought in as part of a large shipment from sources in Asia and South America. This was the big-time wholesale level, where you're talking worldwide operations involving millions of dollars. The original kilo of almost pure heroin would be cut once, with each half sold for fifteen grand, an immediate doubling of the initial price. The major local dealers would then take that once-cut kilo and recut it into half or quarter or eighth kilos to sell to the wholesalers, who would further cut it maybe three or four to one and then pass it through intermediate operators before it got down to the street dealers who actually sold it to the users.

You see stories about drug busts mentioning street values of a million, two million, whatever. Actual street value depends on how a drug is distributed and in what quantities. You can figure, though, as the drug gets divided into smaller and smaller units, with more and more filler being added, that each person along the way expects a 100 percent markup. That's why an original kilo purchased wholesale for fifteen grand could eventually generate a quarter million in street sales, even though the ultimate user pays only three bucks for a deck.

The heroin was generally cut with a substance called mannite, that you could buy in any drugstore. It was used as a laxative for children, and you didn't even need a prescription for it. The drug-gists knew that people buying it in large quantities used it for heroin, but the dealers never had trouble getting all they wanted. It was a white, powdery substance sold in cakes, six inches by one inch, which the dealers would crumble up with their hands. They'd usually work on a kitchen table, making a big pile of this stuff, which was very fluffy and light and therefore wouldn't only weaken the potency of the heroin but also increase its volume. To every ounce of heroin, which comprised maybe one-eighth of a cup, they added half a cup of mannite to end up with a product five times as bulky.

Addicts never had any idea of the integrity of the people han-dling the drug, and sometimes the heroin would be laced with toxic substances. It might even hit the streets without being suffi-

ciently diluted, saturating an area with "hot decks" of pure or
near-pure heroin. You'd find guys dead with needles still in their
arms. Pure heroin kills you almost instantly.

Cocaine, which is what you hear about nowadays, was rare
back then, and you wouldn't find it on the street. It was considered
a cleaner drug, because you didn't inject it like heroin. You
snorted it, and it was mostly favored by money people, like the Hollywood crowd. When you used heroin, you were a derelict, out on
the street, disdained by people and susceptible because of the
needles and your general lifestyle to various diseases. Cocaine was
more fashionable—you know, a ritzy drug for people who could
afford an expensive habit—and considered more high-powered
than heroin because it acted as a stimulant, whereas heroin was a
depressant. One cocaine dealer we busted insisted on telling us
how great it was. You put it on your cock, or the woman puts it inside her, and you both just go crazy—you never had sex like that in
your life.

There was probably as much marijuana as there is today, the
main difference being that back then it was standard procedure to
arrest people for marijuana possession. If you carried nickel bags,
which contained an eighth of an ounce, enough for five or ten cigarettes and worth maybe fifteen dollars, you could be charged
with a misdemeanor. If you possessed more than an eighth of an
ounce, you were presumed to be a dealer and could be charged
with a felony.

Today cops don't even bother with marijuana, except for wholesale quantities. The biggest marijuana case I encountered back
then involved selling to blacks in the entertainment industry.
There was this big stash house in Harlem buying major quantities
and getting calls around the clock from entertainment personalities who would buy by the pound or more. A pound would go for
four, five hundred dollars, and produce maybe a thousand cigarettes. If you bought cigarettes individually on the street, they cost
a dollar apiece.

We occasionally ran into hash, peddled in what was called a
sole, because it was shaped like a foot. A sole weighed about half a

pound, and usually came in from Mexico or South America. Users would shave the hash with a razor and smoke it in a pipe like marijuana, although it was much stronger, more like peyote.

It was funny, but as an arresting officer in drug situations, the forms you filled out required you to ask the person you'd apprehended how long he or she had been users and what was the first drug they'd started on. Well, the vast majority would always say marijuana, which was probably true because that was by far the cheapest and most easily available, and the least dangerous. But when they were too zonked to answer, we'd just put down, *Started on MJ, shifted to H,* so maybe the statistics were a little exaggerated.

Crack was unheard of back then. It's a designer drug, not naturally grown but manufactured in a lab and a lot more potent and dangerous than any other drug.

Since I'm not keeping tabs on the narcotics business anymore, I can't talk much of the day-to-day details. But from what I read and hear from friends still in the field, it hasn't changed all that much except for heroin being replaced by cocaine and crack, and by the whole situation becoming incredibly bigger, with far more people and tons more money involved. Now big-time U.S. operators and those in places like Colombia seem to have endless resources at their command. Some South American cartels probably generate more money than half the countries in the world. And of course everything's much more sophisticated these days, with private high-speed jets and electronic devices and instantaneous communication practically anywhere in the world. And sure, police technology has advanced too, but not even an outfit as widespread and well-funded as the Federal Drug Enforcement Agency can come close to matching the resources of the big drug dealers on the national level, let alone internationally.

ALONG THE WAY I ASK Johnny, given the association between drugs and crime, and his pessimism about controlling the worldwide cartels, why we don't just legalize everything. The incredible profits are based solely on the product's illegality, so why not make it like alcohol and save ourselves a lot of money and grief and violence and prison space?

Johnny doesn't much like the idea.

"I think it comes down to the fact that a country has to be able to say that a certain kind of behavior is not what we want, either for the individual or the society, and therefore we're going to do everything we can to keep people from getting involved in it.

"You have to remember that as bad as the drug problem seems, it involves a very small percentage of the population, and you have to question whether you want the country as a whole to give its blessing to drug usage and the harm it causes just because that path seems easier and might save some money in terms of enforcement. Will it really? And don't we also have to consider the price we'll be paying by encouraging, or at least allowing, a lot more people, young people, kids, to get into drugs? Crack's big now, like I said. What happens when some lab genius invents an even crazier chemical and starts selling it on the corner or in the supermarket? Do we just say, Well, it must be legal because everything's legal now, so sell all you want because the police aren't going to bother you.

"Actually, the idea of legalizing drugs seems futile, because I don't think the majority of the citizens would ever let it happen here. Also, to be perfectly honest, I think too many people throughout the system, from top to bottom, politicians and lawyers and judges and law-enforcement officials too, at all levels, even some of your so-called do-gooders, are deeply implicated in the drug trade themselves in terms of protection and payoffs and various methods of bribery, and therefore none of these powerful people want the present system to change in any way."

THE MOST INTERESTING CASES were always the ones that led you into strange and unexpected twists, and often took you way beyond where you started. One in particular just went on and on, and what began as the most commonplace situation imaginable ended up in an incredible flurry of publicity the next day.

I was working up in the Bronx with my partner when we spotted this guy who looked like he was angling for sales, so we tailed him awhile and, sure enough, nabbed him in the act of selling a couple of decks of heroin. Nothing unusual there. We'd take someone like that down to precinct, book him, and that'd be the end of it as far as we were concerned. We'd head out and go back to work.

Only again, like the fellow lugging the cloth bag full of coins, the guy tried to save his own skin by ratting on a higher-up. This wasn't uncommon, and we'd generally at least listen to the offer and decide whether to take in whoever we had or try to get a line on someone more important. So this guy said, Hey, give me a break, all right, and I'll take you to a bundle connection who's handling cocaine in a really big way.

A bundle connection was a mid-level guy who people working the streets would buy from. So we said, Okay, show us.

He took us to this house and gave us the apartment number of his connection. We left him downstairs and headed on up. We didn't take him up with us because we didn't want to expose him. We just told him to hang around on the corner there, maybe stand hidden in a doorway or something to see whether or not we came back out of the building with his connection. If we did, meaning we'd made a pickup on his information, then he'd be free to go and we'd forget the whole thing. If we came out empty-handed, we'd want to talk to him again, which is why we had him hang around until everything worked itself out. We weren't afraid of him just walking away. After all, we had his name and description and everything, had checked out his ID, all of that, so could find him easy enough if he tried to run. Besides, it's funny in a way, but once these guys turn on their supplier, they get a kick out of it. They gloat over being involved and in some ways actually become what you could call police oriented. They feel like big shots watching us haul someone out of the building in handcuffs, knowing they're the ones that made it happen.

They also hope for a reward, with the favor being repayable at some time. If for instance we come across him sometime and find him dirty, nothing major but maybe just possession, we'd probably be willing to say, Okay, you helped us out, so we're cutting you loose and now we're even.

In this instance, at first we thought maybe the guy had tried to pull a fast one when we found ourselves upstairs in a perfectly normal apartment, with this husband and wife and two small kids. But we quickly realized that they were what we called ounce dealers, with a batch of coke on the kitchen table that they'd been shaving down with a razor and packaging to sell to their street dealers.

For whatever reason, the heroin supply had dried up at that time, bringing on a flood of cocaine to replace it, mostly from Cuba. This was a Puerto Rican neighborhood, but these were Cuban nationals, who claimed they'd left Cuba because they were opposed to Castro and his Communist government, although that's what all the Cubans who came over claimed. The truth is, we weren't particularly interested. We'd got them for running drugs out of their apartment. Who they were or where they'd come from wasn't our concern. In fact, maybe the street guy turned in these people because the heroin dealers resented the cocaine crowd moving onto their turf, but that guy's motives weren't of interest to us either.

Anyhow, the husband sort of sidled up almost exactly like the street guy—if we just gave them a break, they'd put us onto a *really* big-time connection with a direct link to the major cocaine source back in the Caribbean. Of course, these people had a tendency of making their connections sound a lot more important than they actually were, so you didn't make any promises until the information actually panned out. You didn't want to just end up with some other small-time street pusher from around the corner. In general, we found very little loyalty among drug people. They only worried about themselves and would sell out anybody to protect their own ass. The only thing that made them hesitate was the fear that they'd end up dead. Sometimes we'd make a show of arresting an informer, and keep him in jail long enough to convince the street that he was no friend of ours.

Anyhow, the offer from the Cuban guy sounded worth looking into, and it turned out that the people he offered to lead us to were also Cubans, which was probably dangerous for him, but I guess he was willing to take his chances, as opposed to facing a long prison rap and having his family deported. We checked in with our superiors, who agreed that we should follow up his lead. It was always a priority to thwart an operation as high up as possible, rather than bringing in some two-bit punk who'd just be replaced the next day by another punk.

The guy brought us down to this unpretentious hotel on West Forty-ninth in the theater district and gave us the name and room number of a man and woman who he said were high-level importers and suppliers. If they were that important, we wanted to make sure we had the goods on them before we moved in, so the hotel and especially their room were immediately put under round-the-clock surveillance. By the time all this was set up and manned and we could go home, it was well into the next morning. We'd been on duty about thirty hours straight without any kind of break, a couple of street detectives starting with a routine neighborhood bust who by now might be on the verge of breaking up a large-scale international operation.

Of course we weren't yet positive of that, and as I remember, the surveillance went on for several weeks, during which we took our share of shifts, regularly observing the comings and goings of the young couple that occupied the room, checking the hotel phone records, and tapping into calls to Havana and Miami and Los Angeles. We finally made our move when two other detectives and myself, under the command of a lieutenant, stepped forward as the couple was returning to the hotel. They saw right away what was up, and the woman quickly dropped three marijuana cigarettes to the ground. The man did the same with a glassine envelope of cocaine. That level of possession, though, turned out to be the least of their problems.

We put them under arrest and took them upstairs to their

room, where we found a kilo of cocaine on the dresser, which when cut and doctored would probably sell in single doses on the street for maybe two hundred, two hundred fifty grand. They also had scales and quantities of mannite and glassine envelopes, plus a lot of cash, money under the bed, money in the closet. They knew we had them dead to rights and were very passive at first. They were both in their mid-twenties, well dressed and good-looking. The guy couldn't speak English, but the girl could, so he whispered something to her in Spanish, and she told us in English how they had come to America some months back to escape from Castro's communism, and how they were using the money from drugs to help the anti-Castro forces back on the island. When we didn't seem too impressed, she told the lieutenant that they had two thousand dollars in the apartment which would be ours along with another ten thousand that they'd get as soon as the banks opened if we would just let them go. We added attempted bribery of twelve thousand dollars to the drug charges and took them in.

We afterward learned that this drug cartel also ran a big beauty salon up around Seventy-ninth Street on the West Side as their cover, a high-priced hairdressing operation that catered to entertainers, a lot of them Broadway habit people. It had become known as the Broadway connection. The owners sold cocaine in the ounce category, maybe a week's supply, for around six hundred dollars, no big deal for these show people.

Every paper in New York gave the arrest a huge play. I don't know what story the couple gave down at the precinct or what the Feds learned on their own, but the headlines said the couple had been working *for* Castro, not against him, with Castro trying to save the Cuban economy by moving in on the U.S. drug scene.

COCAINE CASH FOR CASTRO: 2 NABBED went one headline. One referred to CASTRO DOPE RING, another to HAVANA DOPE-RUNNERS. But the photos and most of the stories played up the woman. She claimed she'd been a beauty-contest winner back in Cuba, so that got a lot of play, along with the fact that she'd been arrested here for prostitution. One paper put the fact that she was an ex-model in the first sentence. Another called her a "Havana beauty queen with flaming red hair."

The most widely used picture showed her coming out of the hotel in dark glasses, pushing her chin down into the collar of her fur coat, with this detective right behind her, who happened to be me. All the papers except *Newsday*, though, cropped the picture to cut out my face and just focus on hers.

PAYING ATTENTION: THE WHORE FROM THE BRONX

AL DELLA PENNA ➡

WE TALKED EARLIER as to which crimes get prime attention, from the police and everyone else, but it comes up all the time and there are a few more points we can make.

First, any crime which victimizes a fellow police officer receives top priority, for what I think are good and sufficient reasons. And it's not rare. About a hundred and fifty U.S. law-enforcement people are killed every year in the line of duty. Twenty thousand are injured, sixty thousand assaulted.

Certain practical elements also have to be considered in determining police effort on a crime. Certain homicides, for instance, are lost causes from the word go, and everybody knows it. The most obvious and common category occurs within various crime syndicates, particularly drug gangs. Somebody muscles into someone else's territory, or welshes on a deal, or pulls a fast one, and bang, you got a corpse. Oftentimes both victim and killer are illegals with fake papers and no addresses, with four aliases and six nicknames between them. Where do you start? We're not even talking about some bad guy gunning down a good guy. They're both dirtbags who've been working very hard to keep the police or anyone else from learning the first thing about them.

And how do I approach a crime scene that happens to be a busy intersection with thousands of cars and pedestrians going by every hour? Where do we find the witnesses for my Homicide buddies to question? Who in a neighborhood overrun with drugs and guns is going to start blabbing to a bunch of strange cops they've never seen before? Getting information, collecting evidence, is very difficult.

Even a messy apartment, as opposed to a place as neat as the Lamberts', practically eliminates my on-site effectiveness. Dare I approach the serologist with a dozen ashtrays overflowing with butts? What about a greasy sink up to your elbow in dishes, nondescript piles of clothes tossed everywhere? Am I going to bring back footwear impressions from a kitchen that hasn't been cleaned in a month, collect everything I find in a bedroom shared by four kids and grandma?

I remember vividly one apartment in a slum area where I started chipping out a piece of kitchen wall only to be stopped short by the woman yelling, Hey, what the hell are you doing? I explained, logically enough, that I was cutting out the piece because it had a bullet hole in it. Jesus, she screamed, don't break my wall over that, that's from *last* month! Sure enough, there'd been a previous shooting there only weeks before that had nothing to do with the one we were investigating.

Whenever the police have even the slightest chance of solving a whodunit, regardless of the victim or neighborhood or anything else, they're going to bust their horns trying to do so. They're pros. This is their chosen line of work. In the case of major crimes like homicide, the investigators are seasoned veterans from all sorts of specialties who've worked their way up on the basis of their prior record of success, and they're very jealous of their reputations. They also get a kick out of solving crimes, enjoy sending away some slob who hardly deserves to live, let alone walk the same streets as your wife and children.

Still, spending too much time on a low-priority case is not going to win any cop kudos from upstairs, or much encouragement to keep plugging away. He's going to feel distinct pressure to move on to something that all the world considers more important. The same pressures exist in business, government, hospitals, wherever. If you had unlimited resources, you could do whatever your little heart desired. But most of us have to develop some sort of triage system. As a case in point, New York City has a very large, well-trained police force. It also has two thousand homicides a year, about six a day. How can they undertake a meticulous investigation of each and every one of them?

And sure, the police are no better than anyone else when it comes to certain preconceived attitudes toward wealth, social standing, race, class, connections, all those things. Still, it'd be nice if people didn't assume we based *all* our decisions on the worst possible motives. Maybe they could also remember that we generally get our hands a lot dirtier, spend a lot more time in all manner of unappealing locales, and pay a lot more attention to the dead and wounded nobodies of the world than anyone else I can think of offhand.

Maybe the hardest crime of all to solve, for obvious reasons, is the murder of a street prostitute. Well, Suffolk County had one of those not long ago. Although no one knew where she was killed, the discovery of her body in Suffolk County made it our case, and our cops worked long and hard on it, without any kind of public pressure or outcry to spur them on. Yet when it was all over, the mother of this young and woebegone and brutally murdered black prostitute profusely thanked the white Suffolk County Homicide detectives who broke the case, mainly Richard Reck and John Evers. She lived in the Bronx, where the daughter had lived and hustled. The mother said she couldn't believe the time and effort suburban Long Island cops had spent on the case. If her daughter had been killed in the city, she said, she would have just been one more name on the list of people found dead somewhere that nobody really wanted to bother about.

·   ·   ·

My own contributions in this case were not that vital. Homicide did the real work, although I did run across some pretty out-landish surprises in the firearms area.

Mid-September a few years back a call came into the Crime Lab one afternoon reporting a body seen floating in a small bay near Westhampton Beach on the South Shore. Beaches are no more promising as crime scenes than congested streets, so I remained in the lab while others brought the body into the morgue. I was then asked to view the gunshot wounds, and went down the hall to the morgue to do so.

Waiting for me on the slab was the body of a rather tall black woman, slightly bloated but still fresh, maybe in the water a day or so. My eye was immediately caught by a cinder block, actually a large chunk, maybe two-thirds of a whole block, next to her on the slab and still attached to her body by a short piece of white nylon rope and a wire, like baling wire, that ran through her ab-domen. She'd been shot twice, and the wound behind her right ear revealed a fairly large bullet lodged between her scalp and her skull. The medical examiner removed it for me, along with a simi-lar bullet from her chest that had probably killed her. I'd need to put them under the microscope to get more definite, but felt com-fortable telling the detectives they ought to be looking for a gun in the .38-caliber class, and probably one that didn't produce much muzzle velocity. It was the only way I could explain how a bullet that size could fail to penetrate the skull.

As the detectives followed up on this and whatever else they had, I took to the microscope. As always, I started by measuring the land and groove markings produced when the bullet passes through the rifle barrel, since they'll usually allow me to narrow down the class characteristics of the weapon to, say, a specific Smith & Wesson model, or one of the Colt products or derivatives. But with these bullets, through one check after another, I couldn't find any recognizable pattern of markings whatsoever.

Somewhat shamefaced, I came up with a very inconclusive re-port. If we had a suspect .38, I could have definitely said whether it had fired these bullets, but based on the ammunition alone, I didn't have the slightest inkling as to what brand or type of .38 they ought to be looking for. The best guidance I could give them—and even here I hedged—was that it probably *wasn't* either a Colt or a Smith & Wesson.

Over the next few weeks I had little to do with the investigation, but followed with some interest the work of the Homicide detectives. I may have been the only one, since the news organizations almost totally ignored the case from the beginning.

The victim apparently hadn't been in the water that long, so her fingerprints were still intact and provided a positive ID: LuAnn Peterson, eighteen, Bronx address, arrested a couple of times for prostitution near the Hunts Point Market. I guess it's ironic, but if we didn't have fingerprints on file from their drug or prostitution arrests, most Jane Doe bodies that turn up would remain Jane Does forever.

Our detectives logged lots of miles to the Bronx and back. They talked to LuAnn's parents and to her combined common-law husband and pimp. She'd been a prostitute from age fourteen, they all agreed, and had been out turning tricks the night she disappeared. Her husband became suspicious when she didn't return at the expected time, and reported her missing the next day.

He was very cooperative, and if the investigators wanted leads, he had plenty to offer: one of his own nephews had been convicted of raping LuAnn and sent to prison on her testimony; that nephew's girlfriend had gotten into an altercation with LuAnn at the nephew's trial; LuAnn had accused three men of kidnaping, raping, and assaulting her. There was also a corrections officer who had fathered LuAnn's six-year-old son, and several other men she'd established relationships with at various times, including one guy the husband-pimp knew only by his first name, who he suspected of being her current boyfriend.

It's a stretch to think of Hunts Point as a village, but it sounded like one of those genteel English murder mysteries where everybody in the village is a prime suspect. The police dutifully interviewed all these guys, along with others whose names popped up along the way, administered polygraphs, verified their where-abouts on the night of LuAnn's disappearance. Although they were as unwholesome an assembly of suspects as you'd want, nothing linked any of them to the murder.

Out on the Island, meanwhile, most farmers near where the body had been discovered, in the general Riverhead area, were vis-ited to learn which ones trucked their potatoes or cauliflower or whatever into the Hunts Point Market. Nothing opened up along this line either.

Detectives spent a lot of time around Hunts Point itself, a poor, tough, mostly Hispanic area. Its wholesale meat-and-produce market was one of the largest in the city and a notorious center for hookers. When the truckers arrived early in the morning for their deliveries or pickups, the whores would be right there offering quickies in the cabs of the trucks. The detectives interviewed the girls and showed LuAnn's picture. A number knew her and were aware she'd slipped from view but had no idea why.

Hookers have their own culture, their own shop talk, and gossip among themselves about their johns. Normally, they won't talk outside their circle, especially to cops, but with one of their own done in, they were more than ready to cooperate. The investiga-tors asked about unusual or threatening clients, or guys that would take girls out to the Island. They'd never under any circum-stances, the girls insisted, leave Hunts Point to go anywhere else with a john. This was their home ground, friendly territory. They wouldn't feel safe anywhere else.

When asked about johns coming in from the Island, a couple of prostitutes said one guy in particular drove in pretty regularly to patronize different prostitutes. They gave a description of him and his car, and one thought he came from around Riverhead. So the investigators inquired in Riverhead and the nearby towns, none of which was very populous, about anyone of a certain description who went into the city regularly and drove a certain type and color of car.

All this sounds simpler and more routine than it ever is. A thorough investigation of this order entailed details down to something as insignificant as the type of fence wire used in the area. It's something you delve into from force of habit, without any real expectation of getting anything for your efforts. But that was it, the fence wire, that opened things up.

The wire used to affix the cinder block to LuAnn's body was a standard hardware item, so the same type had been found in a goodly number of area farmyard fences. Then one day a guy in his thirties named Sam Walczyk wandered into the precinct house out there and asked to talk to someone about the inquiries made at the home of his mother and father. That was one of the homes where the right kind of wire had been found, along with white nylon rope similar to that used with the cinder block, so the investigators already had their suspicions about this family. Only, whoa, wait a minute! Sam tells them, *I'm* not the one messing around with black prostitutes. It's my brother, *Herman,* who's running in there all the time banging those whores.

So much for fraternal loyalty on the outer reaches of Long Island or probably, for that matter, anywhere else.

When the police got hold of Herman Walczyk, he denied everything, and to prove his clear conscience, signed a consent form letting them search his property. A mistake, for the search turned up a .38-caliber revolver with two cartridges expended. Confronted with this, Herman spilled the whole scenario, practically minute by minute.

He often drove into Hunts Point, he said, to deliver produce from his father-in-law's farm, and frequently availed himself of the local hookers. After midnight on the night in question, he invited a black streetwalker into his car who pulled a knife on him and tried to take his wallet. He reached into the back to grab a hammer and knocked her unconscious with a blow to the head. This caused him to panic, and unable to think of anything else to do, he drove out to his home on the Island. Along the way the woman revived, and he again knocked her out with the hammer.

The guy, by the way, was married, and seemed to maintain a strange relationship with his wife and live-in mother-in-law, be cause neither apparently questioned his forays into the city or any of his other activities. Still, it struck me as very odd, this guy with an unconscious prostitute alongside him on the front seat, chugging into his garage at something like three in the morning. What the hell would he have said if one of the women had wakened and come down to inquire as to what was going on? He stayed only long enough, he said, to grab a .38-caliber Smith & Wesson, and then headed back toward the Expressway.

I did a real double take on hearing this. One of the few things I'd assured the investigators after examining the murder bullets was that the suspect weapon was *not* a Smith & Wesson. What the hell was going on?

It was still dark, Herman went on, maybe four A.M., when he again found himself on the Expressway. The whole thing must have seemed more and more nightmarish to the guy, because LuAnn regained consciousness for the *third* time and started screaming her head off. Holy shit, he must have thought, and he didn't resort to the hammer this time. He had the gun, and used it to shoot her in the head. This first bullet must have been the one that lodged under the scalp, because he then pulled onto a side road, dragged her out of the car, and shot her in the chest to make sure she was dead.

At this point Herman could have made life very difficult for the investigators who would eventually inherit this case by simply leaving the body there and tossing the gun into the bay. How would anybody have ever traced it back to him? But God knows what the hell was going through his head, and for some unfathomable reason he stuffed the body back into the car and drove back to the damn house *again*, which seemed even dumber now than the first time, when he was only transporting an unconscious woman, not a dead one.

He planned to dump the body into the bay, he told the detectives, without explaining why he chose this more complicated proposition over just leaving it in the woods. In the garage, he removed her clothes and placed her body in what he described as a wooden trunk, which he loaded into his little putt-putt aluminum boat on its trailer, and towed the boat to the Westhampton ramp. He launched it there, and as soon as he got out a bit he extracted the body from the wooden trunk, weighed it down by piercing it back to front with some heavy-gauge wire tied to a chunk of cinder block with nylon rope, and slid her over the side.

Another big mistake. He was still in shallow water, maybe a few feet deep. If he'd putt-putted out past the mouth of the bay, the poor dead Bronx streetwalker would have drifted out into the Atlantic, never to be seen again. But Herman didn't know about water depth and prevailing winds and inevitable tides, and also counted too casually on that Rube Goldberg cinder-block attachment to send her to the bottom and keep her there. He probably just wanted to get this body, which by this time must have seemed the size of the Statue of Liberty, out of his car and boat and hands, out of his miserable little existence forever.

He returned home yet again to grab her clothes and dump them at the Westhampton Landfill, then called it a night. Meanwhile, with the wind and tide and sheltered nature of the bay all playing their part, the body never sank at all, never drifted out, but stayed afloat right where he'd tossed it until some fisherman in a rowboat spotted it the next afternoon.

Eventually Herman Walczyk gave them a signed confession, but in our usual zeal to make the case as tight as possible, several of us went to his house to look for corroborating evidence. I, for one, was particularly eager to go, because those wacky land and groove markings had never stopped nagging at me.

The first surprise was what he called his garage. True, there was space for his car, but the detached structure was more like a barn in size and construction, and contained all kinds of strange, non-garage items. The "wooden trunk" he'd referred to was one of several, some on the floor, some hanging from rafters, which sure looked like coffins to me. They even had lids. Herman had refused to say what the hell they were for, and we couldn't help but wonder if he'd figured on murdering and dumping more people—or had already done so, but saved the boxes.

As intriguing as these were, my professional focus went right to the little machine shop Herman had in there, a couple of oddball lathes and grinders, obviously homemade machines but also fairly sophisticated. He'd used them, along with other tools we found, to work on his weapons. Dismantled gun parts lay about, including some barrels threaded for silencers. Damned if we didn't actually find some homemade silencers too. Maybe oddest of all were a couple of handcuffs he'd carefully fashioned.

I spent a lot of time checking out the gun parts. The guy had been breaking down commercially purchased weapons in order to alter and transpose their components. It looked like he'd even made his own barrels. Finally I came across exactly what I'd been looking for. He had one lathe set up to rout out the inside of gun barrels: the son of a bitch had been grinding off the standardized lands and grooves produced at the factory and replacing them with some oddball rifling of his own. No wonder I hadn't been able to figure out what the hell was going on.

I also found out why that .38 bullet had not penetrated her skull. In fooling around with that barrel, he'd left his tolerances too large, so that a certain amount of gas could escape, thereby reducing the velocity and impact of the bullet. Still, the guy was obviously a skilled machinist and craftsman and he'd done amazing things with those weapons, all of it very much illegal. All kinds of laws banned the manufacture or sale of silencers, or any alteration of a weapon's identifying features.

Herman was eventually sent away on the basis of his confession and the corroborating evidence. But like Ronnie DeFeo, the decisive legal outcome still left us plenty to scratch our heads over. Those coffins alone certainly struck me as creepy, to say nothing of the silencers, the handcuffs, his reason for altering and disguising all those weapons.

Could this guy be a serial-killer nut, maybe even specializing in prostitutes? Frankly, we doubted that. His incredibly clumsy methods, with all that hammer banging and aimless driving around before finally, ineptly, killing the woman, that cinder block wired through her abdomen—everything pointed to a guy who hadn't begun all that gruesome business with any premeditated intent. In other words, everything indicated a rank amateur. Professional or serial killers tend to think things through and plan out their actions. That's why they're able to escape detection long enough to commit all those crimes. But hell would freeze over before you'd find anywhere in Herman's actions the faintest suggestion of thoughtful preparation.

Yet what did all those coffins and gun-altering machines indicate if not a truly fastidious preparation for the undetected killing of people? Even with all his dumb moves, no one would ever have known the woman was dead or have connected him to her disappearance if he'd taken that boat out far enough to make sure LuAnn Peterson's body disappeared into that very large ocean nearby. Surely, we'd never have been able to trace him down through those weird gun-barrel markings he'd created.

Maybe he *was* a serial killer.

But nothing ever developed along those lines for us to follow up on. Suffolk County had by happenstance been handed a very difficult homicide to solve, and our people had solved it after a great deal of very hard work. I recently went to our files to refresh myself on some details, and found over 120 single-spaced pages of reports from various investigators, each page reflecting hours, maybe days, of work, dealing with scores of people and many more scores of items that had been collected, catalogued, tested, and stored. Still, those pages represent only a portion of the complete file, hardly revealing the police work that led nowhere: all those worthless leads and futile interviews with people who didn't know any more about this murder than they did about the theory of relativity. And this is only the police file. Believe me, the paper produced by the DAs in prosecuting the case in court would dwarf our teensy little file folder.

So no, tantalizing as it was, we didn't spend any more time following up on Herman Walczyk. We had our man. He got sent away. The case was closed. LuAnn Peterson's mother thanked Detectives Reck and Evers for the attention they'd paid and the good work they and their buddies had done. We had no shortage of new cases, open cases, that needed the same kind of attention.

Whatever else might be said about Herman Walczyk, he was in a class by himself when it came to firearms tampering. I was so impressed I dropped a note to the sentencing judge. Maybe, I wrote, the warden ought to be warned against assigning Herman to the prison machine shop, or God knows what he might surprise them with on his lathe.

A SUIT AND A HALF

JOHN CUOMO ⇒

ANOTHER CASE THAT STARTED out small and ended up not only bigger but stranger than we ever imagined began with the same familiar pattern of small-timers turning in the people above them. The first step was a petty drug arrest we made of a young Italian hood around Bruckner Boulevard and Tremont Avenue in the Bronx, not far from where my sister Jean lived when she was alive. This kid was a delivery boy for the Italian drug crowd, and he'd drive around in a big Caddy making ounce or two-ounce deliveries of cocaine to special customers. The minute we nabbed him he fingered his supplier, a middle guy we picked up with a full kilo stashed under his car seat. He told us he was delivering it to the people over him, in a house in the Pelham Bay area of the Bronx.

We used to work in conjunction with the Federal drug people, generally bringing them in whenever our busts showed signs of leading beyond a level our own Narcotics unit could handle, maybe involving national or international implications that only the Feds had the resources to counter. They valued our local connections and experience, so the cooperation helped us both.

In this case, the Feds provided information that the man who lived in that house with his wife and daughter was a real character named D'Allesandro but known as Charlie Cigar, because he was never seen without a cigar, lit or not, in his mouth. He was reputedly high up in the Italian drug operation, and they had reason to believe that a lot of big Bolivian cocaine shipments coming into New York, ten or fifteen kilos at a shot, went straight to this guy, who would then divvy it up within the organization. When they learned that the guy we'd picked up with the kilo under his car seat was making a delivery for this Charlie Cigar, they enlisted our cooperation in putting a tap on Charlie's phone line.

It was a perfectly legal tap obtained through the Bronx district attorney's office, with my partner and me in charge of the operation. It was much easier in those days for the NYPD to institute a legal tap than it was for the Federal drug people. I'm not sure exactly why, but I think it had something to do with the Federal laws.

You didn't have to actually get inside a house to place a tap. Once you had a legal order, you could do it through the phone company, and our tap was set up in the back of a Carvel ice cream store not too far from the house. The Carvel store was chosen because the junction box handling the local phone lines was located nearby, and our comings and goings wouldn't be so noticed in a busy retail outlet. The franchise owner was very pleasant to us the whole time, although of course we never let him know who we were tapping, or the purpose of the operation.

That purpose, by the way, wasn't just to catch Charlie Cigar in the act of accepting some incoming kilos, although we wanted very much to do that. But both the Federal agents and the New York Narcotics people also wanted to learn about the whole operation, and the other people involved. Of course, even though Charlie didn't know that his every phone conversation was being recorded, he wasn't so dumb that he'd casually spill names or really important information.

In the same neighborhood as Charlie's house lived this buddy of his, Sal, a lower-level, really dippy street guy. He was sort of

Charlie's stooge, and on the phone with him a lot. But even Sal wouldn't give much away outright, although neither of these guys had any brilliant secret code worked out between them. They would always use the same stupid routine, like, *Don't say nothing, will you?* or *Whatta you talking like that for? Keep your mouth shut, you don't have to talk about those things.*

When they were actually discussing drugs, waiting for a shipment to arrive, his buddy Sal would get itchy and keep pressing Charlie about any news from the higher-ups. He'd refer to a kilo as a suit, and he'd say, *I'm really interested in getting some suits out of this.* One time I remember him saying, *Look, I don't want the whole thing. Just get me a suit, a suit and a half, okay?*

Neither Charlie nor his stooge Sal would strike you as particularly educated guys. They'd both grown up around 116th Street in Harlem, when it used to be all Italian. I remember when we were kids we'd all go down there for Mt. Carmel, the big Italian feast, with all this music and food and everything. It was a great neighborhood, but a lot of the people were recent immigrants, and among the old folks maybe half of them never learned to speak English, and even among the kids hardly any went very far in school.

Anyhow, both Charlie Cigar and his buddy Sal grew up there, then got married and settled with their families up in the Bronx. Somewhere along the line they got into drugs. That was all they did, drugs. Neither one had a job. They spent all their time waiting for what they called a *move*, meaning a shipment coming in from Bolivia. It didn't happen all that often for Charlie Cigar—other guys also received shipments, as the organizations like to keep things spread around to make the flow harder to trace and disrupt. Their role after receiving the cocaine was to deliver it down into the black areas of Harlem, where their contacts would cut maybe six kilos into twelve or fifteen and then spread that all over the city to the smaller dealers. This obviously entailed a humongous profit here for everybody concerned. Although they didn't do much more than serve as innocent-looking fronts for the dropoff in this nice family neighborhood up in the Bronx, Charlie Cigar and even Sal would make enough money on one Bolivian move to support their families in style for months.

Most of the time manning the tap was pretty dull. We stayed on it for months as our main assignment, but thankfully didn't have to sit in the back room for our whole duty shift every day. We'd have other investigations going on, and would also spend time on normal patrol.

My partner at the time, Belmont Cohen, and I would meet in back of the Carvel store around ten in the morning to listen to the tapes from overnight. If there'd been no mention or hint about shipments coming in, or suspicious meetings, we'd just file a report with the office that nothing incriminating had transpired and go out on patrol.

Depending on how busy we got, we'd check back regularly and repeat the process, and then in the evening one or both of us would actually man the tap, since nights were the most active time for Charlie on the phone. Although you never knew. Maybe the whole family would be out or something and the wire would be dead for a whole day or night at a stretch. We hoped, naturally, that if anything did break it'd happen when we were there listening, so we could hustle right over and get the goods on Charlie and his couriers. It wouldn't do much good to find out the next morning that Charlie had picked up and distributed a half dozen *suits* the night before while we were home fast asleep.

Pretty much from the beginning we got feedback that made it clear we weren't totally wasting our time. Sal or maybe some other runners or errand boys would call Charlie, and Charlie would call different people, higher-ups, and it'd always be the same questions, either to or from Charlie: *Hey, did you get a call? When are they coming, when are they coming?* The answer would always be the same. *Stop worrying, when they come I'll give you a call, everything's set.* But we never picked up anything specific enough to act on, so just kept listening and recording everything anybody said.

Now, when you're tapping around the clock, especially with the whole family making calls, you run into all sorts of surprises. Even

Charlie himself, who at least made some pretense of being careful, couldn't really have thought anyone was listening in or he
wouldn't have touched the phone at all. As for Charlie's wife and
his daughter, who must've have been around seventeen, eighteen,
it became very clear that neither of them had even *considered* the
possibility of a tap.

Charlie's wife, for instance, was very jealous of him, because
most nights he'd go to this place on Williamsbridge Road, sort of
an Italian neighborhood social club where guys hung out playing
cards and drinking and joking around. Sometimes he'd go days
too, not having anything else to do except wait for the next delivery. He'd not come back for hours, and his wife would get on the
phone and complain to her girlfriend. *That fuckin' Charlie,* she'd
say. *He ain't kidding me, he's out there fooling around behind my back.*
The other woman would say, *I know just how you feel. I got exactly
the same trouble with my husband.* When Charlie's wife worried
about maybe being pregnant, the other would sympathize and
say, *Well, take hot baths. . . .*

It got to the point where the instant Charlie stepped out the
door his wife would call a private cab company nearby and get this
certain driver to come over real quick so they could follow Charlie
to see if he actually went to the club. He never seemed aware of
this cab tailing him, but always headed for the club anyway. From
everything we learned, and we learned a lot, Charlie Cigar had absolutely nothing going for him on the side. All he cared about was
drugs, and the next move, and the money it gave him. He didn't
give a shit about anything else.

His wife, though, would wait outside the club in the cab to see if
he left to go somewhere else, which as far as we could tell, he never
did. Still, she carried on to her friends about what a rat he was, always running off after dinner and not coming back until two or
three in the morning. *That Charlie, I know he's fucking around, I
know he's got a girlfriend somewhere and I swear I'm gonna catch him
one of these days.*

Then we learned that while she was out in front of the club
checking up on Charlie, she and the driver would have sex in the

back seat. She never mentioned that to her friends. We found out because she'd discuss it over the phone with the cabbie himself, what they did last night in the back seat, or were planning to do tonight. It was really something.

Meanwhile the teenage daughter would invite boyfriends over when the parents weren't home, and while some boys were there she'd get calls from other guys. *That's right, Mom and Dad are out,* she'd tell them, and the guys would jump at this and say, *Really? Can I come over? I'll be right over.* And she'd say, *Oh, no, you can't come. Billy's here, and you know what Billy's doing to me?* She'd giggle and really tease the poor guy, describing for him the sex she was having at that very minute with Billy, while these two detectives were practically falling off their chairs laughing in the back of the Carvel's ice cream shop.

After some time, the talk about movements and guys coming took on a more immediate tone, and we got permission from Carvel's to stay on the tap all night long to make sure we didn't miss anything. And that's where we were, just Belmont Cohen and myself all alone in the storeroom of this ice cream shop at maybe two in the morning, when Charlie Cigar gets Sal on the line and tells him, kind of in a hoarse whisper, like that'd make the whole thing more secretive in case anyone's listening, *Hey, I got a call today, and who do you think it was from? The guys downtown. We gotta meet some people that are coming up here tonight bringing those things, a lot of things, in a suitcase.* Sal gets real excited and says, *Oh, yeah? They're really coming? I'll be right there, Charlie. I'll be there in a minute!* The first thing Charlie does after hanging up is call someone downtown, one of his Harlem connections from what we can figure out, and say, *Listen, those people are here, they're coming up and I'm gonna meet them tonight.* When the connection wants to know where these people are, Charlie gets annoyed. *I don't know where the fuck they are—some hotel on Thirty-fourth and Seventh. They're bringing up the suitcase, that's all I know.*

Okay, okay, the other guy says. *You just get it all straightened out, then come down and see me as soon as you can.*

Right away we notified the Federal office down on Varick Street that the shipment was coming in and we needed help, since we were just two guys with one car and had not only Charlie Cigar to keep an eye on but also his Harlem connection, plus whatever couriers were bringing the cocaine up to the Bronx. The Feds said they definitely wanted involvement and would send up another unit in another car as soon as possible.

The next thing we know Charlie's back on the phone telling the guy in Harlem that the couriers are two Bolivians who just flew into the country, each with his own suitcase, and they'd pass him the stuff from a taxi on the corner of Bruckner and Tremont. Charlie himself must have learned this either in person or over another line, because we didn't pick it up on our wire.

Charlie sounds very jumpy, and so does the other guy. *How the fuck you gonna see them if they're in some goddamn taxi? Make 'em come to the house.* Charlie practically explodes at this. *How can I tell 'em to come to the house, you idiot? They don't know how to travel, they're two fucking spics who can't even speak English. Look, they got the suitcases, they're coming, and we'll get right down to you and your friend. Stop worrying.*

Of course, neither one sounded ready to stop worrying. These shipments didn't come every day, and two suitcases probably meant twenty or thirty kilos, millions of dollars.

We were in something of a turmoil ourselves, waiting for the Feds to arrive so we could decide which of us was going to tail which of them. But it was way after midnight, and even though they were anxious to get in on a collar this big, the agents probably had to be roused out of bed and maybe wouldn't arrive until God knows when. Meanwhile we had to move, so took off in hopes of spotting Charlie receiving the suitcases from the cab.

His car was already gone from his house, so we sped over to Bruckner and Tremont, but they must've already made the meet and left. Maybe they'd changed location. Maybe the Bolivians were still giving directions in Spanish to a cab driver who probably did not, in those days, speak Spanish.

Whatever went wrong, for them or us, we lost Charlie Cigar. We assumed, though, that if he'd made the meet he wouldn't go back home with all that coke but deliver it down to his Harlem contact. Unfortunately we had no idea where the hell that would transpire, but we did have the location of the Bolivians' hotel that Charlie had spilled over the wire, Thirty-fourth and Seventh, so we drove down into Manhattan to give that a shot.

As soon as we got there, we saw what a long shot it was. Four hotels right on that intersection, but by this time in the wee hours of the morning we had nothing better to do, so we went from one front desk to the next asking about any recent bookings of two guys who only spoke Spanish, especially from South America. We got lucky at the second or third hotel, where the clerk showed a couple of men arriving yesterday from Bolivia. We figured this qualified as hot pursuit, so got the key and busted into the hotel room, where we found these two guys who didn't seem to speak English. What we didn't find were any suitcases, or money, or drugs, or anything the least bit incriminating. They had IDs, green cards or whatever, and we took down the basic information and went back outside. We knew what they looked like now, so questioned all these cabbies as they pulled up to the hotel about any fares up into the Bronx earlier that night. After about an hour we gave up and drove back to Carvel's.

Maybe, we figured, there'd be something on the wire, and there was, some downtown cab driver from a phone booth, saying, *Listen, I got these two fucking guys that don't even know where they're going, how the hell do I get to this address?* By this time, Charlie sounds like an absolute nervous wreck, no doubt thinking of all those kilos that he desperately, desperately, doesn't want to disappear from right under his nose, knowing his organization would probably kill him if they thought it was his fault, so he frantically starts giving the cabbie directions to his house: *Take a left, take a right, go three blocks, look for a pizzeria, go down, go up,* all in very great detail.

So that's what must have happened: the meet was pulled off at Charlie's house, not on some street corner, and since it was now maybe five or six A.M., it probably took place hours ago, giving

Charlie plenty of time to pass along the coke to whoever was supposed to get it. Having accomplished that, his only real responsibility, he could now be anywhere, including fast asleep in bed after
his busy night.

Well after daylight, the Federal unit shows up, and together we
decide to make a run straight at Charlie's house. Even without a
warrant, we have more than enough over the wire to justify a pre-
sumption of ongoing criminal activity.

The whole family's up and about by the time we get there, so we
split them into different rooms to let the senior agent and I go
around talking to them individually. Charlie's protesting the
whole time, like, *What are you guys, crazy? I got nothing here, you're
outta your mind. I can't even find a goddamn job. All I do is spend my
time looking for a goddamn job.*

When we get to his wife, she denies everything too, until we say,
Listen, lady, we've been on your wire for three months and not
only has your daughter been fooling around but we're on to that
very good friend of yours, the cab driver. *Oh God,* she says. *Only I
can't tell you anything. He'll kill me if I say anything.* He's gonna kill
you anyhow, we point out, if he finds out about the cabbie. She's
wild by now and promises to help any way she can, only says she's
in total ignorance because he never talks to her. We keep pressur-
ing her and she admits somebody came by that night, but she
wasn't in the room and doesn't know who it was or what went on.
Charlie left to go somewhere and then came back. She swears
that's all she knows, but we still don't let her off the hook and finally she tells us there's a trap in the bedroom.

That was very common in those days, for dealers to have a trap
somewhere to hide drugs and drug money, sometimes very intri-
cate and hard to locate, with hidden electric devices and everything. She tells us exactly where this trap is, in the floor of the
closet outside their bedroom. We fumble around the house a little
to protect her, making it look like we just kind of stumbled onto it.
It had some kind of electric seal that had to be broken with a
screwdriver, and then you had to pry under the edge of the sill to

the closet. The whole section of closet floor lifted up on a hinge, and we figured, *This must be it.*

But there were no drugs, no money. The space could easily hold twenty or thirty kilos, and was probably where he'd stash the coke if he couldn't get rid of it. But obviously he'd passed this batch on. All we found was some crummy jewelry, maybe a thousand, two thousand dollars' worth all told, hardly worth a complicated trap to hide it away.

We never found anything in the house or anywhere else, and whatever was in those two suitcases became, after all our months sitting on that wire, just one more shipment that got into the country and into the city, that got cut and packaged and distributed and eventually sold on the street or hand-delivered to some fancy West Side apartment.

Still, based on what we'd gotten over the wire, we were able to arrest Charlie Cigar and his pal Sal on conspiracy to sell and distribute drugs, and handed the case over to the Feds. For me, that was the end of Charlie Cigar and his wife and daughter and his drug deals and everything else, except for a funny little footnote years later.

After I retired, and following my stint at the Waldorf and with the Helmsleys, Jeannette and I opened our frame-and-art shop in Northport in this very nice tourist area on the North Shore. I was at the counter one day when a kind of attractive young woman comes in, maybe in her early thirties, and I could tell from the way she looked and talked that she was strictly a New Yorker, not your typical Long Island type. Italian, I figured, maybe from the Bronx or the Mt. Carmel part of Harlem. I've always had an ear for that kind of thing. We were having a pleasant conversation about the artworks and stuff, or maybe she wanted something framed—I don't remember that part, only when I made out the sales slip, she gave her name as D'Allesandro, with an address out on the Island somewhere. I said, Your name sounds familiar, what do you do for a living? Oh, she said, I'm a schoolteacher, which sounded right because you could tell from the way she discussed the art and everything that she was a well-educated woman. Did you by any chance, I asked, have a relative nicknamed Charlie Cigar that lived up in Pelham Bay? Oh yes, that was some kind of uncle of hers, who passed away a couple of years ago. Oh boy, I thought, could I tell you stories about your uncle—and your aunt too, with her friendly taxi driver. But what I said was, Well, I used to be a police officer, and had some contact with him. Did he ever get sent away? Yes, he did, she admitted. He spent seven years in Federal prison on a narcotics conviction. Really? Well, that was the case I worked on.

Maybe I shouldn't have told her that, because she could have gotten insulted or angry, but she took it surprisingly well. In fact, she became a regular customer, and we always chatted pleasantly when she came by. One time she even brought along her mother and introduced me to her. The mother was a typical older Italian type, nowhere near as educated or Americanized as her daughter, and since I wasn't all that clear about the mother's relation to Charlie Cigar, I was at least smart enough not to mention anything about him. The niece and I never talked about him again either, but she always knew I was one of the cops that sent her uncle away, which I'm sure stayed in her mind.

I guess what stayed in my mind was something beyond the usual *small world* feeling you get when you discover a connection with someone you bump into in a place as big as New York. The D'Allesandro family that came over to this country and settled in Harlem, muttering Italian and trying to keep up the old ways, not only produced Charlie Cigar but also this really nice, educated woman, doing her best to help and work with children as a schoolteacher—and getting paid less for a whole year of that than her uncle cleared on a single pickup from a couple of Bolivians in a taxi.

FOOTPRINTS
AT THE FIRE

A L   D E L L A   P E N N A   ➡

NORMALLY THE LAB'S crime-response team isn't sent to arson scenes. The way it works, if anything looks suspicious at a fire, the local chief or county fire marshal will call for the police Arson Squad. Even though all Long Island firemen, including the chiefs, are volunteers, they're trained to recognize such signs of arson as a suspicious point of origin within a structure, simultaneous origins in different parts of a building, or a fire that spreads too quickly or burns too intensely for the structure involved. Sometimes the color of the flames or smoke will give a clue as to what's burning or what may have ignited it.

The Arson Squad is automatically called out when, as in this instance, you've had a series of suspicious fires in a given area. But our crime-scene unit goes to a fire only when you've had a loss of life, especially if there's a possibility the fire might have been set to cover up a homicide.

Last year Sayville, one of our small South Shore communities, experienced a number of arson fires within a matter of weeks. None had resulted in deaths, and I hadn't been involved in any investigations. Early one morning in late January, I got a call from the dispatcher at the ME's office who said Sayville was experiencing another fire and that I was being put on alert. The call came really early, around five A.M., and I thanked the guy for waiting until I was already awake, because I'd have hated to be roused out of bed well before dawn just to be told I was being put on alert. Sure thing, Al. Meanwhile, you're on alert.

The winter semester had just begun, and I spent the next couple of hours with some final preparations for the first meeting of my eight A.M. criminalistics class. Naturally, you always want to start off with a good impression, in your snazzy necktie and Sunday-go-to-meeting clothes, with the best shine of the year on your shoes, and that's the way I showed up at the appointed hour and began my usual opening-day routine, handing out schedules, talking about absences and assignments, and in general introducing myself to the students as their friendly but incredibly knowledgeable mentor. As part of this, I informed them that as a member of the county's homicide-response team, I sometimes got called without warning and therefore might not make it to class.

At that exact moment, my beeper went off. Boy, did I get some fishy looks. I did my best to convince them that this wasn't a setup on my part and that I'd have to take a minute to check in. From my office, I phoned lab director Vince Crispino, who said, There's a request for our services at the Sayville fire because they're sure it's arson and there's two bodies inside.

Back in the classroom, I explained to the students that I had to cut out because of a potential homicide at a fire, which they seemed to take well enough. In truth, it probably impressed the hell out of them, having a prof who actually got called out on real-live emergencies.

I drove straight to the lab in Hauppauge, where they filled me in on the exact location and told me the victims were two elderly men. Since the medics on the scene hadn't found any signs of wounds or beatings, and neither body had—in the parlance—been cooked, it was assumed they'd died of smoke inhalation. In fact, they'd already been removed, which isn't usually the case when we're sent out, because we're always very interested in the location and condition of the bodies, and the condition of that immediate area. Nonetheless, the boss wanted me to help the Arson people collect evidence, along with one of our lab specialists trained in the analysis of arson residues and materials of that nature.

The Sayville fires had gotten a lot of publicity, so there was a lot of determination to solve them. Strangely enough, everyone felt they *had* been solved a week earlier, when a suspect had been charged and was now sitting in jail. The fact that his arrest hadn't stopped the dirty work, and that two lives had now been lost, really intensified the pressure. There'd even been a fire the night before, a minor one set in a Dumpster right behind the Sayville fire station, as if someone was thumbing his nose at the whole bunch of us.

The two crew members and I headed out in the van for Sayville, about fifteen miles away, where we located this little strip of mom-and-pop stores on Main Street, including a laundromat, a travel agency, a notions shop, that sort of thing. The fire had been discovered at one or two in the morning and had turned an outside wooden staircase in back into a pile of rubble, and pretty much burned out a connecting first-floor wooden walkway that led to some single rented rooms. The sidewalk stores had suffered mostly water damage. The TV stations had apparently featured a lot of spectacular live footage, so even though there wasn't much left to gape at, lots of press people and onlookers still milled around the taped-off area in the midst of all the fire and emergency vehicles from Sayville and surrounding towns, the Arson and Homicide squads, the fire marshal's people, and now us, the Johnny-come-lately crime-scene unit, more than willing to help everybody solve all their problems.

One thing that hit me immediately was how the Arson people had no picnic at all, despite their protective clothing and heavy boots, because they're usually among the first to arrive and get the honor of poking and prodding around with the flames still blazing away. By the time we got there, their faces and outfits were so blackened they looked like coal miners. They'd already spent hours sloshing through a lot of wet and smoking debris, having to be concerned every step of the way about ceilings collapsing and beams falling on them.

My two crew members had brought along in the van their duffel bags stuffed with special clothing for various occasions and kinds of weather, and as soon as we arrived they put on their heavy jumpsuits, thick socks, warm hats, firemen's boots, the whole bit, because this was a cold, windy January morning with a dusting of snow on the ground and only a pale, weak sun overhead. I, though, was still in my fancy professor's suit and tie, with just a thin scarf for warmth. I hadn't brought extra clothes because I no longer had any: my duffel bag was in the trunk when my car been stolen a few weeks earlier, and the lab hadn't given me any replacements yet. Not only would I freeze in this getup, but I'd have everybody wondering why Della Penna had showed up dressed for his famous imitation of the rear end of a horse. At the same time, I could envision the punk who stole my car showboating around New York in my blue jumpsuit with CRIME LABORATORY blazed across the back in big white letters.

I finally scrounged up some insulated coveralls and a pair of fire boots. My feet were still cold, because rubberized fire boots are designed to keep you dry, not warm. Luckily, I bummed a pair of thick cotton socks from a friendly Homicide detective.

I was then ready to get to work, so checked in at the command post to get the latest update and offer our services to the people already there, since in a crowded situation like that you don't want to step on toes or waste time duplicating each other's efforts. The command post had been set up across the street from the fire site in the parking lot of a modern supermarket mall right next to the Sayville firehouse, where the Dumpster fire had occurred the night before.

The command post is simply a converted bus that can be dispatched to the site of major crimes, modified to provide desks and tables, private areas, toilets, practical things of that nature, including an ever bubbling coffee pot. It can also hook its phone lines into the nearest telephone pole. Maybe most important, it provides a place where investigators can talk to witnesses, interrogate suspects, and converse freely among themselves beyond the ears of the press and public.

For me, with the responsibility for preserving the integrity of a site, the bus has proved a real godsend in a very particular way. Before we had command posts, the practical aspects of a situation could lead people, me included, into some very sloppy attitudes. You'd find yourself in a house with a bunch of other people, and maybe on your initial walk-through, you've determined to keep the kitchen, bedroom, and the hallway strictly off-limits as integral parts of the crime scene. Now, you've just started working and will probably be cooped up in there all day, so you're looking for a place to drop your hat and coat, talk things over with other investigators, maybe gulp down a container of coffee. You don't want to do all this in front of the cameras and onlookers, so you figure, Okay, the living room wasn't involved in the crime, so maybe we can just dump our stuff in there and use that as a kind of makeshift headquarters.

We got cured of this a few years ago when a bunch of us were sitting and standing around a living room, coats tossed on the couch and everything, when someone piped up with, Hey, what's that on the floor over there? Unfortunately, it turned out to be a cartridge shell. Oh, shit, I moaned, are we gonna get reamed out on this! And of course we did, and rightfully so.

Inside the command post at the fire, I talked to the chiefs of the Homicide, Arson, and ID units, who together had maybe a dozen investigators working the area, along with the truckloads of volunteer fire fighters and local police officers, and now me and my crew. They were pretty sure the fire started in the back wooden staircase, and assured me that the physician's assistants hadn't found any suggestion of foul play on the two bodies discovered in their upstairs rooms.

I suggested to the Arson chief, as I usually did at fire scenes, that my crew and I could make ourselves most useful by going around with his investigators, who could best recognize the specialized type of evidence that they felt was worth picking up, which we would then package and document. After all, they were the ones who knew, for instance, how deep to probe into burnt wood and how much of a chunk to gouge out for a sample. We would then maintain possession of all evidence until we logged it in at the lab, thereby establishing a direct and uncomplicated chain of custody. You never want to screw up the chain of custody or make it unnecessarily cluttered. Who found this? Where exactly? Who picked it up? Who marked it? Who transported it to the lab? Who signed for it there? Who ran the tests on it? Who maintained storage through the ensuing months or years? The more often I can answer, *Me,* the better off everyone's going to be.

I also volunteered my group for all the sketching, since that's something else we're well trained for. That meant measuring the precise locations of evidence collection and pacing off structural dimensions. Sure, there are probably architectural records somewhere, but the building might have been modified over the years. Of course, with the wooden stairway and the back part of the building burnt out, I didn't have the corner beams I needed back there to anchor my measurements.

Since the fire had apparently started on the staircase, that became our initial focus. If you're going to find evidence of arson, or any clues to the arsonist's identity, that's where it'll probably turn up. Basically you're looking for signs of an accelerant. True, you could torch a building with twigs or crumpled newspapers or a candle placed under the curtains, and lots of fires have been started that way, both accidentally and by design. But anyone who's ever struggled to get logs going in a fireplace knows it's not always easy. Ignition temperature is up in the five hundred to seven hundred–degree Fahrenheit range. Serious arsonists therefore go for a chemical that's easy to ignite yet burns hot enough to set something else on fire, usually some highly volatile petroleum derivative like gasoline, paint thinner, kerosene, lighter fluid, that type of thing.

In terms of collecting evidence, a material's volatility determines how it has to be handled. If you don't package it properly, before long you're going to weaken or contaminate, maybe even lose, the volatile elements that give accelerants their particular identifiable qualities. At one time we used to collect arson material, such as charred wood that may have been splashed with something, in airtight plastic containers. But plastics are themselves produced from petroleum, and you really don't want to mix petroleum compounds when you're aiming toward a very precise chemical analysis. We switched to glass jars for a while, with screw-top lids, but every time you unscrewed the lid to take a sample, you lost some of that specific atmosphere and diluted the rest with whatever was in the air around you.

Now we use standard gallon metal paint cans, which we buy in quantity from a paint manufacturer. Any volatile material goes right into the can and is sealed in by hammering the metal lid shut. When the chemist back at the lab wants a sample, he punches a tiny hole into the can but immediately plugs it with a rubber stopper. He can then penetrate the seal with a needle to remove whatever he needs without any loss or contamination whatsoever.

Laboratory technology for identifying even trace amounts of gases and chemicals has advanced so greatly that if we make a good collection, and keep it pure, the chemists have an excellent chance of identifying both the general category of an accelerant and its exact characteristics. In one case, for instance, the chemists determined that a gasoline compound contained a certain percentage of alcohol. Since only one service-station chain on the Island sold that particular mixture, the finding saved a hell of a lot of legwork in locating the attendant who filled up a container for a certain customer a few days earlier.

You'd assume that somebody intent on splashing gasoline around the house of some enemy or ex-lover, or the site of his own failing business, would be smart enough to siphon it out of his car tank, with no one around to notice. Instead they show up at some gas station, container in hand, that very afternoon, sometimes even at their regular stations, where of course they're going to be recognized and remembered.

As almost any investigator will tell you, it's not that we're so smart. It's that, thankfully, they're often so dumb.

Following my initial briefing, my men and I joined the Arson teams picking through the debris. Obviously you can't do this until the material's cool. Sometimes, if you try to rush things, the stuff can still be so hot it can actually reignite on you. But we were moving along okay at Sayville, packaging and documenting whatever we got handed. Experienced fire investigators are very adept at using their finely honed olfactory systems, and I've seen them moving around like crabs on their hands and knees with their noses pressed right to the ground. You can hear them going *Hwiff! hwiff! hwiff!* and they'll call out, Here, right here! We got something right here!

I've tried smelling the very same stuff and can't pick up a thing. Maybe it's the reverse of my experience as a kid working in that chicken slaughterhouse. Someone else would come in and say, Oh my God, doesn't that smell make you sick? And I'd say, What smell? These investigators, on the other hand, had attuned themselves to pick up the exact odors they were interested in.

They also will visually note where the darkened surface of partially burned wood takes on the squarish pattern of alligator skin, since this configuration is a giveaway for the presence of an accelerant. By digging into this wood, they often discover a stronger chemical residue in the underlying layers, where the chemical hasn't been as thoroughly burnt off. Arson squads now have a device that they actually refer to as a *sniffer*, which is a rod with a sensitive detector at the end that reacts to the slightest presence of volatile gases. When they spot a large charred circle on damaged walls, with two big blackened arms reaching up and out to form a V, they know someone's almost certainly set an accelerant ablaze at the center of that circle.

They also resort to trained dogs to smell out accelerants, the way other units employ them to detect drugs or explosives. (My friends in the K-9 Squad tell me animals can even ferret out a knife or gun tossed into a landfill or heavy brush. The trainers think the dogs do it by using their uncanny ability to smell something *new* in a given area. God only knows how they do this. The animals, like they say, ain't talking. They just gobble down the doggy treats they get for doing their jobs.)

I got a chance to see the Arson dogs in action out in Sayville that day. As I was moving around packaging items at street level, I realized I ought to at least take a look upstairs where the two old guys died, not wanting to learn afterward that I'd missed something by not snooping around. The Arson and Homicide guys I was working with said, Sure, let's all three head up. With that, they indicated this fire ladder thrown up where the stairway used to be, a kind of freestanding, slanting job that seemed barely six inches wide and was swaying furiously in that cold, bitter wind. Look, I said, my otherwise impressive background didn't include any practice scurrying up and down flimsy ladders, so there's absolutely no way you're gonna get me to put even one toe on that sucker.

They naturally found this amusing but recognized my utter seriousness, so we all headed to the rear brick wall, which was still in good shape, where we found a straight-up-and-down metal ladder solidly bolted to the wall. That, I figured, I could manage, and the three of us climbed up and checked on the relatively undamaged part of the roof behind the burnt-out inner hallway. We found nothing of interest, but noticed the uniformed guy from the fire marshal's office going through his routine with his trained dog.

The procedure he followed, he explained, was to bring the animal to the fire scene, then salt a small area with accelerant and let Fido get a good sniff of it. Then he'd say, *Find!* That's it—just, *Find!* We watched the dog scour the whole area, sniffing away like a bloodhound, finally zeroing in at the top of a razed staircase. He must have caught some residual fumes from the burnt rubble, because he just sat right down and stared at the spot. It was great— the dog didn't blink or move a muscle but just stayed transfixed like that until the handler came over and patted him on the rump and said, *Good boy! Good boy!* and sent him off looking for more.

We left them up there and climbed down to continue searching downstairs, and a little while later I looked up and, lo and behold, coming down that same bolted perpendicular ladder, I saw the fire marshal with the dog cradled in his arms, in one arm actually, so he could grab the metal rungs with the other hand, and it suddenly dawned on me what had been nibbling away at the back of my mind: How in hell had the dog, who was probably no keener about ladders than me, got up there? Now I saw how, only in reverse, with the guy edging down very, very cautiously, whispering something like *Easy, pooch! Easy now!* in the dog's ear, and probably praying with all his might, *God, don't let the dog jump! Please, God, not now!*

For all its splendid skills, it wasn't any kind of fancy purebred dog. It was a mutt, that's all, a plain old Heinz fifty-seven varieties mutt.

Since people were not going to be able to work all day without sustenance, some of us thought maybe we ought to fit lunch into our general coordination of everybody's efforts. To this end, the other leaders and I decided that we'd all stop at the same time, so no one would be left behind to complain, Where the hell is so-and-so just when we need him? We all grabbed a quick burger and hot coffee at this little nearby luncheonette and tried to warm ourselves a tad from the chill that by now had seeped down to the bone.

Almost as soon as I got back on the street, an Arson investigator came up and said, Al, it looks like we got another arson-type circumstance in the building next door which you'd better take a look at.

The building next door, across a narrow alley, turned out to be Republican headquarters for Suffolk County. Someone had discovered a flare, the kind you see at highway accidents, that had been ignited and placed in a basement window. It'd burnt the surface of the wooden louvers and fallen to the ground, without generating enough heat to set anything on fire. The Arson investigator and myself started collecting and measuring at that site and brought over the ID crew to take pictures.

Meanwhile, people had naturally been checking out the Dumpster fire of the night before, which occurred behind and between the firehouse and the Masonic Temple next door, and discovered a big scorch mark on the back door of the Masonic Temple. Suddenly we had, counting the Dumpster last night, not one or two or three but four potential arson sites, all in this little nucleus of stores and buildings straddling Main Street.

A couple of investigators from Homicide and Arson hustled over to the Masonic Temple with me, and while circling the place, we spotted low down on the front of the building, partially obscured by the thick shrubbery alongside the front steps, a dark spot on the otherwise light-colored façade. On closer inspection, the wood down there seemed freshly scorched, without a film of dirt or anything. So it too had probably occurred within the last twelve hours or so. Whoever this guy was, he'd sure had himself a busy evening.

We asked a patrolman to seal off this area and went around to the scorched back door of the temple, which had brought us over in the first place, and found in the residual dusting of snow several clear footwear impressions leading up to the back steps. Whoa, I called out, let's make sure we protect these.

Since this area, unlike the Dumpster, was not a fire site, we assumed the firemen hadn't been poking around back there, which meant there was a good chance the impressions were made by whoever tried to set the door, and maybe the whole temple, on fire. Since this kind of evidence fell directly within my area of responsibility, I said, Look, we have to get on these prints right away. We need pictures and we need casts and we can't waste much time getting them. I was anxious because even in that bitter cold there was enough sun to soften the thin film of snow and compromise the prints. The first thing I did was protect the prints from the direct sun by forming a shield with a big cardboard supermarket carton.

You try to capture footwear impressions, regardless of what they're in, first by recording the precise detail through photography, and then through casting, which can't help but alter the evidence in the process. My immediate concern, therefore, was to grab a couple of photographers for that back-door area. But when you're trying to work cooperatively with other units, you can't go around giving orders to everybody in sight, no matter how wrapped up you are in your own work. If I'd just grabbed the nearest photographer, he'd probably say: Hey, I'm already doing something. My boss told me to shoot here, and that's exactly what I expect to keep on doing until he tells me otherwise.

Actually, no one person exerts official overall command when you have all these different specialists under different leaders, although on a homicide investigation the top Homicide man would normally be deferred to by the others. In practice, it rarely comes down to a strict pecking order. Sure, you have disagreements, with each specialist coming at things from a different angle. But these are all pros, working toward the same end, and the potential friction can usually be worked out by staying in touch with each other.

So I located the ID leader and explained about the footprints in the snow, and he agreed about the urgency and took two men away from photographing sections of the original fire site, which was no longer about to undergo immediate change, and had them follow me over to the back door.

In truth, ID photographers hate footwear impressions. It's a lot more work, a lot fussier, than most of what they do. In order to show the ridges and markings we're interested in, they have to shoot at maybe a dozen angles for each impression, pausing between each click to document the angle of the camera, the angle of the artificial or natural light or combination of both, etc., etc. I can help by sketching the general area and locating the prints in reference to the door and so on, but the technical information they have to compile themselves. To make it even worse, almost all film used these days is high-grade color, which gives you much more vivid pictures, but black and white usually gives better definition of footwear prints, so the poor guys have to keep loading and unloading from one to the other as they go. And to power their electronic flash units, they have to lug around these big heavy battery packs that wear down periodically and have to be taken off to be replaced.

Since it took me less time to sketch than for them to take pictures, I wandered over to the Dumpster for a look-see. The firemen had been back there dousing the fire the night before, leaving footprints all over the place, but I was particularly drawn to one set, a little ways off from the Dumpster but close enough, say, for someone to toss some ignited material into the refuse. I was especially interested because these prints seemed similar to the ones being photographed behind the Masonic Temple.

Whatever you're collecting, you always try to differentiate between actual evidence and the artifacts of the investigation itself. This separate print could easily have been made by one of the volunteer firemen attempting to put out the Dumpster blaze. But since it seemed to match what we had behind the temple, it might indicate that someone fighting that fire could also be the one who had started it, and had tried to start the others.

It wouldn't have been a first. Besides all the psychological reasons, which I'll leave to the therapists like my wife Carrie, volunteer and professional fire fighters have both been known to deliberately set fires for certain practical reasons. Promotions, even your continued presence on a volunteer unit, can depend in part on the number of calls you've responded to and the success of your efforts on the scene. Since volunteers often respond directly from home, the guy who set the blaze is going to be up and moving while the rest are still pulling on their britches. And given his knowledge of exactly what's burning where, he can end up looking pretty good—although he can't show up too early, or look too good, for fear of raising eyebrows. As a matter of prudence with questionable fires, you have to consider firemen along with the other obvious categories, such as anyone with ties to the building or to the owner or occupants.

My personal introduction to this kind of thinking left a real impression on me. I had this student in a class who'd simply stopped coming, for whatever reason. I'd half-forgotten about him until one day I got a call from a detctive I knew out on the eastern tip of the Island. Hi, Al, I've been meaning to get to you about this guy we arrested a couple of weeks ago over in Greenport. What guy? I asked, assuming a connective link to one of my ongoing investigations. No, he said, it was some volunteer fireman who'd confessed to starting a blaze out there so he'd get a chance to show his stuff helping put it out, the town being so small and quiet that he'd got tired of waiting for some action.

I still hadn't got the connection with me. Well, the detective said, the guy told us he learned how to set a fire, including the use of paper trails to let him get away before the main accelerant went up, from this college course where the professor had a whole section on arson. He gave you full credit, Al. Said you were a real good teacher.

Since the prints at the Dumpster were getting more sun than those behind the Masonic Temple, we tied out a big shroud, about the size of a bedsheet, between the Dumpster and a nearby tree to provide shade while I hurried over and got one of the photographers at the temple to take a few quick shots by the Dumpster. Just then the Homicide lieutenant came to me and said, Look, Al, let's not make it too obvious that you're looking at these other areas, or even what it is you're looking for. I saw his point, of course. What with all the TV publicity and the crowds on the street watching our every move, our interest in stuff on the ground would immediately tell the arsonist that he oughta dump his sneakers into Long Island Sound. Unfortunately, I told the lieutenant, we already had this bright yellow shroud hanging from a tree by the Dumpster. The news didn't exactly thrill him, but he finally agreed that since we were working out in the open, it'd be impossible to collect any evidence without at least somebody figuring out what we were doing.

Another exterior check of the Masonic Temple led to the discovery, near a previously ignored side door, of yet another shoe print in the thin layer of snow, putting us very much into a situation of considering just how far we could spread our resources. This new

impression looked different from the ones out back. Maybe somebody had just wandered up to this door, for whatever reason. Then
again, maybe it meant we had two arsonists working together, in
which case we'd definitely want a record of this print too. Regardless of any kind of reasoning, you're always aware that it's your
job to preserve anything that *could* be evidence, on the general
CYA approach, because you know damn well if you don't Cover
Your Ass some inspector is going to mosey along and notice that
print by the side door just as it's melting into oblivion, and he's
gonna say, Of course, you've already got all the pictures we need of
that, right, Al? So I hailed the guy at the back door and he brought
his camera around and took a few shots of this too.

I also collected some blackened pieces of veneer from the back
door and some charred wood and debris from behind the shrubbery in front of the temple. The soil there wasn't frozen hard, and
when we dug up a sample with a spatula, one sniff was all I
needed to realize that the gasoline or whatever had soaked right
down into the ground.

When the photographers had taken all the photos anyone
could possibly want, I moved rapidly on the casting of the prints
by the back door, which were already softening in the afternoon
sun. Casting in snow was just about impossible at one time, because the old plaster of paris compounds gave off heat as they set,
meaning you'd end up melting away the very details you were trying to capture. We now use a variation of the substance employed
by dentists to take impressions of your teeth, which has been designed to produce as little heat as possible. This material is also
fairly light, since you don't want it flattening out the ridges. We
further protect the details by first spraying the impression with a
couple of applications of a Krylon-like acrylic mist to coat the surface. It takes time to dry, but gives you a hard surface that will both
highlight hills and valleys and absorb some of the heat produced.
Along the way you establish authenticity by scratching the date
and site and initials of the collector into the material before it completely sets.

The modern compounds are also somewhat sturdier than the

old plaster of paris casts, which we'd try to reinforce with sticks and twigs or whatever, but today's final product is still fragile and you have to be careful lifting it out not to break it. Anything you have to glue back together makes for a pretty unprofessional, and embarrassing, piece of evidence.

What with all the media coverage, the command post fielded a succession of calls from people wanting to pass on all manner of information. Public involvement is very much a two-edged sword. We're always sensitive, as the lieutenant was earlier, about tipping off the suspect to our areas of pursuit. On the other hand, people can tip you off to things you'd never in a thousand years discover yourself. To get to anything useful, though, you've got to put up with everybody and his Aunt Tilly breathlessly giving you the life history of some harmless local ne'er-do-well, and reporting every empty matchbook found in a gutter halfway across town. One way or the other, the calls always come, and the police always listen in the hope of unearthing a real nugget after they've sifted through all the crap passed along by the cranks and busybodies.

One call that day came from a storekeeper a few blocks away who said his plate-glass display had been smashed the night before. Like all the area merchants, he was distinctly nervous about all these unsolved fires and thought somebody might have attempted to torch his place. A few investigators tromped down and while they were sweeping up the shards they noticed a clear footwear impression on one jagged piece. So off I went to collect and document it on the long-range chance that it might have some connection to the fire.

We also heard from a woman who lived slightly farther away who said she noticed a plastic soda bottle sitting on top of her garbage can with some liquid still in it. Normally, of course, without all the arson publicity, she'd have just assumed some teenager had tossed it there. We would have too. But we sent an officer to check it out, and when he unscrewed the cap he needed only one whiff to realize it was gasoline, so I sent a man down to collect that too.

.   .   .

My crew and I worked until it started getting dark around five P.M., scurrying around picking up anything that might conceivably turn into evidence. It was our hope, of course, that at least *some* of those items we'd so carefully packaged and labeled would prove useful in nabbing the guy whose handiwork had brought all of us out there. It'd be nice, for instance, if the footwear impressions at the Dumpster and Masonic Temple matched exactly, and then led us straight to the bad guy. It'd be nice if the accelerant traces detected in the various locations could be traced to a specific service station, maybe even an identifiable customer.

Of course, these Sayville fires occurred very recently, and so far nothing we've done, nothing we've heard, nothing we've logically analyzed has led us anywhere. I naturally hope the hell they find the guy behind all that dirty business. The investigators are certainly putting a lot of effort into this, and would love to put that guy out of circulation, at least for as long as the courts will allow. I hope too that all the time the fire fighters and the Arson and Homicide and ID and fire marshal's people spent scrounging around and tramping through smoking debris and climbing ladders with and without dogs on that long, cold day, and scraping off charred wood and dealing with all those pig-in-a-poke footwear impressions threatening to melt away in the snow—that all of that will eventually pay off in a neat, clean-cut, rewarding way that'll bring us all to our feet cheering. And those cans and boxes and bags and envelopes of stuff we collected and photographed and tagged and brought back to the lab to be analyzed and catalogued and stored—I hope at least one little piece of all that helps send away the son of a bitch who set those fires and killed those two harmless old men living in their shabby single rooms over a bunch of stores.

Maybe it won't. Maybe not a single thing that all twenty or thirty of us did that day will end up being worth a plug nickel of anyone's time. But that's what we did that day. We used everything we had in the way of skill and knowledge and experience to give our total concentration to a lot of piddly little stuff that it's easy enough for someone to look back on now and say, Hey, Al, why even bother? Like, what's the chance you're ever gonna find the guy you want from some stupid sneaker footprint that you and all those other people spent a whole goddamn day treating like the Hope diamond?

You never know, right? Maybe we'll get the guy eventually, maybe we won't. Hollywood and TV to the contrary, every cop knows it's a damn sight easier committing a crime than solving it. Only we can't just tell the bad guys, Look, you don't have to worry about us. We're home downing a few beers and a bucket of pretzels watching *Monday Night Football* and won't be out there nosing around on any kind of cold ground, so just feel free to screw us to the wall whenever the urge overtakes you.

AL'S CONCERN THAT THEIR WORK might lead nowhere proved, a year or so later, unduly pessimistic. A nineteen-year-old probationary fireman pled guilty to setting the fires, including the one resulting in the death of the two elderly men. He was still in high school at the time, with an admitted alcohol problem, and told police that he joined his fellow volunteer fire fighters in extinguishing each of the blazes he set—which obviously didn't surprise Al.

In corroborating his confession, the police relied primarily on the convincing details he provided, and on a pair of heat-damaged sneakers recovered at his home that exactly matched the footprints in the snow that Al and the ID people had battled so hard against the winter sun to collect.

GOLD'S BUG

WHEN TWO POLICEMEN at the front door roused Johnny and his family from their beds at 2:30 A.M. on a Monday in October, 1972, he realized immediately that their lives might well be ruined. Johnny remembers the details of that night, and of the next year and a half, so vividly that even now, recounting the story, he can't hide the pain, the disbelief, the furious resentment. Yet after twenty-odd years, he manages to recount most of it with a degree of composure. He can even laugh at some of the passing absurdities.

His wife Jeannette responded in the early hours of that October morning, after watching John being locked into the back of a squad car and driven away, by writing what she'd witnessed in her diary. In all the months of frustration and uncertainty that followed, while at home taking care of their three children, aged four, thirteen, and sixteen, she filled 113 pages of small bound notebooks, her firm, dark script sometimes giving way to angry slashes. So we have Johnny recalling it all after two decades, and Jeannette, without knowing

**whether they'd even survive, writing everything down in the
fire of the moment.**

J O H N   C U O M O ➡
P A R T   I

I'VE NEVER TOLD the complete story before, and both Jeannette and I
have very mixed feelings about speaking out. It's still hard to for-
give those who caused us so much hurt, but maybe lessons can be
learned from our experiences. Maybe the suffering we went
through even made us, and our marriage, stronger. Mainly, I
guess, we want our children and friends to get beyond the rumors
and innuendos and newspaper accounts to learn the truth about
that terrible period of our lives, and to realize that during my
twenty years on the force all I ever wanted to be was a good cop.

Actually, there are so many sides to the story, it's hard to know
where to begin, but I'm convinced it started with a homicide investigation that got more and more complicated as we kept digging. What makes it really odd is that in my twenty years on the
force, this was my only homicide. Outsiders find this surprising,
but I never worked in Homicide, only Robbery and Narcotics.

I'd just returned from an operation on my larynx, in '68, and
the inspector in charge of my Brooklyn detective division called
me over and congratulated me. For what? I asked, and he says, I
heard you just adopted your third child, right? This surprised me,
because there's hundreds of detectives in the division, three
precincts' worth, and I never figured any higher-up would know
or care about my personal life.

The inspector then asked how I was recuperating, and I assured
him I was fine, one hundred percent, raring to go. He shook his
head and said, No, he wanted me on light duty without worrying
about regular hours. I told him, No, I'm fine, but he insisted. Just
tell the lieutenant I said you can take it easy and come and go
whenever you want.

But I didn't say anything to the lieutenant and pulled full shifts
with a probationary patrolman, a white-shield man. A couple of

weeks later a call came in that a local insurance broker had been shot to death in his office.

The system on a given tour would have one detective catching all cases the first four hours, the other detective the next four. It turned out to be my turn to catch, although of course everybody who's available responds right away to a homicide. So a whole bunch of us rushed to the scene, including this same inspector, who right away asked, Who's got the case? I said, Me, Inspector. You? Come over here! He put his arm around my shoulder, still being nice, and said, I don't want you taking this case. I said, Inspector, please—why not? He asked who my partner was, figuring to shift the case to him, but it was just this inexperienced white-shield man fresh out of Youth Squad.

We were off to one side by ourselves, and I reasoned with him. Inspector, it's gonna make me look like a fool. People are gonna wonder what's wrong if I can't take a case like everyone else. He also realized he couldn't put this young kid on a homicide while refusing it to me, so I got my way and took over.

Believe me—it was the worst thing I ever talked myself into in my life.

When you catch a homicide, you stay with it until it's broken or they close the case. I stayed on this one for months, spending all my time on it, working along with Detective George Kane of Homicide, who was assigned to the case as a specialist. He was very good, very experienced, and we got along fine.

The victim, Alex Havermeyer, worked as an excess insurance broker. That means he handled unusual risks, like art shows, art galleries, that regular brokers shied away from because the risks and evaluations were too unpredictable. The excess guy charged humongous fees but would insure almost anything, spreading around the coverage with several companies the way a bookie lays off bets. That way everyone got a cut but couldn't get stung too bad because they only had a small piece of the action.

Havermeyer's office was this little storefront with venetian blinds across the plate-glass window in front and a few desks and file cabinets inside, a little bathroom in back, the office itself long and narrow and very plain, nothing on the walls, cheap desks, plain carpet, not at all fancy. We found the body lying face up on the floor, and from the blood on the nearby desk we figured he'd been shot in that chair and slumped forward onto the desk before rolling onto the floor.

It didn't look like a robbery, but a hit. Somebody up real close had put two clean shots in the back of his head. Over the next few hours we went through his files, went through our files back at headquarters, checked out his business contacts and talked to neighborhood people, trying to figure out why somebody would come in and shoot this guy. The first major thing we learned was that Havermeyer was somehow connected with the son-in-law of a reputed Brooklyn Mafia boss. The son-in-law, Richard Gruber, half-Jewish and half-Italian, was also in insurance, also out of a Brooklyn storefront.

So we bring Gruber in, who turns out to be a real dingdong loony straight out of left field. He must have been on some kind of crazy high and starts telling us, bragging to us, about what a big shot his father-in-law is, Joey Ramona, and what great connections the father-in-law has. We recognize Ramona's name and realize we're getting well up into the organized-crime hierarchy.

Still, Gruber is our number-one suspect, and we stay on his tail while seeing what else we can learn. The big thing we find out is that the deceased, Havermeyer, had been brokering insurance on a lot of art galleries in various Brooklyn lofts which, a few months later, are wiped out in mysterious fires. Through the coverage brokered by Havermeyer, various insurance companies would pay off two, three hundred thousand dollars.

We figure we're really on to something, but when we talk with the fire department, the fire marshal, they tell us they could never come up with an arson charge. All they know is that when they get to one of these galleries, everything is burned out so bad they can't even identify anything. The insurance might have covered valuable originals, but whatever went up in smoke could have come from Woolworth's.

As we keep digging, one fire adjuster's name keeps popping up. A fire adjuster is someone licensed by New York State who's called in by the insurance company to a fire site to determine how much loss occurred and whether it was a true loss as claimed. He doesn't work for the insurance companies but provides a service to them on an individual fee basis.

This particular fire adjuster's name was Bobby something, and out of fifteen or twenty adjusters working in New York City, he's the one that keeps turning up on these art-gallery fires. The other interesting thing is he's supposedly the boyfriend of Xaviera Hollander—you know, the Happy Hooker—and when we go in to talk to him he becomes very angry and abusive and starts giving us all this crap about his friends in the DA's office. He says, Get out of my fucking office. If you keep coming around making these accusations, I'll have you thrown off the force, I'll have you dumped from the detective division.

At this point, George Kane and I figure, Hey, we must be getting into a very basic area here, what with the guy carrying on like this. In fact, I wrote it all down in my memo book—which is the daily record every police officer must keep and is considered a very trustworthy source, even as evidence at a trial. I wrote down exactly what Bobby said to us, the threat and everything, and had my lieutenant sign it, and even had a lieutenant from Homicide sign it, so there'd be no question of the date of the entry, etc.

But even with the pattern of Bobby's connection to these fires, we know how difficult arson crimes are to solve. If it's pulled off by a real pro, you may not even be able to tell that the fire was set. Even if the Arson investigators can tell, you still have to find the guy who did it and make a case against him. This is almost impossible, short of catching him running from the scene with a gasoline can. If the people behind the burn have any smarts at all, they hire a specialist, maybe even, if the stakes are big, someone from Jersey or Philly who drives into town one day, does the job, and goes home. Even if you do find him, which isn't likely, you then have to prove he did it, even less likely, and then you still have to prove a link between him and whoever hired him.

So we hit a stone wall. We couldn't get anywhere. The fire mar-
shals agreed it looked very suspicious, and had themselves already
investigated some of these fires. Based on our findings, they looked
into them all again. At the end, though, we had no evidence, just a
lot of funny coincidences going back to this broker Havermeyer,
whose murder we were investigating.

Even though we weren't getting anywhere on the arson connection, the Havermeyer homicide itself produced its own share of
strange coincidences. For instance, a million dollars in negotiable
bonds was stolen out of Wall Street, and the investigators were
using wiretaps. Out of nowhere one day someone says on the tap,
*That's because of that fucking murder out in Brooklyn, when they blew
that Havermeyer guy away.* Later it develops that the detective looking into the bond theft becomes a star witness for the Knapp Commission, which at the time was very publicly investigating police
corruption. Eventually it's revealed that this detective was not
only into the drug trade himself but also a prime suspect in the
murder of a prostitute who worked for the Happy Hooker, another
link to our case. Maybe, we figured, he was spilling stuff to the
Knapp Commission to buy himself protection in case his own
drug dealings ever came out, which eventually they did.

So we got involved in the million-dollar bond theft and discovered even one more connection. Richard Gruber's father-in-law,
Joey Ramona—and Gruber is still our chief homicide suspect—
turns out to have as a sideline an interest in shady stock and bond
deals. What they did in those days, they got young guys who
worked as runners on Wall Street and would either pressure these
kids, or buy them off, to report a fake robbery of the big-money negotiable bonds they were carrying, which would then be passed
through people like Ramona and Anthony Albano up to the next
echelon in the mob, with everyone taking a very nice cut.

To cap it all off, the lieutenant in overall charge of the bond-
theft investigation goes home one night and blows his brains out.
No one ever figured out why, but since he had no marital or financial troubles, no health problems, everyone assumed it had to be

connected to the bond thefts and maybe, therefore, with the murder of our guy Havermeyer. Anyhow, at some point along the way, most of the missing bonds in this case, something like nine hundred thousand dollars' worth, were found in a suitcase being carried by a certain lawyer, so in a way the theft was solved at that level, although they were never able to get to the higher-ups.

Now Gruber's father-in-law, Joey Ramona, was a major figure in the Brooklyn crime family at the time, so we start looking into the mob itself, trying somehow to tie together all these elements we've run into, because by now it's really become very complicated. We've got Ramona's son-in-law, Richard Gruber, as our prime homicide suspect, and his friend Bobby, the fire adjuster who's in on all the fire payoffs, which insurance was brokered by Havermeyer before he got killed, and the prostitute who worked for Bobby's supposed girlfriend, the Happy Hooker, and apparently got killed by this cop who's involved with both the Knapp Commission and the stolen-bond investigation, where the wiretap picks up mention of Havermeyer's murder and where the head investigator, this lieutenant, goes home and blows his brains out, which brings us back to Joey Ramona, who we know has been in the middle of a lot of lucrative stock thefts. So we're running all over the place, Brooklyn and Wall Street and Jersey and even up to Connecticut to talk to the big insurance companies, and we're beginning to wonder, What the hell are we getting into here? But no matter how hard we try, we just can't put the pieces together, and neither can anyone else, including the superiors we regularly report all this to.

All the while we keep hammering away at Richard Gruber and maintain a close eye on him. One day when George Kane and I are staking out his office, a van pulls up and two guys get out carrying rifles—wrapped up in blankets or whatever but obviously rifles—and take them into Gruber's office. So we move right in and find Gruber and the two guys looking over and sort of playing with the rifles. To show you what kind of nut case this Gruber was, he didn't even recognize us. We'd probably questioned him twenty times about the Havermeyer murder, we had had him down to the station, we questioned his family, his wife, his mother, his secretary, everyone in the world connected to him, and the jerk doesn't recognize us. In fact what he says is, Look, guys, I got some cops breaking my balls already on some stupid homicide, so I don't need any more trouble over some little crap like this. Kane and I can hardly believe our ears, that he doesn't know *we're* the cops he's complaining about.

He might've been high on something too. Look, he goes on, can't we just take care of this between us and forget the whole thing? He's trying to bribe us, naturally, about the guns, so Kane stays with him and the others, sort of playing them along, and I head outside to a phone and call the DA's office. What we want is some DA guy with a tape recorder so we can sit Gruber down and say, Okay, Richie, what do you wanna do now? Maybe, we figured, he'd be dumb enough or high enough to incriminate himself on the bribery.

But for whatever reason, the DA's office won't send anybody, so we just arrest the three of them on gun possession. I then call Cousin Al out at the Suffolk Crime Lab, since he deals with firearms, and Al says, Sure, they were stolen last night from a shop out here in Hauppauge. So the guys are booked and released on some kind of bail, awaiting trial on the possession charge, and maybe theft too, I don't remember that detail.

From the beginning, Gruber kept saying he wanted to cooperate, and actually gave us a lot of dope on Havermeyer and his connections and everything. Now he says we should check into one of the men we arrested with the guns in his office, Junior Kirby, as a suspect in the murder. We dig a little more and learn that Junior Kirby also has a forgery charge hanging over him for a four-thousand-dollar check he cashed. We figure that's enough to rate a visit, so we go and let him know about our interest in these two charges, to see if he's got anything worth saying. He's very annoyed at Gruber for sending us after him and says, Sure, he's ready to talk. Only not right now. He'll spill everything about Gruber to a grand jury in the morning. We're stunned, because this could be our breakthrough, although it does seem crazy that even Richie

Gruber would be dumb enough to send us to Junior if Junior just turns around and rats on Gruber.

We arrange for Junior to go before a grand jury the next day, but that night around four A.M. I get a call at home from a detective in Queens who says he's got with him a certain Junior Kirby, who they picked up in a car with Richard Gruber, only Gruber had been shot dead, and the gun was still in the car. I can't believe what he's telling me, so I call George Kane and we rush out to Queens to find out what the hell's going on.

This Junior guy was a strange egg of the first order and he actually seems happy to see us, like we're his long-lost buddies. We ask him what happened and he tells his story, that you really had to hear in his own words to get the full effect. Junior is maybe thirty years old but a real dum-dum, a street type without a brain in his body.

Hey, he says, when I tell you what happened you're never gonna believe me. I'm driving along in this car, it wasn't even my own car, I borrowed it from somebody, and I see Richie Gruber standing on the fuckin' corner, so I pull over and say, Hop in. I don't know exactly why I did that. I'm thinking to myself maybe I shouldn't of, because maybe he knew I was gonna testify in the morning, but I don't know, I figured we could just talk or something. And I say, What's up, Richie? And he says, Nothing much, but maybe we could take a ride out to Coney for a frank on a roll. So I'm driving along the Expressway out there by the airport and all of a sudden I see this gun slide out from under Richie's seat, the rider's seat, and I see him grab for it, so I grab for it too and we're wrestling each other for it and all of a sudden it goes *BOOM!* and Richie makes this funny noise—*AAARRRGGGGHHHH!*—and right away goes like this, stiff as a board, and his eyes go closed and right away I know he's dead, just leaning there tilted like a ladder against the window, and I get nervous and don't know what the hell to do.

So I'm driving around by the airport, out by Kennedy, trying to figure out what to do when all of a sudden I see this fuckin' cop behind me with the fuckin' light going, *Binka-Binka-Binka*, and what can I do, I have to pull over and the cop comes up to me and says, Can I help you? Is anything wrong? No, I tell him, we're fine except my friend maybe had a little too much to drink and I'm taking him home. I show the cop my license and everything and he says, Awright, go ahead. He don't know Richie's dead, naturally, only wouldn't you know it, I get half a fuckin' block away and he comes up again and says, Hey, pull over, I wanna talk to your friend.

Jesus, this real dum-dum, I can still hear him telling it, and it still cracks me up. It was like a movie, we should've made a movie of it.

Of course it was all pure bullshit. He was looking to dump the body was what he was doing. Gruber had been killed somewhere else, because ballistics couldn't find any powder burns, and where was the blood? There was no blood anywhere. What made it even stranger was that the Queens detective catching the case was very blasé about the whole thing, and Junior Kirby didn't even get charged with homicide. The prosecutors let him plead guilty to involuntary manslaughter or something and he got maybe a year in prison, when it was perfectly clear that Richard Gruber, our main suspect in the Havermeyer killing, had been bumped off and if Junior hadn't actually pulled the trigger he was certainly an accomplice in trying to get rid of the body. My guess is that others involved in the Havermeyer murder learned from Junior, this real nitwit, that he was ready to spill stuff about Gruber and decided to bump off Gruber to keep *him* from spilling anything, and wanted Junior to dispose of the body, which of course he didn't do a very good job of.

A very famous, very reputable insurance company ended up paying Gruber's widow something like a five-hundred-thousand-dollar double indemnity, on this man who was shot to death, clearly a victim of a homicide. When we check with them, they say, Gee, we didn't know anything about that. And of course Gruber's widow, collecting the half million with no questions asked, is the daughter of Joey Ramona, the big Brooklyn crime boss who seems to be everywhere.

Ten days later, Kane and I are called in by a Homicide lieutenant who tells us, That's it, word's come down from the DA's office officially closing the Havermeyer case since Richard Gruber, the obvious perpetrator, is now dead and buried.

It never seemed right to us, after all those months and all that running around, that the case should end like that.

We used to report to the DA's office on various cases now and then, where we'd meet with Charlie Hynes, the number-two man, and various assistant DAs. We'd try to convince them that someone should still be looking into all those crazy coincidences and connections instead of just shutting the book on Havermeyer, but we could never get a rise out of them. They'd just say, The case is closed, forget it, it's off the books.

Shortly after Gruber's widow got the big insurance payoff, some hit men walked into her apartment in the middle of a visit from her mother and her father, Joey Ramona, and all three were shot and killed, very quick, very clean, without a trace.

Why, I have no idea. I was never on that case and only saw it in the paper. The murder was never solved, and DA Eugene Gold's office never seemed interested in pursuing any relationship between it and any of the stuff we'd uncovered earlier.

So we ended up with five murders—first Havermeyer, then Gruber, then Gruber's wife and her parents, the Ramonas—and one suicide—the lieutenant from the bond investigation—and to this day if anybody knows what these all had to do with each other, they're not saying.

To me, the whole Havermeyer case and its ramifications led right to, or was even the main cause of, all the trouble I got into. One, we'd been poking around into the Brooklyn mob, maybe stepping on toes there, and two, we'd stirred up resentment in the DA's office by complaining about them not following up on our leads. It'd become perfectly clear to George Kane and me that a couple of regular beat detectives like us just didn't have the clout, the resources, to uncover the whole story, that it would have to be someone a lot higher up to really investigate the kind of stuff we were touching the edges of.

And this was the case my inspector didn't want me to take, that I talked myself into. I still kick myself over that.

PART II

WHEN THEY CAME HERE, to this house, at two-thirty A.M. that night in October, I got out of bed and found these two cops at the door, one a detective sergeant that I recognized, asking to come in. I never should've let them in. I should've demanded a warrant or a subpoena or something, but I had no idea in the world why they were there and just wasn't thinking in those terms.

Right in this living room here, the sergeant says, I've got some bad news, Johnny. I'm gonna have to put you under arrest and take you in to the DA's office. Can I have your gun and shield?

I ask them why, what's happening, what are the charges? The sergeant says he can't tell me anything, he's just gotta bring me in. Again like a jerk, I leave them here in the living room and go back into the bedroom where Jeannette's wide awake now, wanting to know what's going on out there, and I tell her I don't know but have to go with these guys. Then I take a quick shower to wake me up and try to get my brain going.

All this didn't take more than ten or fifteen minutes, and it wasn't noisy or anything, so I don't think the kids woke up. If they did, they stayed in their bedrooms and I didn't see them. By this time Jeannette's got a robe on and she's out here with them when I come back, carrying my badge and gun to give to them, and what I see is this other cop standing behind the little wall there with his hand on his holster, ready to go for his gun, as if they're thinking I'm gonna make a break for it or something.

This has always been such a deep-rooted thing for me. I'd been a police officer for eighteen years and never once been in any kind of trouble. And what I never, never understood was why they came at two-thirty A.M. I mean, I was asleep in my bed, I wasn't posing any threat to the community that required being dragged from my home in the middle of the night. I never, ever heard of them doing that with any policeman, regardless of whatever charges there might be against him—going right into his living room to arrest him, let alone doing it at that time of night, and without a warrant.

But there I am, with no idea of the charge, handing over my gun, my shield. They don't cuff me but take me right out to the squad car and put me in back, behind the mesh screen, with no inside door handles. They head toward Brooklyn, but a few miles from the house stop at this little all-night place and we all go in for coffee. I still have no idea who's waiting at the DA's office, and maybe they don't either, or they wouldn't be so casual about taking their time.

I also begin to get some idea of how sloppy their procedures are when they mention over the coffee that they first went to our old house in Syosset, which we'd moved out of two years before, and woke up the new owners. Hell, they didn't even have my change of address, which eventually was something they charged me with, not filing a change of address, although I did file. The DA's office just lost it or something.

When we finally get to Brooklyn, this big municipal building where they have the courts and everything, the sergeant says, Sorry, I better cuff you now, and we ride up in the elevator to the DA's offices and they bring me in to Charlie Hynes, the top assistant DA at the time and now Brooklyn DA himself, sitting behind this big desk. Hynes knew me, because I'd reported to him a lot on the Havermeyer homicide, and he says, Hey, hello, John, how are you, etc. I sort of look around and see the DA himself, Eugene Gold, sitting behind me on the edge of this desk at three-thirty in the morning with his arms folded, this little sawed-off monkey-looking guy, like a wet noodle, and I swear he's gloating. He's also wearing a goddamn tuxedo. He must've come straight from some fancy social function.

Hynes says, You understand why you're here, don't you, Johnny? And I say, No, I don't understand at all, so maybe you could just tell me. He seems to think this is just some kind of act on my part and says, Before I tell *you* anything, we'd appreciate it if you'd tell *us* the whole story, about that robbery with the three women.

The robbery with the three women? I know what he's referring to but have absolutely no idea in the world what it has to do with anything. These three women had complaints filed against them for robbery in some women's shop, something real petty, and I got the case and had them arrested and charged, and one woman's husband, who was some two-bit shady character, got angry about the whole thing. But what the hell did that have to do with arresting a police officer in the middle of the night?

If you don't want to talk about it, Hynes goes on, we're going to arrest you. I say, First of all, there's nothing to talk about, it was an open-and-shut case. Second, you're not *going* to arrest me, I'm already arrested, they dragged me out of bed and took my gun and shield. Oh, he says, sort of surprised, you've been arrested? I certainly have, I tell him. Ask the sergeant right there who took me in.

I'm really getting worked up and I tell Hynes, They *never* should have arrested me. Why not? he says, very cool, and I say, Because they had no indictment, they had no papers, they had no complainant against me. You just don't arrest a police officer like that, barging into his house without a warrant, without anything. Hynes shrugs, still very cool, and says, If you won't talk to us, I'm gonna place you under arrest. I keep telling you, for Christ's sake, I'm *already* under arrest, but you can do whatever the hell you want because I'm not talking to anyone until I have an attorney.

Okay, he says. That's what you want, that's what you get.

They take me inside and print me, and when the desk sergeant starts to back the prints, you know, with additional information that I'm supposed to sign, I say to him, What are you writing there? Don't write they arrested me in the DA's office. They arrested me in my goddamn living room, and I ain't signing a goddamn thing. (I have all this down somewhere. I wrote it all down the first chance I got.)

They take me to another floor to photo me, and as we're walking along the hallway this captain from my own detective division catches up to us and says, Keep your mouth shut, Johnny, they don't have a thing on you. He must have heard, to be there at that time of night, that one of his detectives had been arrested.

When we get back upstairs, I'm waiting around in this squad room, a lot of desks where the DA's police do paperwork and stuff, but there's only a few policemen around this time of night, and I see this other detective from my unit, Ralph Caccia, who pronounces his name Ca-*see*-a. I only barely know him, but learn he's also been taken in from his home. I'm wondering what he's got to do with all this, although we don't really talk because we'd never been friends or anything.

By now it's maybe six in the morning and Caccia gets on the phone to his lawyer or whoever, and says, with these cops around and everything, Hey, they arrested me, the DA people, after all the fucking money I give them every Christmas. He's actually yelling this into the phone, saying, I give 'em a big fat envelope and the fuckers arrest me. This is a *detective*, on the DA's phone, from the DA's office. I couldn't believe it.

It's almost eleven in the morning before they drag us into court to book us, and by then it's all over the city—TV, newspapers, everything, about these two detectives being arrested, and everybody's taking pictures of us coming out of the DA's office in handcuffs. The fact that the DA's office has all these prepared statements and handouts for the media people makes it that much clearer that the arrests weren't some quick or accidental decision but were thoroughly planned out in order to give Gold the maximum publicity. I keep wondering, though, whether that's why they decided to make the arrests in the middle of the night—to give the story a more dramatic and sensational twist. Anyhow, since they *still* don't have a complainant or an indictment, the sergeant attached to the Brooklyn court becomes the complainant, which couldn't possibly be legal after they had to travel through three counties to arrest me in front of my wife and kids.

They list some chickenshit charges like not filing the change of address, but the main ones, with Caccia and me indicted together, are receiving bribes, receiving a reward for official misconduct, and conspiracy to commit official misconduct, none of which, not one word, is true, at least about me. I haven't the slightest idea what the hell Caccia might have been involved in.

They release us both on our own recognizance, and Caccia's got his car right there outside the building and offers to drive me home. I could never understand that, how he came in his own car and I couldn't. We don't say much on the ride, I guess because we're both totally exhausted. He has the radio on and all we hear is these two detectives arrested for bribery, implicated by some electronic bug that DA Gold had set up in a wrecking lot in Brooklyn.

At home I tell Jeannette and the kids what's going on and try to calm everybody down, although of course I'm a nervous wreck myself, completely wiped out. They keep showing me on TV, and all the papers have me coming out in handcuffs. I'm still stunned, still trying to get on top of things. I call a friend on the force, who puts me in touch with a lawyer he trusts, who says, I know the lawyer you want, a real tough-nut hotshot named Barry Slotnick.

I never heard of Barry Slotnick. Not many people had, although now he's pretty famous. He was the lawyer for Bernhard Goetz in the subway shooting of the four black kids, and for the congressman Mario Biaggi on conspiracy charges along with the Brooklyn Democratic leader. Slotnick's had a lot of big cases, although at the time he was just into his thirties, still making a name for himself.

The next morning I drive into the city to Barry Slotnick's office, and he says, I wanna know this, I wanna know that, really grills me, and I tell him the whole story and he says, Don't worry, you have nothing to worry about. His fee, he says, is ten thousand dollars. I don't have that kind of money, my take-home pay for an entire year wasn't ten thousand dollars, but what can I do? I don't know anything about lawyers, and Slotnick comes very highly recommended. I'm suspended with all this publicity and worry and the whole world feels like it's dropping on my head, and rightly or wrongly I just don't see anywhere else I can turn.

I get a call from a guy I used to be pretty close to when we both lived in Syosset. He says he has a message from Warren Donovan. Now, Warren Donovan was a good mutual friend of both of us, our sons were the same ages growing up and we all coached Little League together, things like that. Only now Donovan is a big-time FBI agent who runs a New York City organized-crime task force and is well connected through that work with Charlie Hynes from the DA's office. Donovan, it seems, knows about what's happening to me and has asked this mutual friend to get in touch, because he doesn't want to contact me directly, which might look like he was taking a personal interest in me because of our friendship over the years. And there was always the chance, of course, that the DA's office might be tapping my line. Even my Syosset friend won't say much over the phone, instead asking me to meet him that night at a diner to talk more comfortably. I agree, of course, but to give you an idea of the shape I'm in, I'm wary of meeting him alone. Here I am, a detective with eighteen years of dealing with every kind of imaginable lowlife out on the street, and I'm worrying about some old friend in a Long Island diner. Anyhow, I call Cousin Al and ask him to come keep an eye on us, and he says sure, he'd be glad to.

At the time I didn't see much funny about it, or anything else, but on the phone Al also told me he's taking this course at John Jay College, taught by some professor who's part of the State Crime Task Force. Guess who, Al asks, is in the class with him? Ralph Caccia. In fact, on the day our arrest is all over TV and the papers, the professor takes the roll and says, Well, I guess Detective Caccia isn't coming tonight, and Al calls right out from the class, Prof, Detective Caccia ain't coming again *ever,* believe me.

Anyhow, I meet my Syosset friend in the diner while Al covers me from outside in his car, and the guy says Warren Donovan is aware of my situation and wants to say I shouldn't be concerned, because the DA's office really doesn't have anything on me but just hopes to use me to help nail Caccia. Well, I wasn't at all sure I wanted to get involved in going after another officer, but I didn't say anything and the friend then says that Donovan thinks it would be a good idea if I dropped by to see him at his office as soon

as possible, where it would be okay for us to have a straightforward, aboveboard conversation.

The next morning I drive in to Manhattan to see Warren and
he's very friendly. How are you, John, how's Jeannette and the
kids, how's everybody? Eventually he asks who's representing me
and I tell him Barry Slotnick and he explodes. Barry Slotnick!
What the hell do you want Barry Slotnick for? He represents all
these gangsters, these hoodlums! Of all the goddamn lawyers in
New York, why him? I say, Because I asked the advice of a friend
and am just trying to get the best I can afford. Warren says, Jesus,
John, we know you're not involved in anything. I've seen the
whole transcript, you're clear—only now you've got Barry Slotnick? I said I'm sorry you feel that way, but that's it, he's representing me. Eventually Warren settles down and it's obvious he's
trying to help me out by playing go-between for the DA's office. All
they want, he says, is for you to testify against Ralph Caccia, who
they got dead to rights on the wiretap and who we all want to use
to get some Mafia people we're after. I tell him I'm sorry, that even
though he's a friend he's also connected to the DA's people and I
really can't talk about this without my lawyer. I can see he's disappointed but he says, Okay, I'll get in touch with Slotnick and set up
a meeting with some people.

Back home Jeannette and I discuss what Warren said about
Barry representing gangsters but decide that's what lawyers do,
represent people in trouble who can pay, and our one question has
to be whether Barry's right for us, which so far he seems to be.

At this time, my mother was dying of cancer in the hospital,
and when I go visit her the next day she says she's seen me on TV
and wants to know if something's wrong. But she's weak and on
drugs and not really on top of things, so I tell her, No, Mom, nothing's wrong, I just made a big arrest, that's why you saw me on TV.
Only of course what she saw was me coming out of the DA's office.
That really got to me, not only my whole family, all my friends,
everybody I knew, but even my mother dying in the hospital, seeing me in handcuffs.

The next day I go back with Slotnick to the DA's office for the meeting set up by Warren Donovan, and everybody's shaking hands and introducing themselves around, Inspector So-and-so, Detective Cuomo, Warren Donovan from the FBI, etc., etc. DA Gold isn't there, but one of his assistants is. Barry opens his briefcase and takes out a little recorder and says, All this is being put on tape, proceed, what do you want from my client? Finally someone says, Why don't you shut that off, we just want to discuss things. Barry says, No, anything we say from here on will be on tape. The police inspector says to me, Okay, let's call a spade a spade, are you willing to testify against Caccia? Before I can open my mouth, Barry says, Don't utter a word, John, that's not a question we deal with at this time. To the others Barry says, We want to know what you think you have against this man after all his good years on the police force. You barged in and took him out of his home and I want to know the facts in this case. Warren Donovan says, Come on, Barry, don't get so excited, we're only after these other people and just want a little cooperation from Johnny. Barry looks them all in the eye and says, My client is not interested in this kind of discussion, and with that he puts his recorder away, snaps his briefcase shut, and says, Let's go, Johnny.

JEANNETTE BEGINS HER DIARY late the day after John's arrest, and in this initial entry (but rarely thereafter) seems self-conscious, almost formal:

TUES. OCT 24—What kind of world do we live in—what injustice—Sgt. did not read rights to Johnny—asked for a drink (while on duty *at time of arrest in our home)—He—Gold—put my husband through indignities a murderer doesn't go through—I pray they all suffer the worst agony ever—Dear God—I am so full of hate—help us all through this black moment of our life—*

Over the next days, Jeannette thanks the many friends and relatives, especially Al and Mary Della Penna, who offered sympathy and encouragement. She seems particularly pained when Johnny is forced to drive into the city to turn in his police equipment, and vows, once he is vindicated, to go to the police commissioner with the full story. She thinks of calling someone she knows at CBS News but reconsiders.

SUNDAY OCT. 29—Received Communion with Johnny—first time together at church for a long time—Good feeling—drive into Bronx to visit Mom C at Albert Einstein Hosp—considering serious illness she looked surprisingly good—Johnny rec'd phone call to have coffee with old friend from Syosset—Johnny suspicious— not to trust anyone except lawyer—

    MON OCT. 30—John left to meet Warren Donovan—at moment "Knight in Shining Armor"—intermediary for DA— Johnny's left eye feels as if lid getting stuck closed—keep telling myself maybe a good lawyer (Barry S—??) always presents worst so when things turn out well he looks good—

Two days later, exploratory surgery on Johnny's mother indicates that the cancer has spread too far for treatment. The next morning Johnny drives in to the DA's office for the meeting arranged by Warren Donovan and follows Barry Slotnick out the door when they pressure him to testify against Caccia. He comes home to find a sloppily scribbled letter in his mailbox with a return address of *Wrecking Lot, Brooklyn,* an obvious reference to the news accounts of Gold's bug in the auto-wrecking lot. The flourishing signature at the end is illegible.

Hi John I' you Mother Fucke crook cop Know you was no Mother Fucken god all you Bravery was Joke and crooken I know all one day we o' would get you. When you spit in Win come back in your Face. You never miss Water untill Well go tired What is profect a man go gain Hold World and loss Soul is Soul is life you would Be up for perection [?] get you monthly payment and all Big money But god say no Job is Wort until my change come I say have some-

thing on you D.A. office on you know you was no good Rember
this all Rome haven end is Side of story how [?] W.R. and you W.?
Well I will get you job pumping Shit you Bum

THE CASE THEY ARRESTED ME for, that robbery in a store by three
women, was this little piddly nothing you'd never in a thousand
years think twice about.

Not long after the Havermeyer homicide, I went into the Robbery Squad in Brooklyn's Twelfth Detective Division, which covered three big precincts, Carnarsie, Flatbush, and Crown Heights.
But back while I was in Narcotics, I had a stool named Herbie
Mandel, and got to know him and his wife, Phyllis, pretty well.
Phyllis was born in Israel, and Herbie was Jewish too, although I
don't know where he was born. Herbie dealt in credit cards, coun-
terfeit, stolen and so forth, and did very well. As my stool, he
passed along information about drug dealers—people selling from
an apartment, or a certain spot in a park between five and six at
night where people coming home from work would score. Not big-
time stuff, but helpful, and in exchange he got left alone as far as
his credit cards went. His wife, who worked in a dress shop, also
had contacts and would pass along stuff, so when we were in
touch I'd usually see them both together.

They weren't street people. Herbie drove a Cadillac, and Phyllis
always dressed nice, although their apartment, which I'd been to
a few times, wasn't anything special.

After a while, I found out that Herbie was also stooling for the
Brooklyn DA's office. He'd say he had to appear up in court but was
sure he'd walk because he had friends over there. He claimed connections right to the top, meaning Eugene Gold himself, but probably was just trying to impress me. I was sure, though, that he had
some kind of access there.

Herbie even said one time I could go to an assistant DA's house
and arrest him on the spot if I wanted, because Phyllis and him
had been there smoking with the guy and knew where he kept his
stash. I told him I wasn't touching any assistant DA and that was

the end of that, except after my arrest the same assistant DA was very active in my case. I was always dying to say to him, I could have locked you up back then, you bastard. I could have sent you away for a long, long time.

Once I transferred into Robbery, I didn't see the Mandels much, although sometimes I'd drop by the clothing store where Phyllis worked to say hello. So when the robbery occurred there, Phyllis called the station and said she wanted to speak to Detective Cuomo. The clerical man asked if I'd take the call and I said, Sure, she used to be one of my informants. Normally, of course, the case would have gone to whoever happened to catch it.

These three women, Phyllis tells me, stole something like two hundred dollars from the pocketbook of the owner, but Phyllis got their license number. The crazy thing was that one of the women had even given her name to Phyllis, and turned out to be Mrs. Barone, the wife of some small-time Mafia guy in the area. I take the information down and a few days later—this was no big deal, after all, a couple hundred bucks—Phyllis comes to sign the complaint. We then charge the women, and before long the husband, Leo Barone, shows up at the station house and comes upstairs looking for me, saying, Who the fuck is this Cuomo guy, where is he, who does he think he's messing with?

Now, Leo Barone was just this real street punk, this petty hood in the Anthony Albano family, but he starts telling me I can't arrest his wife, don't I know who he is and what connections he has? We exchange some pretty heated words until he finally leaves when I tell him to get out of the office before I throw him down the stairs.

He recounts this, by the way, on the tape produced later on, because by now DA Gold has the famous bug set up in a trailer in that wrecking lot. Barone says on the tape, Hey, I went to see this Cuomo guy and he threatened to throw me down the fucking stairs, he's a real bitch, you can't get nowhere with him.

Eventually the three women appear in court, but meanwhile two things happen. One, Phyllis gets operated on for breast cancer. I didn't even know this, because we weren't in touch anymore, but find out she's in the hospital when I try to contact her a few days before the trial to make sure she knows the date, and only then re-alize she won't be able to appear. Two, another detective comes up to me asking about the case. I only knew the guy by name, but of course it's Ralph Caccia. He says, Hey, John, can't we do some-thing for those three women? I say, What do you mean, what are we supposed to do? He sort of hems and haws about wouldn't it be nice if the women didn't get into trouble over nothing. I tell him we have the complaint, we have the complainant, and that's the end of our conversation. He never mentions money, never talks about a payoff, anything like that.

I was naturally suspicious, but he kept everything very general, and I figure maybe he's just a friend of one of the women. That was the only time I ever talked to Caccia, about anything, until we were both arrested and he made that call from the DA's office, complaining about the fat envelope he delivered every Christmas, and gave me a ride home.

On the day the three women go to court, I tell the prosecutor that Phyllis, the complainant, won't appear because she's in the hospital. I figure the case would be postponed, which is the usual procedure if a complainant can't appear. But this time the judge confers with the lawyers and the next thing I know, Bang, Case dismissed.

I never really knew why it happened like that. I do know, though, that I had nothing to do with Phyllis being in the hospital and unable to come, and that I never asked for the dismissal. I wasn't really surprised by it, though. What the hell, seven people had shown up that morning—the judge, the three women, their lawyer, the prosecutor, and me. Why would any judge, with hun-dreds of backed-up cases on his docket, haul all these seven people back into court again over some lousy two-hundred-dollar theft?

But this was the source of all my future troubles, eventually leading to the charge against me that I had taken a bribe to get the case against these women dismissed.

One of the few nice things after my arrest was the Detective En-dowment Association coming forward and contributing something like three thousand dollars toward my lawyer's fee. They'll do that if they feel some detective is getting a raw deal.

Another interesting thing was that Phyllis called to tell me the cops banged on her door in the middle of that same night they dragged me out, only she refused to let them in and sneaked out and hid somewhere. What they wanted, I'm sure, was to get a statement from her about how I didn't pursue the robbery of her store diligently enough, or pooh-poohed her complaint in order to get the three women off. Of course, none of that was true, and Phyllis would have said so. But that may have been why they hung around until almost noon before arraigning us. They were waiting for Phyllis to come and make their case for them, and now, looking back, I wonder if maybe that would've solved everything, for Phyllis to show up and say the whole thing was just a load of crap. Maybe if she hadn't run off and hid—although I certainly can't blame her for it—I would have been back on duty the next day, getting apologies from everyone concerned.

After that, the DA's people never contacted her again. Maybe they realized that nothing she'd ever say was going to help them.

Meanwhile, the charges against me were real heavy, so not only was I a suspended cop, with no source of income to support my family, but I also, according to Slotnick, faced a possible twelve to fifteen years in prison. Maybe worst of all, no one, not my lawyer, certainly not anyone in the DA's office, seemed in the least rush to get anything done. Everything just dragged on and on, excruciating, while all this time I was scurrying around looking for work, for anything I could get. Only every place I went, I had to explain everything all over again, which is enough in itself to drive you crazy, especially when you know half of them don't believe a word you're saying.

For a while I drove one of those airport limousines. Then my old friend from Op Two-Five in Harlem who I was still close to, Howie Hundgeon, helped me get work driving a huge construction truck for a subway tunnel being built under the East River. I think they're still building it. The truck was this humongous monster with all these giant wheels, and sometimes I'd just shit at the thought of driving it through all that traffic and those narrow city streets. Christ, I wasn't any truck driver, or limousine driver either, grubbing for tips. I was a detective. I'd been on the force eighteen years. I won commendations. I won awards. What the hell had happened to my life?

SUNDAY NOV 5—Went to church so angry—late on top of it—had words about condition of house—have let things go—stomach in knots—sharp discomfort on sides and back—appointment with Dr. B. Monday—went into city with Bobby and Marianne to visit Mom C—how she is suffering—Dear God be merciful to her—

MON NOV 6—Dr. B. diagnosed pains as muscular—waited on pins and needles for Johnny return tonite—doctor suggests cobalt treatments for Mom—Johnny strongly against the discomfort—what use if cancer terminal?—Everything seems so hopeless at times—both restless during the night—so many thoughts going through our heads—Suspect a car watching house—possibly DA office—why! ! more harassment—

TUES NOV 7—Looks as though so-called "Knight in Shining Armor" W.D. may have betrayed Johnny—hard to believe—Johnny so trusting—Al and Mary Della Penna (God bless) came over—Johnny feels so comfortable with Al—really great guy—Al read copy of wiretap—unbelievable language—those people must be lowest of low—God pity them—they will surely burn for what they are—Johnny took sleeping pill to get nite's sleep—

THURS NOV 9—Continued feeling of being watched or followed—at times fear for the children's safety—& Johnny's & mine—Johnny very restless tonite—apprehensive of hearing tomorrow—mother sinking each day right before his eyes—concerned about jobs and bills.

FRI NOV 10—Waited all day to hear what happened at hearing—spoke to Mom C on phone—didn't sound too good—Johnny came home really down—hearing postponed till Nov. 30—DA's office wants more time to review case—what case!!!—sometimes

I think lawyer isn't interested enough in case to push—Johnny must get a job somewhere—we're running low—bringing nothing in—(I reread this diary and realize how cynical I've become—bitter and suspicious—little trust but for a very few—)

TUES NOV 14—Johnny's eye troubling him something awful—also his stomach—nerves I hope—scans the want ads and his face reveals nothing but heartache—even some of neighbors who were friendly turn their heads—DAM—everyone—everyone—TV—Radio newspapers—will retract!

FRI NOV 24—Johnny still doesn't have anything definite about a job—leads that cousin Al gave him all fell through, all from former policemen—Lousy, lousy world—can't enjoy anything anymore—

SUN NOV 26—Met Sarah at church and thanked her for our turkey true Christian act of charity—Johnny brought home 2 boxes of canned goods given by Joe Greco—collected for those in need they will help—don't know how long it will be till we run dry—

SUN DEC 3—Another terrible day—TV blasting all day with football—terrible arguing with Danny, Marianne and Johnny—all think I'm insane—really at end of my ropes—dear God—I do need strength—

THE HEARING FIRST POSTPONED to November 30 is now put off to December 15 as the DA's office finally indicts Johnny, along with Ralph Caccia, for receiving bribes, official misconduct, receiving unlawful gratuities, and conspiracy. This naturally produces another outpouring of publicity: 2 DETECTIVES AND 7 OTHERS INDICTED IN MAFIA INQUIRY.

I'M MEETING WITH Barry Slotnick maybe ten, fifteen times, but we still haven't seen all the wiretap stuff, just snippets that've been run in the papers, so really don't know what we were facing. But Barry would say he wanted to see me, or I'd think of a question I wanted to ask, and that'd mean getting into the car and driving all the way into the city and paying tolls and parking and waiting an hour or so to maybe see him for two or three minutes after he got out of court, or between phone calls.

With all these meetings and delays, I'm naturally worried about his fee climbing higher and higher. But by this time my mother had died, and through arrangements made long before between my sister and brother and me, I'm the one who gets the house. The lawyer who'd recommended Barry to me was handling the property sale, so Barry knew what was happening on that end and keeps telling me, Don't worry about my fee. When the house is sold you'll have the money to cover it.

Finally, seeing how the police and DA Gold were stalling, Barry comes up with a way of forcing their hand. Go down, he tells me, and put in for early retirement. That gives them thirty days either to grant you full benefits or put you on departmental trial. If they want to try you, they have to show us whatever evidence they have—which is how we finally got our hands on the tapes from Gold's bug.

These tapes had been played up as the key evidence against me from the beginning. You know, DA GOLD USES ELECTRONIC BUG TO GET GOODS ON BROOKLYN MAFIA, and when Caccia and I were arrested, the stories all claimed it was the tapes that implicated us in getting the three women off on that robbery charge, although Caccia was in trouble over other things too.

This bug that Gold bragged about was set up in a crummy trailer in a junkyard, an auto-wrecking yard out in Canarsie which Gold said was the summit headquarters for the Brooklyn Mafia, and maybe it was. It stood behind this big metal fence with barbed wire at the top and German shepherd guard dogs, but the place itself was real junky, with wrecks and rusty cars everywhere. According to the papers, the neighborhood people wondered why all these fancy Cadillacs kept pulling up to this broken-down trailer in the middle of a junkyard.

What I got a kick out of was the *Times* pointing out that DA

Gold arrived for the press conference in *his* Cadillac, probably prancing and preening all over the place showing off the bug to the reporters.

My question naturally was, Where the hell do I fit in any of this?

It wasn't easy finding out. The bug in the ceiling had been picking up everything said in this trailer for six months, and had produced 1.6 million feet of tape. Barry demanded everything relevant to me, and also questioned me very hard on the whole thing. Were you ever in that junkyard, Johnny? Were you ever in that trailer? Did you ever have contact with those people?

No, I told him, I never been in that yard. I never been in that trailer. I didn't even know it existed until I read about it in the paper. You just wait and see, I told Barry. They may have their 1.6 million feet of tape, but I'll tell you one thing they don't have. They don't have my voice on it.

Eventually Gold's office produces excerpts from the tape and we listen to it very carefully. Nowhere do we hear anything that sounds even remotely like my voice. Nowhere does anyone claim to be me, and nowhere do the police, who'd identified the various voices on the transcript, identify anyone as Detective Cuomo.

Caccia's voice, though, is everywhere. Not only does this detective go to the trailer regularly, but he was a real buddy of those guys. He jokes around with them, not only Barone, the small-time hood whose wife I arrested, but Anthony Albano himself, the big shot. And they don't call him Detective Caccia, they call him Ralphie. He tells Albano about wanting to go to school to become a lawyer, stuff like that. At one point Caccia says to Albano, on the tape, Thank you, Tony. I love you, Tony. I love you.

So they got Caccia via his own voice, his own words. The tape also has Caccia asking for six hundred dollars to get the detective on the case to go easy on the three women—although he never mentions me by name. And the minute the judge dismisses the case against the women, he runs to the trailer and says, See, I took care of everything.

So now we finally discover what they think they got on me—

some Mafia patsy detective, Caccia, was taking money and claiming to be giving it to me to go easy on Barone's wife. And then when the judge dismisses the charges against her, Caccia brags on the tape that he had arranged it all through me. But the only actual mention of me on the tape is Barone saying how, when he came to see me, I threatened to throw him down the stairs.

Still, since the women's trial was what the DA was using against me, I always wondered why Barry Slotnick never seemed interested in getting the full story about how the dismissal had come about. I felt he could have easily shown, one, that dropping the charges was perfectly understandable under the circumstances and, two, that I certainly wasn't the one who'd asked to have them dropped. But he seemed to feel that since I had never gone to that mob trailer or had anything to do with those people, or had shown up even once on all that million feet of tape, that I had nothing to worry about.

So all Slotnick says after we review the tapes is, We're set, John. Don't worry about a thing. Everything's coming up roses.

Only the delays go on and on, and I can't pay Barry because the other lawyer hasn't sold the house yet. That really got me, this house we all grew up in, that my mother and father lived in for forty years, being sold to pay a lawyer to get me off charges that should never have been made in the first place.

Tues Dec 12—Johnny had long talk with Barry, planning, preparing for trial—Barry suggested a private investigator should be hired—more expenses—something else for Johnny to contend with—I don't understand Barry's methods, or some of his answers—Johnny rec'd $175.00 from Terry O'Brien collected from men of 12th Detective Division—Very difficult for Johnny to accept charity like this and yet he knows it puts food on table for us all—

THEY STRUGGLE TO make sense of the rumors passed on by Warren Donovan, by Assistant Police Commissioner McCarthy, by the head of the Detectives Association, by Barry Slotnick and his web of contacts, by Johnny's police friends. On any given day, any or all of these might assure Johnny of their belief in his innocence and their certainty that he'll be vindicated; or tell him the root of his trouble is DA Gold, or the PD, the Mafia, his own lawyer, Caccia's lawyer; that he should at all costs avoid the expense and danger of a trial, that his only hope lay in a trial; that Slotnick was his savior, that Slotnick was his assassin.

TUES DEC 19—Terrible weather—really fed up to here with everything—to top it, went to Klein's (seedy store) in Commack to do a little shopping and tried to charge a $6.00 sweater—after waiting 1/2 hr they tell me no authorization to charge—the gall of them—no balance due—

Johnny goes to Klein's and learns that the credit manager closed their account two days after his arrest, based on what he read in the newspaper. Slotnick reports the DA won't dismiss the charges unless Johnny testifies against Caccia, which both Slotnick and Johnny still view as a compromise of their position. Slotnick sees no hope of a trial before March or April.

SUN DEC 24—gifts very lean this year—Johnny constantly complains of burning pains in stomach—sounds like ulcer—couldn't eat much at all—not like Christmas Eves of other years—became engaged 22 years ago tonite—

Just before the New Year, Johnny goes into the Bronx to clean out the cellar of his mother's house, a tedious and painful task. In January, Slotnick, who'd predicted a trial in March or April, now says the trial date will be *set* then, and asks for an additional thirty-five hundred dollars beyond what Johnny has already given him. Al Della Penna urges Johnny to stay with Slotnick, saying he's gone too far to pull out now. Their conversation is cut short when Al is called out to a homicide scene.

Tues Jan 9—Johnny phoned Barry twice—They (DA & PD) are just waiting for him to break—or come crawling to them—Do wish a job would turn up for him—He gets so bored around the house—a lot to do but can't seem to get in groove of things—

In mid-January Johnny is hired as a security officer at Kennedy Airport at $3.50 an hour, "great compared to limousine service." After a few weeks the job fizzles out and he remains without work until he starts driving the construction truck at the subway-tunnel site in late March.

Sat Mar 3—Long time since writing—have been in slump past few weeks—Johnny depressed—I feel and sense his every mood but try to remain silent so as not to add to his restlessness—Barry called last evening to notify John about an appearance in court Monday—routine for anyone out on bail—but Barry will be on vacation in Mexico—

Sat Mar 17—Johnny really low—so very disappointed in Barry, who said weeks ago he submitted briefs to DA's office—now says he's working on briefs—This is tearing at Johnny's very soul—I want to go down Tuesday to meet Barry but Johnny doesn't want me there—I feel left out and not involved—

Wed May 2—Almost one month since my last entry—Johnny spoke to Barry on 25th of April re: case being dismissed in Asst. DA Hynes' office with no strings attached and assurance of reinstatement—Now Barry changes his story to John's case being dismissed if he testifies against Caccia—In addition Barry insists on full payment of remaining $7500.00 before case is dismissed or possibly goes to trial. He and Johnny have had many words and Johnny doesn't trust him—Barry certainly cannot defend him rightfully after all the squabbling between them—

Jeannette makes no further entries for almost three weeks. Then, for the first time, she connects Johnny's arrest with the Havermeyer case.

THURS MAY 24—Tomorrow Johnny meets with Barry to set a trial date—also to sever his case from Caccia—If they had severed months ago, all would be over by now—How those * * * * *at DA's office are continuing this charade is unbelievable—At times Johnny gives in to all the pressures by crying openly—such hate & bitterness I have for all connected with his arrest. Why Barry up till now has not investigated further back to the homicide case Johnny and George Kane investigated in which the very same DA people insisted on closing a case dealing with stock theft and also a murder—Johnny crossed them at that time and sometimes "revenge" for those in power can be so easy—

AFTER A LOT OF UPS and downs along the way, we find a buyer for my mother's house and I receive a check for the money, and the next day—can you believe this? the very next morning—I get a call from Barry, who must have been tipped off by his lawyer friend the minute the sale went through, saying, Hi, Johnny, how are you? I got great news. The whole case is going to be dismissed out of hand and you're being reinstated by the police. So after all this time, from October until June, Barry finally gets a judge to look at the DA Gold's evidence, and one-two-three the judge throws out the whole case.

But we still aren't out of the woods, because the judge didn't have the authority to reinstate me, but just to recommend it to the PD, which he did, so I still had to go to a hearing on that. Even before then, in July, I had to go before the grand jury on the whole Mafia case, maybe because DA Gold hoped I'd perjure myself or get tangled up in my story, but I just went and told the truth and had no problem at all.

In some ways, things seemed to be finally going our way but, believe me, this was the worst stretch of all, because after the judge threw out the charges I figured, That's it, it's over, I'm free and clear. But no, everything just dragged on endlessly, one thing after another, one postponement after another, and it was along this stretch that I became totally convinced that someone—Gold,

I'm sure—had just decided to torment me. A judge had already thrown out the case, so there *wasn't* any more case, yet they just wouldn't let me go. In July of '73 I had the grand jury. In August I had the PD hearing, where the assistant commissioner reinstated me—but only if nothing bad came out at the PD trial.

The PD trial was set for October, then put off until after the Caccia trial. In February—we're now in 1974—Slotnick, for whatever reason, delayed the department trial until March 1. Then it was put off a couple more times until March 13—a full seventeen months after my arrest and suspension.

The police review board conducting the trial looked over the evidence and heard some witnesses, including Phyllis Mandel. Then the chairman says he wants a word with Barry in private. Barry gives me the thumbs up, like saying, Terrific, we're in great shape. But after they confer, Slotnick whispers to me, You're going to have to plead guilty to one charge. They'll dismiss everything else if you just plead guilty to failing to sign in properly at court, which was one of those chickenshit charges they'd listed against me back at the beginning, along with failing to file a change of address.

At this point, after all that other shit, I'm at the end of my rope. I'm a nervous wreck and in no mood to give an inch to anybody. So I tell Slotnick, No, I'm not pleading guilty to a single goddamn thing. I didn't do anything wrong, and they know it. I'm not giving them any easy way out to save their face after what they've put me through.

Look, don't be a jerk, Slotnick says, not angry, real quiet and friendly, real buddy-buddy. You're getting back pay, full reinstatement to rank, everything. I tell him I ain't gonna do it. He says, Aw, c'mon, John, what are you being so stubborn for? What difference does it make that you take this chickenshit charge? When I still hold out, he tries another tack. He says, John, if you don't go along, they're not going to reinstate you, you're not gonna get your back pay—which was a substantial sum, ten or twelve thousand dollars—and you're also gonna be dismissed from the force and lose your whole pension for the rest of your life.

They can't do that, I said. They can, he said. We'll sue 'em, I said. Do you know what that will cost, John? Do you know what that will entail? And I'll tell you the truth, John, I wouldn't handle that case. It'd be a waste of everybody's time and money over nothing.

I just cracked. I couldn't deal with it anymore. I was a wreck. Okay, I said. I'll do it. So I pleaded guilty to not signing in properly at court. The chairman said, Okay, that's it, everything else is dismissed. You're reinstated.

To this day, I wonder what would have happened if my mother hadn't died, if the house hadn't been sold, if I didn't have the money to pay the lawyer. Would it have dragged on forever before Barry got around to doing what he could have done months back, as soon as we saw the tapes?

I thanked Phyllis Mandel for standing up for me at the hearing, but after that we weren't in touch until some years later, when her husband, Herbie, who may or may not still have been stooling for DA Gold's office, got incarcerated on a big Federal charge. I talked to Phyllis on the phone, and she was really feeling down, all nerves, can't sleep and worried about her baby, and I do what I can to cheer her up and everything. A month later I read in the paper that Phyllis and the baby are both found dead in her apartment, the same apartment where I visited them on more than one occasion.

I couldn't believe it, and it still haunts me, it'll always haunt me, whether her being killed had anything to do with her helping me or was another thing altogether. It was no amateur hit, absolutely cold-blooded. They shot her four or five times in the head, and the baby twice, lying in its crib. The baby too, it was incredible. The case was never solved. Those never are.

I couldn't help remembering what happened to Havermeyer, and Richard Gruber, our chief suspect, and his widow and her mother and father, the Ramonas, who were all taken exactly the same way, in a mob hit that never got solved. And I wonder, you

know, whether maybe the reason I'm still alive is that we never did
figure out all the connections to the big shots in that case.

It's a scary story, and sure, in trying to come to grips with
all its convolutions, Johnny indulges in some guesswork as
to motives. Nonetheless, all this happened, confirmed by police and court records, newspaper accounts, contemporane-
ous notes, letters and diaries. But what of Johnny's last point,
figuring out the connections? Are there connections?

First, some documentable facts:

—Johnny got arrested in his own living room after being
roused out of bed after midnight. The arresting officers did
not produce a warrant or inform him of any charges against
him.

—No one ever justified the urgency of the arrest. Johnny
posed no imminent public threat.

—Johnny's voice is never heard on the million and a half
feet of tape produced by Gold's bug at the wrecking yard. He
is directly mentioned only once, when Leo Barone, after an-
grily arguing with him at the police station, complains about
how tough Johnny is. Even indirectly he's only referred to
when Caccia brags about his influence with the unnamed
detective handling the robbery charges against the three
women.

—No evidence was ever produced that implicated Johnny
in the freeing of the three women, although their release
was the sole basis of all the accusations against him.

—The DA's office never produced any evidence to support
their initial accusations, and when Johnny finally appeared
in court, the judge summarily dismissed all charges and recommended reinstatement.

—At both the hearing and the trial conducted by the
NYPD, all charges were again dismissed—although Johnny
agreed to plead guilty of failing to sign in at court.

—He was returned to duty at full rank and with all back pay and benefits.

These facts are clear. Why, then, was he arrested?

Johnny and Jeannette both feel, not unreasonably, that people within the DA's office and Brooklyn's gangland organizations were out to get him. They assume he was targeted because of his vigorous investigation of the many ramifications—including arson, stock theft, suicide, and multiple homicides—of the murder of the insurance broker Havermeyer.

I have to admit I'm not wholly convinced of the connection even though, as a writer, I find myself *wanting* to believe that Johnny and Jeannette's months of agony resulted from some kind of operatic thirst for vengeance, spawned by an unholy alliance between Brooklyn's gangland lords and unscrupulous, politically ambitious DAs. It could happen. We amiably witness more outlandish events on every newscast, read stranger stories in even the smallest small-town weekly.

Still, I can't find that one persuasive link between the weird outgrowths of the Havermeyer murder and the baffling fact of Johnny's arrest and persecution. For me, I guess, the major problem results from the suspicion that if truly powerful forces were out to get Johnny, they would have easily and quickly destroyed him.

What I'm left with, unfortunately, is a rather lame and undramatic assumption. I think the DA's office made a horrendous mistake in arresting Johnny, being taken in by Caccia's bragging on the tape. So they orchestrated their midnight raid on Johnny's home, hauled him through three counties, slapped handcuffs on him, and distributed their self-congratulatory releases to the media representatives they'd made sure would be on hand. They wanted a big splash and got it, with headlines and pictures everywhere and Eugene Gold receiving the kind of racket-busting DA publicity that goes a long way on the New York political scene.

And then, to the accompaniment of a lot of sinking sensations in the DA's office, they realized they didn't have a single piece of evidence against this decorated veteran detective that they'd arrested with such fanfare. So they shrugged. Hell, they got Caccia, didn't they, and one out of two ain't bad. Knowing they couldn't convict Johnny, they never tried. A year and a half later, with no coverage at all, they shrugged again by not contesting Johnny's exoneration, settling for nothing more than the pathetic, almost ludicrous face-saving gesture of that signing-in charge.

They'd resorted to the time-honored bureaucratic stratagem of letting their mistakes die quietly of old age. Do I believe a big-time, big-city DA's office could exhibit such bungling incompetence? Well, these were the people that sent the cops roaring off into the night to bang on the door of a house that Johnny hadn't lived in for years. Organizational charts do not normally feature a department responsible for publicly admitting mistakes, let alone attempting to correct them. Bureaucracies ignore the messes they create in the confidence that even the dirtiest will eventually fade from everyone's memory and concern. There is no arrogance in the world like bureaucratic arrogance.

Dull as it is, that's my explanation, although I'd still rather believe Johnny's. Anyhow, since this is his story, he gets to finish it in his own words.

AS FOR GOLD, well, a few years later I was working as director of night security at the Waldorf—which is another story I can tell you if you're interested—when DA Gold showed up for some function. I knew he was coming because we always got a list of prominent guests ahead of time, the mayor, the governor, various heads of state, and in this case the Brooklyn DA. I positioned myself near him and the whole time stared right into his face, hoping he'd start wondering, Who is that guy? and then come over and say, Don't I know you from somewhere? Yeah, I'd say, I'm the guy you arrested on that lousy trumped-up charge that practically destroyed my family and ruined my whole life. Remember? Detective Cuomo. John Cuomo, who hates your guts.

Caccia? I'm not sure if he was actually convicted of anything, because there may have been some kind of deal or plea bargain or whatever, but I'm pretty sure he was thrown off the force. To tell you the truth, I never really followed up on what happened to him. I really wasn't interested. I was just sick of the whole business and once I got reinstated with my back pay and everything, I just wanted to get the whole thing out of my mind. Like I said at the beginning, it's been all these years and I've never really gone through the whole story for anyone because I couldn't take having to relive it all again.

But let me tell you what happened to Eugene Gold. First off, he ran for attorney general of New York State but, thank God, lost. (Barry Slotnick also ran one time, for the Republican nomination, but didn't get it.) Then there's this other thing about Gold that I gotta tell you about. I never liked the guy, of course, and the whole time I was aware of him I had this really funny feeling about him. It was nothing I could put my finger on, but he always struck me as somehow odd, even creepy. Well, when Eugene Gold was fifty-nine years old and no longer DA, he got arrested at a law-and-order convention in Nashville for molesting a ten-year-old girl. At his trial, the judge agreed to give him two years probation if he admitted his guilt and put himself under psychiatric care, which he did, and that's the last I ever heard of the son of a bitch.

SECTION III

KEEPING IN TOUCH

AT THE TIME OF Johnny's arrest and through those eighteen months of his dark night of the soul, I was living in California. When I heard from my mother that Johnny was in some vague trouble, I wrote to wish him well but did not hear back and never had much idea what he and Jeannette were going through until he told me the whole story for this book. Nor did I ever understand Al's seven-year separation from his family until we sat down together a couple of years ago.

Over time, it hasn't been easy keeping in touch. Maybe we just weren't very good at it. For the first two decades of my career, I taught at universities in Indiana, Arizona, British Columbia, and California, and the cousins' traditional week-end get-togethers did not begin, unfortunately, until much later. Sylvia and I raised our five kids in those westerly settings, a continent's distance from Long Island, where Johnny and Jeannette were raising their three children, Al and Mary their four. All the children are grown now, many married, some with their own children, and a mere listing of where they live says something about the explosively outward forces within families today.

Johnny has a son in Virginia, a daughter who's just moved from Illinois to Arizona, a son on Long Island. Al's children have stayed closest to home. He has two daughters and a son on Long Island, another son in New Jersey. Mine, born in Arizona and British Columbia, are the most far-flung: a daughter in California, a son in New York City, a son in Louisiana, a daughter in Amherst, Massachusetts, a son in Maine.

John and Jeannette have been married forty-two years. Al and Mary were divorced after twenty-four, and he's been married to Carrie for ten. Sylvia and I, after forty years, are separated.

Working on this book, I've discovered how much I value, and have been shaped by, that early closeness with Johnny and Al and the other cousins—Johnny's older sister and brother, Jean and Alfred, and Al's older sister, Jo, who used to "fix me up" with her coworkers at the insurance company.

I've learned a few things recently about Johnny and Al, and I'm sure, given how closely we've collaborated, they've picked up some choice insights about me. If nothing else, they've got some inkling about how I write and how I feel about this energizing and frustrating craft and art which, after all, must seem as strange to them as chasing drug pushers or extricating a knife from a dead woman's throat will always seem to me.

This book has brought us closer. I don't feel we have to *keep* in touch anymore. We are in touch. But I understand better now how vast the continental distances remain between the worlds that even the closest of us separately inhabit.

A DAY
AT THE CRIME LAB

AL TOOK ME OUT to Hauppauge for the first time at nine-thirty on a bright, surprisingly warm February morning in 1993. We drove from the western campus of Suffolk Community College in Brentwood, Long Island, where he'd just taught his eight A.M. class. The Crime Lab shares the building with, and is under the direction of, the county medical examiner. Only eight years old, the broad stone-and-glass structure stands two stories high with plenty of open space around it. Precinct Four headquarters and the County Office Building are also situated on the sizable site off the multilane Veterans Highway. Come spring, Al assured me, the trees would leaf out and flowers instead of snow would border the walks surrounding the lab. He led me up the wide steps into the expansive marbled lobby with a single receptionist, Lil Yokelson, seated behind a desk far back in a corner. Al greeted her with a "Hi, Lil," and headed toward the other corner, where he removed from his jacket something resembling a credit card and held it against a square of translucent glass on the wall. "Voilà," he said and pushed open the white door alongside, leading me into a room with several secretaries. "You can mostly be on your own, George, and talk to anybody you want, but maybe you oughta start with Vince Crispino. He's the boss, and said he'd be willing to chat."

Vincent Crispino, director of the Crime Lab, is dressed much like Al, in his office wear: crisp shirt and tie, pressed but comfortable-looking suit, and I wonder if Al shouldn't have prepped me on the dress code. I've been around a university town too long, and my sport shirt and sleeveless sweater seem wrong, lacking in seriousness. Maybe to make me more comfortable, or because the heating system is efficiently doing its job, Crispino removes his jacket and clasps his hands on his desk, his tie still neatly in place. Coffee? Coke? Graying a bit, with a trim, grayish mustache, Crispino looks to be in his forties, thick-chested and solidly built. His expression is alert and businesslike, but he's clearly at ease, used to talking with reporters, teachers, visiting pros from out-of-town.

Aware that he's now dealing with an amateur, he patiently explains that although his facility is often called a police lab, that's a misnomer, even though a few of his people, including Al, are "sworn," and he himself spent five years as a policeman. But he's now the civilian director of a civilian institution operating under the civilian authority of the county medical examiner. It's not a typical setup, but no setup is typical throughout the country. Some crime labs are run by police but manned by civilians. Others may be all civilian or all sworn. To further confuse matters, in some jurisdictions the medical examiner's position doesn't even exist, its responsibilities handled by a popularly elected coroner.

"The crucial point," Crispino said, "is that we don't answer to the police, and it's not our responsibility to prove anything one way or the other. Sure, the police and prosecutors are very interested in what we dig up, but so are the defense lawyers, and we're legally obligated to give both the same access. Usually the defense will say, Let me have a copy of everything, and we simply give them the whole file. Even in court, if the jury thinks we're feeding the prosecution everything but holding back on the defense, they'll stop trusting us. We try to lay out the evidence so thoroughly and fairly that neither side has any reason to question our performance."

Crispino holds undergraduate and graduate degrees in medical technology and forensic science, and came to Suffolk County in 1985 after working in hospitals and crime labs throughout New York State. Everywhere, he said, funding's a problem. "We have all sorts of specialized needs just for space alone: vaults and refrigerated storage areas, a garage for examining vehicles, rooms where clothing can be dried and processed. We need big receiving and loading areas, and Al uses plenty of space just test-firing."

About thirty-five men and women work at the lab, twice as many as when Crispino arrived, and since their technical and scientific operations have grown increasingly sophisticated, every new breakthrough means new equipment and new, highly trained personnel. "There's no point spending half my capital budget on some new wonder device if I can't hire anybody to operate it. Al, you know, would love to hook into a system that'd let him immediately compare a bullet to a nationwide open-case file, but it'd take an incredible financial commitment, not only here but in every city and county in the country, to get that system up and going. Meanwhile, we try to keep up with the caseload, and do what we can with what we have."

Jack Mario is an associate director of the Chemistry section, and like Al takes his turn leading crime-scene investigative teams.

"The instant a homicide is reported in Suffolk County," he

told me in his office next to the Chem Lab, "certain things happen very quickly. First, there's the immediate response with as many uniformed police, and as many detectives, as needed, including the police ID section to collect fingerprints and footwear and tire impressions, and to take still and video pictures. A senior Homicide investigator is promptly put in charge of the investigation, providing a clear chain of command from the outset. The county can also provide boats and helicopters and emergency vehicles, including earth movers and backhoes and other heavy equipment to tear up cement, knock down doors and walls, dredge sewers or bodies of water. Then there's the lab itself, starting with the ME and the crime-scene units and eventually including a wide variety of facilities to analyze the evidence brought in to them. With major crimes, particularly homicide, we bring an awful lot of brain and muscle into play in a very brisk fashion, so if you're planning to bump someone off, I'd suggest there are better places to try it than around here."

As part of all this, the Chem Lab handles three or four thousand cases a year, almost all involving drugs. Cocaine is by far the most common narcotic, marijuana the favorite nonnarcotic. In New York City, fifty miles away, Mario says, you'd run into a lot more heroin and crack. In suburban or college areas, you'd see pills, uppers and downers.

The Chem Lab also examines, on a smaller scale, arson materials, product-tampering evidence, stimulants and depressants, hypodermics, tear gas. At one time, chemists accompanied drug agents out into the streets, prepared to perform instant spot tests. If the agents were making an expensive buy, for instance, they wanted to make sure they were getting the real thing. The undercover agents themselves would offer for sale "crack" that was nothing more than ground-up macadamia nuts.

Chemists no longer accompany agents into drug areas, Mario says: too time-consuming, too expensive, too dangerous. They pretty much stay in the lab, preparing samples, checking readouts, writing reports—except, of course, when some 3 A.M. homicide sends Jack Mario riding off with his crime-scene unit.

Both of Al's assistants in Firearms are named George—George Reich and George Krivosta—and George Reich talks to me about being called in as an outside expert in a widely publicized Teaneck, New Jersey, manslaughter trial. He doesn't generally like doing this because it often means disputing the testimony of other firearms experts, but got involved this time because he felt a moral obligation. A Teaneck police officer admitted firing two shots that killed a young man but claimed the young man was threatening him with a gun. The prosecution disputed this, saying the victim's arms were raised in surrender, and brought in two firearms consultants to testify that the bullet holes in the victim's jacket proved that his arms were indeed raised when the shots struck.

"I've worked almost twenty years in ballistics in New York City," George Reich tells me, "and all told attended over twenty-five hundred shooting scenes. On the basis of that and my scientific background, my report said there were so many variables that no true expert could possibly devise a valid test based on bullet holes to indicate where his arms were at the moment he was shot.

"What I think my report did was remove the so-called experts, including myself, from the jury's decision-making process and put the emphasis back where I believe it belonged, in the testimony of the witnesses. The trial lasted two months, but the jury took only seven hours to exonerate the policeman. I like to think they agreed that the testimony of so-called experts can only be used up to a point, beyond which common sense and uncontested evidence have to prevail."

Curious about authorities dueling before a jury, I ask Al
for his thoughts on the matter. "It happens all the time," he
says. "You bring in your psychiatrist, I bring in mine. Any
kind of authority you can get, I can get one better. Lawyers
are always looking to undercut the other side's experts,
and I'll tell you, it's usually dry as dust. You state your cre-
dentials, you identify exhibits, you say, Yes, that is my signature on the tag. You identify the casing in the little plastic
bag, you explain what a casing is, you tell exactly where,
when, and how you found it. On and on and on. At big-time,
highly publicized trials, if the TV coverage suddenly breaks
for a commercial and all the reporters run for the bathroom,
you know that some expert witness is about to take the
stand."

And what of George Reich in Teaneck? "George is absolutely first-rate," Al says, "although with all due respect, I
thought the other guys were too."

And the bullet holes in the jacket? Al shrugs. "I never got
the chance to examine them."

Everybody refers to it as the Trace Lab, but its official title is
Criminalistics Laboratory. Even more than in the other units,
walls and doors and cabinets teem with signs:

CAUTION
COMPOUNDS OF HIGH TOXICITY OR CANCER SUSPECT AGENTS

FLAMMABLE
KEEP FLAMES AND HEAT AWAY

DANGEROUS BIOLOGICAL AREA
DO NOT SHUT OFF WITHOUT NOTIFYING LAB CHIEF OR DESIGNEE

"Criminalistics at one time covered everything," explains
Don Dollar, the associate director, "and we still take care of
everything that's not specifically assigned to someone else.

The Firearms people, Serology, Questioned Documents, were all originally under our umbrella before going off on their own. People think of *trace* minerals, *trace* elements, meaning minute quantities, but here it refers to the traces or prints left behind by fingers, footwear, tires. We're also the unit that analyzes paint, glass, hair, and fiber samples."

The four large laboratory tables that run from one side of the room to the other are equipped with sinks and overhead lights and tiers of labeled drawers, the working surfaces seriously overloaded with microscopes, computers, books, files, documents, evidence samples in vials and bottles and boxes and plastic bags.

Hit-and-run accidents, especially those classified as vehicular homicides, give the section much of its work. If the vehicle left the scene without being identified, the lab starts with the paint particles recovered from the debris or the victim's clothing. A new car may only leave behind microscopic traces. With older cars, the paint can come off like cornflakes. Automobile finishes often have seven or more different layers, and each can be identified and classified microscopically, subjected to microchemical analysis, tested for its reaction to visible, infrared, and ultraviolet light.

The battery of tests can identify about 95 percent of paint samples, no matter how minute, as specifically as *Blue metallic GM paint, used only on '89 C and K series trucks and M series vans.* Paint can also link a crowbar to the window that it pried open, a suitcase to a specific automobile trunk. Almost every material has some sort of coating, and when two objects come in contact there's often a transfer of these coatings.

Glass can be analyzed in much the same way as paint, and since different types of glass are used for different purposes, even minute fragments from an accident scene can allow the lab to identify the suspect vehicle as a car with a broken driver's side window and a shattered left headlight. The Trace

Lab can also identify natural and man-made fibers on the basis of fabric type, dyes used, the pattern of any tears or breaks.

Doller shows me the scores of manufacturers' catalogues and fliers used to back up their work on footwear impressions. "When I came here seven years ago, this file was my pet project, but it just takes too much time and can never be complete, what with thousands of manufacturers and suppliers throughout the world."

He holds up for me the remarkably clear shoe prints made in blood when a pair of killers dragged a body across a kitchen floor. "Al was on that case, maybe he'll give you the details. But all he could make out at the scene were these very faint smudges on the linoleum. He wasn't even sure it was blood, let alone footprints. We couldn't remove the linoleum itself so had to do the enhancement right there with Amido black. That's a stain that reacts with the protein in blood to give you beautiful contrasts of everything you see with the naked eye, and a lot you don't. On this print you can actually read the mirror image of the Reebok logo. Also, since we got two distinct patterns, we were able to tell the investigators to look for at least two suspects, probably men from the size of their feet."

In the Questioned Documents room, Jeff Luber explains that his unit gets called in on all sorts of investigations, including homicide and rape, but most often deals with white-collar and harassment crimes, where it's his job to authenticate signatures or handwriting samples, make typewriter comparisons, examine suspected obliterations or alterations on checks and lottery tickets, identify inks and papers.

With handwriting, he likes to have at least five known samples, and prefers twenty or thirty, to discount normal variations. "We're looking at a lot of details, some pretty subtle, of letter shape, size, and construction, connecting strokes, height relationships, spatial orientation, pen lifts. A legitimate signature is fluid and unhesitating, whereas a forger trying to copy something will be very careful to get it right, so you'll find hesitations, heavy inking in spots, a general sense of slow, deliberate movement."

Luber employs a variety of photographic, chemical, and electronic equipment to identify inks and papers, and has a new electrostatic-detection apparatus that can bring out writing on an apparently blank sheet of paper four or five leaves down into a pad when the top sheet's been written on. "Very useful in white-collar crimes," he says, "threats, harassment, even suicides. Sometimes relatives will tear a suicide note off a pad and burn it, not thinking of the sheets underneath."

As for linking typewritten samples to a specific machine, Luber noted that computers had virtually eliminated that kind of sleuthing. "Old typewriter keys could be matched to the letters on a page through all sorts of individualized differences of strike and alignment and damage. With laser printers and ink jets there isn't any strike, and you don't even have a ribbon to work with, so the variations you get are most often manufacturing defects that might occur in hundreds or even thousands of machines." He sounded as if he missed the battered Remingtons and Underwoods of the good old days, which could be traced to their loving owners as easily as a set of fingerprints.

Less than a year ago, the Serology unit at the Crime Lab was split into two parts, with the new combination renamed the Biological Sciences section. The original unit continues to use conventional procedures to examine bodily fluids brought in as evidence, particularly blood, saliva, seminal fluid, and vaginal secretions. Branching off from that, the new DNA unit represents one of the most important advances in investigative techniques since the introduction of fingerprint classification.

Most people these days are aware that DNA—deoxyri-

bonucleic acid—exists in the nucleus of all cells and governs
the transference of genetic characteristics. The pioneering
work of James Watson and Francis Crick a generation ago in
constructing the first model of the DNA molecule, as reported in Watson's best-selling book *The Double Helix* in
1968, brought the subject to widespread public attention.
The theory was first used in police work in the 1970s, as doc-
umented by Joseph Wambaugh in *The Blooding.* Scotland
Yard went to English geneticist Alec Jeffreys for help in their
investigation of a series of rape murders. Using the DNA
analysis of the seminal fluid found in some of the victims,
Jeffreys was able to tell the police that both samples came
from the same person, and that their prime suspect was *not*
that person. The police then started "bleeding" men of a certain age within the community on a voluntary basis so that
Jeffreys could test the samples. Eventually, because the rapist
went to such lengths to get someone else to submit a sample
in his name, he drew the attention of the investigators and
was convicted on the basis of a perfect DNA match between
his blood and the seminal fluid of the killer.

Shortly thereafter private labs began doing DNA analysis
on a contract basis, at first dealing mainly with issues of pa-
ternity but gradually spreading to criminal investigations.

A DNA profile is often compared to a fingerprint, and in
both instances the certainty of identification is based on statistical probability. In other words, you can't *prove* that a fingerprint, or a DNA profile, is unique. But in both cases the
statistical odds are so overwhelming that the chance of a
given sample being exactly duplicated by a sample from another source is practically nonexistent.

In one of Suffolk County's two DNA labs, Joanne Sgueglia
(pronounced *Squeel*-ia), who until last year worked for one
of the few private DNA labs in the country, offers to illustrate
for me the impressive results that can be achieved through a
procedure developed by the FBI. The whole field is young, of
course, and many of the experts, like Sgueglia, are young

people who studied conventional serology and then decided to specialize in this newly emerging discipline. Dark-haired and olive-skinned, athletically trim, Sgueglia speaks directly and unhesitatingly, with a kind of spare clarity that seems focused much more intently on what she's describing than on the person she's talking to.

"But for the FBI procedure you need a large amount of high-quality genetic material, say a bloodstain the size of a dime. There's an even newer method that amplifies a very small sample in order to test it. But to give you an idea of the progress in the field, we're starting a *third* procedure downstairs that combines the first two, using a very small sample to produce extremely high statistical probabilities."

By far the most common tests conducted by the Biological Sciences section are on whole blood, followed by semen from rape cases, and then saliva, and the vast majority of all these are still analyzed via conventional serological techniques. Only a few are subjected to the DNA unit's more precise and comprehensive, but also far slower and more expensive, tests.

"Since any part of the body composed of cells can provide DNA samples, along with the standard bodily fluids, we've also worked on aborted fetal tissue, with skeletal remains, teeth, and bone marrow. Right now, we're testing skeletal remains, trying to determine whether they're of a missing child."

Typically, the DNA unit's role is to show whether or not a specimen from a crime scene came from a certain individual. "To do this," Sgueglia said, "we analyze four areas of the DNA by means of four radioactive 'probes.' With each one we get better and better odds. For instance, probe one might indicate a one-in-ten chance of a match occurring in a given population group. Probe two is far more selective, maybe with odds of one in a thousand. Therefore the chances of a match on *both* probes becomes one in ten thousand. It keeps multiplying, so the odds against an accidental match on all four probes is well up into the millions. The National Research Council is now perfecting a fifth probe, with a certainty factor approaching infinity.

"DNA's impact can be seen in the abrupt plea changes you now get in rape cases," Sgueglia said. "The defendant starts out swearing he never saw the victim before, but as soon as a DNA link is established, he says, Sure I had sex with her, but it was consensual."

To illustrate DNA methodology, Ms. Sgueglia showed me the results from a recent, complicated rape case. "Remember, you're seeing the easy part, which is what the computers and other expensive instruments print out after all the hard work's been done. In spite of the high-tech look, we're still manually making gels and preparing samples. Before we can run any probes, for instance, we've got to isolate the DNA, use a purification technique to clear out extraneous debris, then go through a procedure to see how much DNA we have, and how good it is, in order to decide if it's even worth continuing. At that stage we take the long DNA molecule and essentially cut it into smaller fragments. It's these fragments that are tested against the fragments from the crime scene. None of this is very automated, and all of it is quite painstaking. The four probes require about a week each, and overall it's eight to ten weeks from the time we receive the sample until the results are in."

The case in question involved a victim and four suspected rapists, with the evidence consisting of swabs from both the body and the underclothing of the victim and DNA samples from each of the four suspects. "The semen had first been tested downstairs in Serology, but their results were only definite enough to eliminate one of the suspects. So they sent us the samples, and the first thing we did, in addition to the standard preparations I mentioned, was to separate the female cells, produced by the victim, from the male cells found in the semen. That's one of the advantages of DNA testing: it allows us to distinguish various parts of a mixture, whereas in traditional serology the many overlaps can interfere with the analysis."

Sgueglia showed me a vastly enlarged printout with four vertical rows of perhaps twenty sausage-shaped markers, each maybe a quarter-inch long. The key piece of information, she said, was the size of the individual markers, and the first vertical column served as a kind of molecular ruler, with DNA samples of known sizes. The second row, she said, "is a control group of two fragments from a known cell line that originated with a single female source, that's been run thousands and thousands of times for test purposes by every DNA lab around the world, so we can all judge the validity and consistency of our findings by making sure our instruments show these two fragments falling within an acceptable size range."

The concept struck me: this woman, chosen for whatever reason as the Unknown Soldier of genetic research, her chromosome fragments now treasured possessions of every DNA laboratory in every corner of the globe and maybe destined to be part of every DNA test conducted for the rest of time.

Sgueglia didn't seem much taken with the idea. She showed me how the markers in the third tier, representing the semen sample from the victim's body, matched perfectly the DNA sample taken from suspect number one. This only represented the first probe, she said, but the next three all showed the same match.

None of the other suspects matched this sample, but the separate semen sample taken from the victim's panties showed an equally definitive match with suspect number four.

"Not only were these findings conclusive," Sgueglia said, "but as you can see, they're very graphic, and very easy to see and explain. Sometimes when I testify in court, I notice jurors nodding even before I finish my explanation, because one look at these charts is all they need. So although the technology is very complicated in terms of molecular biology, the results are obvious and easily understood."

Not long after my visit to the DNA lab, the technique was used not to convict but to exonerate. Perhaps for the first time, a prisoner serving a long sentence for rape was cleared when DNA tests, not yet in use at the time of his trial, showed he couldn't possibly have produced the semen in question.

Would every convicted rapist in the country, already in prison and with nothing to lose, demand these tests? Given the cost involved, the courts seemed unlikely to order the tests at public expense, so probably only wealthy convicts would get the chance to give the dice a roll and see what numbers came up on their chromosome fragments.

As deputy chief medical examiner for Suffolk County, Dr. Stuart Dawson is second in command of the ME's office and of the Crime Lab that operates under it. Sitting behind a desk featuring a microscope, Dr. Dawson apologized with a nonchalant wave for the clutter on his desk, the piles of papers on the floor and on tops of cabinets. The jumble and disarray of his office had apparently become legendary throughout the building, but he spoke quietly, confidently, with a straightforward clarity.

"To begin with, I'm a forensic pathologist, which means I've completed medical school and served my residency in pathology, and now specialize in the analysis of the causes of death. Pathologists normally work in hospitals, where they examine surgical specimens, perform autopsies, and run the hospital laboratory. But I then took a subspecialty in forensic pathology, which gave me five years of residency, including a year-long training program that allowed me to start doing the things I now do here. After a couple of years in D.C., I've been here ten years, first as a deputy ME and now as deputy chief.

"Becoming a forensic pathologist essentially means becoming expert in performing autopsies. Hospital pathologists perform autopsies as something of a sideline, primarily to evaluate the propriety of the patient's treatment before his death. For forensic pathologists, on the other hand, autopsies are our main responsibility, the whole ball of wax."

The medical examiner's office, Dawson said, is charged with investigating certain specified deaths within its jurisdiction. Most of these are "unattended deaths," meaning they occurred without a physician available to sign the death certificate. "We then become the physician of last resort, so to speak, and must determine the official cause of death."

That doesn't necessarily involve an autopsy—a major procedure during which the body cavity is opened up and the vital organs are removed for both gross and microscopic examination. The word itself, Dr. Dawson explains, comes from the Greek *autopsia*, meaning to see for oneself, to view with one's own eyes, but a pathologist can often draw his conclusions merely from an external examination or from the patient's medical history. "When you come down to it, *cause of death* is nothing more than the opinion of the physician signing the certificate. It's an exercise in diagnostic medicine not unlike what your family doctor does when you walk into his office and say, This hurts, what's wrong with me?

"As we're all taught in medical school, the first step in diagnosis is the patient's medical history, gained from asking about his general health, previous problems, and present symptoms, supplemented by a physical and appropriate lab test and X rays. The same procedure is used to determine the cause of death, except we can't interview the patient, can't listen to a beating heart or breathing lung, can't have pain or discomfort described. Therefore we do our best to get the medical history from family and friends, to observe firsthand the condition of the organs and any signs of injury or illness. We also consider evidence from X rays and lab tests. Since the presence of drugs and alcohol is a major postmortem issue, especially in trauma deaths, we have a big toxicology section, whereas your typical hospital makes do with a tiny lab tucked off in some corner.

"We have five doctors doing autopsies. The three deputies do the most, I'm next, and Sigmund Menchel, the chief ME, does the fewest. Full procedures are usually performed in connection with deaths whose causes are not readily apparent or not easy to categorize, although that doesn't necessarily make them suspicious. We also get involved in some deaths for legal reasons. No cremations can take place in the county until cleared by our office. Obviously, once a body is cremated, it can never again be examined, so we have to attest that there's no evidence of foul play.

"Although foul play is rarely involved in the deaths we investigate, we always have to be alert to the possibility, especially with traffic fatalities, drownings, bodies removed from fires. Maybe someone drugged or put a bullet in them first. It does happen, and this very small number of suspected or proven homicides provides the ultimate bedrock of why we're here, beyond our essential housekeeping and processing tasks. Someone could claim, of course, that there are hundreds of murders that we simply fail to detect, and if we wanted to lie awake at night tormenting ourselves over that, we certainly could. My feeling is that a few might slip by, but a bunch of old pros like us won't be that easily fooled by some amateur attempting skulduggery for the first time. Remember, I'm not talking about *solving* homicides. I'm talking about recognizing them as such on the basis of what we do here.

"When a report comes in of an apparent homicide and the body is still at the scene, an ME will almost always respond to help the investigators with on-site observations and tests. We'll usually be the first to closely examine and move the victim, and will also take the body temperature and look for other signs indicating time of death.

"Like everybody else responding to a homicide, we have to be concerned, especially during the kind of final examination an autopsy represents, that our procedures and findings will hold up under possible future challenge. It's not enough to say we dug a bullet out of the victim's chest if someone's going to ask us a year later about an aneurism that may have occurred in the brain. For that reason, and because by training and preference we've developed the habit, every full autopsy entails a thorough examination of the brain, neck, chest, and abdomen."

He paused. Had I ever witnessed an autopsy or visited the morgue where they were performed? No, I told him, but Al had promised to take me by. "I'm sure you'll enjoy it," he said without any noticeable irony.

Al is so accustomed to the morgue and what goes on there that it never seemed to occur to him that my first visit might be something of a shock. He and Jack Mario from Chemistry were standing in the hallway talking, while I listened, about a body that had arrived earlier that day with a knife in its chest.

"They bring him as a homicide?" Al asked.

"That was the report," Jack said. "Probable homicide."

"And now they're not sure?"

"The angle and everything," Jack said. "The circum-stances. They're thinking maybe suicide. I'll go later and take a look."

"I'll go down now," Al said, and turned to me. "Want to come?" It was about as casual as asking me to join him for a cup of coffee, but I immediately felt an extraordinary hesitancy.

Jack Mario's reaction didn't help. He gave Al a sharp look, then turned to me. "You ever been in a morgue before?"

"Well, no," I admitted, but not as an excuse. After all, I'd seen plenty of movie morgues, those austere and antiseptic depositories where the bodies were neatly filed away on sliding pallets behind square metal doors, like an enlarged version of the safe-deposit vault at my Amherst bank. Hell, I could handle that. Al would walk in, find the right file door, slide out the pallet, gently lift the shroud and peer down— while I stood on the other side, the body hidden by the half-raised shroud as I observed Al's professional demeanor and noted his comments.

"Why not?" I said to Al. "If I'm checking everything out, I ought to check everything out."

"I'll go down with you," Jack Mario said. "Some people don't take it well the first time."

We'd been standing just outside Jack Mario's office, and started down the hallway. For whatever reason—all those old cop movies? their mention of going *down* to the morgue?—I was expecting a stairway, an elevator, a way to the basement, the subbasement, the gray, echoing catacombs.

As we walked, Jack Mario touched my arm. "If you get queasy, just spin around and back right out. It happens all the time."

Before I could respond, Al took a sharp right into a spacious alcove and the wide-open doors of the morgue. I spun around and backed right out.

"You did okay," Jack Mario said out in the hall, around the corner. "Most guys throw up."

The visual impact of that stunning instant has stayed with me since, and was a turning point. Until then, despite all the talk with my cousins of homicides and bodies and knifings and shootings, I remained the listener, the observer, the absorbed but composed outsider. One glance into the morgue changed all that.

Maybe I stood by the open doors longer than I imagined, too numb to be aware of time passing, but I'd swear it was only a single glance, because all I've got is a still picture, a tableau, with no movement except for the blood gushing against the backdrop of that arrested display.

The blood also gave the scene its only color, geysers and rushes of brilliantly glistening red. Everything else was white, reflective, paralyzed. And cold—the chill made it feel like a freezer door had suddenly swung open, the air not only cold but moist, fetid, tingling at the nostrils.

Six waist-high operating tables with stainless-steel tops, dazzling lights, six naked bodies, male and female, white and black, one the color of slate, six white robed figures bending under the lights, over the bodies, radiant knives poised, the bodies *opened*, skin and flesh peeled back in great flaps around garish red cavities, organs exposed, organs being handled, while along the edges of those stainless-steel pallets narrow gutters carried off the streams of gleaming blood.

Nothing will ever erase that image, not even Al informing me afterward that the morgue did not contain six operating tables, but only three.

My reaction was so typical that Al shrugged it off, saying maybe he shouldn't have taken me there at such a busy moment. Unfortunately, my thoughts were just as typical, dealing as they did with the banality of death, the nakedness of corpses, the rawness of exposed innards, and most of all our eagerness to let policemen and doctors and nurses and hospital attendants deal with all the ugliness we don't want to face ourselves. I kept the thoughts to myself.

"It *was* a suicide, by the way," Al informed me. "The knife was still in his chest, and from the entry angle, way over on the left side, he must've done it himself, which is what everything else points to, too. Did you notice the angle of the knife?"

I hadn't even noticed the knife. My mind was too busy multiplying everything by two.

"Everybody's pissed about calling three guys out on a weekend homicide that turns out to be a suicide. Next time, we'll work up more gradually to the morgue, okay?"

"Sure thing," I said.

F R O N T I N G

F O R   T H E   B I G   S H O T S

J O H N   C U O M O ➡

AFTER GOING THROUGH all that hell of being suspended and charged
with accepting bribes, putting up with the endless worry and uncertainty for a year and a half, we were so beaten down by the or-
deal, both Jeannette and me, that we didn't feel any kind of elation
at finally being cleared. The last thing in the world we felt like was
celebrating. Even getting my full reinstatement with back pay and
privileges seemed more of a letdown than anything else. Sure, I'd
been cleared, I had the papers to prove it, and subsequently got security clearance for a number of sensitive jobs, which I could
never have done if there was any doubt as to my innocence. But I
had been a good cop for almost two decades, a serious professional
who held the department in the highest regard, and the way the
leadership failed to stand behind me in the face of Gold's trumped-
up charges really poisoned my attitude. To this day, my biggest regret is in going along with Slotnick's advice not to sue the city for
false arrest and a dozen other things. I should have found another
lawyer and gone ahead with the lawsuit, because I'm still convinced I could have won it. But I made the mistake of listening to

Slotnick and letting the matter drop, so regardless of the regrets and the bitterness, I had to put all that behind me and move on.

By the time I was reassigned back to my old command, the Twelfth Robbery in Brooklyn, I only had to put in nine months before becoming eligible for my full twenty-year retirement. Given the mood I was in, they weren't about to get any work out of me. I wasn't the least bit concerned with making arrests. I don't think I made a single arrest that whole time. I just wasn't interested, and nobody complained. The bosses understood my hard feelings and said I could come and go as I pleased without worrying about assignments, and I took them at their word. All I was interested in was running out the string.

But I wasn't some old geezer ready for the porch rocker. I was forty-three years old, in good health and still with plenty of energy and ambition. So my main focus was deciding how to spend the next twenty years before I really retired.

At first I was very concerned about the black mark I'd gotten from all the accusations and publicity. Like they say, the charges get the headlines whereas they bury the proof of your innocence, and that sure was true in my case. With all my police experience, some kind of security work seemed like the logical next step, but any security position would naturally require a thorough background check. I wouldn't know how much those charges had hurt me until I actually applied for something.

I started looking around during my final days on the force, and two job possibilities appeared almost simultaneously. One was a very well-paying, extremely tempting job with Helmsley Spear that I eventually did take, much to my regret. But the other opportunity turned out to be something I'd never dreamed of in a thousand years. I heard about it through a detective friend that heard about it from his brother, which of course is the way these things happen. Anyhow, the brother worked in the police department's Hotel Squad, an elite, prestigious unit dealing with crime prevention in New York City hotels.

The Waldorf-Astoria, my friend learned from his brother, was looking for an assistant head of security, so why didn't I apply?

The current head, Bill Whelan, had longtime police connections, an ex-detective himself whose father had once been chief of detectives. Whelan was getting ready to retire, which meant that whoever was hired as his assistant would have a good chance to move up and replace him.

To tell the truth, I didn't see myself having much of a shot at a job like that, working for maybe the most famous hotel in the world. But I applied anyhow, did the interviews and filled out the forms and everything, at least in part to see if I cleared their security check. I was delighted when they investigated my arrest and reinstatement and said they found no problems. I'd expected to come out clean in that area, but then was really surprised to learn that I was seriously being considered for the job. Whelan even gave me a grand tour of the place, which he was very proud of, and introduced me to the manager and took me to lunch in their elegant restaurant.

The job I'd interviewed for earlier that same day at Helmsley Spear would have paid a few thousand dollars more, but Whelan really made the Waldorf sound attractive. For one, he said right out that he would be leaving soon and they'd like to bring in a man like myself to groom him for the top job. They also offered excellent health and general benefits, a very nice work atmosphere, plus all sorts of other amenities. He even made a point of the fact that the hotel would do my laundry and dry cleaning, so I'd have fresh apparel every day without worrying about it, and of course could take my meals there too. So Jeannette and I talked it over and decided to go with the Waldorf, as the more prestigious job and the one with a real opportunity for advancement.

It was certainly nice having a choice between two jobs, but I couldn't help wondering why all these people were being so nice to me. Eventually I came to the conclusion that some influential people in the police department, seeing the raw deal I got, must have gone out of their way to put in a good word for me. And Whelan, given his own police background, must have been aware of the fact that even though I was in real trouble myself, I didn't turn on a fellow officer like Caccia just to save my own skin.

Whatever Whelan's thinking, I got the job, and on the day of
my official retirement I reported to work, dressed very nicely in a
suit and shirt and tie, as director of night security for the Waldorf-
Astoria, a hotel containing over twelve hundred rooms, located on
Forty-ninth Street, with the attached Waldorf Towers featuring
presidential suites where people like Frank Sinatra and Douglas
MacArthur's widow maintained residences.

Overall, we had a security staff of between thirty and forty people.
At night, we'd have maybe three or four in uniform, not policemen
but staff in police-looking uniforms, who went around and
clocked in on a regular schedule on every floor and in between
were stationed at the various entrances to observe whoever came
in. We felt a uniformed presence helped keep out undesirables and
provided a visibly secure atmosphere. We also had four or five men
in civvies every night to keep an eye on the lobby and the various
lounges, restaurants, and function rooms. They had to be very
presentable, of course, to blend in with the patrons—which was
the term they always used for what most places called guests. All
the security people carried pocket radios, but at night, I was the
only person armed. Days, only Whelan was.

Every evening I'd accompany the cash being transferred from
the office and the different stores and shops to the cashier, then es-
cort it to the auditing department. Whelan did the same during
the day. We also maintained tight security on the patrons' safe-deposit boxes, using the nearby switchboard operators to keep an eye
on the area, along with camera surveillance and security personnel. The last thing we wanted was any losses of cash or valuables a
patron had deposited for safekeeping.

In addition to these everyday matters, I had three major responsibilities.

The most straightforward was to arrange security for elite functions and for distinguished international guests—kings or prime
ministers or UN leaders. We would double or triple up with our
own people or go to private agencies for supplementary guards,
armed or otherwise. Active police officers weren't supposed to

moonlight at that time, so the agencies were staffed mainly by retired policemen, although a lot of active guys took these jobs
under various guises because they needed the money.

My second concern dealt with thefts, either by employees or patrons. Everybody knows that even crummy roadside motels are
plagued by stuff disappearing, but I never realized the dimensions
experienced by a high-class place like the Waldorf. My job was to
do what I could to keep the losses down, but the insurance company generally agreed to cover the hotel for what was judged a
normal pattern of loss. I was stunned to find out that the acceptable figure, the amount considered standard and not worth getting excited about, was a million dollars a year.

My third responsibility was a much bigger problem at night
than during the day, and that was dealing with prostitutes. When
people hear this, they usually say, *Prostitutes at the Waldorf?* That's
right, I say, prostitutes at the Waldorf. I could tell you all about
them.

As for thefts by patrons, you're mostly talking individual items
of silverware or towels, even doorknobs or faucet tops. A lot of
times it's just a matter of grabbing a souvenir on the way out. This
can add up to significant figures, but you're dealing with so
many petty instances that you don't want to waste too much time
over it.

With the staff, you run into larger-scale situations more demanding of your attention. The hotel would hold periodic management meetings on this, and would ask me to devise ways of
controlling employee theft and of identifying the guilty parties.
One time we suspected that certain maids might be stealing from
patrons. I arranged to rent a camera, which we hid in a hotel room
set up to look like it was occupied. We put in luggage, hung stuff in
the closets, unmade the bed, and then when the maid let herself in
to clean, the camera would automatically come on. I would view
all the films, but if the maid came across the cash we'd left under
the pillow, say, she'd put it aside to make the bed and then slip it
back under the pillow. So we never caught her or any of the other

maids in the act, but we figured word must have gotten around, and I got commended by the management because the thefts dropped off very suddenly and dramatically.

The biggest scam during my time there involved the theft of large quantities of linen. The Waldorf maintained a daily inventory, and when we saw shortages developing in our stock of expensive table linens, our preliminary investigation indicated that something was happening on the loading platform. We set up a personal surveillance system whereby a security person secretly observed activities from a vantage point and discovered that some platform workers were operating in cahoots with the laundry-truck driver. When the driver delivered clean linen, he was supposed to take back the used linens loaded into canvas wheelers. But he'd arrange the soiled stuff to form a top layer, under which piles of clean linen would be sneaked onto the truck, that the driver would then sell off, probably to some other hotel, splitting the money with the platform workers.

I caught another employee carrying out a scheme right in the main lobby where he worked the reception desk. Again, we'd gotten complaints, so I observed him surreptitiously for a period of time. He'd take the mail that was left at the desk, not only letters but notes, packages, papers, and hold them up to the light to see what was inside. In some cases he'd actually slit them open, and if there was any cash, which there often was, he'd help himself to at least part of it. Often patrons didn't know how much money had been sent to them, or how much they'd deposited, so few people were suspicious, especially since he did a very neat job of resealing everything.

Even though I'd caught him red-handed, this guy was a long-time employee with no blemishes on his record, so I had to make my case strongly enough to forestall trouble with the unions, who were very protective of the employees. What I did was have him admit in writing to his activities, on the understanding that we would then not press charges but simply let him go, and after that the union naturally wasn't interested in protecting him.

We also dealt with thieves that specialized in the various hotels throughout the city. We kept pictures of many of them in a file built up over the years, and made sure our security people were familiar with the photos, since we were always on the lookout for known professionals. Most were men, well dressed and with a great deal of pure nerve, who would walk around whatever hotel they'd selected and use any means they could to get into a room. Sometimes, by one ruse or other, they'd get a maid to let them into what they claimed was their own room. Another favorite trick, when they saw a maid cleaning a room with the door open, was to pretend to be the occupant coming back for something they'd left behind. Or they'd just hang around a floor near checkout time, and if any guests left the door open behind them when they went to check out, which people often did, the thief could be in and out of the room in a flash, stealing whatever hotel property wasn't bolted down.

The professionals also used picks, and in those days before electronic locks they could probably get into any room in the hotel, except maybe the supersecure ones in the Towers, and in seconds could strip the place of whatever cash and jewelry and valuables had been left behind. Certain pros would try to enlist cohorts on the staff to tip them off to which patrons would be going out for the evening, or to give them access to the house phone to call up to see which rooms were unoccupied. Sometimes they'd watch people going to the safe-deposit area to take out valuables. It might mean they were getting everything together to check out tomorrow, and maybe would leave those valuables in the room when they went to dinner.

They really had a lot of balls. Some would just watch the registration desk, and if they saw a couple checking in and smelled money, they'd either try to get near enough to hear the room number or else wait till the couple got on the elevator and then hurry up to the desk and say, I just missed my friends who just checked in a minute ago. Where did they go? Sometimes the clerk would fall for it and say, Oh, you mean the Fitzgeralds? In room

303? I don't think anything that crude happened much in places like the Waldorf, where the clerks were too experienced to be taken in so easily.

In general, with the Waldorf's high-class personnel, there wasn't much going on among the staff that concerned me. But the hotel was naturally very protective of its reputation, and if lapses did occur, it would often fall to me to maintain the standards. It wasn't just a matter of pilfering or getting involved with thieves. In fact, the weirdest situation I ran into there had nothing to do with stealing at all.

I caught this one guy masturbating in this little inside corridor behind the Bull and Bear, the main restaurant there. The corridor was used primarily by waiters and busboys hurrying back and forth between the restaurant and the kitchen area, so it wasn't all that public. Still, it wasn't exactly private either, and I was just walking along one night when I spotted this guy I didn't recognize hunching off in a corner by himself, whacking away. I grabbed him and said, What the hell are you doing? Do you work here? What the hell's going on? He was just this young kid, a busboy, I think, that maybe had the hots for one of the waitresses or something, and I hauled him up to my office and said I was going to call in the police to arrest him for public disturbance and a violation of the health code unless he signed the paper I drew up. So he did, saying, Mr. Cuomo caught me masturbating on this date, in this certain location, and I agree to leave voluntarily and not come back.

With the prostitutes, I introduced new ways of enforcing the rules that seemed to work out better than previous attempts at controlling them. The Waldorf policy basically came down to practical matters. We didn't frown on patrons having prostitutes come to their rooms on a call-girl basis. That was a matter of a patron's choice, to invite someone to his room as long as the person didn't violate the safety or decorum of the hotel. At the same time, we didn't want street girls strolling in from Forty-ninth Street and openly soliciting or creating an unseemly atmosphere.

That was the distinction I had to work with. The management would even say to me, Look, Johnny, it's all right if the girls frequent the bar—Harry's Bar was the main one, the famous one—as long as they're appropriately dressed and don't become pests or cause any kind of disturbance. It was, after all, a public gathering place. Although we had the right to keep out undesirables, even known prostitutes had to be treated under the same general conditions imposed on everyone else. We even suspected that some bartenders helped set up the girls, but there was no way to be sure. Our main determination was to keep the girls from walking the halls or openly offering their services.

The biggest problem with the prostitutes didn't actually involve their primary activity of turning tricks, but the secondary one of rolling patrons. We had a lot of that, because the prostitutes knew what a racket it was for them.

For instance, I would receive a complaint from a patron, a man traveling alone on business, that an amount of cash had disappeared from his room in his absence. The truth, often, was that he'd come back to the hotel for the night, probably bombed out of his mind, and when he got out of his cab, one of the girls on Lexington, the streetwalkers, would hit on him. Hey, honey, you wanna invite me upstairs? I'll show you a good time. So he'd bring her into the hotel, or maybe give her his room number so nobody would see him escorting this streetwalker through the lobby. The prostitute herself would use a side entrance, or slip someone she knew a few bucks to let her go up after him.

Sometimes she would use various diversionary methods to get his attention away from his wallet, but the standard ploy was for the girl to quickly remove her clothes and get him all excited and then suggest he probably wanted to take a shower. She'd have noted, of course, where his wallet was, still in his pants maybe, or stuck in a dresser drawer, and as soon as he got in the shower, she'd grab the cash. She wouldn't take the wallet itself because she didn't want anything on her, even for an instant, to connect her with this guy. She'd just grab the cash and run and then, maybe right away that night, maybe the next day after the guy sobered up, he'd report the robbery. I was at a business dinner, he'd tell me, or a Broadway play with some friends, and when I returned, all the cash in my room was gone.

A lot of men would be reluctant to report anything, feeling either guilty or stupid about the whole thing, so we always assumed it went on even more than we heard. But if there was an appreciable amount of money or jewelry involved, or if the girl had maybe grabbed an envelope along with the cash that contained important company documents, the guy had to report *some* kind of theft to qualify for the insurance, or to explain what happened to the company paperwork he'd been carrying.

So he would fill out the forms, reporting a burglary by unknown persons in an unknown manner while he was absent from his room, and listing the missing items, maybe even padding it out a bit for the insurance. I would then be stuck with this report, and would have to respond to it. If it struck me as bona fide, I would immediately report it to the police, to the Hotel Squad itself if it involved a significant loss.

But first I had to make the decision whether to believe the guy or not, although it really wasn't that hard spotting the fishy stories. In an actual burglary, for instance, you'd almost always find evidence of forced entry. Even a burglar who got in by stealth would be rushing to get out as quickly as possible, tearing through drawers and tossing things around, leaving the room in real disarray.

The most compelling indication of a real burglary would be the fact that the man was traveling with his wife or family. In that situation, I would always lean toward believing him. But I'd be immediately suspicious of a man on his own. When I mentioned this to someone, he said, You mean if I was traveling alone and my room was burglarized, I'd be better off not even reporting it because no one would believe me? That's right, I told him. Even if you messed up the room yourself, the security people would probably spot that as just your cover for the fake story.

Whenever I had to deal with a suspicious report, I'd interview the complainant to give him every benefit of the doubt. You have

to remember, I was a very experienced detective who'd been involved in lots of interrogations over the years and had a good feel
of how honest a guy was being, how well his story held up under
scrutiny. Often the recounting would just get weaker and weaker
with every word the guy said, with every hesitation and evasion
and guilty look. I'd give him plenty of rope to hang himself and
then might inquire about his home phone number, and business
number too, in case I had to get in touch with his wife or business
associates. I had no intention of doing any such thing, but the guy
would start sweating bullets. I'd feel my way along, of course, and
at some point would say, There wasn't by any chance a guest present in your room sometime last night, was there? I'd explain that
we'd often had trouble with some of these girls brought up to the
rooms, and that we weren't making any sort of moral judgments
but just trying to determine what really happened and the hotel's
responsibility in the matter. Of course, if he felt he'd be just as
happy to forget the whole thing and not file any report of any
kind. . .

Generally he'd jump at this opportunity. I'd tell him it was probably a wise decision on his part, and if he was interested in keeping this sort of thing from happening again, maybe even in getting
back at the girl who'd robbed him, then maybe he'd take a quick
look at a file of pictures I happened to have in my office. I'd assure
the guy that there'd be no public report, that nothing would be
said to anyone, but that we would appreciate his cooperation, and
we often got it, mainly because the guy would be so pissed at the
girl who took him for a ride like that. This sort of handling, at any
rate, avoided a lot of insurance claims against the hotel and all
sorts of potential legal wrangling.

The photo file was probably my main contribution to the handling of prostitutes at the Waldorf. If any of my men came across
obvious streetwalkers or even higher-level prostitutes openly soliciting in the bar or hallways or anywhere else, I'd have them
brought up to my office. I would then interview the individual
prostitute, take a couple of Polaroid pictures of her, and have her
sign a statement saying, I was picked up by security officer so-and-

so, at this time, on the twenty-seventh floor, etc., etc., and brought to office of supervisor of security John Cuomo. I understand that if I am again found in this building I will be arrested for trespass and turned over to the police.

Actually I had a standard form, and all they had to do was fill in the blanks and sign it. They wouldn't give their actual names or addresses, of course, but that didn't matter, because we had their pictures on file if they came back, which really cut down on the number of girls we had to deal with over and over. The photo file also discouraged them from rolling their johns, because now the victim might identify them so we could put the police on their tail. In New York City at the time, a girl could be arrested for prostitution, or soliciting prostitution, or even loitering. Even just standing on a corner: if three or more women were standing on the corner, a cop could run them in.

Most of the street prostitutes were either black or Puerto Rican, and they hung out chiefly on what we considered the bad side of the hotel, which was Lexington Avenue. Very few would be walking around the hotel, because they'd be spotted right away in their typical streetwalker garb. Also in those days we didn't have many black or Puerto Rican patrons, except for foreign women who had an altogether different look. The white prostitutes working the hotel would usually dress very nicely and try to pass as patrons, but at the same time they were trying to drum up business and so wanted men to recognize them for what they were. They'd come up to me sometimes when I was just walking around, not having any idea who I was, and say, Hi, where you from? I'd say, Oh, Illinois, around Chicago, why? Just wondering, she'd say, you here on a convention? Just business, I'd say, and she'd start asking about maybe coming up to my room. What for? I'd ask. Oh, just for talking, she'd say. Talk, entertainment, whatever you want. What I'd usually do is seem very shy and reluctant at first, to make them really commit themselves, and then get them to name a price. Once they mentioned money I could nail them for prostitution. I'd then tell them who I was and why we didn't want them hanging

around, and bring them to my office to get the Polaroids and statement for my file.

Sometimes when I'd try to move in on suspicious-looking
women, they would see me coming and rush straight out the door.
Maybe they'd been tipped off to my description by some other
girls, or could just spot a certain coplike look in my eyes.

I really enjoyed my time at the Waldorf, and had real hopes of
staying on and moving up when Whelan retired. Along the way, I
even completed a course in hotel management to give me a better
background for the work, and the bosses seemed pleased by that,
so I assumed they had plans for me. But unfortunately it didn't
work out that way, and I remained only about ten months, all told.

What happened was that when Whelan actually began making
moves toward retiring, the expectation I had of being considered
to replace him seemed no longer in the works. The first word I got
of this was when the hotel manager called me in to say that they
were going to start interviewing other people for the position. It
became clear that various political considerations had come into
play, involving people with far better connections than I had, and
although I never got the whole story, it ended up that they hired a
detective from the Police Department's elite Bureau of Special Services, and I took that as a sign that I probably ought to look elsewhere.

It wasn't easy giving up that job. It was unique in a lot of ways,
with the opportunity to meet all kinds of interesting people and
get involved in the big functions and celebrations and annual din-
ners. I met presidents, governors, all kinds of show-business
celebrities. Cardinal Spellman, of course, was right around the
corner at St. Patrick's, and on a number of occasions we'd also
have Bishop Francis J. Mugavero from Brooklyn. Whenever he attended some big event, Mugavero would hold a hospitality reception in a suite, with a complimentary bar and a very classy spread
of all sorts of fancy Italian food and appetizers, but the bishop
himself, he was just a real regular guy. People would go up there to

wish him well and he'd chat with them just like anybody else. I'd be invited too, and I'd go up and, you know, I was very moved by meeting a man like that, who was both such a high, imposing figure in the Church and at the same time such a friendly person. He'd shake my hand and I'd be real uptight, not knowing how I was supposed to act or anything, and he'd say, Cuomo, Italian, eh? Where'd you grow up? Where do you live? How long you been working here? Things like that were really special to me, not what you'd expect on your normal job, and I knew I'd miss it.

A retired police lieutenant who'd been employed by Helmsley Spear as corporate security director for all their properties, the same person who'd mentioned a job there almost a year earlier, told me the position was still open. I got back in touch with them and received another interview with the fellow I'd originally applied to. He was close to Harry Helmsley in the parent organization and showed the same interest in me he had the first time. You come highly recommended, he said. You want the job, you got the job.

The fellow's name was James Early, and he was that kind of guy, very direct and decisive, almost crude, you could say, without the smoothness you'd expect from a guy in his position. He said, Tell me, Johnny, what are you making over there at the Waldorf? I think it was around seventeen five, a decent salary in those days when you'd get a raise of maybe five hundred a year. He just waved away my answer and said, We'll give you twenty-five, how does that sound? I said, Gee, that sounds pretty good, and he said, You start next week. I'm sure if I said I was making thirty, he'd have offered me forty. What the hell did I know?

The job was with one of their subsidiaries, Owners Maintenance. Since the company was incorporated, New York State required three corporate officers. Harry Helmsley was president, as he was of the parent corporation, Helmsley Spear. An accountant type served as treasurer, and I became the required third officer as vice president for corporate security.

It all sounded pretty impressive. Of course, knowing now what happened to Harry Helmsley and his wife Leona, you'd have to be crazy to get involved with them. But I'd never heard their names before, and all I knew was that Harry had made multimillions as a real estate tycoon and that Leona took a special interest in the hotels they owned. No one had any inkling Leona would end up in prison and Harry would stay out only because he'd become so old his lawyer got him off for ill health.

Anyhow, I was very grateful for the job and the big raise, and I started with a great deal of enthusiasm. Helmsley Spear owned a great many major properties in New York, including the Empire State Building and One Penn Plaza, which was something like sixty stories high with a couple of million square feet of office space. They also owned hotels like the St. Moritz and the Sherry Netherland, and the one he built just for his wife, the Park Lane, along with many other hotels, office buildings, and apartment complexes.

The part of the job they emphasized in hiring me was the supervision over whatever security problems might arise at any of their properties. Some were similar to what I experienced at the Waldorf, such as thefts by employees and others, which for Helmsley Spear also entailed the loss of very expensive equipment in office and industrial buildings and on various construction sites. We also had to deal with general instances of vandalism, loitering, prostitution, that sort of thing. Finally, the organization faced certain security problems in dealing with the unions. In fact, James Early, this tough Irishman who came up from the East Side slums, worked for the parent corporation as their labor-relations expert, and it wasn't long before he got me involved in that and helped bring about my departure.

As it was, I wasn't on the job very long before I realized that my actual security responsibilities were very minimal. Sure, on occasion they'd ask me to look into something, but all their properties had their own security forces, and these people were perfectly capable of handling whatever came up, leaving me with very little to do. Why, I began to wonder, did they even hire me if there was nothing for me to do?

I discovered that the key was my watchguard's license, which they'd told me I had to get and which I did easily enough, based on my law-enforcement experience. The license authorized me to hire guards and to fingerprint and do background checks on applicants through the BCI—the Bureau of Criminal Investigation down in D.C. That's why they wanted me, so they'd have someone properly authorized to hire security people. Then I learned that most guards I hired for Owners Maintenance did not actually end up working for us, but instead for the many commercial and industrial tenants of the Helmsley Spear organization. The way I understood it, firms renting space from Helmsley would customarily hire their security people through Owners Maintenance. Delta Airlines, for instance, which had three whole floors at One Penn Plaza, got their guards through my office. In addition, Helmsley's commercial tenants, of which there were something like two hundred in One Penn Plaza alone, would lease their janitors, window washers, elevator operators, handymen, just about everybody needed to maintain the property, from Owners Maintenance.

Once I realized they hadn't hired me for regular security responsibilities, but only as a figurehead so they could use my license for the hiring of guards through Owners Maintenance, I again began thinking of moving on. The final straw came through one of my few involvements in actual security work. Some people in the parent organization called me in one day and said they were getting a lot of pressure from one of the service unions. The main leaders were two Puerto Rican workers, both porters, one who cleaned up outside One Penn Plaza and the other inside. There were rumors, I was told, that these leaders might have arrest records that they'd lied about on their applications, so the organization people asked me to do a background check to see if that was true.

This wasn't what I'd been hired for, but I figured, Okay, if they want a check, I'll run a check. Since these were service workers, not guards, I didn't have the authority to use the BCI records down in Washington, so I got in touch with some police contacts I still had and said, Look, can you do me a favor and let me see the yellow sheets on these guys? Lo and behold, what came back were pretty impressive arrest records for both guys on various charges. This apparently was exactly what the corporation wanted, and they then fired the guys for falsifying their applications by not declaring their arrest records.

This immediately became a big issue, since the union was very unhappy about these guys being fired, and we were hit with picketing and strike threats and union fliers handed out with my picture on them making me the scapegoat for Owners Maintenance, as the guy who'd been out to get their leaders. I wasn't at all happy about this development, and even less about the Civil Liberties Union coming in to defend them. The issue went to court, where eventually it all came down to whether the company could investigate them at this late date, and whether I had the right to use the means I did to produce their yellow sheets.

With all the lawyers bickering in court, I really couldn't tell you exactly what kind of authority I had, although I know that investigations like that go on all the time. The court then said I had to divulge the source of my information, but there was no way I'd reveal my police contacts, and I was really concerned over being declared in contempt or even convicted on some civil-rights charge. Even though Helmsley Spear provided me with a top lawyer, they were only concerned about their own ass, and I knew that if I had to hang for what they asked me to do, they wouldn't shed any tears over seeing me hang.

That was the turning point, even though I was never charged with anything. The union guys were reinstated by Judge Motley on the basis of my refusal to reveal my sources, and I decided to end my days as corporate vice president in the big-money world of high-flying New York real estate.

When the Helmsleys hit the front pages some years later, with jokes about them on the talk shows and everything, I learned along with everyone else about all the other, far more extensive shenanigans they'd been involved in. The treasurer of Owners Maintenance was convicted along with the Helmsleys, so of our three corporate officers, I was the only one who got out un-scathed. During the trials, I'd just shake my head and say to my-self, John, you thought you were lucky to find that job back then—but the real luck came when you decided to get out before they had you going down with the rest of the ship.

GUN HUNCHES

HAS THERE EVER BEEN a mystery novel or cop movie in which the solution wasn't ingeniously revealed by a hero who breaks free of the restraints imposed on him by his superiors to go charging off on some loony hunch? It's a treasured cliché of crime fighting, but both Al and Johnny claim there's some truth to it. Cops swear by their intuition, and will cite chapter and verse with the least encouragement. Do they conveniently forget hundreds of wild-goose chases while glorying in the one instance that paid off? Do they embellish that one instance during each retelling? Maybe so, Al admits, as he prepares to relate his own hunch story, which he swears he hasn't had time to embellish because it happened barely a month earlier.

AL DELLA PENNA ➡

I WASN'T EVEN ON CALL that week when our deputy director Bob Genna phoned me at home just before midnight to say someone had discovered a body in a basement. Would I be good enough to take it since the duty crew was already out on an earlier homicide? The victim lived alone in Yaphank, he said, about a mile down the road from County Police Headquarters, and his body had been found by relatives. It looked like he'd been shot, Genna added.

I agreed to go, since we regularly fill in for each other when needed. Genna said he'd also come and bring along one of the young assistants in Serology, Diane Alia, who was interested in observing us in the hopes of eventually becoming a crew member herself. We'd also be joined by Jack Mario, a lab chemist who normally directed his own crime-scene unit. Genna said he'd go directly to Yaphank with Diane Alia, while Jack and I could meet at the lab in Hauppauge and drive out in the crime-scene van.

Since I go to bed around nine-thirty, nighttime calls usually rouse me from a deep sleep. My first stop therefore becomes our all-night doughnut shop for a giant container of their steaming wide-awake coffee, to be consumed on my one-handed drive to the lab in Hauppauge. I keep the radio off and concentrate on whatever knowledge I've already picked up about the scene I'm going to encounter. Might there be footwear impressions, a possible forced entry, tire impressions, gunshots, Homicide panting to learn what kind of weapon to look for?

I'm also aware of who'll be working with me, what their specialties are, who's handling the measurements, the castings, the documentation. Will we need special equipment not already in the van? I try to list in my head the specific things I'll want to look for on the walkthrough. Let me do this, let me do that, let me make sure I don't forget this other thing. I'll think of things I might have missed some previous time, errors or oversights I don't want to repeat.

And I'm always aware of the weather and any problems it might present. In the winter, you hope you're going to be inside. In summer, especially when the body's been discovered after a period of time, you pray you won't end up in some cramped, sweltering closet. You don't always get what you pray for.

Between the coffee and the driving and the thinking ahead, I try to get all my gears oiled up and spinning. You always run into surprises, but try to keep them to a minimum.

When I pulled into the parking area this night and saw our sparkling new van out there, my reaction was, How nice! The duty crew took the old rattletrap and left us the beauty! Only it was so new I hadn't yet been issued keys for it, and couldn't find any on the key board inside. Okay, Jack Mario will have a set.

But Jack Mario arrived keyless too. We're both frustrated now, because our homicide scene's growing colder by the minute, with our boss among those waiting for us there, no doubt telling the young serologist how lucky she was to get the chance to observe a couple of hotshot old pros like Jack and me in action.

Maybe, Jack suggested, someone had left for the day with the keys still in his pocket. He phoned a coworker at his home nearby, waking him up at one in the morning. Yes, the guy mumbled, he had keys. Off Jack zoomed in his car, leaving me still bearish and muttering as I envisioned our happy murderer boarding a nonstop to Tahiti.

Within minutes the *old* van chugged into the parking area, and the two guys returning from the previous call, who'd heard all about our homicide on the radio, hopped out and thanked me for agreeing to fill in. At the same time, they couldn't resist joshing me about what a snap their scene was, what we call a "grounder," an easy hopper to the shortstop. Standard street shooting, body already removed by the time they arrived, nothing to look at except a couple of bloodstains on the pavement. Ours, on the other hand, sounded more interesting: prominent guy, alone in his house, dead as a doornail in his basement. Still, as they were quick to rub in, they were heading home now from their dull little case, whereas we fill-ins hadn't even begun.

At which point, my predicament must have suddenly dawned on them because their grins disappeared. One reached into his pocket and very sheepishly offered me a set of keys. The funny thing, he said, is we *had* the new van, but realized you guys would need it more than us, so drove back and switched. We just forgot to leave the keys is all. Sorry.

So now I had both vans and both sets of keys at my disposal, but no Jack Mario. Eventually Jack roared up and jumped out, all very Hollywood, triumphantly dangling his keys before my face. I dangled mine right back and, more than a bit agitated, we sped off together in our shiny new van.

We arrived in a nice wooded area of Yaphank, big suburban houses, lots of land around them, but our place was a little more rustic. We drove up this long dirt driveway, through trees and everything, and were flagged to a stop by some patrolmen in a large dirt area cluttered with patrol cars and maybe a dozen tractor-trailer rigs. A Homicide detective said Bob Genna was already at the house, which lay at the end of the dirt road that continued beyond this large truck area. The victim, a guy in his forties named Buddy Packer, used his twenty-six acres here both for his home, set back from the public street, and for his trucking-and-hauling business.

Jack and I walked from there, checking for tire or foot impressions. The dirt was bone dry, but sometimes you luck into a puddle that'll yield nice prints. We saw nothing this time.

Bob Genna had been waiting for us as anxiously as we'd been waiting to get there, and he hurried forward to meet us on the road as we neared the house. After their initial forays inside to make sure there were no more bodies, no suspects lurking about, the police had cleared everyone out to keep things clean for our walk-through. First, Genna passed along what he'd learned. Buddy Packer, living alone, hadn't seen his girlfriend since they'd gone out Friday night—this being Sunday—and hadn't called his ex-wife either, who he kept in regular touch with. When some sisters and brothers couldn't get him on the phone Saturday or Sunday, a whole bunch of them, six or eight all told, in four cars, had came over together a few hours earlier. The first thing that made them suspicious was Buddy's pickup truck behind the house, where he never parked it. Inside, they found his body on the base-ment steps, where it still lay, more or less untouched.

Genna, Jack Mario, and I, with Diane Alia coming along to ob-serve, began our walk-through, all wearing our standard lab-issue dungarees. Diane was the age of our daughters, a bright, lively young serologist eager to learn everything there was to know about crime-scene investigation. We conducted our walk-through by starting from the garage and moving into a small mud room, past the dinette/kitchen area to the carpeted hall off the bedrooms and the door to the basement. From that door we could see the body of a large, heavyset man face down on the wooden stairway, his head on the bottom steps, his feet halfway up the flight. The body was partially wrapped in a couple of regular bedroom quilts, and he'd been losing blood from the head area.

Since Buddy Packer was the exclusive occupant, with no one else possessing any proprietary interest or right to privacy, we were free to search the whole house. The cellar itself would be the obvious starting point, but the only way down was via the steps, with a good chance of disturbing the body. Besides, the unfinished wood railing might be receptive to prints or stains that we wouldn't want to smudge, so we decided to skip the basement until the ID people photographed and dusted the stairway. We could then help the medical examiner inspect the body, the quilts, the nature of the wounds, before removing the body and giving us easy access to the cellar.

Of course, the first patrolmen on the scene had to go into the cellar to determine whether the victim was still alive, and to search for other victims, for weapons and suspects. We didn't in-quire as to how they navigated around the body. They had their job; we had ours.

Going back into the garage, we retraced our way inside in a more deliberate manner. The first thing I discovered was a small eye-level gouge in the standard tongue-and-groove wood paneling that ran from the mud room through the dinette and into the kitchen. From the floor right below the gouge, I picked up a casing that looked like it came from a .22 cartridge. Not much farther along, just into the dinette, I found an expended bullet on the floor. It was what we call a .22-caliber short, with a fairly low velocity. That, along with the hardness of the oak paneling, probably accounted for the bullet merely gouging the wood. Since it showed no evidence of blood, the bullet had probably not struck Buddy Packer or anyone else before ricocheting off the wall and falling to the floor.

In the living room we noticed a small cardboard gun box, empty but labeled for a Beretta .22 pistol, that jibed with the bullet and casing we'd found. Since people who break into houses rarely carry their weapons in labeled boxes they leave behind, the .22 would probably have been Buddy Packer's. Maybe the gouge in the paneling meant he'd taken a shot at his intruder.

In the kitchen we discovered that the refrigerator was unplugged, for what reason we hadn't the foggiest notion, and the food inside was losing its chill.

By shining my flashlight parallel to the linoleum a couple of inches above the surface, I found something even more interesting: faint smudges that looked like bloodstains that someone had tried to wash off. Let's stay out of the kitchen, I said, until we see what we got here. Not long before at a homicide in Wyandanch, our Trace Department used a new technique with Amido-black solution on a bathroom floor to enhance footwear impressions we had no idea were even there.

I spread out shrouds to protect the linoleum while we continued searching the kitchen, spotting on a counter *another* gun box, this one for a Smith & Wesson 9-mm handgun, bigger and more powerful than a .22. There was no gun, but the box did contain two loaded 9-mm magazines. By the same reasoning, we assumed this gun too had probably belonged to Buddy Packer, not an intruder. The Formica on this countertop curved up at back in a standard splash guard, a damaged section of which revealed an embedded bullet. It looked like a .380, and I made sure we got good photos of it and then chipped around it with a hammer and chisel until I could pop out a square of Formica containing the bullet. Like the .22 we found earlier, it had no bloodstains so probably hadn't hit anything other than the wall.

When I started searching through the drawers of that counter, Diane asked me why I bothered, since they were all closed. Maybe they hadn't been, of course, when things were happening, and sure enough, lying innocently in one drawer we found an expended .380 casing that visually seemed to match the bullet I'd just taken out of the Formica.

Since a .380 is roughly the same size as a 9-mm, the Homicide detectives wanted to know if a 9-mm Smith & Wesson could have fired the .380 dug out of the wall. I told them I didn't think so, which they were not happy to hear. It meant we were now dealing with three different guns and bullets, a .22, a .380, and a 9-mm, and hadn't even learned yet what kind of gun and bullet had actually done the guy in.

We found more broad smears or stains, not droplets, on the hall rug near the basement door. If a person is shot and subsequently keeps moving, trying to escape or whatever, you generally get well-defined droplets on the walls and floor. The stains we were looking at would more likely have been created by a body being dragged along the floor.

All along we suspected the homicide might have resulted from a burglary, yet the house was full of apparently authentic Indian relics and artifacts—blankets, pottery, artwork, etc.—and nothing seemed disturbed. Had the burglary somehow been aborted before the thief could take anything?

As always, we kept up an ongoing conversation with the Homicide detectives, trading information back and forth as things unfolded, and got a real jolt from them. Barely a week earlier, Buddy Packer had reported to the police coming home at night to find two burglars, who he could only identify as being Hispanic, already in his house. They took him downstairs—why was this guy, dead or alive, always ending up in the basement?—where they tied him to a Lally column and proceeded to burglarize the house of various items and over a thousand dollars cash. They also took his Lincoln, leaving him with just his old pickup to get around in. It wasn't clear why they'd ignored his Indian collection. Maybe they didn't think it was worth anything. Could they have later realized their mistake and come back for it, or was the murder an entirely different operation by entirely different people? A guy would have to be monumentally unlucky, though, to be hogtied by burglars one week and shot to death by different ones the next. It could happen; you never knew.

We started thinking that maybe last week's robbery had left Buddy jumpy enough to start carrying around a .22 for protection. So on the second intrusion, whether by the same guys or not, he'd pulled his gun and taken a shot at them, but missed, thereby giving us the .22 that gouged the wood paneling. And then either he or they had fired another shot, this time with a .380, that had ended up in the Formica after also missing its target. As for the Smith & Wesson 9-mm missing from its box, God only knew what that weapon had to do with anything.

We also learned from Homicide that Buddy Packer's friends and neighbors all spoke of him as a very nice guy, well liked, with no known enemies. He did, however, have a tendency to get in over his head financially. He owed money all over the place, personal debts, business debts, which had everybody wondering if last week's burglary, which the cops hadn't found overwhelmingly convincing in the first place, might not have been staged for an insurance payoff. Only how would that tie in with this week's murder? There'd also been talk of possibly shady stuff in his trucking business, and he'd recently been indicted for illegal dumping in Jersey. So Homicide had plenty to chew on.

Eventually we got to the body, after working with the ID people setting up the areas to be dusted and the photographs and videos we wanted. We followed the ME down the steps and slid the body off them and onto the cellar floor to give the ME room for his prelim, intended mainly to provide a tentative cause of death. In this case it appeared to be a single small gunshot to the back of the head, most likely by a .22.

Anything else would have to await the autopsy, and the ME already had a morgue wagon standing by to take the body to the morgue. The problem that immediately arose involved getting 250 pounds of what was literally and figuratively deadweight up these very steep and narrow steps to a spot level enough for a gurney. One of life's mysteries to me is the certainty that the morgue wagon will always arrive with only one man aboard. The assumption, I guess, is that there'll be lots of young, strapping policemen around to help transport the body wherever the hell it has to go. Of course, not many young policemen, strapping or otherwise, are eager to develop much expertise in this specialty, so I'm usually the one who ends up being conscripted, as I was this time, along with the equally unthrilled Jack Mario and Bob Genna.

I have learned, though, to make sure when a body is being moved up or down at any angle to go for the up end, since the weight naturally tends downward. So Jack and I led the way up with the feet, while the driver and Genna struggled manfully with the arms and shoulders below us. Actually, we all struggled, cramped into that impossibly tight space, and I could feel my back screaming at me with each wrenching step.

When Jack and I finally got the feet up to the door, huffing and cursing and grunting, I couldn't help thinking of Archie Bunker and his son-in-law trying to get through the same doorway at the same time, with neither willing to give way for the other. Well, either Jack or I would have happily let the other go first, but we couldn't manage that without shifting even more weight onto the poor guys beneath us, so we forced ourselves and the feet through at the same time, like sausages. Then we had to make a sharp turn in the narrow hallway, sort of pulling the body along until the guys below managed to squeeze through the door themselves with the torso.

Through all this, Diane stood to one side politely observing us sweating and straining. She had these gigantically long nails, so afterward we couldn't resist razzing her on them, saying she'd better get them trimmed if she wanted to do crime scenes because she'd be expected to pitch in and help move bodies just like everyone else. Oh, I can't trim them, she said. They're not mine. I can't even get them off.

I was stiff as a board for days from all the lugging, and the morgue driver, the youngest of us by far, is still out with a sprained back. Maybe we need more sophisticated techniques, with winches and pulleys like piano movers use, to relocate large, heavy, and inert objects from down wherever to up wherever.

After all the hours we'd spent working the scene, we brought back to the lab a decent collection of evidence: the two gun boxes, the two bullets and casings we'd found, and after the ME's autopsy, the bullet that killed him, which we were all pleased to learn was a .22 that matched the one we'd found on the floor, so at least we didn't have a fourth gun to worry about.

Don Doller also developed some lovely footwear impressions using the Amido black on the kitchen linoleum, which I think he showed you, and probably even bragged about, when he showed you around the Trace Lab. He was even able to extract similar footwear patterns in blood from the quilts. This plus the blood-stains on the hall rug seemed to confirm that Packer had been shot in the kitchen and then dragged through the hall on the quilts and dumped down the stairs.

But even though our lab people did a good job at the scene un-covering all sorts of ballistic and other evidence, you don't always get a correlation between your success in gathering evidence and the usefulness of the evidence in tracking the bad guy down. So even though we had all this stuff neatly bagged and labeled, Homicide really didn't know where to begin. No one could even guess why Buddy Packer's body ended up on the cellar steps. As for motives, had Buddy Packer been mixed up in a criminal feud, a turf war? Had some loan shark gotten impatient over his long-standing debts? (His woeful financial situation was confirmed when all those big rigs in the parking area were repossessed shortly after his murder.) Maybe the burglars from the week be-fore—if they existed—had come back again and somehow ended up killing him this time. And then there was the girlfriend/ex-wife situation, normally an area Homicide paid a lot of attention to. In this instance, Buddy seemed to have gotten along just fine with both of them.

The investigators had come up with only a single lead. One of Buddy's mechanics who'd been having trouble with his wife had slept over at Buddy's a few nights. That would have given the guy some knowledge of the layout and Buddy's possessions and habits, but what did that prove? Nothing else suggested the mechanic was a guy who'd repay his boss's sympathy by killing him.

My microscope tests on the bullets and casings we'd brought back showed that the .22 that killed Packer was fired by the same small handgun, probably a Beretta, that fired the bullet that had gouged the wood paneling and fallen to the floor. We did not possess that gun. The 9-mm shells from the gun box seemed to have played no part in the murder, and we did not possess that gun either. The bullet in the Formica indeed proved to be a .380, as I'd suspected. Since we did not possess that third weapon, and it wasn't a .380 that had killed Packer, none of this information seemed of very much help or interest.

Even so, I checked into land and groove impressions on the .380 to see if I could determine the kind of gun that fired it. Often I can only designate a certain *class* of weapon because of the commonality of many markings. In this case, though, the rifling was unusual enough for me to be fairly certain the bullet had come from a Sterling .380 handgun. A small manufacturing firm in upstate New York, Sterling had gone out of business and I didn't often run across their products, but besides making a vague mental note of the situation, all I could do was add the bullet to our open file.

Here's where the hunch came in. As we receive the continuing flow of all firearms items confiscated for whatever reason in Suffolk County, we have to decide how to handle them. We might have bullets but no gun, gun but no bullets, maybe both but no suspect. If the item's linked to a major crime, it naturally receives priority treatment. But we get most guns on illegal possession, and usually just check to see if they're in working order, if they've been discharged recently, if they show any unusual or suspicious features. Unless something looks fishy, we then forward them directly to the property bureau.

Our evidence file, by contrast, contains only those firearms items connected to open cases involving crimes against persons, such as robberies, assaults, and homicides, but there's never any shortage of them, and our files keep growing all the time.

With all this always in mind, a couple of weeks ago I'm going through a batch of illegally possessed guns when I come across a Sterling .380. Now, although Sterling was a small firm, hardly in the league of Colt or Smith & Wesson, they still produced hundreds of thousands of .380s, most of which were probably still floating around. This one had come in from Mastic, down on the South Shore, as a Possession Four violation. That's the least serious possession charge, referring to an unloaded weapon with no appropriate ammunition at hand, the sort of thing I'd normally pay no attention to at all.

But I get what I can only describe as this vague feeling, no more than a kind of idle curiosity, and figure I'll at least go as far as checking out the report on its confiscation. Even this much interest is unusual, because these things are usually cut-and-dried. In this instance, it turns out that some guy whose name meant nothing to me got into an argument with his ex-girlfriend and started brandishing around this empty gun. She called the cops, who hauled the guy in and routinely sent along his gun to us. My brain is still telling me, So what?

Then I check the times and dates in the police report. The gun brandishing in Mastic took place Saturday afternoon, maybe twelve hours after Buddy Packer's murder, which the investigators had set around midnight on Friday.

Of course, Packer was killed by a .22, but a Sterling .380 had been in the house at least long enough to fire a bullet into the Formica. Wouldn't it be a hell of a thing if the gun brandisher's Sterling .380 had actually been in Packer's house, only a few miles away, at the time of the murder?

Very offhandedly I mentioned to my assistant George Krivosta that maybe I'd just mosey downstairs and test-fire this gun just to see what I come up with. He reacted exactly as I would have. What, are you crazy? You're gonna be wasting your time now checking every Possession Four against every open homicide in the file? I gave him a little shrug and said, Look, I got a hunch, that's all. In true professional fashion, George lets out a roar and gently suggests what an intelligent man might do with a hunch like that.

To give some idea how unusual this interest of mine was, in my whole twenty years in the lab I have never once succeeded in matching any possession gun against my open-crime file. Never. Not once. And in order to make a valid comparison, I have to take the weapon downstairs and test-fire it into the tank and then microscopically compare the test bullets to the twenty or so open-case bullets of the same type in my file. We're talking maybe thirty, forty hours of glass time. Even when we've had some cause to suspect a connection between two weapons, we've never come up with anything. So I had absolutely no historical precedent on my side, clearly justifying George's more than skeptical reaction.

Only I happened to be the boss, so I flipped him the old cheerio and headed down to the water tank where I test-fired the Sterling with some nice fresh ammunition. Then I spent a couple of days, far more time than I had any right to allocate on what I had, trying to match up those test bullets microscopically with the .380 we plucked from the Formica. All the results were inconclusive, though, because the Formica bullet's impact had damaged its markings. I couldn't say yes, I couldn't say no. But we'd also recovered the casing from that bullet in the kitchen drawer, and casings don't get battered on impact, because there is no impact— they just pop out of the weapon. That casing had been routinely sent to ID to be dusted for fingerprints, so I called them and urged them to expedite it back to me as soon as possible. Sure, they said. There'd been no prints anyhow.

Almost as soon as I got this casing from Buddy Packer's kitchen drawer under the microscope, my knees started knocking. Even at first glance, the markings closely matched those from my test-firing. But close wasn't enough; the match had to be exact. So I went back to the bullet dug out of the Formica and to the test bullets, and spent a great many painstaking hours squinting into the eyepieces of my dual microscopes before I felt ready to make a definitive statement. The bullet from Packer's kitchen Formica definitely came from the .380 Sterling the guy in Mastic had brandished at his girlfriend only hours later.

I called Homicide for Vinnie O'Leary, the chief investigator on the Packer killing, only he wasn't working that day. He'd been putting in so much overtime on the case that his boss wanted him to take some time off. I called him at home, figuring he'd be as excited as I was, and that turned out to be an understatement. Who was this guy waving the gun? he asked, and I gave him the name from the police report but it didn't ring a bell, so he asked where the guy lived, and when I gave him the address, I heard an actual gasp over the phone. Holy shit, O'Leary said. That's two doors down from Packer's sleep-over mechanic.

From that point on, things moved quickly. O'Leary scooped up the gun brandisher, one Carlos Rivera, who was out on his own recognizance awaiting arraignment on fourth-degree possession and menacing. The judge hadn't required bail since the charge was deemed minor, which turned out to be a real break for the investigators, O'Leary said. If Rivera had to post bail, it would have placed him in a different category insofar as being under suspicion, and would have made interrogating him much more difficult. As it was, he could be questioned as a material witness, and he readily admitted frightening his girlfriend with the empty Sterling .380, although naturally he insisted he never meant any harm.

More important, he was also adamant on never having been near Buddy Packer's house or knowing the first thing about any kind of robbery or murder. The investigators believed him, but wanted to know who else had access to his gun. Oh yeah, Carlos said. His brother Miguel, who everybody called Mike, shared his apartment and had borrowed it overnight on Friday. O'Leary must have let out another gasp, because that, of course, was the night Buddy Packer was murdered.

So they grabbed brother Miguel, alias Mike, and he spilled what he claimed was the whole story. Yes, he'd borrowed his brother's gun, and had been in the house when Buddy Packer was killed, although he hadn't done the dirty deed, the other guy had. What other guy? This guy who lived a couple of doors down named Freddy Shore—none other than Packer's sleep-over mechanic. Mike then proceeded to give a full recounting that, as he progressed, sounded at least in part self-serving.

It all started the week before the murder, Mike said, when Freddy Shore told him about his boss, who lived in a house hidden in the woods loaded with cash and other stuff of value. Freddy said he couldn't do anything himself, because he'd of course be recognized if the boss happened to pop in unexpectedly. But why, he suggested, couldn't Mike and some like-minded friend wait till the house was empty some night and just slip in and help themselves, and then split the take with Freddy since he was the one that tipped them off to the opportunity? So Mike and his friend moved in on the house, and when they were surprised by Buddy Packer's return, they overpowered him and tied him to a Lally column down in the cellar while they finished looting the place.

The following week, Mike said, Freddy Shore started getting very nervous. Buddy Packer was making a big stink about the robbery, snooping around and asking questions and talking to the police, and Mike suspected Freddy was worried that if the cops found Mike and the other burglar, they might be so ungentlemanly as to turn him in as the instigator of the whole thing. Anyhow, Freddy told Mike that they had no choice: Mike and his friend had to go back and kill Buddy Packer before he screwed them all. Mike's friend said he wanted no part of killing someone in cold blood, and pulled out in no uncertain terms. Mike said he tried to pull out too, but Freddy wouldn't let him, and forced him to go along by promising that he, Freddy, would be right by his side. Freddy then pressured him into borrowing his brother's nice big

Sterling .380, a serious heavy-duty weapon perfect for bumping someone off.

So it was Freddy the mechanic and Mike Rivera who staked out Packer's empty house Friday night, waiting for him to return so they could kill him. They waited in the dark, Mike said, Freddy outside and Mike himself in the garage with the .380. He started fooling around with the gun, he said, and it accidentally went off. He didn't know what or where the bullet hit, but found the casing on the floor and put it in his pocket. Then he went into the kitchen, where he did some *more* fooling around with the same gun until the damned thing went off again, the bullet this time lodging in the Formica. Again he searched for the casing but couldn't find it, and this became the one we discovered in the kitchen drawer, where it'd obviously fallen without him noticing it. He was so concerned with not leaving the casing behind, he said, he unplugged the refrigerator and shoved it away from the wall to search behind it.

The part we all wondered about was whether anybody could possibly be stupid enough to keep playing with a gun until it went off a *second* time. Sure, Mike wanted the cops to believe that those two shots were mere accidents, and that all the firing with the Sterling .380 took place before Buddy Packer even arrived on the scene. And it wasn't, after all, the Sterling .380 that killed Buddy, but the single .22 bullet lodged in the back of his head, which probably came from Buddy's own little gun.

Anyhow, through a combination of physical evidence, Mike's version, and a certain amount of speculation, Homicide concluded there was almost certainly some kind of scuffle when Packer returned, with Mike taking a couple of wild shots with the .380 until either he or Freddy Shore got Packer's .22 away from him, missed him once with it, giving us the bullet that bounced off the oak paneling, and then got him in the back of the head and killed him with the next bullet.

According to Mike, of course, Freddy Shore shot him—as Packer was on his hands and knees pleading for his life with this former employee who he'd befriended by taking him into his home. But Freddy showed no mercy, Mike said, and killed the guy in cold blood for "no reason at all," which seemed an odd thing for Mike to say, since he'd already admitted that was their whole intent in going there together, to kill the guy.

Anyhow, there are still some odds and ends which everyone's trying to clear up before the trial. We never recovered, for instance, Packer's .22, which was no doubt the murder weapon, and we're still waiting for permission from the new owners of the house to search the garage area for that first bullet that Mike says went off accidentally. If we find it, and can plot out angles and things of that nature, we might get a lot better idea of the circumstances under which it was fired.

But Mike Rivera's story answered at least some of our questions. Now we know why the fridge was unplugged. We also learned why Packer's pickup was parked behind the house, where he himself never left it. They were hiding it, Mike said, so that if some relative or neighbor came by they'd think Packer was away and wouldn't go inside. And dumping the body down the cellar steps? Well, with the same sort of brilliance they'd shown all along, they figured that if someone did go inside they'd still think Packer was away and so would just leave. To the same end, they'd washed most of the blood off the linoleum. Maybe they were counting on no one *ever* finding the body.

Mike Rivera and Freddy Shore are now awaiting trial for murder. The third friend from the week before will be tried for that robbery. Of all the guys scooped up because of that funny hunch I had about that Sterling .380, the only one not in jail facing a very long prison term is Carlos Rivera himself, the gun owner whose brandishing got everything going for us.

The fact that Miguel, alias Mike, was so ready to talk was certainly a big break for everyone concerned in this case, and people are often surprised at the number of suspects who voluntarily confess to all sorts of heinous crimes. Some guys, like Terry Harrington in the murder of Barbara Lambert, seem eager to tell everything. Others clam up at first but gradually start revealing important details or, as with Ronnie DeFeo, regale you with one confession after another, each more farfetched than the last. Some never give you word one. Their lips are sealed. These are usually the more disciplined types, who've carefully plotted out the crime and remain in strict command of their feelings and actions. William Patterson, for instance, who purchased a rifle the week before and drove a thousand miles up from Georgia to shoot his wife, has never admitted anything.

Of course, you don't just plunk someone down and say, Talk! First of all, an accusatory tone generally produces an automatic denial as a defensive reaction. The experienced detective has learned to be patient, and is adept at sensing moods and feelings, anxieties if you will. He waits for the right moment, the right button to push to encourage the guy to talk.

A lot of people will say, Hey, we know how you encourage someone to talk, you put him under a glaring light and pound the shit out of him with rubber hoses. Well, I'm not claiming that never happened, but I will say it's a kind of Hollywood cliché from the past and not at all representative of today's better-educated, more highly trained law-enforcement professionals. Also, as I mentioned earlier, the Supreme Court has significantly shifted the focus of investigations from the obtaining of confessions to the gathering of physical evidence. Before Miranda and the other landmark decisions, getting a confession, one way or another, was often crucial in establishing a case. Today that's not at all true, and police have to follow stringent guidelines in obtaining a statement. Investigators therefore put much more emphasis on establishing a rapport with the suspect and gaining his trust, because no one's going to talk to some cop that's threatening to jump all over him. The investigator will express a certain amount of sympathy and understanding. He'll say things like, Well, why don't you tell me your side of the story? I'm sure you had reasons for what you did. I'm sure something was bothering you, something drove you to it. What was it?

Commonly, the guy starts by offering excuses. She was coming at me with a hammer, which is why I pulled my knife. The other guy threw a punch, so I conked him with a bottle. The officer won't condone any of this, but he'll make every effort to listen with understanding and sympathy. He wants the guy to feel that he's at least getting a fair hearing.

Investigators know that a suspect, in his own mind, has probably convinced himself that he had good reasons for doing what he did. It's just human nature then for him to want to make a case for himself, complete with all his reasons and excuses and explanations. Not that listing all these for some detective in the station house will do him any good, but still, people want to at least try to vindicate themselves.

Of course, once a lawyer appears, the chances of getting a statement drop to zero. The first thing a lawyer says to his client is, Shut up, I'll do the talking here. But the very self-justifying impulses that make a suspect *want* to tell his story to anyone who'll listen are the same impulses that discourage him from calling a lawyer. The shrewd investigator will of course play on this. He'll say something like, Why don't you get it all off your chest now, before we get embroiled in lawyers and procedures and all that crap, with everybody pushing and pulling you a hundred different ways and giving you orders about what you can or can't say. Why don't you just say whatever you want now, in your own words, without anyone else twisting it all around on you?

The key element is often nothing more than the personality, or the tone, of the individual investigator. Maybe one detective hits a stone wall with a certain suspect. The rapport, the chemistry, just isn't right. He'll then let someone else try to strike a better chord. The suspect's got to feel, for whatever reason, that the detective he's dealing with, although part and parcel of the law-enforcement apparatus that's accused and arrested him, will treat him honestly and fairly, will stick to his word, won't trick or deceive him. And of course the suspect *wants* to believe that somebody, even this cop, is willing to show some sympathetic understanding of his plight.

Sometimes little, very specific, details can help break down the natural distrust of cops. One detective, aware of the suspect's worry about his wife being stranded without their car, arranged to have someone drive the car home to her. This in itself was enough to convince the fellow that the officer was a decent human who he could feel comfortable talking to.

These days most confessions occur *after* we've accumulated enough evidence to make the charges stick. The investigators enjoy the luxury of not really needing a statement and therefore aren't tempted to resort to anxious or desperate tactics to obtain one. Conversely, the suspect's awareness of the evidence against him also serves as an inducement to fessing up. After all, he knows he did it, and he knows the cops know it too. So his only recourse, in a sense, is to try to make the best possible case for himself in terms of explanations and extenuating circumstances. In the course of doing that, he'll often not only admit his guilt but reveal enough specific details to confirm it.

The word *confession,* by the way, is never used. It has all the wrong connotations. Instead, the detective might say, Why don't you just give us your recollection of the events? or The truth of what really happened? or The circumstances exactly as you re-member them. And you never push for the whole story in one big gulp, because the prospect of telling *everything* might be so daunt-ing that it'd strike the guy dumb. You take little steps, go for small details. You don't ask, Why did you shoot your ex-wife? You ask, What were you doing at her house that afternoon? Maybe he'll say, Look, I just stopped by to pick up some clothes. Well, there's your first step: he admits he was at the house. Then maybe you ask, What did she say when you showed up? Did you get the clothes? What did you do with them? You confine yourself to one piece at a time, gradually reconstructing the whole puzzle.

The familiar tough-guy bravado you're often dealing with can distinctly work to your advantage. These are guys that enjoy pushing people around, that are very macho and cock-of-the-walk in their attitudes. They enjoy thumbing their noses at all our mealy-mouth ideas about law and justice and fairness, and actu-ally take pride in the very activities that got them arrested. So very often the impulse to talk, even to a cop, comes directly from their show-off mentality. Sure, I let the guy have it. I wasn't gonna take any crap from a punk like that.

The positively weirdest example of that occurred just recently, and had all of us really shaking our heads over it. A couple of guys were murdered in a drug situation. Three suspects from the same gang were placed at the scene, one white and two blacks. When the cops picked up the white guy, he confessed to being the killer. I had the gun, he said, I pulled the trigger. But when one of the black guys learned of the confession, he became infuriated. Hey, he screamed, throwing an absolute tantrum, *he* didn't shoot those guys! *I* shot them! You think a goddamn white guy would have the guts for that, could handle a gun like that?! Don't believe a fucking word he says! I'm the guy that pulled off those killings!

THE SAUCE, THE SAUCE IS EVERYTHING

IN 1991, AFTER SPENDING fifteen years working together to turn the Wilkes Gallery into a successful business, Johnny and Jeannette gave it up, sold their house in Northport, and moved to a sprawling desert retirement area near Phoenix, Arizona—the first of the cousins, beyond my wife and me decades earlier, to move more than a few miles from the Bronx. Their bright and spacious new house was still receiving its final touches from workmen clattering and banging about while Johnny and I concluded our interviews there. We sat on the stone patio, shaded from the desert sun beneath the large arch of the house, facing the newly planted shrubs and trees of their yard, the bird feeders, the leisurely golfers moving through the soft knolls of the course across the way, close enough for us to watch them putt out on the tenth green. Beyond the golf course, maybe ten or twenty miles away but dominating the scene nonetheless, the bare and rocky purplish mountains rose to the north.

Johnny swims and golfs almost every day, both knees having been successfully operated on. He visits the local track, takes the inexpensive flights to Nevada for a day at the casinos, dines out with Jeannette and their new friends, and those old friends who've also retired nearby. Jeannette volunteers at a Phoenix art museum, keeps busy fixing up the house, organizes and deals with their visitors. "One of the things that made us hesitate about coming here," she says, "was the feeling we'd never see our family and friends again. I think we see more of them now than ever. They just keep coming." Both seem happy, and I don't think either would consider moving back.

J O H N   C U O M O   ➡

AROUND THE PERIOD OF the Waldorf and the Helmsleys, before Jeannette and I settled in at the Wilkes Gallery, I pursued a few other situations that seemed attractive. After all, when you're still in your mid-forties, with only a modest pension to count on, you keep your eye open for opportunities.

Actually, I was still on the force when an old and dear friend, Patty Biase, brought a couple of very promising investments to my attention. Patty and I had been born only a day apart, had grown up together around Pelham Bay, had even been drafted into the Army on the same day back in the fifties, so there'd always been a real bond between us. Patty spent more time in the service than I did, with the counterintelligence division, and had been active in busting up a European drug ring tied into the Army. He'd even received a presidential citation, and when he left the service he qualified for a good job with the Federal Drug Enforcement Agency. All this time we'd remained friends, and the wives and us would often spend a night out or take vacations together. Since I was attached to Narcotics for the NYPD, for maybe five years Patty and I would help each other out on various cases, further cementing our strong relationship.

Like me, Patty had an innate gambling passion, and he fulfilled a longtime ambition by getting together enough cash to purchase some trotting horses. In those days a few thousand dollars could get you into that kind of operation, and the key wasn't how much money you invested but how well you picked and trained your horses. Well, Patty found this place out on the Island where he boarded and trained the horses and worked them out during the winter. But when the expenses ran a little higher than he'd figured, he asked whether I'd be interested in becoming his partner. After talking it over with Jeannette, I bought in for a modest amount of cash. Besides, we liked and trusted Patty and knew he'd always been a real student of the trotters. Since we were both still in law enforcement, we had relatives stand in as our representatives, with their names on all the paperwork. I'm not sure of any specific regulations against it, but the general feeling was it wouldn't look good, so we didn't advertise our involvement.

At one time we had eight or nine horses, and they did all right by us. Patty had a good eye for horseflesh, and we'd engaged a veteran trainer. We picked up nice money in purses at Yonkers Raceway and other tracks, but mostly profited from betting on ourselves. When we knew our entry had a good shot at winning, we'd back him heavily, always with good odds because no one had ever heard of this little two-man operation we had. We took home some pretty handsome winnings.

Then Patty decided to leave the DEA, even though he was a widely respected agent with good prospects, because he wanted to go into business on his own. He asked me to sell him back my portion of the stable, which I did, as he planned to use the profits from the trotters for another investment he had in mind. To give you an idea of the potential of the trotters, on our last day as partners, actually our last race, Patty bet heavily on our entry at something like fifteen to one. The horse took the race, and Patty's winnings from that one bet completely funded his buyback of my whole 50 percent of the stable.

He then bought into a brand-new steakhouse chain, securing the very first Bonanza franchise on all of Long Island. Again, we're not talking big money, for an outlet in a chain no one had ever heard of. His restaurant quickly became successful, and he made plans for a second one on the Island, again approaching me

with a partnership offer. For some reason, I'd always been attracted to the restaurant business, ever since running that little
café at the government-surplus depot after World War II. At one
time my first retirement desire was to go to Brooklyn College to
study restaurant cooking and management, but it was an expensive two-year program that we couldn't have afforded on my
pension.

I was still on the force when I considered becoming Patty's partner in the second Bonanza, given my good feelings for him and
knowing how well he'd done with the first. It would have, I think,
left Jeannette and me set for life. But it wasn't meant to be, because
just then all of Patty's plans ended in a real tragedy for him and his
family. Patty was thirty-nine years old, a real healthy bull of a guy
who'd always been physically active. Well, he and his wife and another couple went out together for New Year's Eve to some place in
Syosset when out of nowhere he keeled over and died from what
the doctors said was a heart attack.

Patty had always been a very warm, popular man, with hundreds of friends, and his wake was a huge affair, with people from
all walks of life and lots of FDA and law-enforcement types from
all over the country. I was one of the pallbearers, and during the
wake all people talked about was the shock of him going so suddenly, with a lot of speculating about foul play being involved.
After all, he'd taken part in some very large-scale investigations
with the DEA, and for years he'd believed that certain powerful
drug traffickers might try to get back at him for sending them to
prison.

The autopsy was itself questionable, with the damage to his
heart not the sort associated with a typical heart attack, but more
consistent with somebody introducing a drug into the system that
could damage the heart. But nothing ever came of the rumors,
and that was the end of my Bonanza opportunity, with the very
sad death of one of my closest friends.

Not long afterward, another friend presented me with another
restaurant opportunity. Joe Flynn wasn't at all like me. He was a

lot looser guy, more of a free swinger. Joe too had been a detective,
retiring a few years before me, and through some connection had
bought a couple of restaurants down in Pinehurst, North Carolina, one featuring Chinese, the other being promoted as a "New
York style" hamburger joint featuring hamburgers on English
muffins, something I never once heard of in my whole life in New
York. For some reason it went over fabulously down there as a true
big-city treat.

Pinehurst was a small inland town not far from Fayetteville,
with a famous country club that hosted a nationally televised golf
tournament every year. The golf hall of fame was also located
there, along with area colleges, and with one thing and another,
Joe Flynn's two restaurants were doing okay. Whenever he visited
New York, he'd always rent a big suite at the Waldorf, take people
out for dinner, throw lavish parties. It was good for business, he'd
say, although it was also just his style, the way he liked to do
things. You could see he truly enjoyed spending money, and he always gave the impression of having plenty more where that came
from.

One day we got talking and he said his real ambition was to run
a classier, more upscale restaurant. Well, he'd heard about this
closed-up restaurant down there that he saw as a surefire winner
and would just love to reopen. It'd gone defunct only because the
owner had been killed in a car crash, and it had a prime location
right next to the Pinehurst Hotel and just off the famous country
club. The restaurant was called The Gray Fox and had been popular for years with the country-club crowd.

I was on my way out at Helmsley Spear and very ripe, you could
say, to get bitten once more by the restaurant bug. To give you
some idea of how much it was on my mind, when I was at the
Waldorf, I'd sometimes walk into the big kitchen just to talk with
the cooks and service workers and see how they set things up and
went about their work. Jeannette and I hadn't yet taken over the
Wilkes Gallery, so when Joe invited me down to look things over, I
went and immediately fell in love with what I saw. The town itself
was nice and attractive, the restaurant big and impressive, with a

slate roof, an alcove, a little garden. It could seat maybe sixty people, with an imposing fireplace and a balcony for small tables. Of
course it was old, and after being dormant over a year would need
money for repairs and sprucing up.

The only snag was Joe Flynn himself. Not that I didn't like him,
or didn't trust him. He was a great guy, and struck me as one hundred percent honest and honorable. Only for a guy that always
had money to spend, he was now, it turned out, broke. His problem was simple. He wouldn't just spend money, he'd squander it.
He was also a very, very generous person, an easy mark for anyone
with a hard-luck story.

After I'd visited North Carolina, Joe said we could reopen the
defunct restaurant for very little. But after he got me excited about
the possibilities, he confessed that he happened to be a little short
right now. If I'd put up the money to get us started, he'd repay me
as soon as possible. Maybe that should have scared me away but,
as I said, I knew him to be an honest, standup guy. Beyond that,
the operation really didn't call for that much cash, and since a
restaurant had previously done well in that location and Joe had
made a go of his other two Pinehurst ventures, the potential
seemed very real.

Jeannette, though, wasn't crazy about moving to North Carolina after all her life in New York, and we agreed that at the beginning she'd stay in Northport with the kids and I would come
back weekends until we saw how it worked out.

I put up the money I'd gotten from Patty Biase for my half of the
stable, found myself a condo down there, and set about getting the
restaurant opened. Most of the work fell to me, because Joe was
busy running his other two restaurants, but he still wanted a big
say in all important decisions, as did his wife, who was down there
with him. What we should do, he said, is open an Italian restaurant. The town didn't have any Italian restaurants, so we could really fill a void. I said that sounded okay to me, again banking on
Joe's experience in giving him the benefit of any doubt I had.

The hiring of a chef was typical of how they'd take over. Joe
said he was good friends with the owners of this famous Italian

restaurant in Manhattan, supposedly frequented by big-name celebrities. It was Joe's kind of flashy, showy place, and he'd often eat there himself when he was in New York. On a trip north Joe took me there, gladhanding everyone in sight, although it seemed that his friendly connection with them was mainly as a big-spending regular. Anyhow, he told them we were looking for an outstanding Italian chef for this very fancy restaurant we were opening. The people there practically smacked their lips: A chef? An Italian chef? We got just the man for you, he's in Italy, very good, very experienced, dying to come to America. He'll be perfect, just what you need. On the basis of what they said, not even knowing whether or not he'd be a legal immigrant, we agreed to pay his passage and left it at that.

Back in Carolina, I continued getting the place ready while we waited for the chef to show up. But now Joe was saying it'd be a big mistake to spend too much money on renovations, the main point was just to get open, waiting to use the profits to fix things up. So we cut corners everywhere and didn't do much besides painting the insides and general cleaning.

Our much-touted master chef, Silvio, finally arrived from Italy. He barely spoke English, but that was the least of it. His only cooking experience, it turned out, consisted of making cakes, cookies, and bonbons on a cruise ship. What he was, in other words, was a pastry chef, the last thing in the world we needed. But he was some kind of *paisan* from the chicken farm up in the hills that the New York relatives wanted to get over here. We were too close to opening day to find another chef, so were stuck with him. I should say *I* was stuck, because Joe, whose great friends had foisted this guy off on us, kept saying he'd work out fine and went back to his other restaurants.

Silvio didn't have a clue about anything, including what he needed in the kitchen. He kept making all these stupid demands, and Joe and his wife would back him on everything. He's the chef, they kept saying, he knows what he's doing. So Silvio in his broken English would say, We gotta have this, we gotta have that. And everything had to be authentic, real Italian provisions, which in no way could be found within a hundred miles of Pinehurst, North Carolina. We brought in meats and cheeses and fresh pastas from Philadelphia and New York, and sometimes the whole shipment would be ruined because it wasn't properly packed or iced. Joe Flynn even had us ordering Italian bread from some New York bakery that he said made bread that you couldn't match anywhere else in the country. You'd think a goddamn pastry chef would at least be able to bake a loaf of bread. I was really beginning to wonder whether Silvio could do anything.

The worst thing, when you consider that we were advertising this absolutely authentic Italian restaurant, was that the guy couldn't even make tomato sauce. The sauce, I kept telling him, the sauce is everything. The truth was *I* made better sauce than he did, and I spent hours trying to teach him how, but he never got it right. I was ready to ship him back to the old country, in a box if necessary.

The grand opening finally came, with the restaurant now called La Volpe, which is Italian for "the gray fox," or at least "the fox," and Joe pulled out all the stops. To begin with, he wanted only invited guests, including our families from New York. Jeannette and our daughter and my sister and brother came down, for instance, and Joe told me to put them up in a luxury golf-course condo and charge it to the business. It was all carte blanche, the best of everything regardless of cost. Oysters on the half-shell? Sure, on the house, anything you want. He stocked us with expensive booze and kept it flowing like water. Listen, John, these are good people, very good people, let's send over a bottle of champagne. Naturally it had to be Dom Perignon, at something like forty-two bucks a bottle. The dumbest part of all was that the expense of this luxurious grand-scale opening was for people, like all the guests from New York, who'd probably never set foot in the place again. Meanwhile, we couldn't afford to repair the slate roof or paint the front door.

He even insisted on a maître d', not just for the opening but afterward too. I said, Joe, these people don't need some guy in a monkey suit greeting them at the door. Christ, I'll be here, I can greet them, it'll be fine.

Anyhow, we were open, and we kept waiting for the place to take off, but it never did. Part of it was the food. We can't serve this food, I said to Joe. Just taste that sauce, how can anyone even eat it? We're never gonna survive with a goddamn pastry cook making the tomato sauce. On top of that, we had all kinds of trouble getting stuff shipped in. We gotta have tortoni, Joe would say, and I'd say, Where are we supposed to get tortoni? We'd end up with a guy driving down two hundred miles from Richmond, Virginia, to deliver frozen tortoni.

And the worse Silvio cooked, the fancier he got. He kept putting all these delicate exotic-type dishes on the menu that no one down there had ever heard of. They could tell what it tasted like, though, and people just stopped coming in droves. We should've been serving pasta, meatballs, chicken cacciatore, pizzas. They'd have gone for something like that, I think.

We finally dumped Silvio, and Joe Flynn brought in a local chef he knew, who was at least an improvement, but the situation was really wearing me down, what with traveling home every weekend on top of all the pressures and worries down there. I'd close up the restaurant Saturday night at eleven and drive all night to get home Sunday morning, only to turn around and head back first thing Monday to open up for Monday night, twelve hours of hard driving each way, desperately groping the whole time for some way out, the big break that'd put us over the top.

I actually worked out a deal with the Pinehurst, the biggest hotel around, for them to give their overflow dining-room crowd coupons good at our place, which would have helped a lot, but Joe Flynn brushed the idea aside. He was always like that, his wife too, knocking anything I came up with.

Joe's main problem, I'm convinced, was that he always had to think big. He couldn't be bothered with details, and had no sense of how taking care of little things could make everything else easier. His great brainstorm was to start a Pinehurst tennis tournament, as part of the world tour with huge money prizes and worldwide press and TV coverage to lure in the top international players. It'd be like the big golf tourney there. It was a perfect example of Joe's kind of thinking. He didn't care about getting fifty more customers a week. He wanted a scheme that'd make us overnight millionaires.

And, like always, he had the perfect connection to guarantee success, another terrific friend, this time some TV actor named Edd "Kookie" Byrnes, who had been on the series *77 Sunset Strip.* Well, the idea never got off the ground. It was a complete bomb.

About six months of that backbreaking schedule, working and worrying and commuting, was all I could take, especially since the place just wasn't making it. I told Joe I was sorry but I couldn't manage anymore, it was too hard on my family. He said he understood and agreed to buy out my share of the business and pay back what I put in for his share. Although naturally, this being Joe Flynn, he confessed to being short of ready cash just at that moment. But he promised to pay everything back within a year, and since I'd always believed him to be an honorable man, I went along. And he did exactly what he said, he paid back every penny without ever missing a single payment.

That ended my fling as racehorse owner and restaurant investor—more or less stumbling from Yonkers Raceway to Bonanza to La Volpe in Pinehurst, North Carolina, home of the golf hall of fame. You could say it was a string of failures and missed opportunities, but you have to remember that I started out with only a modest amount of money, our life savings, and ended up with that same amount, maybe even a few dollars more, which was still available for the right investment. This time we found it right under our nose, where it'd been the whole time: the Wilkes Gallery.

We knew what we were getting into when we bought the gallery, in a prosperous area of nice shops, because Jeannette had gained real insights into the business while working there part-time. We steadily expanded all the time before selling it to retire here in

1991. It isn't a very dramatic story, but I guess success usually isn't.

A real turning point was when we got the school-district work, framing all their certificates for retirement, for academic and athletic awards. On the basis of that, the VA hospital came to us, and we'd sometimes frame as many as 250 pieces at a time for them. And Jeannette, with her artistic touch and design background, consulted with the VA in picking out the art and displaying it for them when they opened a new wing. We expanded the gallery into a much larger space, took over a big Hallmark line, sold art supplies and unusual crafts and artifacts. But it didn't come easy. All those years we worked long hours six days a week, including Sunday afternoons. I'd remember how, maybe sixty years earlier, my father and your father, George, worked together in a fruit-and-vegetable store. Times were hard and they didn't do as well as Jeannette and I did, but running our own store certainly made me appreciate how hard they must have worked at it.

People would comment sometimes how strange it was for a street detective to end up framing artwork and selling giftware. I never thought the connection was hard to understand. Maybe the popular picture of cops as shoot-'em-up, push-'em-around bullies doesn't leave room for this part of a policeman's makeup, but most cops I knew went into law enforcement because they wanted to be out there mingling with people, talking and interacting and observing. They never wanted to hide behind a desk or work in a stockroom or library. They enjoyed seeing what people were like, learning what made them tick. Although of course the mixture you encountered out on the street included a lot of mean and dangerous people, the real dregs, which you didn't get at the Wilkes Gallery. But that was certainly all right with me.

I'd run into enough of those types to last me a lifetime.

DAY TWO
AT THE CRIME LAB

IT WAS JUNE BEFORE I got down from Massachusetts again for another day at the lab. The memory of my first visit in February was still vivid, and will probably always remain so. It wasn't just the unexpected jolt of the morgue. I was also taken by the thought of the Crime Lab—a modest building, modestly staffed, full of quite normal people in quite normal rooms—as the hub of all crime detection in a county of a million and a half people. Everything ended up there: the finger- and footwear prints, the stolen and wrecked cars, the hundreds of photos and sketches and notes documenting each crime scene, the endless reports of endless interrogations, the bullets, the guns, the bloody clothing, and, of course, the bodies.

With all this in mind, I casually decided to pay attention to crime stories in the newspapers, not the daily litany of murders and rapes and assaults and burglaries, but items of a more general nature. I wasn't sure exactly what I was looking for, maybe a sense of the importance of the issue to editors, and by extension to the public. I also wondered if I might find anything like a consensus out there, about anything.

The undertaking could most charitably be described as idiosyncratic, with no pretense to completeness, fairness, or organization. I kept at it for a couple of months, but followed only two papers: the Springfield *Union-News*, my regular source of news about the cities, towns, and rural areas of western Massachusetts, and *The New York Times*. I didn't include any local or national TV news, documentary and feature accounts. If I had, everything that follows could be multiplied many times over.

The answer to my question about consensus came quickly. For everyone supporting a caning in Singapore, someone else denounced the practice as barbaric. For every argument for outlawing guns or legalizing drugs came another demanding that we keep guns legal and get tough on drugs. The battle lines were drawn everywhere: stricter punishment vs. more rehabilitation, more jails vs. more probation, money for education vs. money for cops. Even more complicated and contentious differences arose over welfare, family values, parental responsibility, curfews, boot camps, religion in the schools, violence in the schools, illegal immigration, police corruption, political corruption, public apathy. Three strikes and you're out? Absolutely! Never! The death penalty as a deterrent? It only makes sense. It makes no sense at all. And both sides of every issue arrived lugging suitcases full of studies proving their point.

I wasn't surprised by the debaters as much as I was impressed by their ferocity. The lion may yet lie down with the lamb, but the guns and the antiguns, the punishers and the rehabilitators, the social critics and the champions of personal accountability, are not in our lifetime going to break bread with one another.

The *Union-News* ran a Mike Royko column headlined CONGRESS DOESN'T HAVE A CLUE ABOUT COPING WITH CRIME. Well, who does? I began to see that everyone does. Only, my clue is better than your clue, which I'd just as soon not even hear about.

As to my more general curiosity about how these papers handled crime, let me, with no real faith in statistics, pass along a few statistics. The moment I started clipping, I realized I'd have to file by category or would never again find anything. Even though I'd miss an occasional issue or forget to go back to something I'd noticed earlier, my folders now contain the following number of stories in the following categories:

Drugs: 24 items, including a plea for legalization by Dear Abby and a Sunday feature, THE DRUG FIX, with several experts demanding "a new strategy in the war against drugs" while disagreeing totally as to what that strategy should be.
Guns: 12
Police: 26 items, advocating more and better police, fewer but better police, better-paid police, better-trained police, better-educated police, more honest police, more sensitive police, tougher police, more public support for police, more police walking the beat, more computers for police, better guns for police, no guns for police, don't trust your police, thank God for your police.
Solutions: 25
Toughness: 13
Statistics: 11
Miscellaneous: 14

I counted 125 items. In addition, I was (un)fortunate enough to run head-on into an extensive *Union-News* series under the rubric FIGHTING CRIME/SAVING OUR COMMUNITIES. This was not some timid article-a-day deal. This was a series to end all series. A prefatory "To the Readers" note revealed the oceanic nature of the deluge to follow:

> *A team of 37 reporters, editors, photographers and artists worked for three months to assemble a comprehensive look at crime in our region. Over the next four days, our readers will have the opportunity to not only become more knowledgeable about this serious problem but also learn what we can do about it.*
>
> *It's important that readers understand that this is not an attempt to tell them how bad things are. We are providing information that is useful in their daily lives. This is an effort to educate. Knowledge is power.*

As an English prof, I've always considered myself a dues-paying member of the knowledge-is-power crowd, but even a professor can spot overkill when it threatens to drown him. On Sunday, May 1, 1994, the paper ran no fewer than *thirty* features on crime. We're not talking about snippets, but long, profusely illustrated articles with multicolor graphics and loud headlines. The lead story took top-center of page one:

YOU CAN'T HIDE

FEAR OF CRIME CASTS ITS SHADOW ACROSS WMASS.

Inside, the various sections competed with one another for spectacular coverage. The "Home" section presented a half-page drawing, titled A SAFER HOME, tagging sixteen danger spots of a typical residence. The "Living" section began with a huge, lurid headline: DOMESTIC (boxed in red) VIOLENCE (in large black caps). "Business" informed us WORKPLACE VIOLENCE EXACTS TOLL—TERRIFYING IMAGES PROMPT EMPLOYERS TO TAKE PRECAUTIONS. "Leisure" ran a red-and-black column down the left edge of the page, tracing TV violence since the fifties, and led with an imposing color photo of Arnold Schwarzenegger aiming a handgun right at the reader for an

article entitled TAKING DEAD AIM—VIOLENCE, CRIME GRAB SPOT-
LIGHT ON-SCREEN. "Emphasis" assured us, unequivocally, EPI-
DEMIC OF VIOLENCE SICKENS U.S.

And these were merely the *lead* articles, followed by much
more of the same inside the sections. Reeling from these
screaming headlines, I could only think of the minister's
note in the margin of his sermon: "Argument weak here—
Pound on pulpit!"

Even "Sports," that sacred preserve memorializing daily
encounters of no significance whatever, got into the act.
They seemed rather lame about it, though, and could only
come up with a single article, VIOLENCE IN SPORTS INCREASES
AMONG PROS, AMATEURS. During my brief newspaper experience, we loved to run internal contests designed primarily to
make someone else in the newsroom squirm. Whoever was
on the Sports copy desk that evening would be a shoo-in for
"Feeblest Headline of the Year," almost rivaling James
Thurber's marvelous WHO HAS NOTICED THE SORES ON THE BACKS
OF THE HORSES IN THE ANIMAL HUSBANDRY BARN?

Sportswriters, I've always believed—and I speak as a fan,
a lifelong follower of games—are not comfortable in the real
world. Give them even a whiff of relevance, and they turn as
craven as whipped dogs. Their colleagues in Business or
Fashion or even Home may salivate at the thought of being
turned loose on CRIME, but they do not. That's why certain
young scribblers, including those cheerful ne'er-do-wells
permanently banished, usually for good reason, from the
news desk, the city beat, the editorial offices, decide to become sportswriters in the first place. They're honest enough
to admit that they simply do not give a damn about anything
important, and therefore end up enjoying themselves and
helping their readers do the same. God bless them, I say.

After wading through the 125 clippings in my files, and
the 30 items celebrating the first day of the series, I didn't
bother to count, let alone read, the dozens and dozens that
followed on succeeding days. For me, at least, the point had

been made, although I'm not sure exactly what that point was. I found myself greatly looking forward, however, to another visit to the Crime Lab, where the fervor was as strong but more focused, more restrained, and where no one spoke in headlines.

And this second day was to be Al's, concentrating on his work in ballistics and at crime scenes. He prepped me for the visit the night before over a beer in the living room of his and Carrie's place in Plainview, about fifteen miles west of the Hauppauge lab, just over the line in Nassau County.

AL DELLA PENNA ➡

UNTIL ABOUT 1960, physical evidence collected by police was minimal, usually either firearms or fingerprints. Confessions were what you were after. You questioned lots of witnesses, interrogated suspects, pushed for a signed statement: I admit it, I done the dirty deed, I shot Aunt Martha and sold off her diamond brooch for dope.

The Supreme Court's Miranda decision in 1966 changed all that. Not only did the court strengthen the rights of suspects and curtail the way confessions could be obtained, it also warned the police, in essence, not to rely on a confession as their solitary evidence. So police were suddenly forced to broaden and improve their procedures, and did so by reaching out to the theories and practices developed by a French scientist, Edmund Locard, back around the turn of the century.

Locard originated the use of scientific methods in police investigations. Go out and collect real data, he said, and then develop laboratories to analyze, interpret, and present this data as convincing testimony. But it was only after Miranda, many years later, that we learned to do just that, and base our whole approach to criminal investigation on something far more solid than someone's bleary-eyed confession to a murder that he would later completely disavow in court. And although I doubt if anyone foresaw this from the beginning, it's turned out that the emphasis on physical evidence has been especially valuable in the prosecution of one-on-one, unwitnessed crimes such as rapes, assaults, homicides, where you often have nothing to go on but what the criminal has unwittingly left behind.

We were still in the earlier stages of this shift when I came into the lab, and things have of course changed enormously since then. Maybe we haven't quite moved from the Stone Age to the Space Age, but it sure feels like that sometimes.

I'd been a patrolman for seven years in Suffolk County when I moved inside in 1968. The whole Crime Lab employed maybe ten people then, less than a third of what we have now, and my only firearms background was some modest armorer's training in the Marines, plus whatever you happened to pick up as a police officer. Since there were no specialized schools, you read and studied on your own and attended the training sessions run by major manufacturers. Mostly you learned on the job, working on the guns that came through the door.

We were much less compartmentalized in the lab then. Even though I was in Firearms, I was expected to help out wherever the need was greatest. We had a lot of narcotics coming in, so I'd drop into the Chem Lab and see how they operated, learn their basic procedures. The same with Serology and the other units, and it's been valuable over the years to understand the other guy's perspective, even though the details we learned back then are pretty archaic now.

Into the seventies, we had precious little to work with inside, and even less an idea of what to look for outside. We'd go to a homicide scene, maybe scrape up some blood, bag some stained clothing, pick up any bullets or casings. We never sketched anything, rarely took measurements, wrote skimpy notes. When we got back to the lab we'd say, We think this is blood on this shirt. Is it? Can you say whose? And they'd tell us it was definitely Type A, which meant the detectives could now limit their search to a mere 40 percent of the total population.

We also had people taking photographs, usually one guy from

ID toting a Graflex with huge flash attachments and one-shot bulbs, like the old newspaper photogs lugged around.

Beyond that, we had the capacity to collect and categorize fingerprints, although we had to do all the matching by hand, and could generally only confirm whether or not a suspect already in custody produced the prints on the gun. You had to use the naked eye just to classify a print into a general category that would include thousands, even millions, of prints, depending on whether you used a local, regional, or national base. If you narrowed down to burglars or rapists or drug pushers, you'd still have to deal with an incredible number of files and a very tedious search prone to all sorts of errors and oversights. Even today, fingerprints are rarely used in a cold search, although the technology is available to move in that direction with computer imaging and national data bases. Back then, of course, a cold search was just about impossible.

At rape scenes, our basic tool was ultraviolet light. We knew prostatic fluid produced a fluorescence under it, so would pass the UV over the bed or car seat or whatever looking for fluorescence. It told you what sheet or upholstery swatch to bring in, but not a hell of a lot more. It was worthless as far as identifying its source.

In those days, however, it was standard procedure to take a sample of blood from whatever suspect we had in hand. We were provided with a kit for this purpose containing a small lancet, and would jab the guy in the finger and squeeze a couple of drops into a vial with a preservative. Eventually the practice was eliminated as being too invasive, although it wasn't just the civil-liberties people who complained. The police union said we were crazy to be drawing blood. What the hell medical background did we have? One of these days, they warned us, we'd be sued for millions by some guy claiming the lancet we'd pricked him with gave him some godawful disease.

The fact is, lab people didn't go out much back then, and never thought of protecting the crime scene. We'd just drive up in our little Ford, with a supply kit the size of a fishing-tackle box, and grab anything in sight. Now we have this monstrous van containing every conceivable piece of equipment ever deemed useful, and we'd never barge in on anything. We'll even pull back sometimes and go sit in the van to talk things over before making a move.

I look now at the DeFeo file, six murders in a prominent family, and it's really *thin*, maybe half an inch thick. We recently resolved a case that no one ever heard of that produced enough paper to fill three whole expansion files.

I went to a digging scene a few weeks back that really shows the changes that have taken place. It was a Jane Doe situation where the body was accidentally discovered by some Korean wood walkers, who frequently roam around looking for wild herbs for healing or whatever. They spotted a hand sticking up from what turned out to be a shallow grave. Years ago, we would have said, Okay, we got a body here, let's dig it up and get it back to the morgue to see what the ME can tell us. Now it's, Don't touch a thing, get tarps down so we don't make footprints, get photos from this angle, from that angle, from every angle before anyone even touches a shovel. Even after we started digging, we'd stop every inch or so to take more pictures and collect more soil samples. We wanted them from every level. Suppose one guy digging the grave left at a certain point and the soil mixture on his shoes was different than on the shoes of whoever stayed behind and kept digging?

It used to be we'd spend an hour or two at a typical crime scene. I remember one old boss saying, What the hell have you guys been doing for three hours? You got some kind of boondoggle going for you out there? Now we average a good eight or nine hours, with twelve or even fifteen not that unusual. We'll spend three hours just waiting for the casting materials to dry.

One big advantage of all these changes is that we're no longer asking the Homicide detective, for instance, to wear too many hats. A detective's invaluable expertise lies in interview and interrogation. He's extremely good at knocking on doors and establishing rapport with people, at making on-the-spot assessments of honesty and credibility. He's also adept at drawing conclusions from all the facts and clues and conjectures whirling around him during an investigation. But he's not trained to gather, or package, or preserve, evidence, so he's not asked to do that anymore. We'll take care of it, we tell him. You go with your strengths and we'll go with ours.

And when you're collecting evidence, the basic rule is to handle everything as little as possible. On occasion, you'll actually get instances of an officer picking up a cassette player and turning it on to see whether it's working, or what's on the tape inside. Right at the beginning Locard said, You can't touch anything without changing it. When you walk into a room, you modify it by what you bring in, and later modify it by what you take out. He called it the exchange principle. Somewhat later a German scientist, Werner Heisenberg, set forth a parallel idea in his uncertainty theory. He said you can't measure both the speed and the location of an electron at the same time, because the measurement of either distorts the other. Therefore, he said, nothing is ever truly certain, and when we're talking about evidence, in spite of the marvelous advances, we're really only dealing with levels of approximation. Still, any bit of information about a crime is helpful, and you never know where that final piece that solves the whole puzzle will come from, or even if it exists, but it's what you're always trying to unearth.

Our growing awareness of safety and ecology concerns has prompted lots of big changes in the lab. I don't know if you've ever noticed, but I've had something of a hearing loss for years. I'm sure my military experience had something to do with it, but a lot comes from my first years in the lab. In those days, somebody would say, Stick a little cotton or something in your ears when you're firing, and we figured that would take care of any problem. And this was in a lab about the size of a large bathroom. Really. I'd do my microscope and paperwork at my desk and then close the door so I wouldn't bother anyone else and do my test-firings into the water tank squeezed right into the same tiny room. Sometimes I think it's a miracle I can still hear anything.

Labs and morgue areas have always used all manner of toxic, cancer-causing, liver-damaging, skin-burning, eyesight-threaten-

ing, and otherwise nasty and noxious materials, and no one ever
gave that much thought either. I remember working with some
shot-shell wadding that had been removed from the leg of a guy
wounded during a robbery. A technician had preserved the
wadding in formaldehyde, traditionally the standard procedure.
Only suddenly nobody wanted to go near it. Everybody said, You
got it, Al, it's your evidence, you take care of it. Well, I'd learned
enough not to want any part of it either, so I went back to the
technician and said, Look, I'll keep the specimen, but do you have
some way of disposing of the formaldehyde? Oh sure, he said, and
strolled over to the sink and poured it down the drain. Good Christ,
I yelled, what the hell are you *doing* with that?

He sort of blinked at me and said, What am I doing with what?

I'VE ALWAYS FELT THAT the gift of a good teacher is the ability
to re-create his own enthusiasm in his students. After an
evening listening to Al talk about the Crime Lab, I couldn't
wait to get back to it, wondering how I'd managed to miss so
much the first time. It was another pleasant, warm day, with
the young trees on the Crime Lab grounds in full leaf, the
bushes bountiful, the flowers blooming.

In his office, Al checks the messages on his L-shaped desk,
crowded next to a tall white file cabinet. The desk drawers
are finished in blond wood, the top in ebony, although little of
the black surface shows through from beneath the scattered,
uneven piles of books and papers and pads. He prepares
himself for the tour he's promised me by draping his suit
jacket over the back of his chair. The collar of his striped
blue shirt remains buttoned at the neck, his tie fastened in a
wide knot. He does, though, fold back his shirt cuffs. Because
he is an on-duty police officer, he wears his leather holster
looped over both shoulders. Under his left arm hangs the
Austrian-made Glock 9-mm semiautomatic pistol adopted
as standard issue by Suffolk County a few years back. To balance the weight of the gun, from the right side of the holster

dangles a set of Peerless chrome-plated steel handcuffs and a magazine of 9-mm cartridges about the size of a cigarette pack. As a longtime habit, although hardly consistent with his otherwise very businesslike detective look, Al carries wherever he goes through the halls and labs and offices of the Crime Lab a quart-sized plastic water jug with an attached plastic straw, its phosphorescent reds and yellows and oranges standing out gaudily against the beige walls like something snuck in, or left behind, by a kid on a class outing.

"I keep refilling it all day long," Al explains. "I even drank tons of water as a kid. Do you remember?" When I shake my head, he says, "I thought novelists were supposed to be very observant, and remember everything, but maybe it's only true for detectives."

Al starts me this time where the work starts, in a small pair of rooms where Muriel Bernzweig, the evidence clerk, receives and logs in the items received from throughout the county. Muriel is a Crime Lab veteran of some twenty years, having begun as a secretary back when incoming evidence was handled by detectives. Muriel helped out and learned. As her abilities and aptitude came to the fore, she gained both the responsibility and the title. It's not an easy job. The lab doesn't deal with minor infractions, but with homicides, rapes, suicides, traffic fatalities, violent assaults, which means that Muriel receives an awful lot of clothing soaked or stained with every imaginable form of liquid and solid gore. Any item she handles, clean or otherwise, could well convict or absolve someone of a major crime, and she's responsible for maintaining the faultless, invulnerable link in the evidentiary chain of possession. She seems to manage it in an unruffled, almost maternal manner, attentive to detail but at the same time cheerful and friendly, reminding me, for the few minutes I watch her work, of a Norman Rockwell town librarian, although she's not cataloguing murder mysteries here but the emblems and vestiges left behind when real blood flows from real bodies.

Al riffles through the Evidence Analysis Request forms waiting to be sent to the appropriate sections, showing me those that will end up on his desk.

—A bullet given to police by a North Amityville resident who noticed a hole in his siding and retrieved the bullet: "He wants to know who fired it. Unless the bad guy's been bad before, and we got a record of it, the chances are not good."

—A victim's shirt from a shooting scene to see if its condition is consistent with a gunshot wound: "Seems like overkill, since they've got the victim and it's obvious he was wearing this shirt when he was shot. They're probably interested in powder burns, anything showing how close the gun was. Maybe they're suspicious of the victim's story. Just because he's been shot doesn't necessarily mean he's been shot the way he says."

—An expended bullet from a recent shooting in someone's home, not found during the initial search, eventually retrieved by the victim's wife while cleaning: "Routine exam and checks against the open file."

—A revolver recovered during a robbery investigation: "They want to know if it's a working weapon, which would elevate the charge from second- to first-degree robbery. Shots were fired at the scene, so the gun's obviously working, but they want us to put it in writing."

—A gun possibly used in a suicide: "Again, there may be some question about what actually happened, because they suspect this gun may be inoperable."

—A pistol taken from someone arrested under a search warrant: "Contraband. Routine checks against the open file."

—Two Glock 9-mm, standard-issue police sidearms—the same as Al's—submitted with a Weapons Discharge Report: "Every instance of a policeman discharging his weapon, whatever the cause or circumstance, requires a full inspection and report. Here a patrolman reported firing one round into a suspect vehicle fleeing from a buy/bust operation. Since there were two officers on the scene, we automatically get both guns, without being told which was fired. We have to determine which one it was, and whether a faulty safety or other defect might have caused it to fire accidentally. The officer, for instance, might be saying the thing went off without his even touching the trigger, although of course we're not informed of any of that. We just check out the guns and make our report, which the department considers along with all the other evidence to decide whether the officer was warranted in using deadly force toward a moving vehicle."

—Articles of clothing from an attempted murder: "Again, the investigators want to know if the condition is consistent with a shooting, and whether there's any trace evidence to indicate distance. Routine."

He takes a drink from the plastic straw of his water jug. "Let's just follow some of this stuff through."

Since she's got limited space in the receiving area, once a day Muriel Bernzweig transfers recently acquired items from her temporary lockers to the main-evidence vault across the hall. Al opens the thick door of the main vault by sliding his credit-card-sized ID pass over the wall glass in a circular fashion. I've learned that the glass area on the wall is called the *reader*, and that it not only allows access to restricted areas but eliminates sign-in sheets by automatically recording everyone who enters. Noticing a bullet in a plastic bag on an IN tray just inside the door, Al picks it up and simultaneously pulls a magnifying glass from his pocket, playing it back and forth, unaware of—or maybe just tired of hearing jokes about—the Sherlock Holmes parody. "It looks all right," he says, "but under the microscope the identifying marks may have been squooshed off by bones or whatever."

Lines of parallel metal shelves fill the spacious, yet dreary and oppressive cinder-block room. The shelves are crammed with all shapes and sizes of bags, boxes, crates, containers. "Evidence is unfortunately not designed for neat filing, and you never know what's coming in next. You just hope the circus bareback rider isn't murdered on her horse tomorrow."

All big drug hauls are examined and shipped out as soon as possible, Al says, because you don't want millions of dollars' worth of anything lying around.

Each lab section has one aisle as its retention area, designated simply by a scrap of paper with FIREARMS scribbled on it, or SEROL, or CHEM. The weak, grayish overhead lights accentuate the gloom, and although I can't pick up any separately defined odors, everything in the room seems to have made its own sour, moldering contribution to the dankness.

Reminded of an incident, Al chuckles and shakes his head once, briskly. "Ever since I took on more specialized responsibilities, I don't usually get directly involved with suspects. Some years back, though, I was the only person available at a rape site to take a blood sample from the suspect. I'd been a policeman long enough to know that you don't get that close to a reputed bad guy without knowing what he has in his pockets, so I told him to empty them. He did, bringing out the usual stuff plus this big wad of tissues. What the hell you got all those tissues for? I asked. Oh, he said, I use them to wipe my ding with."

Showing me the great clumps and clusters of bags filled with stained clothing in the Serology aisle, Al makes a face. I haven't said anything about the smell, but maybe my expression gives me away. "Actually, it's only a *little* odoriferous because everything's dry. The wet stuff is either frozen or kept in the walk-in refrigerator-vault next door. That's a real consideration, handling those items. You can't just toss a shirt into a plastic bag because any blood will break down in that environment and the bacteria that develops will alter the very properties the serologists want to extract. And however you package the shirt, don't put the gory knife in with it, because once you commingle the fluids you compromise both as evidence.

"The only time the Firearms area gets clothing is when there's a gun involved, but that adds up over time, and every once in a while I have to dragoon my two Georges in here to clean up some of this stuff. It's not pleasant work and there's a tendency to hope it'll go away. We shouldn't even be handling clothing, because it's a low-priority item that we'll probably never do anything with. But we're supposed to get it, so we get it."

He shows me a dozen or so rifles in plastic bags, not nearly as many as I expected, then indicates the real cache further back, shopping carts and canvas wheelers overflowing with chaotic accumulations of rifles and handguns, each bagged and tagged but pointing every which way. Al points out fifteen cardboard crates shelved on top of one another, and opens just one crate to show me the twenty or more manila envelopes inside, one handgun to each.

"You hear about all these programs these days to get guns off the street, with all kinds of incentives encouraging people to turn in their firearms. Hell, there are millions of weapons out there in the hands of God-knows-who, and I for one would be delighted at the thought of melting down every last one of them.

"Well, Suffolk County voted a trade-in recently, with excellent cooperation from local merchants and businesses in the way of discount coupons and cash bonuses, and it was enormously successful. Something like fourteen hundred guns were turned in.

"Of course, we all have our own little patch of the garden to hoe, which is always uppermost in our minds, and when I was first informed of the program, which I had nothing to do with setting up, my immediate reaction was, Holy shit, am I gonna have to *deal* with all that stuff?

"And there was actually some talk along those lines, about having us hotshot ballistics experts inspect and catalogue and run tests on every single weapon to see if we might be able to connect this thing that showed up on our doorstep with some unsolved homicide from the year one.

"Believe me, I sweated bricks over that. What we're talking about, literally, is *thousands* of hours of paper shuffling and cataloguing and glass time on the very far-fetched possibility of possibly connecting one weapon with one open case. Thank God, my impassioned pleas, along with the program's promise that all weapons would be treated anonymously and not investigated, convinced the powers-that-be that we in Firearms should not even *look* at these weapons but simply forward them directly to the Property unit for a decent burial.

"What came in, by the way, was a bunch of old rusty cheap crap. No criminal in his right mind, no matter what promises you made, was going to walk in anywhere with a weapon that might be of any conceivable interest to us. We got mostly nice grandfatherly types who dug this piece out of the dank recesses of the cellar where it'd lain untouched since World War II, figuring, Hey, if I can get free burgers and fries at McDonald's for it, why not?"

Walking past the aisle entrances of the storage room, we encounter a huge metal safe, maybe six feet high, six feet wide. "A throwback from some town station before the police went countywide. I think they lugged it here to lock up drugs. God only knows what's in it now." Each of the two metal doors has a huge knurled handle; Al yanks on one and steps back, amazed when that door easily swings open. It's four inches thick, and so are the walls. "For years I figured it was locked and nobody could find the key." He pulls the other door open and we peer in at stacks of old ledger books and thick file folders. Al pokes around, craning to read the tabs. "Hey, here's Big Barry!" He flips through the folder and pulls out Bob Genna's crime-scene sketches, with broken lines showing the probable movements of the three victims, a stick drawing for the cleaning woman's body, arrows for the trajectory of the shots. "That's what's here, I guess, dead files. Probably the only reason this monster's still taking up space is no one knows how to get rid of it."

Toward the back of the room an automobile hood leans against the same wall. Al's section also handles the identification of toolmarks, the evidence left behind when metal strikes metal, "be it a knife, a hammer, an axe. The hood came from a homicide scene outside a bar where one man plunged a knife, again and again, into the hood of the other man's car. Maybe he figured it was like shooting a cowboy's horse. Anyhow, the car owner then grabbed the knife and stabbed the first guy to death, so we have to see if we can link the knife to the hood dents. The problem is duplicating the angle of the plunge, whereas bullets will always go the same way down the same barrel."

In the rear corner, darkened by the shelves cutting off what little overhead light reaches back there, Al shows me a life-sized stuffed dummy in jeans and a sweater, flopped over what looks like a library cart, its legs dangling from one end. The head is made of sheeting topped with a curly wig. "It's just a regular old store dummy that we got years ago as a body stand-in for crime-scene classes. We could make it male or female and give it all kinds of fatal wounds. Then recently an off-duty police officer, at home with his family in this residential neighborhood, stepped outside when he heard some kids hot-rodding up and down the street. A conversation ensued between him and one of the hot-rodders, and when he reached in to turn off the ignition, the driver hit the power-window button and roared off with the officer's arm trapped inside. The officer's body was slung out at an angle and slammed against one car after another parked on that street, and he ended up dead."

Staring at the dummy, Al makes a little movement with one side of his mouth. "We've got it weighted down with sand now because the officer was a big, strapping man, and we're running tests with it dangling outside a car to see if we can reconstruct the angle of a human body at different speeds."

Inside the office he shares with his two Georges, Reich and Krivosta, Al sits at his desk fingering a sealed plastic bag, turning it over a few times to examine the handgun, magazine, and single cartridge within. For the first time, I notice how long Al's fingers are, how delicately he holds the package in his fingertips. "Manufactured by RG Industries. I've been to their factory. Used to be a division of Rohm, in Germany, but Congress banned all imports of cheap handguns, so the parts are still German but long lines of Cuban women in Miami assemble them."

Carefully he removes the gun from the plastic bag and cracks it. "No matter how many times you pick up the same gun, the first thing you do is make sure it's unloaded." He peers with one eye down the barrel. "When the barrel shows a lot of lint, like this one, it's a good sign it hasn't been fired recently."

While I look over his shoulder, he fills in the checklist he maintains:

Semiautomatic, .25-caliber RG pistol
no sign of dusting for prints
nickel finish
rifling: 8R
length of barrel: 2.5 inches
overall length: 5.5
shape of firing pin: round
trigger pull: not applicable, less

condition: good
condition of barrel: dusty, lint
safety check: thumb left side, working

"*8R* means eight grooves of rifling curving to the right. *Less* means it's hammerless, a single-action, semiautomatic."

He pokes around on his desk and finds the paperwork. "Guy was robbing a check-cashing place in Commack when someone called the cops. Guy runs out and jumps in a Dumpster to hide, wherein he's later discovered by the police and arrested.

"It's funny, but bad guys seem to be partial to Dumpsters, not only for themselves but also for getting rid of guns and knives or anything else they don't want found on them. Maybe they realize how much cops hate searching them, especially on hot, muggy days. You're dealing with major-league smells and messes, in very close quarters, and never know what your hand's going to bring up next out of the muck.

"Anyhow, the gun and cartridges were recovered from this Dumpster along with the robbery suspect. It sounds pretty straightforward, but I'm not happy with the way it's been handled. First of all, they shouldn't have used staples to seal the bag. Lawyers can destroy the whole chain of custody by showing how easy it is to remove staples and neatly fit them back into the same holes. Also, since the magazine and cartridge were retrieved separately, they should have been packaged separately. Worst of all, since the gun was not recovered on his person but only in the same area, they should have immediately dusted it for prints to look for a direct link between the guy and this gun. Even if no prints were found, we'd look a lot better and more believable if we at least had the sense to look for them instead of just *assuming* the guy and the gun belonged together because they ended up in the same Dumpster.

"Anyhow, they want us to see if it's operable so they can

charge him with armed robbery, and see if it matches up to anything in our case file, so let's start by going downstairs and shooting a few rounds into the tank."

Al takes four fresh .25-caliber cartridges from his collection and marks each by hand with what looks like an enlarged pencil. He also marks the unfired cartridge that arrived with the gun. "This is a battery-operated electric vibrator with a carbide tip that I'm using to make indexing marks, so later I don't have to revolve each bullet three hundred sixty degrees to get my bearings on the microscope. Of course the two Georges have their fun with the idea of a vibrator with a hard tip. I said it was actually a scriber with a vibrating tip, but that didn't help."

In the basement, Al uses his ID card to let us into a gray, empty, vaultlike room, our voices echoing, the air frigid. They don't heat the empty areas, he explains, although he's quick to point out that this is the best facility he's ever had. He flicks on the fluorescent lights to reveal the firing range with its round bull's-eye targets seventy-five feet away. "We use the range just to test operability. Since we also want to test this weapon against the file, we'll use the recovery tank."

The tank's in an adjacent room, a rectangular stainless-steel tub, ten feet long, five or six feet wide, containing about four feet of water. A metal tube as big around as a stovepipe is attached by metal brackets to one edge of the tub, angled down toward the water.

"I'll use the case gun," Al says, "to fire the four new cartridges and the one from the Dumpster. We shoot down through the tubing, which is at a twenty-six-degree angle to make sure the trajectory isn't so steep that the bullet will hit bottom, or so flat as to let it skip across the surface or carom upward. It may not seem so, but the water resistance is enough to stop anything we shoot into it before it reaches the back of the tank."

We both put on ear protectors and I back off a few feet. He

loads the gun, puts on safety glasses, and fires five times down through the cylindrical tube. Five casings pop out around him; five bullets strike the water with hardly any splash and settle to the bottom about halfway toward the back. The air is acrid now, stinging to the nose and eyes. The ventilation system is designed to exchange the air every six minutes, Al says, without sounding convinced, then reaches toward the wall like a pool-hall player picking up his cue. "After experimenting with all kinds of exotic devices for recovering the bullets without getting all wet, we found the perfect method." Using a stick with a lump of soft clay at one end, he dexterously retrieves the bullets one at a time. "You probably don't remember this either, but we used to fish out coins from street-corner grates this way, except we used chewing gum."

On the way back upstairs, we visit the collection of firearms he's amassed over the last couple of decades, much more neatly arranged here than in the evidence vault: small handguns on wall hooks, large handguns on trays and racks, rifles and shotguns on yet more racks, taking up every bit of wall space in a room the size of several living rooms. Al estimates four hundred rifles, twice that many handguns. Also machine guns, submachine guns, cane guns, bayonets, ornamental swords, hand grenades, a pistol with a shoulder extension that allows it to be fired like a rifle, a spring-propelled knife that can be hurled twenty feet with considerable force and accuracy, an ivory-headed cane that fires a very large, very powerful .410 shell.

He points out a double-barreled rifle on a tripod with a rotating crank handle, looking like a prop from a parody of some World War II movie. "The crank makes it semi- rather than fully automatic and therefore legal. Collectors love militaristic-looking weapons, even an aberration like this. They stick them in their living rooms."

I mention that my son Michael read somewhere of a gun

disguised as a beeper. "I've heard of it but haven't run across one yet. There's also a gun out there that looks like a belt buckle. The FBI issues bulletins on new weapons, and not just for us. If some patrolman on the street sees a guy aiming a beeper at him, it'd be nice for him to know it ain't necessarily a beeper. Most people assume oddball weapons like that are illegal, but the truth is you're free to do anything with a disguised or funny-looking piece that you can do with any other kind of gun."

The collection serves as both a reference file and a source of working parts when they want to test-fire a defective gun. Al has personally worked with a good many of the weapons. He picks one up and says, "I handled this .35 in 1982 when it came in from a homicide in the Hamptons," and proceeds to discuss the ballistic details.

One of his toughest challenges involved a rifle recovered from a burnt-out building, where the heat left it incredibly warped and distorted. "What I had to do there was reconstruct the whole weapon using parts from a different weapon of the same type in our collection here, except for the barrel itself, because the barrel's what gives you the identifying marks on the bullet.

"Those marks, by the way, were developed after it was noted that early weapons, using a smooth barrel, sent the bullet off on a rather drifting, erratic flight. So spiral grooves were cut inside the barrel, giving the projectile a rapid spinning motion that allowed it to maintain a more stable, accurate course.

"The irony, I guess, is that the very advances like the rifling in the barrel that made firearms such successful tools for murder and mayhem also made them a lot easier for us to categorize and track down."

On the way out, he reaches behind him to flick off the lights, and as the huge room goes dark I realize that what most impresses me is the fact that many of these thousand or more weapons got here because they were used to kill someone in the otherwise pleasant, civilized county of Suffolk, New York.

On a coffee break on the second floor, still thinking of that room full of weapons, I ask Al about gun control. He has a few thoughts on the matter.

"From a moral or ethical point of view, I think gun control is a good concept, given the widespread criminal use of firearms. Yet from a practical point of view, I have real doubts as to its effectiveness. I've worked thirty years in New York State, which maintains very strict control over handguns. They must be registered, you must apply for a permit and undergo tests of character and background, submit to fingerprint checks, all that. I can tell you, though, that in the vast majority of criminal handgun situations I've encountered, the gun was unregistered and illegal, either stolen or obtained from out-of-state or from an underground dealer. As far as I can see, the law has not affected violence in the state."

I point out that homicide laws haven't eliminated killings, that no laws have ever eradicated the crimes they prohibit, but they're still on the books. The NRA argues that criminals will simply ignore gun-control legislation. Well, sure they will, because that's what *makes* them criminals, their refusal to obey the law.

"That's the ethical consideration, which I totally agree with. But if you're asking me as a practicing professional whether I think those laws will do—or have done—a lot of good, I would have to answer no. Now, if we can conceive of a total, absolute ban of all guns throughout the whole country, preventing even a single firearm from becoming available to a single one of our two hundred and fifty million citizens, there's no doubt murder and assault and all violent crimes would be greatly reduced. But I don't think such a ban would be politically possible, given the constitutional issues of Federal vs. state power, and the strong, almost fanatical opposition among certain groups and throughout certain sections of the country. And how on earth would we ever enforce such a law?

"Maybe our best bet would be to make it *very* punitive for any crime involving a gun. It won't stop—nothing will—your husband-and-wife or jilted-lover killings, or your drug-turf murders, but it might give pause to the guy moving in on the 7-Eleven. But we've got to be very clear: we don't care if it's ten cents you're taking, if you're packing heat, you're going away for a long, long time.

"Only then you get into plea bargaining, overcrowded prisons, the cost of incarceration, etc., etc. Nothing's simple, right? We keep coming back to the very basic question of a criminal class, and why we have one, and what we can possibly do to keep kids who are living under the worst of all personal, family, and economic situations from deciding that the *only* way out of the hopelessness of their lives is to start pushing drugs or robbing stores. Because, you know, as horrible as prison seems to you and me, who have nice homes and stable families and can reward ourselves with a night out at a good restaurant, time behind bars isn't all that scary to someone whose life outside has never rewarded him with a goddamn thing.

"Getting back to guns, I must admit that even after all these years, I don't truly understand a lot of the psychology involved. For instance, the minute a war ends, the manufacturers start designing their sport guns to look like the most recent military weapons. Everybody who went over to Vietnam saw this *beautiful* thing called an M-16, a .223-caliber, in other words a mere .22 that ran three thousand feet per second, with fifty grains of weight to the projectile, a little bastard designed to blow the kneecap apart when it struck, and yet so light, so fine. At that point, Colt says, Hey, we won't be turning many of these out for the troops anymore, so let's make ourselves an AR-15, a semiautomatic sport rifle that's the spitting image of its military counterpart. They're

snapped up by the thousands, only, Christ, I wonder, what
would anybody *do* with a weapon like that?"

Back in his empty office, Al picks up the ringing phone.
"Sergeant Della Penna here, how can I help you?—Oh, hi,
Bob . . ."

Listening, Al takes a swig from his refilled water jug as I
move around the office, looking at the fading, dog-eared
posters tacked on walls over the three desks and the file cab-
inets and the bookshelves: Smith & Wesson Handguns—
Small-Frame   Revolvers,   Medium-Frame   Revolvers,
Large-Frame Revolvers—SPEER Bullets—Rifle Bullets,
Handgun Bullets, Grand Slam—Wilson Arms Custom Gun
Barrels—Gun Drilling, Gun Reaming, Gun Rifling—RUGER
Security Six Double-Action Revolver, Field-Stripped View.

"No, I'm not sure which George handled that—And what
homicide in Jersey are you talking about?—The size of the
shot? Well, sometime's it's eradicated as you use that shell, so
you can't tell afterward. Look, give me the case number, and
I'll have the right George get back to you when he shows
up."

A typical situation, Al explains after hanging up. "One of
our Homicide detectives has a union-organizer-type murder
out here on the Island—the organizer was murdered—and
now thinks it might have had some links with a homicide
over in Newark he heard about, and wonders if we can make
the connection based on the shells."

He takes the five test bullets he fired downstairs into the
narrow area behind his office and sits at the comparison
microscope designed to view two bullets at the same time, rotating each on its axis 360 degrees looking for correspond-
ing lines, usually of microscopic size, that match perfectly on
both bullets. "It's like the split screen they use for baseball
games, so you can watch the pitcher and the runner on first
at the same time."

He places two of the fresh bullets in the wax holders of the two microscope stages. "We'll go through the four bullets looking for duplicate characteristic markings, as opposed to individual markings on a single bullet. Once I find a repeatable pattern, I can go to my question file to look for matches there, just in case our Dumpster friend maybe robbed other places too, maybe even left a bullet behind that we got our hands on."

Hunched over, Al peers, adjusts, peers, adjusts. "You start with the lowest magnification, because it'll give you the most detail. The more you increase the magnification, the more you exaggerate every movement and shudder. You also reach a point where everything is so enlarged it's unrecognizable."

He keeps fiddling with the knobs. "I'm having a tad of difficulty lining these up via those scribe marks I etched in before." Peering intently, he makes a minor adjustment to one knob. "This isn't the least bit automatic, and can be a very slow process, really a judgment call. Ah—okay now. Take a look."

He slides off the stool and lets me bend down to the twin eyepieces. The two bullets, magnified by a factor of eight, seem identical, the hairline scratches matching perfectly.

"Normally, I'd examine all the test bullets, but let's just take these two for now to compare against the open file. I know the barrel of the case gun has eight land-and-groove impressions, twisting to the right, because I counted them before, and now I've verified that count on the bullet. That gives me my classification—.25-caliber, 8R." At the rear of the crowded room, he pulls out a file-cabinet drawer, flips through a section, and lets out a brief laugh. "This saves a lot of work—I can note that I reviewed the file for expended bullets of that class and found none. I have, in other words, covered my ass.

"However, I have lots of expended .25-caliber *casings* from recent homicides and assaults, so the question now is: Do I have a compelling reason to start the whole process over again with the casings from the test-firings so I can compare *them* to the file items? Well, we're dealing with armed robbery, which is classified as a violent crime. Yet it would not be at the top of our list. Lab policy requires that we make comparisons in all crimes against a person, but in this instance no one was killed or even assaulted. The gun was not discharged during the crime. A fingerprint check of the suspect has not turned up any priors. Given all that, I'd have to receive some positive input from someone—my supervisors, the detective running the investigation—before I'd decide to spend hours and hours of glass time on this, as opposed to some other case."

Through the open door connecting to the office, we see and hear the two Georges return together and sit at their desks. It's late morning by now, lunchtime, and both are straightening up their desks, glancing at papers, making notes. I follow Al back into the office and they look up as Al begins to speak, but just then a message blasts down on us from the ceiling loudspeaker, full of the screeching unintelligible vibrato of a bus-station sound system. Al continues speaking, but no one in the room can understand him *or* the announcement, and he gives up almost exactly as the announcement ends.

"Was that for us?" George Krivosta asks.

"I wasn't listening," Al says.

"I think it was for us," George Krivosta says.

"They know where to find us," Al says, at which point the phone on his desk rings and he grabs it. "Sergeant Della Penna—Right—I spoke to Bobby Henn on that, the union organizer—Let me see which George it was, I got three here at the moment." He holds the phone to his chest. "Which one of you handled the Panone case a couple of weeks ago?"

"Not me," I assure him.

"Me," George Krivosta says. "Shot in the driveway."

"Newark's on the phone," Al says. "Talk to them."

"What for?"

Another announcement begins, maybe a repetition of the first, but no clearer this time. The volume's awfully high for an office this size.

"What for?" George Krivosta repeats, shouting now.

"Bobby Henn called before," Al shouts back. "But this is the guy in Newark. Pick up, and I'll hang up."

George Krivosta picks up, but is still talking to Al. "What the hell's Newark . . . ?"

"They got a case that might relate to the Panone shooting."

When the announcement ends, George Reich, the only one really trying to listen, says, "I think that was for us too."

"Another one for us?" Al cracks up. "What are you guys doing, taking in laundry? Someone's calling in to say they want their collars starched?"

"Dollar extra for starch," George Krivosta says. He holds his phone to his ear, then makes a face. "There's no one on."

"We're usually better organized than this," George Reich informs me. "I think we're getting giddy."

"Having three Georges in one room is what does it," Al says. "It forms a critical mass."

"Al's your cousin," George Reich tells me. "Make him let you go to lunch."

"Pick up your shirts before you leave," George Krivosta advises. "Rolled collars, right? Eight-fifty, no tipping."

"Let him tip," George Reich says.

"C'mon back with me, George," Al says.

It takes the three of us a moment to realize he means me. I again follow him into the microscope room where he removes from the file cabinet a baggie containing three .25-caliber casings. "It's a long shot that just occurred to me," he says. "Maybe we can tie these to the Dumpster gun." He affixes the file casing onto the left stage of the dual microscope, a test-fire casing from the Dumpster gun on the right, and studies them through the eyepieces. "Nice concentric markings," he says, in the soft, dreamy voice of someone deep in concentration. "You could fall in love with markings that clean."

I assume he's found something, made the match, but he shakes his head and returns the casings to the proper baggies. "Miles off," he says, "just as I expected."

Why'd he bother then?

He shows me the name on the file baggie: BRANCH, George.

"Wouldn't that have been something?—*The Fourth George Reveals All!*"

Over lunch at a neighborhood restaurant, Al turns reflective. "Like everyone else, police love to clear up backlogs of paperwork. Take burglary, for instance. We mentioned before how it's always tough to solve. He's gone, you don't know where he came from, where he went, what connection he might have to the place he broke into. Do you automatically dust down every inch of an eight-room house for prints? Did friends, family, neighbors ever visit? What about the plumber, the TV repairman? Forget it, unless you either catch the guy in the act or some lucky cop stops him for running a light with a trunk full of loot.

"When the police do get a burglar redhanded, they'll ask if he's pulled anything else like that, maybe encouraging his cooperation with a plea-bargain deal. So they tour the area with the guy in the back seat. This house, he tells them, that house, the big red house on the corner. And if those places actually have been robbed, the cops can in one afternoon close out a whole bunch of open cases, which gives a real boost to their batting average on the yearly report."

On the drive back to the office, we move to a case he figures will never boost anybody's average.

"A major issue in the Kennedy assassination, of course, has been the movie frame showing his head going backwards. Why would it be flung backwards if he'd been shot only by Oswald, indisputably from behind?

"Surprisingly, there's practically no data on this issue. If you asked a convention of medical examiners how many had ever witnessed an execution by firing squad, or someone being shot in the head under *any* circumstances, I doubt if you'd get a single positive response. I'm not sure there've been any motion pictures either, except for the Zapruder film itself in Dallas. So in spite of the thousands of hours spent analyzing those crucial frames, there's nothing to compare them to. Some experts say it's impossible for the head to be thrown backward, or brain matter to be scattered backwards, by a shot from behind. Others say the human nervous system can behave in odd ways, and the enclosed high-pressure environment inside the skull could produce an explosion that would send internal matter in all directions.

"The other major issue is whether Oswald's bullet could have passed through Kennedy's body and struck Governor Connally without being far more mangled than it was—the "magic bullet" theory. Here I'm on more comfortable ground, and from a ballistics viewpoint I'd say that the big, mean projectile fired by Oswald was easily capable of doing just that."

"Let's start here, where the morgue wagon brings in the bodies." We're at the back of the building, on the ground floor, in a hallway connected by a set of wide doors to an outside parking area. "In addition to those relatively few homicides that the Crime Lab spends so much time on, the morgue processes all unattended deaths and scheduled cremations, all motor-vehicle and other accidental deaths, and all deaths deemed suspicious for whatever reason. I'll get you the numbers after."

Maybe twenty feet down the hall, away from the doors and toward the morgue, each arriving body is weighed on a large corrugated metal scale, flush with the floor and preset to discount the weight of the rolling stretcher. In an adjacent room, the body can be X-rayed if called for. Across the hall, the bio-hazard room stands locked behind a warning sign. "If we're dealing with an advanced state of decomposition, or a communicable disease or other risk, the body will be scooted right in there for the autopsy. It's just a one-table version of the regular morgue, but isolates the whole package from the perspective of both odor and contamination. It's even got a separate, totally isolated ventilation exhaust system."

Closer to the morgue, Al opens a thick metal door and ushers me into a refrigerated room big enough to contain perhaps a dozen empty, waist-high canvas stretchers on wheels lined side by side along the walls. Seven more, right inside the door, contain corpses only partially and haphazardly covered with shrouds. They are gray and stiff, eyes wide open, bizarre in their expressions, and I stare at them without any real sense of what I'm feeling, except that I find myself noting that each actually *is* identified by a tag tied to his big toe.

"Some are awaiting pickup by funeral directors. Some are John Does that'll either be claimed or receive the necessary clearances before being buried in a potter's field somewhere."

On the wall outside the door, where it can be monitored from the hall, the temperature gauge reads thirty-nine degrees Fahrenheit.

"During an autopsy," Al explains, "a pathologist can often calculate time of death by such signs as the digested condition of the stomach contents. But investigators at the crime scene always want information *right now*, maybe even before the ME arrives, and have different ways of making on-the-spot estimates.

"The basic principle is simple: once death occurs, certain processes cease, and others begin. Knowing the rates at which postmortem manifestations proceed gives you a decent estimate of how long they've been going on. Body temperature, for instance, can be compared to the temperature of the premises. Once a body reaches the ambient temperature, though, it stays at that point, so after a day or so, you have to rely on bodily decomposition.

"Lividity—or *livor mortis*—is the grayish blue or light purplish color gradually taken on by the skin after death when the blood settles at the lowest point of gravity. Its presence in certain areas therefore can tell you how the body was lying and whether it might have been moved. *Rigor mortis* also follows a measurable sequence: from none, to some, to total, and then back to none again as the body reverts to its normal looseness."

Any of these processes, Al says, can give investigators the immediate information they crave, because all take place at inevitable rates and in a manner that no one can fake, or reverse.

In the spacious recess in front of the morgue's open doors, we encounter Dr. Stuart Dawson, the deputy chief ME who'd talked to me months back. He stands, clipboard in hand, viewing two uncovered male bodies side by side on stretchers.

Barely a minute has passed since I honestly couldn't sort out my reactions to confronting seven toe-tagged bodies in a refrigerated room, and here I am, casually running into two more, and studying them as calmly as Al and Dr. Dawson. Is that how long it takes to become inured, dispassionate, professional?

Nonetheless, I'm careful to face away from the morgue doors, and am very aware of the cold air blowing out on my back.

Al asks Dr. Dawson whether a certain Jane Doe has been buried, and I realize he's referring to the woman dug up from the shallow grave stumbled upon by the Korean wood walkers. Nothing's developed on that, Dawson tells him. The autopsy didn't lead to anything, and she's been turned over to Social Services for burial arrangements.

Al makes that characteristic movement at one corner of his mouth: *What can you do?*

Dawson turns back to the bodies on the stretchers, and so do we. Both men look to be at least fifty, maybe older. One has a purplish scar across his abdomen. The other's chest, shoulders, and arms are resplendent with red-and-black tattoos—animals, names, flowers, curlicues. "A real picture show," Al comments.

Dr. Dawson nods. He's wearing a white jacket cut like a suit jacket, revealing his tie, and glances back and forth between his clipboard and the bodies. He's out here to decide whether to perform full autopsies on these bodies or to make do with a simple external, in which case the body will not be dissected. A blood sample, though, will be extracted by a needle inserted into the pericardium, the sac around the heart, and a urine specimen taken with a needle into the bladder.

According to the reports of the physicians' assistants, both deaths appear to have occurred naturally, and neither body shows signs of trauma. Still, Dr. Dawson hasn't made a final decision yet and remains in the hall, examining the bodies and taking notes as we turn around and Al leads me, watching my face this time, through the open doors into the morgue.

It's not nearly as busy as on my first visit. We're greeted cheerfully by two men in white gowns standing near a desk to the right that I hadn't noticed last time. A male body lies on the farthest table, maybe fifteen feet away, its gaping, vividly red body cavity flapped open as a young female pathologist in a green lab gown traces a line from ear to ear around the back of the head with a wide-bladed instrument, then pries into the incision until she can flip up the skull and expose the brain.

Dr. Stephanie Horowitz, Al tells me, a young deputy ME and one of their two women pathologists.

Watching her without moving any closer, I recall, for what surely must be the first time in ages, that as a kid of twelve I started working in a butcher shop on Castle Hill Avenue in the Bronx, where I became proficient with the carving and boning knives, the cleavers and saws, lifting sides of beef from the hooks and slamming them onto wooden chopping blocks to dress them quickly with sure, darting movements. And Al worked at a poultry slaughterhouse—what on earth does any of this mean?

Al introduces me at the desk to Pete Strebel and Bruce Haber, pathologists' assistants in charge of morgue maintenance and record keeping who also work alongside the MEs during autopsies. Like most of the people in the building, they're used to visitors and readily provide the numbers that Al promised earlier. In the first six months of the year, 2,038 deaths were referred to the ME's office, with maybe two-thirds of those cremation checks, claimed by private doctors, or handled elsewhere. Since January, therefore, the morgue has performed about 200 externals and precisely 403 full autopsies.

A plastic wipe-off poster board on the wall has been filled in with a black crayon to give the name and morgue number of the procedures scheduled for that day, the assigned pathologist, whether a standard or external autopsy is scheduled, whether ID photos, fingerprints, or X rays are indicated.

While Dr. Horowitz continues to work over the body on the back table, Al stands beside me with his arms folded as I examine the other two parallel tables, concentrating on the details that I missed during my split-second view earlier. Each metal examination table has an attached square sink at one end. Along the edges, what I saw as a gutter drain for the blood is actually a one-inch pipe. "No drain," Al says. "The surface is pitched toward the sink, and the pipe provides a steady stream of water to flush everything down that direction."

A platform next to the sink holds a balance scale, a plastic cutting board, and a variety of specimen jars. A newspaper-sized pad of tear-off sheets pinned to the wall over each table has a list down the left margin—heart, right lung, left lung, liver, right kidney, left kidney, spleen, brain, thymus—with horizontal spaces for recording the weight of each organ and the pathologist's comments.

"That's your standard autopsy," Al says, "which entails the examination and removal of all major internal organs and the preparation of tissue samples for our own labs or to be sent outside. The entire brain is also removed for both gross and microscopic examination. When the weight and condition have been recorded and necessary tissue samples taken, the larger organs are usually sewed back inside the cavity, so that instead of being disposed of, they can remain with the body."

Al's wife, Carrie, has some therapy clients scheduled for early that evening, so Al and I have dinner by ourselves. We both eat heartily, and over the meal I check out my notes with him.

TALES OF
SPANISH RAYMOND

JOHN CUOMO ➡

THIS STORY I DON'T ENJOY telling all that much, because I end up looking dumb and not in control of things. Being a cop all those years, a detective, you get used to being in control.

Anyhow, there's always been a certain degree of the gambling instinct in my life. Even in my teens, I was a big poker player, so I've been gambling in one form or another for forty, fifty years. Some men don't start serious card playing until their thirties or so, and I like to think my additional experience gives me an advantage. The truth is I'm a good poker player, very good, with excellent success over the years. Maybe this story goes to show that no matter how smart you think you are, an experienced policeman *and* card player, you can still be taken.

Over the years I've enjoyed casinos, both for the gambling and the whole feeling. After we took over the Wilkes Gallery, I even applied for a security job at the Tropicana, a big Atlantic City casino, and would have enjoyed the atmosphere. They seemed ready to take me on, but the gallery was doing very well and we didn't want to give that up and move the kids and everything, so I dropped the idea.

From Northport, I'd take one-day junkets down to Atlantic City, which was a short hop on the commuter plane out of Islip, and spend my time at the tables. Now, here in Arizona, I fly up even more regularly to spend the day in Vegas. In addition, Jeannette and I usually vacation in the Caribbean after Christmas, either for my birthday in January or hers in February, because Jeannette really loves it down there.

For my part, I always distrusted the Caribbean gambling, and still do to this day. I insist the casinos there are definitely against the gambler, and are allowed to do things that would never be allowed in Vegas or Atlantic City. For instance, their crap tables seem to have extra felt padding so the dice bounce around a lot more, which makes me very suspicious. And if the dice roll off the table for any reason, they put them right back into play, which they would never do in any casino in the States, where they'd right away discard them or at the least inspect them *very* closely to make sure they haven't been switched or altered.

The crucial difference is that Caribbean casinos are owned and operated by the government, so there's no supervision *over* the operators. American casinos are privately owned but operate under extremely close state scrutiny.

On the particular trip I'm talking about, Jeannette and I flew to Puerto Rico in February for her birthday at one of the very finest hotels down there. We went on a limited-type junket operation, which means I agreed to deposit a sum of cash, in this case five thousand dollars, with the casino. The agents in New York who arranged the junket would in essence tell the hotel, *Don't worry about this fellow, he's a player,* because naturally they'd get a piece of the deal too. The arrangement was that the hotel would comp me—provide as complimentary—not only our stay, including food and beverage, but also airfare, which all told would run a few thousand dollars. To qualify, you had to be known by the junket agent, which I was. Beyond the five thousand cash I deposited, I was granted a twenty-five-hundred-dollar line of credit, which was pretty standard for me at most casinos. They were comfortable with this, based on what they assumed I'd lose at the tables over the four days of our stay. But it was also a good deal for us, thanks to all the freebies, and because I don't gamble to win but only not to lose, and wasn't obligated to bet any specific amount of money but just to show good faith by putting in a reasonable time at the tables. My assumption was that I would play in my usual manner and maybe drop a few thousand, which was what a vacation like that would cost anyway.

As soon as we arrived and registered, I went up to the cage in the casino and put in the five thousand, because you don't want to carry that much cash around. Since our room wasn't made up yet we were still in our winter clothes from New York, whereas everyone else was in shorts or swimsuits or various tropical clothing, so we found some shade at poolside and were enjoying their nice complimentary lunch when this guy comes by, dressed in shorts and flashy shirt, the complete tourist outfit, and strikes up a conversation. Hey, howya doin'? You people just get in? I say, Yes, we just flew in from New York, and we indulge in the usual small talk before eventually he says, Hey, Johnny, you play poker ever? Well, once in a while, I tell him, and he says, Well, a few guys get up a little game over here every afternoon, you think you'd be interested?

Just to be polite, I thanked him very much and said I might. But I knew he'd spotted us as new arrivals because of our clothing, and I had no more intention of playing poker with him than with the man in the moon.

I forgot all about him as soon as he left, and for the next three days we went about our own business in our usual way, having a lovely vacation, with Jeannette on the beach a lot while I spent my time at the tables, maybe dropping a few dollars here and there but nothing spectacular or unexpected. On the morning of our next to last day Jeannette and I get up for breakfast and our dip in the ocean and we're sitting on the beach, with me already getting bored with the sun and everything, when another character, not the one from the first day, drifts over dressed in beach attire and starts in with the same approach: Howya doing, good morning, nice day, etc., etc., and then how boring it is at the moment because the casinos don't open until after lunch. He brings up the idea of whether I might be interested in playing a little poker, and since I don't know what to do with myself the rest of the morning, this time I admit that I might be, and he says, Well, we're gonna get a few guys together for a friendly game over there, pointing to a side area with tables. Okay, I tell him, I'll meet you. Jeannette said she couldn't understand why I wanted to play poker when I could sit on the beach with her, but I explained that I never liked sitting on the beach. I wanted something a little more interesting to do. So she said the usual things, you know, Be careful, I'll meet you for lunch, etc., etc., and I said, Sure, sure, and left.

Since I hadn't brought money down to the beach, I went up and took four hundred dollars from our room safe. Downstairs, there were already four guys at the table getting ready to play. The guy who'd approached me the first day wasn't there, so except for the guy who'd invited me a half hour ago, I didn't recognize any of the men. They were in their fifties or so, from Wisconsin, Michigan, that sort of thing, and one from Louisiana, all typical tourists in straw hats, floppy shorts, flowered shirts.

Everybody introduced themselves and shook hands all around, and the guy from Louisiana, with this glittery gold chain around his neck, took out a plastic bag with a deck of cards and a bunch of tiny plastic colored disks for chips. What say we all buy in for a hundred dollars? No one objected and I asked what stakes we'd be playing for. The Louisiana guy, with a real heavy southern drawl, says, How about one-to-five? Now, a one-to-five dollar range was definitely high for me. One-to-two was more my speed, but the others just shrugged, so I went along.

Everybody slides over a hundred to Louisiana for one-dollar and five-dollar chips and we begin. All goes perfectly normally and pleasantly with the usual small talk, and I'm pretty much holding my own. I even get on a hot streak and before long I'm up four hundred dollars and thinking, Boy, this is great, what a nice relaxing way to spend the morning.

The Super Bowl had just been played, and the guy on my right gets me talking about it and I say, Yeah, I lost a few bucks on the game, things like that, sort of diverting my attention. Afterward I realized that's when they must have made their move with the deck, because right then someone says, out of nowhere, Why not make it pot limit? Everybody else agrees but I'm a little hesitant, so they say, Tell you what, we'll make it dealer's choice, and even though I'd never played pot limit before, again I go along. After all, I figure I'm doing all right with these guys, none of whom strike me as being all that good at the game.

That throws the game wide open, because if the dealer declares pot limit it means you can bet up to the amount already in the pot, which can very quickly become an appreciable sum.

That's what the dealer goes for on the next hand, pot limit. The first three cards I'm dealt are all tens, two in the hole and one showing, so even though I'm still reluctant about the stakes I figure I'm off to a terrific start. The high card bets five dollars, and I bet ten, and somebody says there's sixty dollars in the pot and bets sixty, and I call the sixty. The game continues with pretty heavy betting all around, and one guy drops out. I eventually draw two eights, so I'm holding a full house, and the Louisiana guy, he's just showing a pair of fives. Nonetheless, he's betting heavily too and I begin to be concerned that he may have two more in the hole for four of a kind. Then someone else draws a five, so I figure the best he can have is three fives, which I can beat with my three tens full.

We continue playing, and when it looks like a few guys might have something good, the betting really heats up. At one point the Louisiana guy, still with just two fives showing, puts in two hundred and fifty dollars.

My immediate reaction is, Two hundred and fifty dollars! I can't go in for that! But goddammit, I've three tens full! So I say, I thought we were playing a sociable game here. I didn't even bring that much with me. They say, No problem, Johnny. You got credit in the casino, right? Besides, we trust you, we're all friends here. We'll just make a note on the side of however much you're light and keep the game going.

With that, I put in the two fifty, and Louisiana says, I don't think you got much, Johnny, so I'm gonna raise you five hundred.

From this point on, I don't remember exact amounts at every step, although I do remember the cards dealt to each of us, and the exact order, which I guess proves I'm what you might call a true dyed-in-the-wool poker player, because the cards stay in my mind even years later, whereas the money doesn't.

Gradually the other guys drop out, leaving just me and Louisiana, and based on what he's showing and what I know I have—three tens full—I go ahead and raise him, say, another five hundred. He draws a queen and I know the fourth five is out, which means he can't have more than fives full. Still, he says, God-damn, Johnny, I don't know what the hell you have there, but I'll tell you what, I'm gonna raise you a thousand.

Again, that makes me pull up and think, because I'm already light around sixteen hundred bucks. Listen, I say, this is getting ridiculous. I mean, I should raise you because I don't see how you can possibly beat me, but I'm just gonna call you, so I match his thousand dollars and say, Let's see what you got. With that I turn up my two cards in the hole and show my three tens full. The guy says, with that real heavy drawl rolling into a kind of chuckle, Well, I'll be a son of a bitch, John. Look at this, I got three queens full. And goddammit, he does. All along he had two queens in the hole.

I'm absolutely stunned at this point. Hell, I lost twenty-six hun-dred dollars on that one poker hand, on top of the four hundred I brought with me in cash, meaning that in a half hour I'm down three thousand dollars. A couple of guys get up and say they have to head on for one reason or another, Thanks for the game, Johnny, all that sort of stuff, leaving me with Louisiana and the guy who'd originally invited me to play.

I say to Louisiana, who's taking it all very casually, not gloating or anything. Look, I lost and that's it. I'm an honorable man, so if you just wait here I'll go over to the casino to get the cash and be right back with it. Oh, sure, he says, that sounds fine, I'll just wait right here.

I leave the two of them and go up to our room first to use the bathroom, and Jeannette takes one look at me and says, What's wrong? Nothing, I tell her, probably not in the world's friendliest voice. Just leave me alone. I go to the casino, which is just getting ready to open for the day, and tell one of the floor bosses that I've run into a little problem and need some money from the cage, say around three thousand dollars. So he has me draw a marker for three thousand in chips, and I take the chips to the cashier, who gives me the three thousand in green.

I go back out to where the two guys are waiting, count out twenty-six hundred, and hand it over to the Louisiana guy. My head is absolutely spinning and all I can say is, That was some game we had, that was really amazing. I was still dazed, trying to understand how I could possibly lose so much money so fast.

When I get back to Jeannette she again says, What's the matter, John? You look so angry, you look so bothered. I say, You won't believe this, Jeannette, but I just blew three thousand dollars. She screams, THREE THOUSAND DOLLARS! And then, without even blinking, says, They must be con artists, that must've been some kind of scam. To show the state I was in, I tell her, No, I don't think so, they seemed like just regular guys. But even as I was saying it, I guess somewhere in the back of my mind a little voice was saying, Hey, Johnny, maybe she's brought up an interesting point here. . . .

All through lunch it's running through my head that maybe I *was* taken, which with my background, my experience, was a particularly galling thing to admit. It keeps eating at me and that afternoon I start a little investigation of my own by going to see the casino manager. They bring me into an office in back, where a woman assistant manager says very pleasantly, Yes, Mr. Cuomo, what can I do for you? I explain I'm a retired detective here with my wife from New York, and that I put five thousand dollars in the cage upon arrival, with an additional line of credit, which she naturally understands to mean that I'm a good customer, a trustworthy patron. I tell her the whole story and say I'm convinced I was set up within their facility, and with the aid of someone working in their casino. Oh, she says, how can you possibly say a thing like that? Because, I point out, they knew I had money in the cage, and even knew I had a line of credit. And two different guys approached me on two separate occasions, which clearly wasn't just random.

She keeps saying she can't possibly imagine anything like that happening and is really sorry I feel that way but there's nothing she can do. Okay, I say, you're the assistant. Let me talk to the top manager, the person in charge. He'll be back tomorrow, she says, and I say I'll make a point of seeing him before we leave, although the truth was I didn't have much hope in that direction.

I hardly slept that night, knowing we were flying out the next afternoon and wondering what the hell I could do before then. At this point, what with the markers I'd taken out to cover general gambling losses, plus the three thousand in markers after the card game, plus various cash withdrawals along the way, the five thousand cash I'd deposited wouldn't even cover me. I figured I owed them an additional twenty-five hundred dollars, pretty much my whole line of credit, and was feeling very, very disheartened and embittered about that.

Our plane was scheduled for three the next afternoon, and since the day was rainy we took this little jitney bus around noon that ran back and forth between our hotel and the sister hotel down the road. The bus was a typically very nice setup, with cocktails on board and everything, and we had decided to visit the other casino, which was just opening up. We played roulette for an hour or so and were standing in the lobby with Jeannette saying, Look, all the shops are closed, since it was midday siesta time. And who do I see coming down the escalator but the guy who'd invited me into the game yesterday, and had waited with Louisiana for me to come back with the money.

Jeannette sees my look and asks, What's wrong? and I mutter, That's the son of a bitch who took me in the card game.

As he gets off the escalator I go over and grab his wrist and say, C'mere, I want to talk to you, do you happen to remember who I am? And he says, in a very lively, friendly voice, trying to ignore my own tone of voice, Oh, hi there, how ya doing? Sure I remember, we had a drink together last night. No, we did not, I tell him. I'm the guy you took for three thousand dollars in that goddamn card game yesterday. I always carry my police shield, my retired shield, and I pull it out, still holding him by the wrist, and stick it in his face and say, You picked the wrong man this time. I'm a New York City detective, and I know people here in Puerto Rico, and I want you to understand that I want my money back and I want it back now.

All of which was pure bluff, of course. I didn't have the foggiest idea how to go about dealing with this guy. And he was still protesting that he didn't even know what I was talking about. He kept saying, Jeez, John, take it easy, what are you getting so excited about, let go of my arm, will ya? But I could see I had his attention and said, Bullshit, no, I won't let go of your arm! Then, not shouting or anything, just spelling it out firmly right into his ear: I—want—my—money—back—now!

This seems to work, and he says, Okay, okay, in a really hoarse whisper, just give me the time, where can I meet you? Back at our own hotel, I tell him, in the big circular bar in exactly one hour. Okay, he says, don't worry, you'll get your money, I'll personally deliver every penny right into your hands.

I can't say I was very confident but figured it was the only shot I had with our plane leaving in a few hours. Maybe I was hoping he'd show with the money because yesterday, when they trusted me, I'd showed with the money.

Anyhow, I turned him loose and went back to Jeannette, who'd naturally been watching open-eyed, wondering what's going on, and I assured her everything was just fine. Let's get back on the bus, I said, the guy's gonna meet me in an hour with our money.

We hop on the jitney, and while we're waiting for it to start I pour myself a drink and am just sitting there trying to relax when I look out the window and spot the *other* guy walking by, the real culprit from Louisiana, and immediately I'm in a rage again. Without even thinking, I jump off the bus and grab the guy by the throat. Actually I grab him by his goddamn glittery gold chain and I'm twisting it hard as I can and bending him back over this railing on the street, all the time yelling, You son of a BITCH! I got you now and I'm not gonna let you go until that other son of a bitch comes back with every cent you screwed me out of.

Of course, the guy had just been walking along minding his own business, not expecting some enraged maniac to leap off the jitney and attack him, so he's really flustered and I'm doing all I can to keep him that way, rattling him around pretty good and finally getting him down on the ground still in this real death grip around his throat. All along he keeps rasping, What the hell's going on, are you crazy or something? Then he starts yelling, Police, police, I'm being attacked, get the police! I say, Fine, you want the police, let's get the police, and I start yelling right along with him, Police, police, someone call the police!

Sure enough, a hotel security guard comes running out of the casino, a heavyset, no-nonsense Puerto Rican who wants to know what the commotion's all about. I flash him my shield and say, This guy ripped me off last night, get the police here and I'll give them the whole story. Only we're right in front of the hotel, and all the guard's concerned about is these two wild men creating a scene that might disturb the patrons, so he quick hustles us inside while I yell back to Jeannette, Everything's all right, I'll be back in a minute.

The guard ushers us into the security office, where Louisiana immediately starts screaming at the guy behind the desk that he wants me arrested for assaulting him on the street. I try to be calmer, explaining I'm a retired New York City detective, which right away gets their interest. They start asking where I worked and one lights up and says, Hey, you worked the Bronx? I was born in the Bronx! That's where I grew up and went to school!

Suddenly it's like we're old friends, and they're very sympathetic and only want to know how they can help me. I ask them to get the local police, because I'm not worried about any assault charge and think the cops might scare Louisiana into giving me my money back. Meanwhile, with the security people just standing there watching, I'm doing my best to shake him up on my own, telling him in no uncertain terms what I'm gonna do to him. You son of a bitch, I say, you owe me twenty-six hundred dollars. You give it back to me or so help me, I'll break your knees. You think I assaulted you outside? I'll show you a real assault. I'll break every bone in your body. I'll leave you crippled for life. But even though he's just a pudgy, slow kind of guy with this real mushy Louisiana drawl, he stands right up to me and keeps shouting back that he's gonna have me arrested, I choked him, I broke his hand, I tried to steal his goddamn gold chain. What I'm actually thinking is, Holy shit, here I am in this foreign country, what the hell am I getting myself into?

We're still going at it when we hear sirens outside and two local policemen come barging in. These two don't speak English as good as the hotel people, so a security man begins explaining the whole deal. Of course, he's in no rush about it and I keep glancing at my watch because, one, I'm supposed to meet the other guy who said he'd bring my money back to our hotel, and, two, our plane is leaving in an hour or so and I know Jeannette's out there on pins and needles wondering what the hell's going on.

When the cops learn that I'm a former New York City detective, they also ask me in their broken English about the Bronx, especially about the Fort Apache section, because they have friends and relatives living there. Without any forethought I just happen to say that one of the people up there that I know is Spanish Raymond.

Now, Spanish Raymond is a story all to himself, and the mere mention of his name completely changes the whole situation. I know Spanish Raymond? Do I really know him or am I just making it up? Oh no, I say, that's the God's truth, and it was. I used to see Spanish Raymond around all the time in Harlem. He'd invite me into his restaurant for dinner, or if I went there with someone, he'd spot me and come over to the table to shake my hand and ask if there was anything special I'd like, anything he could do for me. We'd even have a drink together occasionally when I was off duty. It wasn't that we were *friends*, because we were both aware of our different positions and interests, but we had a definite relationship.

Spanish Raymond, you see, was probably the richest, most powerful Puerto Rican in either the United States or Puerto Rico. In certain areas of the Bronx, he completely controlled the whole numbers operation. And this was before the state lottery came in, when everybody played the numbers, and whatever money was bet on them ended up in the pockets of Spanish Raymond. We're talking about an enormous operation here, millions of dollars changing hands every day, and all his private preserve. He became a multi-, multimillionaire, with very wise investments both in the States and throughout Puerto Rico, where he must have owned half the goddamn island and became very famous, a national hero.

I'd been in regular touch with him for years back when I was in Narcotics. The key was that Raymond focused strictly on numbers, with no interest at all in narcotics, so there was no conflict in my seeing him. Now, if Raymond got in hot water over his gambling activities, I couldn't help him, and he knew this and didn't expect help. That was always clear. His restaurant, for instance, which was a very legitimate and highly profitable operation, was situated right in the middle of a Harlem area with heavy drug and prostitution and drunkenness problems that Raymond did not want going on right around his establishment. So we kept that locale clean so his patrons didn't have to fight their way through any unpleasant activities.

I naturally didn't go into all this detail with the Puerto Rican cops, or point out that Raymond probably wouldn't even remember who I was. The mere mention of his name was enough, and it'd be no exaggeration to say that from that moment on the cops and security people looked at me with awe. All they wanted were stories about Spanish Raymond, which maybe they figured on impressing their friends with. I made it clear, however, that getting my money back was uppermost in my mind, and since they were now very much on my side, they said, Okay, how can we help you? Hold on to this son of a bitch, I told them, while my wife and I go back to our hotel. If the other son of a bitch shows up with my money, you can let this one go. Or break his legs, if you feel like it, throw him in the river, drown him—I don't care. If you guys are too shy for anything like that, I'll make sure Spanish Raymond hears what happened to me down here and, believe me, *his* men won't be shy about taking care of these guys.

I shouted this out right in front of Louisiana, wanting him to fully appreciate my seriousness, though I couldn't really tell if he did or not.

Jeannette and I grabbed a cab back to our hotel, where I asked the security people to keep an eye on us in their bar to make sure nothing funny developed. We ordered a drink and waited and waited for the other guy, with our bags right there for a quick get-away once time ran out and we had to leave. Jeannette went to the ladies' room to get ready, and this impeccable-looking American came up and introduced himself as the manager who'd been out of town the day before. I forget his name but knew of him by reputation as one of two brothers born and raised in Vegas who were involved in the upper management of casinos in Puerto Rico as well as Vegas and Atlantic City. He informed me, remaining very cool the whole time, that he was aware of my situation, and what could he do to help? Well, I said, he could start by getting me my money back. Unfortunately, he said, he was heading for a very important meeting. Then he sort of snapped his fingers and out of nowhere appeared this very large Puerto Rican man, Santiago, who he introduced as head of security. He'll do whatever he can for you, the manager said, so for about the nineteenth time I told *this* guy my story, stressing even more than before my terrific friendship with Spanish Raymond.

By this time Jeannette's back and tugging at me saying, C'mon, Johnny, we gotta go, we'll miss our plane. Santiago said, in perfect English, You go right ahead and catch your flight, Mr. and Mrs. Cuomo. We'll take care of everything.

So we caught our flight, with no sign of the money from the poker game and with me still owing an additional twenty-five hundred in markers. They didn't mention the markers and neither did I, although I assumed I'd eventually have to pay them off to protect my reputation with them and all the other casinos.

I didn't give up, though. When I'm taken advantage of, it eats at me, and I become very intense and determined. Back in New York, I got on the phone practically every day to the hotel and spoke to everybody I could. Pretty soon they got real sick of me, and whenever I actually got through to the manager he was always running off to an important meeting in Vegas or wherever, one excuse after another. Still I hung in there. Eventually I wrote them a long, detailed letter about how I'd suffered both financial and physical jeopardy on their property, and how I'd personally apprehended one of the perpetrators and turned him over to them, etc., etc. On the basis of all this, I wrote, I expected full restitution of the losses I'd suffered in the crooked poker game. One of our gallery customers, a stenographer, typed it up for us, so it looked very businesslike.

A few days later, instead of me calling him, the manager called me.

Look, Mr. Cuomo, he said, sounding kind of worn down, we don't know the gentleman you're accusing of cheating, and there's no way we can get the money back that you lost in a private card game with which we had no connection, but we value you as a client and want to see you satisfied. What can we do for you?

Maybe, I said, you can make up for that crooked card game on your premises by canceling the twenty-five hundred dollars in markers I owe you.

Done, he said.

You're an honorable man, I said, and I look forward to future pleasant stays at your hotel.

No, I never got in touch with Spanish Raymond. It'd been years

since I'd seen him. A man like that knew tons of people, and he
might have just given me this blank stare. Cuomo? Cuomo? I don't
remember any detective named Cuomo.

Or maybe he would have said, Why are you recounting all this?
Anyone who gets taken at poker by a bunch of pudgy white guys
in flowery shirts isn't getting any sympathy from me.

EXTRACURRICULAR
EXPLOITS

AL DELLA PENNA ➡

UNTIL RECENTLY, I drove a 1990 Honda Accord, not fancy or expensive but sporty looking, a dark-red two-door coupe still sparkling with its showcase gloss. Nothing identified it as a policeman's car. I'd learned my lesson when after long hours at a crime scene, I returned to find my antenna bent into something resembling a pretzel. I'd also heard of officers whose windows got smashed and tires punctured. Any deterrent effect of a police ID on your car also serves as an invitation, even a provocation, especially in the neighborhoods we're often sent into.

I now respond to all calls from home by first stopping at the laboratory to pick up the crime-scene van, which I then drive to my destination. It makes good sense, of course, having all my equipment at hand when I arrive, but the truth is I started the procedure mainly to protect my car.

Carrie and I live in this condo situated on a small line of similar residences, with angled curbside parking facing the entrances, and last Labor Day weekend I was returning from my early morning run, stepping into our little entryway, when I was struck by the open space out front. It wasn't even something I'd consciously noticed. I just had this funny feeling, like, Hey, something's wrong here. I actually stared at the spot for a minute before it finally sank in: my car was gone. I tried to convince myself that I must have parked it somewhere else last night, but knew that wasn't true. I just stood there with my hands on my hips, looking hopelessly one way and another. You goddamn jerk, I kept saying, your goddamn car's been stolen!

I'd of course dealt with enough other people under similar circumstances, but they were other people, because things like this only happened to other people. This was me, a savvy thirty-year cop who'd seen and dealt with just about the whole gamut. The one thing I'd never been was a victim. I was always the guy in charge, the one on top of any situation who was very good at figuring things out and knowing what to do next. I felt incredibly stupid, completely helpless. What could I do? Stand there muttering and cursing and staring at that empty space all week? Where the hell would that get me? The car—my car, not someone else's—was gone, and it must've been my own dumb fault.

Having to announce the news to Carrie was a real downer. Having to report it to the police was even worse.

We live right over the line in Nassau County, so I called the 911 number and they sent a patrolman. The guy was nice enough, taking everything down and being very sympathetic. Then I said, kind of sheepishly, I know you're gonna get a chuckle out of this, but I'm also a police officer, a detective sergeant in Firearms out at the Suffolk County Crime Lab. He did get a chuckle out of that, especially since there's this friendly rivalry between the Nassau and Suffolk cops. They don't give a shit who they steal from, he assured me when he stopped laughing.

He filled out his report: time and circumstances of theft, suspicious activities, location of keys. I assured him I'd locked the car and taken the keys, but he seemed a little dubious when he found no broken glass on the street to indicate forced entry.

Everybody thought it was a big joke. One wiseass neighbor actually said it was too bad I wasn't out there when the guy tried to zoom off, because I could have just drawn a bead on him and fired away. Are you crazy, I said, shooting guys for stealing cars? Like stringing up horse thieves in Dodge City?

After a few days a Nassau detective came by, saying half a dozen cars had been stolen around the area that same night. They'd picked up a suspect, a non-English-speaking Hispanic who admitted that he and several other Hispanics had been brought to the neighborhood by some guy who would point out a certain car to them, which they would then hot-wire and drive to a specified location for a fee. The inside members of the gang would then drive the cars to a chop shop where, within hours, they'd be broken down into parts or completely changed in appearance.

Okay, so I'd never see my Honda again. Since I was already tired of driving around a rental, I pestered the insurance company to pay up so I could buy a replacement. Normally, they won't settle a claim for at least thirty days, in case the car reappears in good shape. But I kept after them, and finally the woman at the insurance office said, I'm going on vacation Monday and don't want you bugging everybody else too. I'll cut you the check ahead of time if you just promise to leave us alone.

Once I cash that check, of course, I'm home free. The car belongs to them. And since the Honda was barely a year old and in excellent condition, I came away with a pretty good settlement, which I put toward a brand-new Toyota Camry that I immediately started driving around.

A couple of days later, I got a call from some garage in Brooklyn saying they had my Honda. They'd traced me down through the police reports, but were sorry to say the vehicle was totaled and then abandoned. They thought I might want to check the trunk for personal effects. I told him I appreciated the offer, but that it was the insurance company they wanted to call. Come down anyway, he said, they won't want any personal stuff.

So I checked it out, but everything I'd kept in the trunk was gone, my bowling ball and golf clubs, my crime-scene clothing bag containing jumpsuits and various footwear. It took just one look at the car itself, though, for me to realize how I'd lucked out with the insurance. If the clerk hadn't rushed me my check to take off on vacation, this total wreck would have still belonged to me when it showed up, and I wouldn't have collected beans.

I couldn't believe the car hadn't been chopped up or even disguised. The only alterations were to replace the side windows with glass tinted as dark as New York allows, making it almost impossible to see into the car from outside. I have no idea why they went to the trouble. Some teenage fad, like one-way sunglasses years back? They also installed a fancy curlicued chrome frame around the license plate, but incredibly didn't switch the plate itself. So somebody had been tooling around in a hot car without even bothering to slap on new plates.

Stolen cars are not my specialty, but the Nassau investigator came up with a theory. What likely happened, he said, was that the guys who stole the car probably left it unattended somewhere on the way to the chop shop, at which point someone else, maybe even one of the Hispanics the ringleaders had hired for the dirty work, proceeded to steal it from them for their personal use.

What the hell did that say about you—having your car stolen *twice?*

Over the years I've gotten real personal satisfaction in learning everything I could about my specialty, which is the surprisingly voluminous and complicated field of guns and ammunition. Most firearms examiners share this fascination, and most are also avid hunters and gun collectors. Some have whole rooms and walls full of museum-quality items, on which they've expended a good deal of money.

In this regard, I'm a real anomaly. I'm not in the least interested in guns away from work, and have an absolutely zero passion for collecting them. Besides my standard-issue Glock 9-mm police handgun, I own only two weapons, both commemorative. One I bought for the Suffolk Police Department's twenty-fifth anniversary, when it was strongly suggested that all section chiefs purchase this special Smith & Wesson .38-caliber revolver in honor of the occasion, with the proceeds going to some worthy cause. The other, a Ruger 9-mm semiautomatic pistol, I felt equally obligated to obtain when I was elected president of the international firearms association. That's it, two handguns, both stuck in a drawer at work. I never use them, never even take them out to look at or show to people. If I never saw them again, I wouldn't miss either one.

I don't even own a rifle, and never have. Every time I've gone hunting, I've had to borrow a gun, and nowadays I only go because it gives me a chance to be with my son, Al, Jr., who could happily spend days out there in the woods going after all kinds of game to put on his family's table.

Personally, I *hate* the woods. I hate being cold, hate getting up at four in the morning not for a pleasant, invigorating jog but for a bitter, exhausting, daylong trek spent lugging a very heavy rifle through all manner of strenuous, vexatious terrain. I don't even like the shooting aspect, and of course half the time you never shoot anyway. You never see an edible animal. All you do is tramp and sit and tramp and sit. I hate it. It disrupts your normal regimen, puts blisters on your feet, and fouls up your bowels.

Not surprisingly, my son contends that I'm the worst hunter he's ever seen. Mainly he objects to the fact that I always head into the woods with a radio and a cigar. That's why we never see any animals, he says. The ones that are too deaf to hear the radio can smell the cigar fumes from the next mountaintop.

Still, almost every November during deer season we head upstate for the Adirondacks, and every time I drag myself home swearing never to go again. Carrie pays no attention because she sees how much I enjoy being with my son and knows nothing could keep me away next year.

Much of my attitude toward hunting can probably be traced back to my early experience. By the time I moved into the police laboratory from my regular patrolman's beat, while in my early thirties, I'd been out hunting a few times with friends without any memorable results. Then one November a new neighbor moved in across the street, a Navy recruiter who was a dedicated hunter and wondered if I'd head up to the Adirondacks with him to show him around. Sure, I said, fine. So I borrowed a rifle—which should have tipped him off to the kind of hunter I was—and on the appointed day we both got up before dawn and drove north through a depressingly cold and heavy rain. The fellow himself, though, was pleasant and easygoing, and in spite of the weather we were doing just fine our first few hours in the woods until early in the afternoon we somehow got separated.

Naturally it wasn't the newcomer learning the ropes but the local expert who ended up hopelessly lost. Because all I really knew about the Adirondacks was that they composed a monstrously large area of rugged mountains and dense, often impenetrable woods. And since they were well north of the city and of some elevation, they could also get bitter cold in November.

It was a terrible experience. The rain kept coming down without letup and I spent hours and hours walking through wet brush and soggy woods without the slightest inkling where I was or which way I was heading. And then with really depressing suddenness it got dark. I gave up hope of getting out that day and set about making myself some shelter. I fashioned a very crude lean-to barely big enough for me to get under, actually nothing more than an overhang of wet branches I'd sawed off bushes and trees with my trusty hunting knife.

I more or less settled down under that for the night, with no food, no more water, no sleeping bag, and thoroughly soaked clothes that wouldn't have been warm enough even under the best of circumstances. Nor did I have any matches. I mean, I was as totally unprepared as you could get. Even if I'd had the brains to bring matches and keep them dry, everything was so wet I don't know what I could have gotten to burn. I was never a Boy Scout or anything—as a kid I never *knew* a Boy Scout—but seemed to remember there were ways you could find stuff for a fire in any weather by dragging stuff out of caves. I had no idea how I'd ever find a cave and was deathly afraid of them anyhow. I wouldn't stick my hand inside a dark, cobwebby cave for all the kindling in the world. I've always had generally unpleasant feelings toward large spiders, and was even less interested in stirring up some mother bear ready to kill to protect her cubs.

So I froze my ass off through what was probably, all in all, the most miserable night of my life. Hey, I'd grown up in the Bronx and lived my adult life in well-populated areas of Long Island. At heart I am, and will always remain, a city boy. In addition to signs on every corner telling you exactly where you are, I'm accustomed to streetlights, an occasional illuminated window or storefront, headlights going by. During that endless soggy night in the Adirondacks it was so pitch black I literally couldn't see my hand in front of my face.

And the familiar, unthreatening sounds I'm used to come from cars, from planes circling JFK, from a neighbor's TV set, or maybe an occasional drunk on the street. When the rain finally died off that night, it brought every sound that much closer and left me shivering on my little pile of leaves under that flimsy overhang listening to a *lot* of animals making a *lot* of strange, loud, and unsettling noises. People said there were bears in those woods, and I believed them. They also talked of mountain lions, which I at least half-believed. What animals I was hearing, I had no idea, but it seemed like every untamed beast within ten miles of me was restlessly roaming through the darkness doing its own animal thing as noisily as possible for no other reason than to absolutely scare the *shit* out of me.

After what seemed like forty or fifty hours, it got light enough to convince me it was morning, although the sky was still too dark and overcast for me to find the sun. This was unfortunate, because the only plan I'd devised overnight was to follow the sun as soon as it rose, to at least keep me heading in one direction rather than endlessly circling around on myself.

I'll tell you, I prayed about as hard as I could for that sun to come out, and eventually it did. It's what I think of as my own private miracle. I prayed and prayed and suddenly there it was, blazing through this one opening in all those black clouds.

It stayed out just long enough for me to line up a mountain

peak as being due east, and I set off in that direction, very thirsty and very hungry, and hiked, and hiked, and hiked through the whole morning and into the afternoon without encountering a single person or building or road or sign of human existence. I did spot a couple of airplanes overhead, and waved and shouted furiously at them. That was my big hope, flagging down somebody going two hundred miles an hour ten thousand feet up in the air.

The one other bit of woodsy lore that I seemed to remember was that if you ever got lost in the woods, you should simply find a stream and follow it, because that would inevitably lead you back to civilization. Well, I found a stream, and I followed the hell out of it for hours, and I have news for the Boy Scouts. When you follow a stream long enough, what you come to is a swamp in the absolute middle of nowhere, where you stand every chance in the world of sinking in up to your armpits. I know. I practically did.

Just about when I was beginning to admit the dreadful prospect of having to spend yet another long, dark, wet, and *very* hungry night in the woods, I encountered two hunters. They, thank God, knew exactly where they were, and showed me on their map how I'd ended up some twelve miles from where I'd lost my buddy the day before. I'd swear I'd covered a lot more miles than that, but most of it had probably been pretty zigzaggy.

Anyhow, they got me back, famished and grumpy but otherwise salvageable. I thanked them profusely, without mentioning what I did for a living. If they'd asked, I was prepared to tell them I sold vacuum cleaners door-to-door.

Oh yes, my reunited partner, the Navy recruiter: he said he'd reported me missing as soon as he realized we'd probably gone down two different sides of the same mountain and therefore could not hear each other's shouts. The rangers spent a few hours searching for me, but headed home at the first sign of nightfall. They were not about to wander around in the dark to rescue anybody short of the Queen of Sheba. In the morning they gave it another shot, but only in the immediate area of my disappearance. That was standard operating procedure for them. Either the guy would come stumbling out through dumb luck or bump into somebody with a better sense of direction, as I did. Barring either of those flukes, they assumed his dry white bones would be discovered come spring, with its melting snow and gently blooming flowers.

I thanked the rangers for trying their best and even joined in laughing off the escapade, but didn't tell them, any more than I did those two hunters, my name, rank, or serial number.

Probably my most rewarding experience in law enforcement didn't result from any individual case or specific achievement, but rather came about in a cumulative manner. The International Association of Firearms and Toolmark Examiners is the only worldwide organization in my field. It was founded in the late sixties by a group of examiners in Chicago to let members get to know each other and discuss mutual concerns, new developments, improved techniques. I joined in 1970 after I moved into the Suffolk lab, and over the years performed in a number of offices until in 1989 I was elected president.

The organization has about 650 active members, and as president I had the standard organizational responsibilities of planning and chairing the annual convention, overseeing the editorial staff of our magazine, coordinating various standing committees. Probably my most important, and least predictable, task was to act as spokesman on any matter affecting our members.

Two really explosive issues came to light during my term. One began as a bitter, but seemingly local, confrontation between the two agencies that share law-enforcement responsibility in Los Angeles—the police department and the sheriff's office. There's always been a lot of overlap between them, and since each naturally considers itself superior to the other, they've had a history of rivalry and distrust. We got involved when this bad blood came to a head in a widely publicized case that hinged, purely and simply, on the findings of a single firearms examiner.

The crime was one that's become all too familiar, and lurid enough to ensure sensational national publicity—a series of murders of area prostitutes. It's since occurred in places like New York, where this guy Joel Rifkin confessed to something like seventeen murders in 1993. Whatever the psychological root causes, it's the kind of crime that can really baffle the police. Unlike LuAnn Peterson, the prostitute whose body was found floating off Long Island, and who had a fairly stable circle of family and friends back in the Bronx, most streetwalkers are very transient, without local connections, and known only by assorted aliases. So what you get, as in the Rifkin murders, is some nut case murdering seventeen women with hardly a single missing-persons report being filed.

In Los Angeles in 1989, the police had discovered three bodies but didn't have a suspect. One night a couple of LAPD patrolmen stopped a car when they recognized the woman inside as a prostitute who plied her trade in that locality, and lo and behold, behind the wheel was a sheriff's deputy. They arrested him for cocaine possession and confiscated his service handgun from the trunk.

If that wasn't grief enough for the deputy sheriff, the chief firearms inspector of the LAPD tested the handgun and announced flat out that it had fired the bullets that killed those three prostitutes. Up to this point, our organization had no particular interest in the case, since the firearms aspect seemed fairly routine. But then the attorney for the deputy sheriff brought in an independent expert who said he found no link at all between the deputy's gun and the murder bullets.

The furor got even worse when two other experienced outside examiners also failed to find a link.

We were thrust into the middle of the controversy when I started getting calls from TV stations and the LA *Times* and papers throughout the country about this dichotomy in our ranks. I said I wanted a lot more information about it before taking any kind of stand, but it never got to that because the sheriff's deputy was quickly exonerated and the LAPD chief, Daryl Gates, who later ran into some trouble himself, forced the Firearms chief to retire and dumped his whole Firearms section with him.

My organization's main role was in putting the pieces back together. For one, our ethics committee drew up guidelines and protocols for dealing with future disagreements between professionals and called for the establishment of accepted criteria for what we call a "match" between a bullet and the gun that fired it. It's a highly technical situation, and yet subjective in many ways, nowhere near as cut-and-dried as we might like. We also helped arrange for some of our retired senior members to spend a few years grooming a whole new Firearms unit for LA, set up under civilian authority outside police control.

All in all, that local confrontation in California led to all-important national ramifications for our organization, and we spent a lot of time promoting job training and core curriculums at the state education facilities, and for standardized testing and certification programs. We also supported the FBI, whose examiners were members of our organization, in adding firearms courses at their forensic-science school in Quantico, Virginia.

That year, 1989, also marked the time when many states and municipalities, spurred on by mass shootings in places like McDonald's, became interested in banning assault weapons. I got all sorts of frantic phone calls and letters from state legislators and other interested parties, all wanting me to provide an unequivocal definition of whatever it was *they* wanted to ban. But *assault weapon* is basically a military term, referring to any weapon capable of being used in anything that could be defined as an assault. It's essentially meaningless in any exact firearms sense. Are we talking about an automatic that keeps firing as long as you hold your finger on the trigger? A semiautomatic that cycles to feed the cartridges but requires you to pull the trigger for every shot? A revolver that spins one notch after every firing to supply another bullet, but which you have to cock each time before you pull the trigger? Or a single-shot shotgun that won't even eject the spent casing but makes you unload, reload, cock, and fire each time? Then of course you have all kinds of doctoring that can alter the firing apparatus, or make some relatively innocuous sporting rifle *look* like something the Pentagon might call an assault weapon.

We'd struggle to come up with something useful but discovered no one cared a hoot about precise nomenclature. We like to think of ourselves as impartial scientific investigators, but the politicians wanted no part of that. Both sides were just looking for some convenient "expert" testimony they could use to whack their opponents over the head. I found it a real education.

The whole experience of being president was an education. I didn't even realize, to tell the truth, how truly international the group was until I found myself in almost daily communication not only with the FBI and other agencies throughout the United States, but also from Europe, from Africa and Asia, from South America. These people would want my opinion on one thing or another, and Jesus, when I gave it, they would listen. All in all, pretty heady stuff for a high-school dropout from the Bronx who, without a couple of breaks here and there, could have spent his life cutting up turkeys at a Long Island poultry farm. So I guess I'm allowed to be a bit proud.

COP STORIES:
ITALY AND BEYOND

TALKING ABOUT A BOOK in progress has always been uncomfortable for me, and I've said little to friends about this one. Their strong reactions therefore surprised me. It ought to make interesting reading, I kept hearing, because everybody knows cops and criminals are two sides of the same coin.

Well, I'm not sure I know that. Nor have I seen any research supporting the idea. It was, of course, a cliché long before I started this book, and will remain a self-righteous part of the public consciousness long after I've finished. I suspect it's rooted in a kind of intellectual and economic snobbery. Since criminals and cops have both typically come from the lower classes, it's an easy, albeit sloppy, step from there to the assumption that people from *those backgrounds*, unlike the rest of us, have all been stamped from the same mold. Poor kids have never had many ways of getting a leg up on the American dream, and as Johnny said earlier, the NYPD was one of the few places where a high-school dropout from the Bronx would be judged on his readiness to work and learn. But if one group of poor kids tries to rise out of poverty by breaking laws while another hopes to do so by enforcing them, don't these opposite choices suggest more differences than similarities?

That we're so eager to take the cop/criminal parallel as self-evident reveals more about us, possibly, than about the makeup of either cops or criminals.

At one time I did some modest reading and thinking about a subject that still interests me: comedy. Why do we laugh? What do we gain from humor? Why are certain subjects and persons considered so inherently funny that we've made them perpetual targets of our jokes?

One thought has stayed with me: we make jokes about subjects that worry and mystify us, and about people we fear. For subjects, we can begin with sex and religion, move on to all varieties of civilian and military authority, science, bodily functions, style, social rituals, marriage. For people, we have bosses who can't figure out their precise function, let alone who they're supposed to meet for lunch, while their secretaries have figured it all out on their first day and have been keeping the business afloat ever since. Although if we're afraid secretaries might really be running things, we can console ourselves by laughing at those who can't spell or type, who spend hours chatting on the phone with their boyfriends, who take dictation perched on the boss's knee and promise to attack their IN box the minute their nail polish dries. Absentminded professors. Repressed nuns. Drunken priests, kings, and judges. Mad scientists. Power-hungry generals, double-talking politicians, doctors thinking of their golf games in the middle of the heart bypass, lawyers chasing ambulances, neurotic psychiatrists, artists whose masterpieces win prizes when hung upside down, dim-witted sex kittens with baby-doll voices, construction workers leaning on their shovels, athletes muscle-bound all the way to the top. As antidote to the husband/father as family tyrant, we have all the comic strips, situation comedies, and TV ads featuring brisk, competent wives whose dithery husbands are forever napping on the couch, refusing to ask directions even when, as always, they become helplessly lost, and incapable of cooking, sweeping, changing a diaper, or taking a wrench to the kitchen sink without flooding out the whole family.

In terms of this book, we have both the bumbling "dese and dose" criminals enshrined as charter members of The Gang That Couldn't Shoot Straight and the equally inept and hilarious Kops, Keystone and beyond. Peter Sellers peering through his magnifying glass as he hits his head on a crossbeam. The cop carefully writing out a parking ticket while the masked robbers behind him shoot their way out of the bank. Why can't you ever find one when you really need him? Coffee-counter stools. Glazed doughnuts.

We laugh to get back, to disarm, to bring down. Only through ridicule and scorn can we confront, if only for that instant of laughter, the forces that intimidate us.

I wonder if any of us has the slightest idea if, or why, or how, cops are really like criminals. But the easy parallels, like the jokes we tell about them, sure as hell make us feel better.

J O H N   C U O M O ➡

MY FATHER, WHO WAS BORN in Italy in 1892, was a strong but quiet man who kept many things to himself, so much so that we knew very little about his early life beyond certain rumors and assumptions that had been passed down. In my case, I learned more last year, when Jeannette and I visited his only surviving sister in Italy, than I ever knew before. Our trip there occurred exactly a hundred years after he'd been born in the village of Arguello, a few miles outside of Pompeii.

His name was John, Giovanni really, and he was brought over here by his father when he was twelve, right after the turn of the century, but only for a visit before they returned to the farm in Arguello. Then my father, still only in his teens, left his father, his whole family, behind to come to America by himself. What we all understood, although I'm not sure my father ever *said* this, was that his father was very harsh, very mean to him, and he more or less ran away. No one seemed to know exactly how he managed to get the money or papers to come here. Whenever we asked about that, or his reasons for coming, he would just well up with tears and walk out of the room. We'd say, Dad, Dad, why did you leave? He must have realized we wanted to know because we were family, because it was part of our lives too, and we wanted him to share it with us, but he would never divulge anything about that part of his past.

My mother would say, You know your father, if he doesn't want to talk about it, he won't. He had a very hard life there, she would say, and you shouldn't make him bring it all back. Even many years later, when we kids were grown and he was retired, we'd say, Dad, why don't you take Mom and go back to where you grew up and see your family again? He absolutely refused. No, he said, I don't want anything to do with anybody over there.

When my father arrived in this country to stay, his main connection here was our grandmother, yours and mine and Al's, who was a Cuomo and had her three children, all unmarried, living with her—your father, also named John; Al's mother, Camille; and my mother, Helen. Grandma Cuomo was some kind of aunt to my father, and since he had no place to go she took him in with the family as more or less another son.

He went into the Army during World War I and served overseas and fought in the battle of the Argonne Forest, and maybe others too, and eventually made sergeant. That always impressed me, this totally uneducated kid from a farm up in the hills in Italy who couldn't read or write and had to learn English as he went along, working his way up to sergeant. Maybe he received what they called a battlefield promotion, but we never knew, because it was one more thing you couldn't get him to talk about.

I wonder sometimes, if he was alive and knew about this book, what he'd think of his son talking so much about himself.

It was through his Army service that he got his citizenship, and he returned to marry my mother. She was also a Cuomo, of course, some kind of second or third cousin, which was common at the time, and extremely common in the Italian villages, where just about everybody was related to everybody else.

My father worked at different jobs, mostly in vegetable stores, including the one that he and your father owned together. But what I most remember, because it really caught a young kid's imagination, was the job he had during the thirties working an ice-cream route with a horse and wagon. I was maybe six at the time, and he'd take me with him sometimes. This was the end of the horse-and-wagon era, and I remember how good he was with horses. In the middle of a hot New York summer in those days you'd often see a horse drop to the street from exhaustion. I remember him leaving his own wagon at the curb and running over to this other horse that had collapsed, giving it water and washing it down until it was all right.

He never did become educated, but was always very quick with numbers. He'd take me to the vegetable store and I'd be amazed at how he'd multiply and divide and figure prices and weights in his head. This also showed in his card playing. He was always a card player, especially poker and pinochle, which I guess is where I got it from, and my own knack for numbers and odds.

During the Second World War, when I was around ten, he got a job as a warehouseman out at Fort Totten, on the Island, and continued working until he retired in the late fifties.

As a World War I veteran and active Legionnaire, he volunteered for what they called the Air Patrol during World War II. People don't seem aware of that now, but there were fears then that we'd be bombed, and the Air Patrol provided a round-the-clock spotting service. Lots of times I went with my father up to City Island for his tour of duty as an aircraft spotter. I remember you coming too, George. It was a real outing for us, almost a game, a couple of twelve-year-olds staying up at night to spot enemy planes with binoculars. I remember really cold nights on this long dock with a bitter wind blowing in off the water. When we got too cold, we warmed up in an enclosed room back on land. If a spotter saw a plane, he phoned in a report to headquarters, a certain kind of plane at such and such a height and direction, and they'd record it on this chart and decide if it was a regular flight or some German bomber coming over. I don't think we could tell one from another, but I can still see my father studying these books of black silhouettes so he could identify the different planes. I don't know what would have happened if we ever spotted anything really strange or threatening. Maybe all the air-raid sirens in New York would start blaring and everybody would turn off their lights and run down into their basements.

By the time my father retired from Fort Totten in the sixties, which was about fifty years since he'd left Italy and had any contact with the family he'd left behind, one day he received a letter from his two sisters over there—or maybe their lawyer, I'm not sure anymore—informing him that they were selling the old farm and moving into town. I guess they wanted authorization from him as one of the legal heirs to the property, and to arrange for his share of the proceeds.

I remember my sister Jean either going herself or getting my father to go to a lawyer friend at the American Legion, and some correspondence on the situation, but the upshot was my father refused to sign any papers or have anything to do with the sale. He never received any money or further notice of the transaction, and we figured, Well, it was just this little farm up in the hills somewhere. What could it be worth anyhow?

For the next twenty years or so, no one thought about it again. Then we received our first real word about the family in Italy when my nephew Donald, my brother Alfred's son, tracked them down while he was working over there. He said there was still a legend in the village about my father leaving. The legend said he would never return until they built a bridge over the Atlantic. That was how strong his feelings were.

Then in the late eighties, a few years ago, Jeannette and I made our first trip to Italy and attempted to find the family. But every time we mentioned the name Cuomo in Arguello—or his sister's name, since she'd been married many years—the townspeople would say, Oh yes, they came from this farm up in the mountains,

a very healthy place to live up there, with clean air and everything. Beyond that, we never found out where they lived now. For
our second trip, though, we did research ahead of time and made
contact with my father's last surviving sister, my Aunt Genoveffa,
and made arrangements to visit her.

The whole family had moved to a town called Buscarelli, which
was the next train stop from Pompeii, and when we arrived they
picked us up at the station and took us to this imposing house in a
compound that you entered through a gate, and that contained
several very nice houses. Aunt Genoveffa had been much younger
than my father, probably now in her late seventies, but very lively
and obviously overjoyed to see us. From the minute we arrived, we
were treated like royalty, and very soon other relatives started arriving. It seemed like the whole town was flocking there, but actually they were mostly family, aunts and uncles and cousins and
whatever, some coming all the way from Rome just to meet us.

The interpreter for everybody was Aunt Genoveffa's granddaughter and namesake, who everybody called Genny. No one else
in the family spoke English, so it was absolute chaos the whole
time, but we were really thrilled. Every time we turned around,
the doorbell was ringing and someone new was arriving, everyone
throwing their arms around us and kissing us. We'd arrived
around eleven in the morning, and in the middle of all the excitement Aunt Genoveffa started cooking up this enormous feast for
everybody, and by two in the afternoon we sat down to this real
Italian-style meal, course after course of pasta and steak and
salad and different kinds of cheeses and olives and nuts and wine,
and finally these wonderful pastries.

During the meal the schoolchildren started coming home in
their little uniforms, and they'd hug and kiss us too, and then
someone would stand up to give them a place at the table and put
a plate of spaghetti in front of them. All along, people were getting
up and down at the table, because we must have met fifty people
that day, and naturally there wasn't enough room for everybody
to sit down at once.

Through all this we were trying to talk to everybody and they

all tried to talk to us, so it was very chaotic the whole time, especially for the poor granddaughter Genny, who did a wonderful job
translating but could barely catch her breath the whole time, let
alone get the chance to sit down and eat. Thanks to her, though,
we did learn a lot about the family.

For one, we discovered that three of Aunt Genoveffa's nephews
were policemen, one in Naples, one in Rome, one in the very elite
Carabiniere. Now these were my cousins, although I'd never
known about them or vice versa. It was almost like a revelation to
me, that I kept shaking my head over. Was there something in the
family genes that turned us all into cops?

The aunt's house, by the way, was a spacious and very beautiful
home that she shared with her daughter and son-in-law and their
two grown children. It had beautiful furniture and lamps and pictures that Jeannette really noticed and commented on, and the
most luxurious bathrooms you ever saw. The son was in the mar-
ble-and-tile business, and the bathrooms and halls were con-
structed with very impressive marble and tile work. We didn't go
into the other homes in the compound, but you could see they
were very impressive too, each with its own little garden and vine-
yard, and as we talked to people we gradually became aware that
all the surrounding homes were occupied by family members. The
whole compound, it turned out, belonged to Aunt Genoveffa,
who'd bought the land and built the houses for the others with the
money from the sale of the old farm. Apparently the healthful reputation of the air and the climate up there in the hills meant that
the property was worth a *lot* of money to the buyers, who turned
it into a very fancy health spa.

In all the hubbub and excitement, this didn't sink in right away,
but later in the afternoon after most of the relatives had left, the
granddaughter who'd been doing all the translating said to me,
You know, John, Grandma is a very wealthy woman now, and she
wants you to know that at the time the farm was sold—which of
course was when my father got that letter he refused to have anything to do with back in the sixties—she sent him his share of
money. I said, Gee, I don't know about that. It was a long time ago

and of course my mother and father have now both passed away, but I don't think he ever got any money like that. Oh yes, she said, Grandma says we definitely sent him money.

I didn't argue, because who knows after all these years, although I'm sure my father never saw anything like the kind of money that Aunt Genoveffa obviously had. It occurred to me then that, even though I'm sure their hospitality was totally sincere, at the same time they maybe thought we'd come after all these years to lay claim to my father's share of the money. Of course, that was the farthest thing from our minds, and we just let the whole thing drop, and all parted in very good spirits.

In fact, they insisted we should stay longer, for as long as we wanted, but we had trains to catch and everything. They insisted then on taking us to our next destination, and so the son-in-law, who drove a Lamborghini worth something like seventy thousand dollars, took us on this wild ride down the mountain roads to Sorrento, where we caught our train.

On the train, we ran into this very friendly conductor who told us that he had been born in Queens, New York, and said his parents had gone back and forth between America and Italy until finally, twenty-two years ago, deciding to stay in Italy for good. We had a nice conversation with him, but meanwhile everything we'd learned about Aunt Genoveffa and her beautiful house and all her prosperity had finally begun to sink in. I think we were particularly impressed by the fact that the farm, which we'd always written off as a couple of scrubby acres up in the hills that my father ran away from, was now some ritzy resort providing expensive vacations for the upper crust. What would have happened if my father had ever gone back, or had even paid attention to that letter from Italy offering him his share of the sale? Jesus, all those millions of Italian immigrants coming to America to make their fortunes, and here we had this whole family who'd stayed behind and could have bought and sold our house in Pelham Bay a hundred times over.

Maybe the best thing to come from the visit, besides meeting all those wonderful people, was that the granddaughter Genny, who did all the translating, said she was dying to come over and see America. Jeannette told her, Come anytime you want, we'll show you around and introduce you to everybody. And I said, Make those cousins of mine come too, the three policemen. We'll put them up and I'll get Al to come out to Phoenix and we'll all sit around over a beer trading cop stories about Rome and Naples and the Bronx and Brooklyn and Long Island, all over the place, and we'll let you sit over in the corner there, George, and take notes.

I PLAN TO BE THERE. Meanwhile, in January of 1994, Johnny celebrated his sixty-fifth birthday in Arizona. Jeannette spent months organizing it, all along insisting it was a surprise, that Johnny had no inkling. I think he had an inkling.

The cousins from Italy couldn't make it, but all the American ones showed up, along with Johnny's children and grandchildren and a lot of new and old friends and neighbors, and some ex-cops he'd known for forty years—including Howie Hundgeon, who'd leaped out of a squad car and raced into that Harlem hallway back in the days of Op Two-Five to rescue a raw and uncertain rookie from his encounter with a screaming madman on the stairway above.

Howie Hundgeon's become something of a heroic figure in my mind, although he'd no doubt be uncomfortable with that thought. He's a quiet, not very large man, a gambler and card player who even as he was enjoying himself at the party was looking forward to the next couple of days in Vegas. He had thick blondish eyebrows, a gaze that seemed very steady and self-contained. It was hard to imagine him getting excited about anything, or letting on that he was excited. You got the impression that there wasn't much he hadn't seen, or anything that would catch him off guard. Howie Hundgeon hadn't only allowed Johnny to survive. He was the cop who showed Johnny, one-two-three, exactly how you went about surviving.

A single image from that party remains above all others.

In her phoned invitations, Jeannette told everyone that Johnny didn't need or want gifts, and would be embarrassed to receive any. Instead, we could bring a stuffed animal.

A stuffed animal? What in hell was Johnny going to do with a stuffed animal?

Jeannette explained that although Johnny rarely mentioned it—he certainly hadn't to me, and I was writing a *book* about him!—he was a regular volunteer in a local hospital for children with incurable diseases.

At the party, one side of the very large room, on the apron of a raised stage, was lined from wall to wall with fifty, seventy, a hundred stuffed teddies and Raggedy Anns and alligators and Snoopies and firemen and puppies and cats and just about every other imaginable form of stuffed boy, girl, and beast, mythical or otherwise, furry and beribboned, round and bright and grinning, for Johnny to take to the kids in the hospital the next day.

POSTSCRIPTS

THOSE THREE COP COUSINS in Naples, in Rome, in the Carabiniere, brought to mind that my mother's father, Michael Vogt, patrolled Central Park in the early 1900s as a mounted policeman, on a horse that he groomed, cared for, and visited after he retired. My few memories of him are vivid: a man in his seventies, gray mustache, thin wisps of gray over his ears, given to contented silences but gratifyingly indulgent to his only grandson. I remember waiting for him in front of our 178th Street walk-up apartment, excited by expectations of ice cream and Crotona Park, running to him as soon as he rounded the corner from the trolley stop on Tremont Avenue. He was a formidable figure, erect, vigorous, with powerful shoulders, looking as if he could still wear his uniform with authority—and tall, strikingly tall, a looming giant of a man.

More than a half century after his death, my mother came upon his official police ID photo in a box of ancient snapshots. The print had aged into furry sepia tones, but the lines of the height chart behind him remained in sharp focus: my grandfather was five feet eight and a half inches tall.

These days, Johnny remembers my father, his uncle, as a habitual card player and chronic gambler. My father and I were close. During my several stints working at Taller & Cooper, we commuted from the Bronx to Brooklyn in his car, worked alongside each other on the shop floor, ate our bagged lunches on a bench near his grinder or on the factory roof if the sun was out. After work, we'd stop with the other guys for a beer before heading home. I don't remember him ever playing cards. I don't remember him ever gambling, except for the quarters that most of us tossed into the hat for the baseball pool.

Is Johnny misremembering, or did I somehow miss the one trait he recalls above all others? Did I simply refuse, for whatever reasons, to grant that memory its place among those others that are now, for me, my father? After these questions, it's only a short step to wondering what memories your own children, your own grandchildren, will preserve.

In committing ourselves to this book, Johnny and Al and I thought of it as something our children and grandchildren might value, and agreed not to lie, contrive, distort, invent, or inflate. Given our human limitations, it wasn't always easy living up to that superhuman pledge, since we had no choice but to make selections of selections, to deal with memories of memories. We began to understand the absurdity of that winnowing process which labels vast areas as trivial, to be discarded forever, while declaring a few odd moments worthwhile or illuminating, maybe even true.

I'm no longer altogether sure Taller & Cooper *had* a usable roof, or allowed us to eat our lunches out there. Could it have been Rogers Peet, a different group of workers, years before or after, my father nowhere in sight? It might even be a scene from one of my novels, maybe suggested by a recollection, maybe invented in response to some narrative necessity.

Still, let's not knock memory. No matter how full of holes it may be, how humdrum its chosen darlings, it goes a long way toward making us us, and allowing our lives to become our lives.

GEORGE CUOMO has published novels, stories, and poems, and has received awards from the National Endowment for the Arts and the Guggenheim Foundation. *A Couple of Cops* is his first book of nonfiction.

ABOUT THE TYPE

This book was set in Photina, a typeface designed by José Mendoza in 1971. It is a very elegant design with high legibility, and its close character fit has made it a popular choice for use in quality magazines and art gallery publications.